Lifelines and Risks

Lifelines and Risks

Pathways of Youth in Our Time

Robert B. Cairns and Beverley D. Cairns

CAMBRIDGE
UNIVERSITY PRESS

Published by the Press Syndicate of the University of Cambridge
The Pitt Building, Trumpington Street, Cambridge, CB2 1RP
40 West 20th Street, New York, NY 10011–4211, USA
10 Stamford Road, Oakleigh, Melbourne 3166, Australia

First published 1994

Printed in Great Britain

Library of Congress Cataloging-in-Publication Data

Cairns, Robert B., 1933–
    Lifelines and risks : pathways of youth in our time / Robert B.
Cairns and Beverley D. Cairns.
        p.   cm.
    Includes bibliographical references.
    ISBN 0-521-48112-0 (hc). – ISBN 0-521-48570-3 (pbk.)
    1. Youth–United States–Longitudinal studies. 2. Socially
handicapped youth–United States–Longitudinal studies. I. Cairns,
Beverley D. II. Title.
HO796.C245 1994
305.23'5'973–dc20

94-29549
CIP

A catalog record for this book is available from the British library

ISBN 0-521-48112-0 hardback
ISBN 0-521-48570-3 paperback

Contents

Foreword   vii

1   Lives in progress   1

2   Taking a long look   8

3   Growth and aggression   45

4   Stepping stones to violence: developmental roots   68

5   Social networks and the functions of friendships   90

6   Shadows of synchrony   130

7   The self and the other   147

8   Dropouts, throwouts, and runaways   167

9   Life and death   194

10 Risks and lifelines: the opportunities of a lifetime   221

11 The developmental perspective: puzzles and proposals   239

12 Extending lifelines: intervention and prevention   258

    Notes   274

    References   288

Foreword

Fifteen years ago we gambled that we could plot the course of social development of individuals from childhood to maturity. Our goal was to identify some lifelines that could be made available to vulnerable youth. We believe that developmental investigation is the backbone for behavioral study; it yields information on the pathways of life that can be obtained in no other way.

We also feel that behavioral research and social policy should be mutually supportive. To this end, we hope to make our findings accessible to an informed public. On this score, we think that the most important ideas can be clearly stated, and the simplest statistics are more often than not the most robust.

Several technical reports of our work have appeared, or are due to appear, in archival journals. This means that the methods and analyses have already passed the filters of peer review which evaluate rigor and reliability. One happy side of this investment in technical articles is that we are free to be less technical in this book. We have tried to keep the quantitative presentation to a minimum, although we slip from time to time. Colleagues should consult the technical reports for critical details. A companion volume, *Methods and Measures for Longitudinal Research* provides detailed information on the psychometric properties of the measures and how to use them.

Our research vision has remained constant through the years. The work is ongoing, now funded by the National Institute of Mental Health and the National Institute of Child Health and Human Development. Earlier we received support from the National Science Foundation, the W. T. Grant Foundation, and the MacArthur Foundation. The Spencer Foundation has been our own lifeline at critical times. Marion Faldet deserves our special thanks. When we began, few federal or private foundations in the United States wanted to commit funding for more than two or three years, much less the span of a generation. The lack of continuous support required us to convince critical peers every two or three years that the work was worthy. That helped keep us focused. Each of these grants is a public trust and we are grateful for the confidence that they represent.

This book represents the efforts of a dedicated team. Besides ourselves, key members over the years have been Tamara Ladd, Holly Neckerman, Lynda Ferguson, Lori Musick, Becky Premock, Man-Chi Leung, Adrienne Himmelberg, Lynne Marschke, Kate Raiford, Lisa Buchanan, Louis Gariépy, Scott Gest, Shane Greene, Laura Sadowski, and Gary Peterson. Each one made distinctive and important contributions to the research, including the preparation of this volume. Not only was there a melding of disciplines – psychology, social work, education, internal medicine, psychiatry – there was a unity of purpose. At earlier stages, Jane Perrin and Kathryn Hood were especially helpful.

Our professional colleagues have been invaluable. David Magnusson has been an inspiration and a friend, providing personal and intellectual support over the past ten years. Beyond advice, he has opened to us the raw data files of his longitudinal project in Stockholm, and helped us understand its relation to our own data. Urie Bronfenbrenner and Norman Garmezy deserve our appreciation for their insights into the discipline and personally for their wise counsel and support. We thank Harry Yamaguchi for criticizing an early version of the manuscript and for urging us to complete the task in ways that would enhance the science. Tokio Honda, Carlos Santoyo, and Keith and Sheila Holly spent their sabbaticals in our laboratory. Their research contributions and critical comments on earlier drafts of this volume were invaluable.

The title of this book was suggested by British ethologist John Macintosh on a stroll down Franklin Street in Chapel Hill several years ago. John suggested "The Life Line", a title that seemed well suited for the stories of the lives of 695 persons from childhood through adolescence.

The volume has taken seven years to write. The central ideas have remained, though the data have grown richer. Editor Farrell Burnett deserves credit for holding us to the task and helping us through the final stages of preparation, review, and publication. This first volume is concerned with vulnerability and resilience in development. Succeeding volumes will focus on successful adaptation, families, and the multiple roles of social networks.

The help and cooperation that we have received from teachers, counselors, principals, superintendents, probation officers, judges, and county clerks across the country cannot be overestimated. A special kind of assistance came our way when Dwayne Powell, the nationally syndicated editorial cartoonist for the *Raleigh News* and *Observer*, donated an original drawing to this study to become the logo and to provide identity for the subjects. It is still uniquely theirs and continues to generate pride in participation. Our thanks to Jan Powell in helping with special needs.

Ultimately, however, the success of this work reflects the willingness of children, adolescents, and young adults, along with their parents, friends and spouses, to open the windows of their lives to us. We began by giving them small gifts, and by the end, it came full circle; they have begun to give us small gifts. The real gift was their cooperation and trust. It is to them that this volume is dedicated.

Beverley D. Cairns
Robert B. Cairns
Chapel Hill

While the incidents and cases described in this book are based on studies of real persons, the names, locations and other biographical details about the participants have been changed to preserve their privacy and anonymity.

ONE

Lives in progress

I don't have a best friend around here except for one; that's the teacher.

Jane (10 years old)

Just trying to get through one day at a time, and never – and I know there's gonna be worries. I know you've got to have pain in order to have happiness. I realize that. You've got to have pain sometimes in your life, but for the last couple of years, that's all it's been. There hasn't been very much happiness.

Jane (20 years old)

Developmental pathways evolve in time and place, so it is necessary to describe anew for each generation the trajectories of individual lives. As Jane's reports suggest, there can be lawfulness of individual development in the midst of change. Webs of influence operate across time to constrain an individual's actions, coerce choices, and create novel opportunities. Certain lifecourse patterns have enough in common to be described as developmental pathways. This book provides an account of pathways of youth in our time, the generation that came of age in the 1990s.

Common-sense beliefs are difficult to examine objectively. Attempts to tackle critically the problems of living are further handicapped by the limited methods of the science. To clarify the nature of developmental pathways in our time, we will rely upon four separate though related sources of information. Each source has its own distinctive strengths and weaknesses, and they provide a compelling story if analyzed together. And compelling it must be, since some of the conclusions we reach on pathways and how they can be modified defy both common sense and the assumptions of contemporary psychology.

1

Our primary information source is firsthand observations of 695 representative children as they became teenagers and parents themselves. Over the past fourteen years, we have seen young people like Jane through the lens provided by their schools and through the eyes of their peers, their spouses, their parents, and their grandparents. Even more important, they shared with us their thoughts of themselves as they were growing up. We became privy to their friendships, their failures, their successes, their marriages, their loves, their children, their imprisonments; in short, to the events and feelings they experienced in the course of living. Virtually all of them continued to be involved with this study through the end of high school and into their own adulthood and parenthood. Much of this volume is about lives in progress.

The second source of information is the work of colleagues who have undertaken similar investigations in other places during this time. Several longitudinal studies in Europe and North America have recently matured and these results have revolutionary implications for understanding the pathways of living.[1] Happily, this area of science tends to promote cooperation rather than competition. The problems are broad enough to stimulate collaboration among researchers, whose goal is to advance understanding of youth.

Over the past decade, we visited the laboratories of colleagues throughout North America and Europe to talk about their findings, discussed the problems they encountered, and studied their data in order to understand why their findings agreed or disagreed with ours. Because of the different values and standards of societies and the rate of change in these standards, researchers do not have to be embarrassed by differences that emerge across countries, regions, and time. The challenge is to understand what the differences mean.

The third information source involved studies conducted with colleagues and students. The work has been designed to replicate and extend specific findings or resolve particular discrepancies among investigations. No single study can do the job of solving the complexity of human development. The infrequency of some events demands that the researcher look to special samples in order to zoom in on particular relationships and outcomes.

Toward this end, we have been concerned with special problems encountered by youths who grow up in the 1990s in the inner cities of the United States, where there are escalating rates of homicide, violence, and substance abuse. We made observations, examining the schools and the emergency department of a major trauma center. We also became involved in a state-wide study in North Carolina of 1,300 youths who had been identified as extremely assaultive and violent. To check on the generality of the observations, we collaborated in investigations in

Hong Kong and Taiwan with students and colleagues. Such cross-national information helps to determine which relationships and outcomes are limited to the United States, and which may be more broadly applicable.

The fourth empirical leg upon which this book rests is actuarial and epidemiological. We consulted national and international reports on education, health, and crime to clarify what "in our time" means in cold numbers. For example, the Statistical Abstract of Sweden for 1990 indicates that the majority of live births are to unmarried women. This finding is consistent with the 1990 US Census Bureau that most African-American infants are born to single mothers. A similar trend is apparent in white mothers. Such national data help account for the fact that most of the children born to teenage participants in our longitudinal sample lived with only one natural parent by the second year of life. The national and international statistics suggested that our young people were simply representative of a major shift in western societies, their norms, and expectations.

In addition, a collaborative investigation with social historian Stephen Schlossman took us into the juvenile court records of Los Angeles County to track the trends of problem behaviors of girls from the turn of the 20th century (Schlossman & Cairns, 1993). Schlossman's work indicated that sexual promiscuity and incorrigibility were the major crimes for girls from 1910 through 1950. But the patterns of crime for juvenile females in the second half of the century are not unlike that of juvenile males, including arrests for assaults.

More generally, records of health, families, and education help plot the nature of the changing landscape in which development occurs. The obligation of research is to understand social change rather than lament it. But records are themselves fallible and their accuracy may depend upon how the characteristics are measured as much as when they are measured.

The perspective of developmental science

The melding of these perspectives, the direct observation of individual lives, the generalizations from contemporary longitudinal investigations, the findings of modern epidemiology, and the influence of historical changes on people and society, seems necessary to tell the story of human development. Neither part is sufficient in itself. But the task of weaving together these perspectives on development has been hampered by the methods of the component disciplines. These limitations of the methods and analyses of behavioral science have been infrequently discussed by those of us who employ them, but are real nonetheless.

A shortcoming of analytic procedures typically employed in modern psychology and sociology is that they usually begin with a reduction of the causes of behavior into component parts, either by experiments or by statistical models. For example, one aim of developmental psychology has been to pinpoint the causes of a given behavior, say, aggression. Is it regulated by early family experiences, genes, hormones, peer influences, deficient social perception, or association with deviant peer groups? Studies designed to address this issue indicate that all of the above variables seem to have some identifiable contributions. However, there is little information on how these factors are woven together in individual lives.

The problem is that behavior patterns like aggression represent a fusion of factors; they are determined by multiple "causes" acting together. It has become increasingly clear that any well-designed study will identify several factors that have an influence. Virtually any sane expectation will be "statistically significant" if the study is competent. The problem remains to determine how these factors are organized and weighted during the course of individual development. The task of intervention must ultimately deal with the acts of individuals, not disembodied variables.

Developmental science refers to a new synthesis across disciplines that has evolved to guide research in behavior and biology.[2] It brings attention to the holistic nature of behavioral study, to the role of time and timing in understanding individual functioning, to the special properties of behavior in biological adaptation, and to the correlated nature of events without and within the person. According to this perspective, the puzzles of human development will remain unsolved so long as our procedures treat problems of adaptation as if they were separate entities, unrelated to other features of each person's life.

For instance, it has become increasingly obvious that the problems of youth tend to co-occur and that the focus must be as much upon the individual in context as upon variables, such as school dropout and teenage parenthood. We began our longitudinal focus on individual lives because our view of development demanded that we study each life as a whole. It also required that we adopt procedures that would make such an integrated view of behavior possible.

There has been a growing recognition in the physical and biological sciences that complex systems have their own laws (Gleick, 1987; Kadanoff, 1986; Lorenz, 1983). These laws may be as simple and fundamental as other laws of nature. This proposition is particularly important when the special properties of behavior are considered, because maturational, biological, and experiential factors are inseparably fused in development. Our task in this book is to identify the lawfulness that exists in the seeming chaos of youthful development.

The youth

One of the paradoxes in the longitudinal study of human behavior is that investigators and participants travel together through space and time. Any serious attempt to understand the trajectory of development and change demands as large a slice of the lives of the investigators as the lives of the participants.

As a group, the 695 children and their families that we observed in conjunction with this volume represent a broad slice of American life.[3] They include the privileged and the poor, female and male, African American and white in about the same proportion that one would expect to find nationally.[4] Over the past decade, they have dispersed throughout the United States and abroad. Some were in the thick of the Iraqi war, some were in college or university, some were working or looking for jobs, and some were staying home to take care of their babies. A small number are in prison or other institutional care, and a few have died. By systematically tracking them each year, we have managed to keep contact with all of them, and have recently interviewed virtually all of the original group who are still living.

There were some persons who, as children, were judged to be headed for trouble in their adult lives. Other children by virtue of their own competence, personal dispositions, and community and family status seemed destined to have a smooth road ahead, or so it appeared until new problems emerged for them in youth. The problems took many forms, sometimes family breakup (by separation, divorce, accident, or homicide), running away, dropping out of school or being thrown out, being ostracized by peers or former friends, becoming a parent while still a child, or substance addiction. The total information set has permitted us to take a cross-sectional look into these lives at several points in time and to compare the statistical snapshots that they provided with broader national and international pictures of youth. It has also permitted us to track the emergence of problems and subsequent solutions as they occurred in these lives.

Much of this volume will cover phenomena and outcomes that seem as if the story could end no other way. That would be a mistake, however, because *most* young lives today have twists that are as subtle and complex as the roles described by Dostoevski in *The Adolescent*. While one of our conclusions is that we are much closer to explaining these phenomena than has been recognized, we have had plenty of opportunity to be surprised. It is from errors in expectations that we can learn the most.

Looking ahead

Our aim is to describe a new way to understand children and youths who are at risk from serious problems of living. Toward this end, we bring together information about developmental changes in the person with developmental changes in the social and physical context in which she or he lives. This simultaneous focus on person and context is something we do every day. We accomplish the feat automatically and unconsciously in creating views of ourselves and of others. But the methods of the social and behavioral science have traditionally led in a different direction. The dominant research strategy has been to remove the person from the environment, then dissect each into separate variables and elements. The problem of how to recombine the elements to represent adaptive, resilient, living people continues to beguile. The Humpty-Dumpty problem is at the core of modern behavioral study.

Our solution has emerged because of new trends within modern developmental science. Accordingly, the study of individual development is a holistic science. That means that its study requires an integration of methods ordinarily assigned to the separate disciplines of sociology, psychology, epidemiology, social ecology, and psychiatry. The work has taken longer than we anticipated because the science is still in its formative stage. Where appropriate methods and analyses were unavailable, we had to revise existing techniques or invent new ones. One of the advantages of this new orientation is that the facts on the development of people should be clear enough to be accessible to anyone who is interested. Looking ahead, we have three objectives in preparing this book.

First, we describe some of the major behavioral and psychological risks of youth and what are the lifelines. By risks, we mean the events or characteristics that have the potential to produce serious and permanent impairment of psychological and emotional development, or injury or death. The specific risks that we will consider include violence, deviant social groups, school dropout, suicide, threats to self-esteem, and substance abuse. By lifelines, we mean the events or opportunities which potentially lead to changes from pathways associated with deviant or destructive outcomes. The lifelines may emerge externally as people (parents, friends, teachers, spouses, lovers, relatives, or children) and opportunities, or internally through shifts in values, beliefs, and biophysical status.

Second, we describe the "hidden competence" that exists in virtually all children and adolescents.[5] Certain resilient teenagers succeed, despite the odds against them. But exceptional cases should not be divorced from an understanding of the normal trajectories of development, lest exceptions be taken for the rule.

Third, we will outline how normal development is achieved in the transition from childhood to adulthood. Accordingly, the "biological lottery" of adolescence will be described, along with the adaptations in early adulthood.[6] In the following chapters, we evaluate the role and functions of self-esteem, the freedom of youth, the buffers of early experience, aggressive and violent behaviors, and the capacity for resilience.

TWO

Taking a long look

How did you find me here? I just can't believe you found me. I know you said you would, but I didn't really believe you. Will you find me again next year . . . promise?

Melissa (5th grade)

Melissa was crying when she said it. She had just lived through a miserable, wretched year that seemed more like 19th century Dickensian England than near-21st century America. She and her brother had been abandoned by their mother, placed in a foster home, removed from it to live with their mother again, then rejected again by the mother after three weeks, placed in an emergency home care center for sixty days, then in an orphanage. In the course of these moves, she had been assigned a different surname from the one we knew her by in the 7th grade, and moved to a different part of the country. She was honestly puzzled as to how we had located her. We found her over the next several years as well. By the time she was in the 10th grade, her life had changed for the better, due in large measure to the acceptance and support of her original foster parents who had re-entered her life.

Descriptions of procedures are usually presented in fine print for the eyes of experts, as if the methods were too esoteric for nonscientific readers. That is an illusion. In point of fact, the techniques adopted in research are the heart and soul of the science. If the measures are weak, misapplied, or inappropriately coded, the statistical analyses will necessarily yield trivia. Even behavioral observations are never "mere records". Filters exist at several levels, from the lenses of the observers to the syntax of the recording scheme and the statistical transformation of the data.

We will also report how the longitudinal investigations are conducted. This will include an examination of the "dirty bathwater" of research, including the stuff that gets tossed out before a cleaned-up version is published. To understand what the findings mean, raw accounts of how the research is done can be more important than exhaustive statistical data analyses.

On longitudinal design

Longitudinal research is a design of choice from the developmental perspective. In behavioral investigation, *longitudinal* refers to a temporal dimension rather than a spatial one. It designates investigations where persons have repeatedly participated in measurements over a significant span of their lifetimes. Textbooks usually contrast longitudinal research designs with *cross-sectional* designs (where people of different ages are seen on one occasion in order to make comparisons of various age groups). It can also be contrasted with *retrospective* designs, where investigators ask subjects to recall earlier experiences and thereby reconstruct the temporal dimension through the mind of the subject. Or it can be compared with *social history analyses*, where information about a person recovered from some institution (e.g. school, hospital clinic, police, factory) is linked to that individual's current functioning. Compared to these alternatives, longitudinal designs are inevitably more expensive for participants and researchers alike in terms of time, cost, and commitment.

But what is the difference between studying groups of people at 10, 15, and 20 years of age and, say, studying a group of persons for each of the 10 years between 10 and 20 years of age? In both cases, one would have reliable information on the average changes that occurred over the ten-year period. The advantages of cross-sectional procedures seem obvious in terms of economy and lack of measure contamination by repeated assessment. However, age-related averages are only part of the story of development. Jacob Wohlwill (1973) and William Kessen (1960) have observed that longitudinal investigations are required to go beyond age-related descriptions and clarify individual processes of development and change. Longitudinal studies are necessary to identify individual difference predictability from one age to another, their stability over time, and the rates and types of individual change. Perhaps most important for our consideration of lifelines and risks, longitudinal information is required to identify the periods of greatest risk and phases most susceptible to change in youth. Moreover, longitudinal information is required to identify the permanence or instability of interventions introduced.

One alternative to the laborious study of people over time is simply to ask individuals to recall critical events in their past. After all, each of us should know what happened in the past as well as anyone. This use of the subject as an autobiographer seems not only efficient, it permits people to participate actively as expert witnesses on their own lives. While this use of self-reports seems attractive and inexpensive, the evidence indicates that personal retrospection provides an extremely shaky foundation for science. In this regard, modern studies of human memory provide robust evidence on the fallibility of personal recall (Ross, 1989). Memories of personal life experiences tend to be selective, projective, and inventive. Memories represent in varying measure an amalgam of the person's present concerns and his/her constructions of the past. Typically they provide more information about present circumstances and attitudes than those of the past.[1]

Earlier hospital, school, work, or arrest records provide a way to transcend the limitations of personal recall. But objectivity in scientific measurement must also be concerned with the use of official records that were collected for a different purpose. Given the burden for service, for example, emergency department physicians must sometimes choose between careful paperwork and careful operations. Small wonder that backward analyses of historical records sometimes yield information as inaccurate and incomplete as personal recall, but the shortcomings arise for different reasons.

Longitudinal designs are not without pitfalls. Some of them have been summarized in Kessen (1960) and more recently in Magnusson and Bergman (1990a) and Loeber and LeBlanc (1990). The problems range from the issue of data quality and confounding to the problems of biased sampling in selective attrition. There is also the time and age factor. Usually the effective lifetime of the investigation extends beyond the effective lifetime of the investigator. People who had the foresight to initiate the project and design the measures are often not the ones to complete the major analyses and interpretations. Then there is the possible problem of the people being studied getting to know the assessments and researchers too well. This problem can show up in such ways as anticipating questions and tests, to covering up critical information because it is embarrassing. When there is slippage between the aims, the measures, and the secondary analyses and interpretations, errors may increase.

There is the special problem of mistaking temporal sequence with causality. This is the error of assuming that events which occur before a given outcome may be safely interpreted as causes of the outcome. That is an illusion.

Subject loss and lack of cooperation loom as a special problem in longitudinal studies of aggressive and antisocial behavior. People who are most likely to be lost are those who are at greatest risk for school dropout and other deviant outcomes (Cairns, Gariépy & Hood, 1990; Farrington *et al.*, 1990). One important factor is the social network in which subjects are embedded. The network can promote continued involvement and cooperation. The maintenance of the sample also interacts with the issue of data quality, in that the instruments used should take into account the cost (both perceived and real) to participants and the information that the procedures will yield. Quantity of information should not be equated with quality. Subjects may be overwhelmed by the number of questions and the level of their intrusiveness. Further, researchers may be tyrannized by the amount of data yielded. On this count, nothing can substitute for a thoughtful, *a priori* analysis of instruments. Moreover, repeating exactly the same lengthy battery of inventories over multiple assessments may diminish, not enhance, the value of the study. If behavioral novelty and developmental changes are anticipated, the procedures should be age-appropriate and relevant to the person's motives and interests.

Progress and pitfalls

Over the past two decades, the longitudinal study of human behavior has become an impressive enterprise in psychology, sociology, and criminology. The effect on the disciplines has been nothing short of revolutionary, the field has achieved a more precise account of human behavioral ontogeny over the past ten years than the preceding ninety years of this century. A large debt for this progress is owed to such pioneering investigators as David Magnusson in Sweden, Lea Pulkkinen in Finland, Michael Rutter and David Farrington in England, Paul and Margaret Baltes in Germany, and Jack Block and Leonard Eron in the United States, among others. One index of this progress are the recent publications of the European Science Foundation's Network on Longitudinal Studies and Individual Development. Six volumes recently published by the ESF Network constitute a core contribution to a basic methodological and theoretical paradigm shift. Two methodological volumes are particularly important for guiding research design and analysis (i.e. Magnusson & Bergman, 1990a; Magnusson *et al.*, 1991). Four additional volumes published by the Network are concerned with substantive issues. These include problems of aging (Baltes & Baltes, 1990), the prediction of psychopathology (Rutter, 1988), biological correlates of behavior dysfunction (Rutter & Casaer, 1991), and developmental change (de Ribaupierre, 1989). The forging of alliances across disciplines must have been a heroic task, because the researchers bring different sets of methodological and theoretical tools. However, collaboration and thoughtful compromises seem essential in order to reach a common high standard of interdisciplinary activity.[2]

Despite the progress and potential of longitudinal study, some fifteen years ago we decided that there were a number of shortcomings in the available data that had to be corrected. These shortfalls arose in part because of the nature of the phenomena investigated, and in part because of residual limitations in research tools and analyses. Some of the limitations included:

Forgotten girls. Girls have often been under-represented in longitudinal investigation. Gender bias has been particularly strong in studies of conduct disorder and violent behavior where, until recently, females were omitted completely as participants. This under-representation of females persisted even in the face of strong evidence that implicated females as a primary cross-generational link.

Slippery scales. Different criteria have been employed in arriving at judgments of altruism, aggression, and social isolation, among other personality patterns across ages, across investigations, and across societies. Accordingly, attempts to generalize across investigations requires careful attention to the operations of measurement and analysis to determine the ways in which compatibility may be established.

Attrition and missing persons. The loss of participants (e.g. through a failure to find them in follow-up, or their failure to cooperate) is a continuing concern for longitudinal researchers, with some studies reporting greater than 50% attrition. Failure to keep track of participants occurs easily within an open society, and it is often the most important participants who cannot be found or who refuse to cooperate. Times are shifting and recent reports indicate much higher rates of successful tracking than even ten years ago.

Phenomena lost. There has often been an insensitivity of psychological measures to developmental change because true novelties in behavior and morphology arise in adolescence and early maturity. Phenomena are "lost" by measures and statistical techniques that obscure these ontogenetic changes, either by virtue of static categories or by standard score transformations and nondevelopmental metrics and analyses.

Illusionary families. Researchers who conduct longitudinal studies of family influence frequently restrict their sample to children who live with both biological parents and at least one sibling. And both parents must agree to cooperate. Although such sampling is necessary to identify "intact families", we know that most young parents and young children nowadays do not conform to the standard intact family of the

1950s and 1960s. Post-modern families – those in 1990 and beyond – in America and Europe show considerable diversity in structure. Only a minority of young families fit the stereotype of two natural parents who are married and living with two or more children. For example, most women in Sweden under the age of 25 who bear children are not married. And if the research is restricted to children at home with intact families, most children will be eliminated prior to sampling.

Lost signs. Because of the expense of longitudinal research, intervals between observations often range from two to five years, and that is responsible for a loss of information about critical events in the past (i.e. "lost signs" from the past). Significant changes may occur in a life trajectory over short intervals, and it seems reasonable to expect that observations/interviews of adolescents should take place at least annually.

Replication. The most powerful evidence for the reliability of a phenomenon is its independent replication. On this score, many of the classic longitudinal studies are $N = 1$ investigations, because no attempt was made to select independent cohorts (i.e. cohorts are separate longitudinal samples of persons within the framework of the same investigation). Generalizations from the study must be limited to that sample, and the sample has already matured.

It should be noted that there are good reasons for many of the limitations. Consider, for example, the scarcity of females in longitudinal studies of conduct disorder. Omission of girls from studies of conduct disorders has been the outcome of rational design decisions, not oversights or gender bias. Relative to boys, few adolescent girls were arrested for antisocial or violent behavior. To maximize returns, longitudinal investigators focused upon behavior problems in males where the incidence is higher. As the technology of longitudinal research has developed over the past ten years, investigations have become increasingly sensitive to these issues, and steps taken to address them.[3] Decisions about design grow out of the aim of the work, and the samples, measures, and analyses are relative to the goals of the study.

The Carolina Longitudinal Study

Despite the pitfalls and high-risk nature of longitudinal study, there is now a growing consensus that there is no substitute for carefully collected and precisely analyzed longitudinal data. When we began this work we hoped to avoid the more obvious hazards of research design. And if we did not avoid them, we wanted to be able to preserve some new information on the nature of development, even if the broader project failed. As it turned out, the safeguards that we instituted for protection had scientific merit in their own right. The research has not shrunk since it began; on the contrary, it has expanded to meet the new issues and to answer the fresh questions that arose.

The design

The Carolina Longitudinal Study (CLS) design could be described as a multiple-cohort, multiple-method, multiple-level longitudinal investigation.[4] The research has multiple cohorts, because two different samples of subjects (i.e. cohorts) were selected which differed in age. The cohorts were studied separately but simultaneously in successive years on an annual basis through the end of high school. After three years, the two groups overlapped in coverage because one group began annual assessments when they were in the 4th grade and the other group began assessments in the 7th grade. It was multiple method, because several measures were used to define each significant variable. That is important because measures of behavior and psychological characteristics are suspect when applied at different ages, due to possible errors of measurement and/or errors of conception. Any investigation of this magnitude requires assurance, or measurement protection, by the use of several different measures of presumably the same characteristic. The research was multiple level, because it permitted several levels of analysis. That is, it seemed important to be able to zoom in to study individuals and homogeneous subgroups and to zoom out to study the entire sample and its properties in any given year. Within each cohort, subgroups of the most aggressive boys and girls were identified at the beginning of the study, along with control groups of individually matched nonaggressive children (matched with respect to classroom attended, age, sex, race, physical size, and neighborhood).

It was longitudinal, because we saw each participant every year. Longitudinal analyses are essential to clarify issues of individual continuity, growth trajectories, and changes over development.[5] The design also permits a person-oriented analysis of individual ontogeny.[6] Given the possible cultural dependency and generational dependency of longitudinal findings, it seemed especially important to determine the stability and generality of the present results. As shown in Table 2.1, we experienced a high rate of recovery throughout the several years of the study.

This work may also be described as 695 experiments. In this regard, each of our participants, along with his/her family, friends, schools,

Table 2.1 CLS recovery rate through 1990

Cohort I								
Grade								
4th	5th	6th	7th	8th	9th	10th	11th	12th
Year								
1981–82	1982–83	1983–84	1984–85	1985–86	1986–87	1987–88	1988–89	1989–90
N^a								
(220/220)	200/220	(194/220)	(191/220)	(198/220)	(209/219)	(214/219)	(217/219)	(217/219)
Recovery rate								
1.00	0.91	0.88	0.87	0.90	0.95	0.98	0.99	0.99

Cohort II								
Grade								
			7th	8th	9th	10th	11th	12th
Year								
			1982–83	1983–84	1984–85	1985–86	1986–87	1987–88
N								
			(475/475)	(456/474)	(446/474)	(446/472)	(461/472)	(466/472)
Recovery rate								
			1.00	0.96	0.94	0.94	0.98	0.99

[a] Embedded in each cohort are subsets of males and females who were judged to be extremely aggressive on the basis of school nominations by two or more principals/counselors/teachers. Non-nominated subjects were individually matched on the basis of sex, race, classroom attended, and physical size.

spouses or live-ins, and children, constituted a separate study in progress. Each person originally enrolled was considered important to the investigation. We were unwilling to write off any individual as dispensable or lost. Given the goals of our work, we rejected the assumption that attrition in some portion of the sample was normal and permissible. People who "disappear" in the course of longitudinal research may be those whose lives have undergone the most radical or distinctive changes. To the extent that they remained the same or changed in outlook, they may provide the data that outline the limits of malleability. Moreover, idiographic sources of control can be extraordinarily powerful in the lives of individuals. If all dimensions must be shared by the entire population, the most important influences in the construction of a particular life may be ignored. We will try to be sensitive throughout to both levels of analysis. We will also describe selected individuals and their circumstances.

Although the CLS will be the focus of much of this volume, it does not stand alone. Prior to the CLS, we completed a full-scale study to serve as a dress rehearsal for the measures and the methods. This work was conducted in a nearby city of 135,000 people, and involved a one-year longitudinal investigation of three grades of a junior high school. Preliminary studies were also conducted with several hundred younger children in order to establish the measurement properties of the instruments. Since the CLS began, we have undertaken simultaneous investigations of particular issues. These include, for example, investigations of the short-term stability and cohesiveness of social networks and friendships and the cross-national replication of our findings on social organization of peer groups.

Three other investigations stimulated by our findings on the prevalence of aggressive behavior and violence will also be discussed in this volume. One study was based in Los Angeles and dealt with the role of violence in traumatic injury and death in children and adolescence. A second study concerned the social affiliations, social networks, and gang membership of 500 African-American youths in a large city in the south-east of the United States. A third study addressed the relationship between suicidal and aggressive behavior, as represented in a special state-wide sample of 1,300 assaultive and violent adolescents. Other collateral investigations were undertaken, including the analysis of trends in juvenile delinquency of girls in Los Angeles in this century, and studies of social networks and behavior in children in Taiwan and Hong Kong.

The original sample

We began collecting data for the primary CLS in 1981, following two years of preparatory studies to establish measures and refine the research design. For the CLS, 220 children in the 4th grade were selected from 4 different public elementary schools (Cohort I), and 475 adolescents were selected from the 7th grade of 4 public middle schools (Cohort II). The average age of Cohort I at mid-year was 10.2 years; the average age of Cohort II was 13.4 years.

Overall, the sample was representative in race and socioeconomic factors. Twenty-five percent of the participants were minority status. The proportion of African-American participants in the study was virtually identical to the proportion of the African-American population in the communities selected for study. The mean family socioeconomic status of the sample was near the national average. The scale of socioeconomic status that we used, the most recent revision of the Duncan scale, was based on parental occupation. The higher the status of the occupation, as judged by a national sample of respondents, the higher the numerical score.

The full range of occupations was represented by the parents or guardians of our participants. The parents included the chairman of a medical school department in a major university, attorneys, regional sales managers, small business owners, truck drivers, domestics, farm workers, and the chronically unemployed. Following the scale, a numerical score from 11 to 87 was assigned to each family based on the highest job level in the family (i.e. the primary wage earner). The average was 30.2 in Cohort I and 31.6 in Cohort II, close to the national mean of 34.5.

All children in the designated classrooms were invited to join, without regard to selection factors (such as intact families or age and number of siblings). We required a signed statement of permission, indicating the informed consent from parents and children, prior to participation.

The extended sample

Every child had a carer of some sort – parent, stepparent, orphanage house parent, foster parent, grandparent – and those were eventually included in the investigation. Grandparents who were not primary carers were also interviewed. In the schools, we attempted to identify the social network in which the children and adolescents were embedded. This required that we obtain information about the friends and peers of each of the original participants. As some became parents, we have seen their children. All of this was done with the consent and support of the participants and the others.

The idea behind such extensive data collection was that each person was embedded in a context of influences. Given that assumption, it was not sufficient to measure the individual; we had to assess the effective social context of which the individual was a part. On this view, the effects of parents and grandparents are not just historical, they are also contemporaneous agents who contribute to the quality and direction of the individual's behaviors and attitudes. As the circumstances change, so must some features of the individual. Peer influences we believed were not merely a phenomenon of adolescence, so it was necessary to identify social groups prior to and following puberty.

The original settings

We felt that the settings where development occurs would be important to understand both the individual and the problems of the age group. So a brief description of the communities where the children grew up is in order. The participants were initially located in the public schools of five communities that we will call Georgetown, Walnut Valley, West Hill, Van Ness, and Marysboro in a mid-Atlantic state .

Walnut Valley, West Hill, and Van Ness are located in suburban metropolitan districts, according to the 1980 US census. In each community, people who did not commute to their jobs worked in manufacturing (furniture, textiles, agribusiness, electronics, assembly), business, or services. Though similar on several dimensions, the communities have certain distinguishing features. West Hill, for example, has a four-year liberal arts college as well as a facility for the care of children whose families have disintegrated. Van Ness is the site of a major national textile corporation. Its residents are proud of the trips that the local high school choir takes annually to the White House, and a recent graduate of Van Ness High School was selected as a Rhodes Scholar.

Georgetown and Marysboro are located outside the metropolitan area and designated rural in the 1980 census, but Georgetown was shifted to a metropolitan suburban designation in the 1990 census. Both communities had been established during the Revolutionary War, hence the names reflect the British origins of the early settlers. The towns have been in a county that has been historically agriculture and agribusiness, but which has become increasingly influenced by manufacturing. Each of the towns has its own elementary, middle, and high schools. It would thus be possible for a child to continue throughout his/her entire career from preschool through high school in the same system. Georgetown was within commuting distance of a national center for research and light industry, hence the shift from 1980 census to the 1990 census from the rural to suburban classification. Marysboro was more distant, but within an hour's drive of another metropolitan area. Both were small towns in the center of a rural area.

This provides a brief look at the character and demographic properties of the communities. But it is not as easy to identify the community as it might seem at first blush. In any longitudinal study that extends longer than a decade, the place where the observations begin cannot be assumed to be the same as the place where the observations continue. This is the case even when children remain in the same house from infancy through adolescence. Over time, changes in the environment may be due to shifts in family residence, age-related changes in mobility and personal definition of the environment, and/or secular changes in the character of the communities themselves. Over the period from childhood to adulthood, children may move from one house to another, from one community to another, or from one state or country to another. In this regard, change *per se* may be less important than the reasons for change. Is the move due to a shift in parental employment, to family breakup because of death or divorce, or to a pattern of chronic migration and instability? Does the change in the character of the community reflect a national recession or expanding growth and local economic opportunities? The reasons for environmental change are doubtless as important as the details of change.

For children and adolescents, definition of the community was age-dependent. Once adolescents in this region reached 16 years old, they qualified for driver's licenses, and cars were available for most of them. On Friday and Saturday nights it was commonplace for some teenagers in Georgetown to drive to nearby cities. Change in the boundaries of the community at this stage reflected an age-related expansion that had been going on since early childhood, and which would accelerate throughout the transition years.

Each of the communities themselves underwent changes, some major and some minor, over the decade. All of the communities suffered from the deep recession that occurred in 1982–83, and the dominant manufacturing facilities in the region became depressed. This "economic downturn" became translated into a major loss of income for a significant number of families whose children were involved in our observations. But there were also periods of economic growth, where some sectors of the community prospered.

Some of the changes that were observed in the decade were specific to the communities. A brief rundown of the changes illustrates the point.

Walnut Valley's biggest change involved the opening of a final link of a nearby major interstate freeway which made travel and commuting to the research and industrial centers even more convenient than it had been.

Van Ness, on the other hand, changed little beyond a shift in the public ownership of the dominant national corporation which controlled much of the local economy. In the mid-1980s, the company was restructured by a leveraged corporate takeover, the consequences of which were devastating for the local economy. In addition, prominent local clothing and hosiery mills were merged, and the larger companies either shifted their manufacturing operations or merged. The closing of local plants forced many of the parents to shift jobs, or to leave work entirely.

West Hill fared better in the economic merry-go-round of the 1980s. In part because of the stability of the local college, the community seems to have changed least over the decade. It continues to be a popular residential area for people who are employed in management and the professions, in addition to the faculty of the college.

Georgetown benefited from its proximity to the national research center, in that there was spillover of people, jobs, and prosperity into Georgetown and its surrounds. The county and the community struggled to maintain their essential rural character. It is a battle partially lost in the 1990s, due to its popularity as an exclusive retirement center for the region and the East Coast.

Marysboro remained in 1990 pretty much as in 1980. Of the five communities, it was the one most distant from the metropolitan centers in commuting distances and attitudes. Its main industries (poultry, furniture manufacturing) suffered as much as the rest of the region during the recession, but there were no major plant shutdowns. Although improvements were made in the federal highway on the outskirts of the town, and a new shopping mall was built, the town still had no movie theater in 1988. But it had superior high school football and basketball teams. Some of our longitudinal participants who participated in sports in high school eventually won athletic scholarships to college.

This sketch of the communities is provided because the settings for development can clarify individual pathways of life. Depending on where they live and the circumstances of their families, children can be affected by events as broad as perturbations in the national interest rate and its effect on industrial expansion, or as local as the widening of a two-lane road into a four-lane highway.

These were the communities of origin; that is, the towns and cities where participants lived when we first met them. In the course of growing up, many participants and their families moved. By the age of 19, only half of the individuals lived in the county where they were first located. In the first year, a significant portion of the participants dispersed to distant points – north to Alaska and south to Ecuador – as well as other rural and urban areas of the United States. One of the tasks was to find these young people and their families, which was not easy for those who sought to lose the past and create new lives. Any effort to identify the person in context must recognize that the contexts are likely to change over time along with the person.

Cooperation and trust

The first requirement for conducting research with adolescents and school-age children is to win the cooperation and trust of the schools, parents, and the students themselves. All this must occur before the first day of data collection audit must continue every year of the study. To conduct research, we could not have permission withdrawn by the school, the child, or the parents. The problem of survival was compounded because we had no official status in any of the locations in which the studies were conducted. We remained only so long as the parents, children, teachers, principals, and administrators would permit.

Typically we found cooperation, helpfulness, and a genuine desire to assist. We discovered that most people in most schools across the country were extremely helpful, as were most parents and guardians. Perhaps the most important element in maintaining individual cooperation was to secure support from the community at large and the effective social unit which the participant was a part of. The levels of participation increased in the schools as they got acquainted with us over a three-year period. Participation rates, determined by the proportion of children/parents who signed and returned informed consent permission forms rose from 50% of the 7th grade in the first middle school to 89% in the last 7th grade. Each year the study continued, the original subjects and, until subjects were 19 years of age or older, their parents/guardians were informed and their participation solicited.

We wanted to convey respect to each person for their time and for their opinions. Due to school policies, we did not pay teachers or counselors, despite the time they spent helping us. Instead, we provided modest gifts meant to show our appreciation. Because we believed that the best single gift for a teacher was an excellent book, we spent a lot of time selecting interesting, attractive, and useful volumes. For the school, relevant books on the state and its history were presented to the school library. Beyond these institutional gifts, we sought to ensure that the children, parents, teachers, principals, counselors, and school secretaries were uniformly behind the project. For example, we brought flowers on special occasions to celebrate or to express sympathy. Refreshments were sometimes provided for faculty meetings, when it seemed appropriate. But we also tried to maintain a low profile in the institution and play down our own role in the activity.

Sports were big in the lives of the young people with whom we dealt, and one of the most impressive gifts in their view was an autographed poster of the basketball players from our university. Yes, we knew the stars and would say "hi" for our participants. It did not hurt that, during the course of the study, the team was a perennial contender in the NCAA "Final Four" national championship. Other participants did not care about sports, but they did care about their future academic careers. When school counselors wanted to bring the potential students to the campus, we provided tours and refreshments.

Beyond the home and school, public and state agencies provided assistance to the project. These included the courts, residential psychiatric facilities, social service agencies, probation departments, and other locations for the treatment of deviant or disturbed adolescents. None could be taken for granted, and every new contact was a challenge. All required patience and persistence.

Throughout the research, we have been aware that one individual could jeopardize the whole endeavor. Virtually every school had one ill-tempered, suspicious, or neurotic person, and some had more than one. In each case, the critical issues had to be dealt with sensitively and rapidly. Even after the project got off the ground, it could crash at any stage. These problems were potentially compounded because we needed cooperation year after year.

An illustration of the above is in order. In our first day at Walnut Valley Elementary School, the school counselor and the school principal agreed to permit observations in 4th grade classrooms. The research team was directed to Vivian Wright's class to begin, and Mrs. Wright agreed. The two observers were puzzled when, on the third consecutive day of observation, Mrs. Wright made critical comments to her class about the University, class visitors, and psychological research, all while the observers were present and concentrating on coding 5 second behavioral observations.

How was the research team instructed to handle the challenge? It remained calm and continued the observation protocol until the end of class. At that time, the senior researcher thanked Mrs. Wright for her willingness to permit the observations and told her that the observational series was completed. The next day, the team brought her the gift volume given all teachers that year, along with a note of gratitude for her help.

We learned later that Mrs. Wright had a long and difficult history of problems with the school administrators, parents, and students. The assignment of this classroom to the research team was a draconian but pragmatic test. It was obviously the most difficult classroom in the school, as the counselor and principal were doubtless aware when they made the assignment. Through the remainder of the study, this administrative pair seemed convinced that we passed the test, and they provided strong support to the research team. Eventually, Mrs. Wright did so too and requested that the research team returned to her class the next year.

Pitfalls of a more or less serious nature could arise any day. We expected to be challenged in one way or another, even though permission had been granted by the district superintendent and the school's principal. Some of the tests were trivial. In one school, we had to appear at 6:15 a.m. to meet with the principal each morning; in another, we had to prepare 350 individually addressed permission letters to be distributed in 2 hours. But more serious problems occasionally arose. These included institutional machinations, where superintendents, counselors, teachers, and principals became singled out for criticism and possible firing because of their cooperation in our research. In other cases, we became inadvertent pawns in ongoing feuds and personal quarrels.

Beyond institutional politics, we sometimes became peripherally entangled in other ways, such as situations where the parent of one participant became sexually involved with the parent of another participant. This complicated our attempts to obtain parental interviews. In another situation, a parent reportedly became the lover of one of the teenage participants. Other relationships facilitated cooperation, such as when a young woman, whom we had known since the 4th grade, married a young man from another cohort.

One of the dilemmas we encountered was how to track participants who escaped from prison and were "on the run" from the police. Should we interview them when they were fugitives, and possibly be implicated in their subsequent capture, or wait until they were apprehended by authorities? We chose to be patient.

Then there were the everyday dilemmas. It was usually most convenient for the research team to see participants in schools, but our convenience had to be weighed against intrusions in the teaching program. This particular problem was negotiated separately with the administrative and teaching staff of each school, and the academic performance of each child. We also had to deal with the problems of everyday life. Subjects and parents showed selective memory for appointments, and teachers sometimes forgot to return assessments and rating forms.

At each stage of the research, it is necessary for investigators to balance their responsibility to participants, schools, and parents on the one hand, and their responsibility to the research program on the other. Ordinarily, these two commitments were not in conflict. In the present case, it helped that one of us had had experience in school administration and was acquainted with the multiple problems that confront teachers, parents, and participants.

The cooperation of the participants themselves could never be taken for granted. Each year they received small gifts, and smaller children got smaller gifts. For participants in the 4th grade, we began with paper stickers and pencils featuring the logo of neighboring universities. These school-related gifts to participants escalated each year, until the 12th grade when each received a see-through solar calculator. High-school seniors were also given a special T-shirt designed for them by a nationally syndicated cartoonist. Virtually all participants liked the gifts, and some have preserved them from year to year. If the participants had already dropped out of school, we provided a token payment of $20 for continued participation in the study in addition to the other gifts.

We were obligated by our beliefs and professional ethics to ensure that no one would be hurt by his/her assistance. In the course of this investigation, we became acquainted with incidents that were illegal, embarrassing, and harmful to the participants. We were bound by a promise of confidentiality not to reveal identifying information about individual lives, and this extended beyond participants to all persons who cooperated with us. Although the quotes in this volume are verbatim, the identity of all participants has been concealed by changing key features of the descriptions. The names and places are disguised, but not the incidents. Unlike therapists and teachers, we did not attempt to alter the course of any lives, nor did we break the confidence that had been assured.[7] The overwhelming majority of persons in schools and communities throughout the country that we have contacted have gone out of their way to help us. Many of the participants, after years of receiving gifts, reciprocated in later adolescence and gave us gifts to express their affection and respect. We now have a collection of ceramic dishes, T-shirts, photographs, pictures, and pens.

Although we tried to keep a low profile in day-to-day activities in the schools, we felt it important to keep students and teachers fully informed about the investigation. We helped student reporters prepare stories about the project for school newspapers, conducted workshops for teachers and counselors, and met with the administrative boards of school districts. An attractive pamphlet was printed which answered the ten most frequently asked questions about the project. This was distributed to members of school boards, parents, participants, and teachers. As the work progressed, we were invited to meet the leaders of the State Legislature and Senate regarding recommendations on the prevention of school dropout. These activities reduced misunderstanding about our work, and they provided a protective buffer when potential problems arose.

Lost and found: the problem of attrition

All longitudinal studies are vulnerable to sample attrition, and our research was no exception. Loss of participants means that the information obtained may be biased toward the most stable and conventional members of the community. It is not safe to assume that participants will be lost at random. Reasons for sample attrition are multiple, but the participants become "lost" because of family breakup, parents or guardians move to unknown destinations, the child's custody gets changed, or the adolescent may have run away from home, or joined the military. Other participants were not lost at all; they simply no longer wished to participate or their parents withdrew permission.

Tracking participants has required considerable travel, mostly by automobile, covering approximately 60,000 miles per year. Traveling was not only an expense, it was also hazardous. Two automobiles were totally destroyed in the course of the first ten years of the study, and another one was worn out. In the first years of the research, we deducted the mileage from our taxes, bought new cars, and kept the research team on the road. Personal safety of the researchers beyond the highway was always a concern, and the concerns intensified as participants got older and geographic locations became more diverse. Subjects were located in places as diverse as the mountains of Alaska to the inner cities of Los Angeles, New York, and Washington, DC. In inner-city schools, armed security personnel were routinely present at points of entry and in their halls. When it was necessary to track participants who lived in the part of the city which had the highest crime rates and drug-related murders in the United States, researchers traveled in pairs. Visits to homes elsewhere were made with discretion. With ever-present backup, we gained confirmation, reliability, and protection. In the first ten years of study, these safeguards proved effective; there have been no instances of personal harm to any investigator due to threats or attacks in the community. The safeguards also make for better science, in that observations are confirmed by having two separate observers.

In 1990, at the end of the tenth year of the study, all 695 participants in our original research sample were relocated. A small proportion were no longer living (0.6%), and some declined to be interviewed (1.3%). In mid-1990, the sample had become national in scope.[8] The participants lived throughout the United States, from Alaska to Florida, and California to Massachusetts. The status of the sample through the end of high school is shown in Table 2.2. Locating most of the participants was routine; the task was not a major issue for six out of ten participants. The remainder were found with increasing difficulty. At the time, this tracking and recovery was something of an oddity in the literature, and it still remains extraordinarily high. It is now common for investigators to find that they can relocate a high proportion of their subjects, and recovery rates in excess of 90% are becoming standard.[9]

Participants who drop out of school before graduation were a special challenge to locate, even when they did not leave the community. The problems were multiplied when they migrated across the country. Finding these "lost" participants required ingenuity and stubbornness. No simple recipe can be written, because new problems continued to present themselves. The job was made easier when close relationships were established with people in key positions in the school system and the community. They could then be relied upon for directions and clues

Table 2.2 Number and proportion of subjects who moved and distance they moved

	Index of distance moved[a]						Sum
	0	1	2	3	4	5	
Females	223 (0.75)	19 (0.05)	20 (0.06)	18 (0.05	12 (0.03)	20 (0.06)	362
Males	251 (0.76)	21 (0.06)	11 (0.03)	17 (0.05)	14 (0.04)	16 (0.05)	330
Combined	524 (0.76)	40 (0.06)	31 (0.04)	35 (0.05)	26 (0.04)	36 (0.05)	692[b]

[a] Movement index increases with distance, namely:

"0" No move: subject found annually in schools originally assigned (if school dropout, then lived in same area as original school).

"1" Subject found in same district, but in a school different from original assignment.

"2" Subject found in new school district, but in the same county.

"3" Subject found in nearby county (i.e. ≤ 50 miles).

"4" Subject found in distal county but in the same state (i.e. > 50 miles).

"5" Subject found in different state or different country beyond the United States.

[b] Data were combined across Cohort I and Cohort II. Three subjects died in Cohort II prior to 4th wave, hence were not tabulated in this summary.

as to the current whereabouts of the individual, and they sometimes provided invaluable assistance in gaining the participant's cooperation and confidence.

When participants were "lost", one or more of the following steps were taken. The order in which the steps were taken depended upon the circumstances:

o Schools. Records and personnel acquainted with the participant were contacted for information about the current residence of the participant.

o Relatives and friends. People acquainted with the participants were contacted to obtain information on where they now lived. This proved to be of special importance when the participant had a brother, sister, or cousin who has remained in the original school system.

o Former employers. The places where the participants or parents were employed were contacted, and information was sought about where they might have moved.

o Postal service. Registered letters were sent to the child or parent with a request to forward, or we requested that the post office provide us with the new address.

o Telephone directories. A search was made of the telephone directories in the city or state to which the individual was believed to have moved.

o Neighborhoods. Inquiries were made in the neighborhood with former neighbors or acquaintances on the whereabouts of the participant and his/her family.

o Research records of participants. A review was made of all original data obtained from the participant in order to abstract information on relatives who could be contacted, jobs of the parents, concerns about moving, and other clues to the participant's whereabouts.

o Research records of peers. The preceding step was repeated in the original data of all friends or relatives who were in the study.

o Residential directories. A search was made of the residential directories of the communities in which the individuals were reported to have moved or earlier resided.

o Public records. County and state records were searched to obtain information about the current residence of the participant or his/her parents (e.g. the drivers' licenses recorded in the Department of Motor Vehicles; birth certificates, death certificates, and marriage certificates recorded in the office of the County Clerk).

On occasions, we found some potential sources who were not willing to cooperate. Other participants and/or their families actively avoided being found because of difficulties with creditors or the law, or fear of getting discovered in one or another illegal enterprise, from drug dealing and prostitution to car theft, smuggling, or incest and child abuse. Lack of cooperation also arose in cases of disputed guardianship between parents, or between foster parents and biological parents. We discovered early on that refusing permission is not always a matter of forgetting to return a permission slip. It can take the form of passive avoidance, failing to show for interviews, and a variety of other techniques.

Other sources sometimes did not cooperate because of institutional policies. Schools and employers occasionally would not provide the information without additional guarantees and the approval from the person to be contacted. On these occasions, schools were often willing to serve as a middleman to relay the request to the participant, who then contacted the researchers. An example of how we proceeded in one case illustrates our problem-solving strategy.

Danny Suitor moved from Georgetown after the 5th grade reassessment. We had been told by the school personnel that Danny moved to another state, but the school had not received a request for records from the new location, and no forwarding address had been provided. The research team succeeded in tracking his movements through two states, but drew a blank after a move away from Florida. Upon re-examination of the original transcripts, it was discovered that Danny said he had a sister, Nicole, who was 3 years younger, and might possibly still be living in Georgetown. When Georgetown Middle School was contacted, it was learned that a Nicole Suitor was indeed enrolled. As part of the divorce settlement, Danny had gone with their father, and Nicole remained living with their mother. She said she thought they (father and son) now lived in a small town outside Wheeling, West Virginia, but she did not know their address. The research team learned that a Samuel Suitor held an unlisted telephone in Trenton. By checking all high schools in the area, we found only one school with a student by the name of Danny Suitor. A helpful school counselor confirmed that this student was in fact our participant. Through the counselor, Danny agreed to take home information that we supplied regarding the project, along with a parental consent form. The son and father agreed to participate, and all forms were returned to the school. The research team traveled to West Virginia and completed the annual assessment battery. Danny reported among other things that he was planning to drop out of school within the month. If the team had failed to find him through the school, the relocation might have been even more difficult.

Danny represents one of the hard to locate participants. The tracking involved family breakup, multiple moves into different states, helpful school teachers and counselors, listening to original tapes, willingness to travel, a couple of lucky breaks, and plenty of persistence. Ordinarily, the relocation was accomplished in the same year as the loss, with few gaps in the research record. Danny was an exception. The more difficult cases were those in which participants were "on the run" to avoid arrest for felonies or imprisonment for parole violations, were permanent runaways, were school dropouts who moved to other states and changed their names (because of their own marriages or parental remarriage), or were assigned to foster home placement or adoptions that involved several moves and one or more name changes.

Are the returns of tracking worth the costs? No simple answer can be given without detailed information about the actual characteristics of the individual participant. You may argue that the individuals who become lost are more likely than those who are easily found to have experienced further difficulties in living. Hence, the lost participants may be seen as a special risk sample, according to Eron and Huesmann.[10] On the other hand, the participants who are "lost" may experience such a sharp shift in living circumstances as to lead to enduring changes in their lives and subsequent behavior. In our experience, some of the more serious problems and dramatic changes took place in the lives of individuals who would have been entirely lost from standard longitudinal tracking. What is a risk to one child may be a lifeline to another. Given the goals of this investigation, to identify naturalistic shifts in circumstances that could bring a turnabout in a life trajectory, it was imperative that we attempt to relocate all participants.

In general, we found that becoming lost was more often a risk than a lifeline. Children and adolescents who were difficult to find year after year were the ones who were at greatest risk for problems in school and in the community. These results are summarized in Tables 2.3 and 2.4. We found, for instance, that there was a greater likelihood of early school dropout if the child/adolescent moved from one residence to another. This effect held for both males and females, and it held in both groups of participants. The risk for dropout was consistently three to four times as great if moves had occurred, regardless of gender or sample. Further analysis indicates that the dropout was not merely an effect of moving *per se*. Even prior to moving, individuals who would change residence differed from those who would not on those behavioral dimensions predictive of dropout; namely, aggression and academic incompetence (as measured by grades failed or ratings of academic performance). They did not differ on socioeconomic status (SES), and only marginally on measures of popularity and peer

Table 2.3 Early school dropout following moving in CLS by gender and cohort

		Remain in school		Early dropout		Total	Statistical evaluation
Cohort I							
Females	No move	185	*(0.92)*	15	*(0.08)*	200	
	Move	29	*(0.63)*	17	*(0.37)*	46	
	Total	214	*(0.87)*	32	*(0.13)*	246	χ^2 (1) = 26.13, p < 0.001
							Contingency coefficient = 0.31
Males	No move	152	*(0.86)*	25	*(0.14)*	177	
	Move	29	*(0.59)*	20	*(0.41)*	49	
	Total	181	*(0.80)*	45	*(0.20)*	226	χ^2 (1) = 14.84, p < 0.001
							Contingency coefficient = 0.25
Cohort II							
Females	No move	62	*(0.85)*	11	*(0.15)*	73	
	Move	23	*(0.53)*	20	*(0.47)*	43	
	Total	85	*(0.73)*	31	*(0.27)*	116	χ^2 (1) = 12.10, p < 0.001
							Contingency coefficient = 0.31
Males	No move	67	*(0.92)*	6	*(0.08)*	73	
	Move	20	*(0.67)*	10	*(0.33)*	30	
	Total	87	*(0.84)*	16	*(0.16)*	103	χ^2 (1) = 8.40, p < 0.001
							Contingency coefficient = 0.28

acceptance. The last effect suggests that, although there may be quite different reasons for moving depending upon SES, those participants whose families did change residence tended to differ from peers in terms of behaviors that were associated with school failure and interpersonal difficulties.

The lesson is clear. Participants who are most likely to be lost from longitudinal studies are not random cases. To the contrary, they are likely to be those people who are at greatest risk for problems of living and health.

Measures and observations

The heart of any investigation lies in the objectivity, replicability, and validity of the measures it employs. The public transduction of empirical phenomena into theoretical constructs distinguishes this enterprise from common sense and clinical intuition. In the study of social patterns, validity is hard won, and slippage may occur at any step of the design-measurement-generalization process. In the absence of a standard for longitudinal assessment, we proceeded cautiously in the selection and refinement of measurement instruments. For this reason,

Table 2.4 Problem behaviors associated with moving

Assessments prior to moving	No move	Move	ANOVA Significance
Cohort I			
Females			
Aggression (ICS-T, 7th grade)	2.50	2.95	–
Popularity (ICS-T, 7th grade)	4.89	4.33	*
Academic competence (ICS-T, 7th grade)	5.25	4.48	*
SES	28.84	29.67	–
Grades failed (prior to 4th grade)	0.25	0.37	–
Males			
Aggression (ICS-T, 7th grade)	2.70	3.56	*
Popularity (ICS-T, 7th grade)	4.90	4.60	–
Academic competence (ICS-T, 7th grade)	4.75	3.81	*
SES	32.74	27.63	–
Grades failed (prior to 4th grade)	0.26	0.43	–
Cohort II			
Females			
Aggression (ICS-T, 7th grade)	2.48	3.08	*
Popularity (ICS-T, 7th grade)	4.77	4.48	–
Academic competence (ICS-T, 7th grade)	4.90	5.04	–
SES	32.52	28.57	–
Grades failed (prior to 7th grade)	0.14	0.46	***
Males			
Aggression (ICS-T, 7th grade)	3.24	3.82	*
Popularity (ICS-T, 7th grade)	4.48	4.09	*
Academic competence (ICS-T, 7th grade)	4.28	3.76	*
SES	30.41	33.82	–
Grades failed (prior to 7th grade)	0.45	0.53	–

– Not statistically significant.
* $p < 0.05$.
** $p < 0.01$.
*** $p < 0.001$.

we spent two years in preliminary study to ensure that the procedures were sensitive to the phenomena that we wanted to focus upon.

This last point brings up a major trend in measurement. In Chapter 1, we offered the idea that the puzzles of human development require researchers to study each life as a whole. This general proposition goes beyond a vague commitment to individuality, integration, and holism. It has strong implications for how the business of science should proceed. Among other things, it implies that multiple levels of measurement are required rather than focus upon single variables, single tests, or single contexts. One of the reasons is that behaviors, for the most part, are limited by the momentary features of relationships and contexts.

Behavioral actions and cognitions – the stuff of psychology – have a special status for biological adaptation and integration. In the accommodations of human development, particularly social patterns, the actions and counteractions of other people constitute major extra-organismic sources of behavioral organization. These actions are at the interface between the internal constraints of the individual and the external constraints of the setting. Some actions, including self-concepts, are tailored for specific functions, such as providing reasons for getting out of bed in the morning. Other actions, such as those dictated by social etiquette and styles, are more strongly constrained by the immediate context. Several domains of activity are organized within the individual and provide mutual constraints. But synchrony does not mean substitutability. Each system is organized in its own terms, and self-reflections may be poorly associated with the judgments that most people share about you.

The practical implication of this brief excursion into the modern theory of assessment is that we had better be careful about how and what we measure. Self-reports such as survey interviews or tests are necessary but not sufficient. We also need objective observations of behavior, taken by independent researchers, which can provide information about unconscious actions that are beyond the individual's own awareness. Other informants and outside the extended "self" of the family are important as well. This includes information from peers and teachers. Other individual measures include contemporaneous records from schools, the courts, and the state. These have clear limitations, but they help transcend context and permit us to bridge the gap between individual measures and epidemiological statistics.

Then there are measures of the world beyond the individual. In life, the environment is not a single thing; nor is it a stable, unchanging entity. To the contrary, at any one stage, there are multiple contexts of life, including different individuals and groups that are important for the person. In these contexts, each of us potentially has different selves. This means that the longitudinal measurement of individual actions must identify the multiple social contexts for the person: the family, best friends, peer social groups and networks, the spouse, and the children. It is also critical to identify the several physical contexts afforded by the home, the school, and the community. The behavioral phenomena that we observe in individuals over time represent a complex equation that incorporates all of the above.

If all this sounds complicated, it should not be surprising. The scientific issues involved in tracking lives in progress are considerably more profound than they appear at first. At each stage of measurement and analysis, investigators must bring together several layers and levels of assessment in order to make sense of individuals.

In the light of the fallibility of single information sources, we employed multiple measures of each quality or characteristic. We also thought it essential to understand the source of variance that each measure captured before we attempted to combine the components. That was no small trick when the procedures employed extended from information from teachers, peers, parents, social networks, the courts and probation departments, school records, school yearbooks and newspapers, and interviews from the individuals themselves. In addition, parents and grandparents participated in semi-structured interviews when subjects were in late adolescence.[11]

Data tyranny is a special hazard in longitudinal work. In order to have sufficient statistical power to conduct multivariate analyses, a reasonably large number of participants must be studied on repeated occasions. More participants and more measures inevitably lead to more data. The problems are compounded by the accumulation of data year by year. Computers help, but nothing can substitute in the analysis for a clear statement of aims of the research and the establishment of priorities.

Accordingly, we adopted a minimalistic strategy in data collection, following guidelines summarized by Cairns & Moffitt (1992).[12] Two of their points are especially worthy of note because they are opposite to the assumption that more is better. Specifically, the points are:

o Greater depth of understanding is not always associated with greater coverage or length of assessments, in that the costs of extensive subject participation can outweigh the returns.
o Given the limited amount of unbiased information that can be obtained from any single information source, including the self reports of participants, there may be surprisingly little information loss. Attention should be given to minimize the demands of the assessment upon individual children and parents. Where possible, the assessments should be "subject friendly" and/or take advantage of involvement in other normal functions (e.g. preschool and school activities, health checkups). (Cairns & Moffitt, 1992)

In general, priority was given in all measurement to "brevity consistent with clarity and reliability". To avoid becoming over-whelmed by the details of the work, we provide only short descriptions of the nature of the instruments that were employed during the school years.

The backbone of the yearly contact was a semi-structured face-to-face interview conducted annually with the subject. The interviews were tape-recorded and information was obtained about social networks, friendships, conflicts, perceived parental attitudes, and other domains.

Our interview procedures differed from those employed in many other contemporary research settings, and a comment is required to clarify the nature of the information obtained. Our semi-structured procedures were modeled after those pioneered by R. R. Sears and his colleagues in studies of child rearing and development, and extended by A. Bandura and R. H. Walters in studies of delinquency and M. Rutter and G. Brown in psychiatric investigation.[13] The interviewers were extensively trained to follow an interview protocol. It was semi-structured because the interviewers permitted the subjects to give extended answers (as opposed to multiple choice), and to express their concerns in their own words as opposed to the items and constructs defined by the interviewer, and there was an explicit interview protocol to be followed, along with standard probes to gain additional information. On the other hand, this method differs significantly from "survey methods where subjects are given explicitly defined categories of response form which they must select" (e.g. Elliott, Huizinga, & Menard, 1989), and it differs from clinical interviews, which provide modest or loose structure.

The format permitted explicit definition of domains of analysis and scoring for, among other things, social networks, conflicts, and friendships. In addition, the interview was modified as the subject's age and circumstances changed. For instance, the interviews for participants who dropped out of school were modified so the questions were consistent with their current life circumstances. Similarly, as subjects entered new stages of the life cycle, questions were added (e.g. on work satisfaction, pregnancy and parenthood) and others eliminated. The interview core continued to be its concern with relationships, conflicts, and social networks.

In addition, the subjects and their teachers annually completed a brief test (Interpersonal Competence Scale), which originally consisted of a series of fifteen items for the teacher and eighteen items for subjects (including three "filler" or distractor items). Consistent with the minimalistic bias, we attempted to keep the interview and related test procedures brief. This succeeded for the initial years of measurement (interviews were approximately 20–30 minutes in length), but in later years they grew longer (i.e. 45–60 minutes in length).

Beyond these annual measures directly from participants and teachers, information was gathered from the school yearbooks, newspapers, and reports from schools on school dropout. Detailed information on the procedures is given in the technical papers that we have published and which are cited in the References (see Cairns,

Cairns, Leung, & Ladd, 1994, for a detailed description of the methods and measures). In brief, the fourteen domains of information in the school period include:

1. Social networks. Composite cognitive maps of the social network and social organization of the classes and schools were developed on the basis of information provided by participants and peers. The networks yielded information about the persons with whom each participant affiliated, or if he/she had no affiliative group. Information on networks and friendships was collected annually.

2 "At risk" and non-risk control. Identification of children who were at high aggressive risk, along with matched non-risk control subjects, were obtained prior to the beginning of the study from teachers and principals when children were in the 4th grade (Cohort I) or 7th grade (Cohort II). The "risk" definition is discussed more fully in Chapter 4.

3. Social cognitive interview. Self-reports and self-cognitions, derived from individual interviews that cover the self, family, and peers, along with perceptions of friendships, recent conflicts, and goals for the future. As we indicated above, the interview was age-graded and circumstance sensitive. The semi-structured interviews were conducted annually and tape-recorded.

4. Direct behavioral observations. Extensive, week-long observations were made which employed synchronized, multi-level observational procedures in school classrooms and physical education classes. These observations were made for all subjects in the high risk and matched control participants upon entry. It occupied much of the research assessment time in the first three years of the investigation. Additional observations were made after three years.

5. Interpersonal competence scale (ICS). Ratings by teachers, counselors, and parents yielded assessments of behavior in the school or the home on four separate factors i.e. social acceptance (popularity), peer conflicts (aggressiveness), academic performance (academic competence), social relations (affiliation) and a summary dimension (social competence). In addition, subscales of the ICS tapped appearance, athletics, emotionality, as well as withdrawn and shy behaviors. These ratings were available annually as long as participants remained in school.

6. Interpersonal competence scale self-reports (ICS-S). Participants rated themselves annually on the same scales employed by teachers, permitting the longitudinal plotting of self-attributions and comparisons with sources outside the self. This information was available annually for all years of the investigation.

7. Peer nominations. Each year, participants and peers provided a "cognitive map" of the social network, nominated best friends, boy/girlfriend, and people with whom they have had recent conflicts, thereby providing peer assessments of each participant's behaviors. This information was available annually, but it is most reliably interpreted for the first two years of the investigation.

8. Maturation. Each year observers rated participants on dimensions of physical maturation and attractiveness. For those subjects who were in school, annual ratings were obtained from teachers. In addition, photographs were obtained from school annuals, or the subjects agreed to be photographed. Both males and females rated themselves on physical attactiveness each year, and females reported their age of menarche.

9. Academic progress. School performance and failure was determined from counselors, teachers, and the participants. The information from the school included school grade placement, graduation, school dropout, and serious problems of attendance. This information was available annually.

10. Delinquency and crime. These measures were obtained from court records, reports from probation officers, self-reports, Department of Motor Vehicle records, visits to detention facilities and prisons, and published records of arrests and court actions.

11. Marriage and births. Information was obtained from county records, self-reports, and direct interactions with the spouse and/or infants in year-to-year assessments. This information was collected on a continuing basis from newspaper reports.

12. Family status and runaways. Changes in family composition, runaways, and familial attitudes were determined in the annual interviews with participants, late adolescent interviews with parents, and visits to the locations where the participants lived.

13. Employment. Various economic data, including teenage jobs, automobile operation and ownership, were obtained from the participants themselves and, in some instances, visits to the workplace. This information was collected annually from mid-adolescence.

14. Health, accidents, and mortality. Information was obtained from participants, from school personnel, newspaper reports, the Department of Motor Vehicles, and, in the case of death, the Office of the State Medical Examiner.

The tasks of collating, organizing, and retrieving the information from multiple sources occupied as much time and effort as getting it in the first place. Hence we had a primary concern with ensuring the accuracy and quality of each record.

These procedures are summarized in Table 2.5. They are described in greater detail in several technical reports on the research. Our aim in this table, and in this volume is to provide an understandable overview of the kinds of information obtained and why we sought it. This does not, of course, substitute for a detailed description of the precise methods and variables.[14]

Data quality

The question of data quality refers to the reliability and validity of the raw information and the measures. Confidence in the information obtained on a specific issue can be no stronger than the weakest link in the process of sampling, measure design, data collection, transcription, transduction, and analysis (Bergman & Magnusson, 1990). Accordingly, we felt that it would be misguided to assign the primary data collection to the least informed or most naive members of a research team. Exactly the opposite research strategy should be followed, if history is a reliable guide to the achievement of future progress. The essential contributions of Alfred Binet, Wilhelm Preyer, Sigmund Freud, Jean Piaget, J. M. Baldwin, Zing-Yang Kuo, T. C. Schneirla, and Arnold Gesell may be traced, in large measure, to instances where the investigators themselves participated in the data collection.

But in the evaluation of contemporary research, the involvement of the primary investigators in the collection of human data is usually viewed with question, or suspicion. Presumably the closer investigators are to the data, the more likely it is that their biases will influence the outcome of the work. So assistants who are employed at the first stage of data collection should be naive with respect to the purposes of the study and the meaning of information. And the professional message to students and colleagues is that intellectual responsibility and seniority is tantamount to graduation from the tedium of data collection.

One difficulty with this modern definition of research roles is that people whose responsibility it is to understand the subtle organization of behavior patterns have become insulated from direct contact with them. Distance inevitably dulls the researcher's perceptions of the critical elements of the phenomena to be explained. So we spent considerable time in screening, training, and advising all research personnel who had direct contact with participants, schools, and families.

Fourteen people were involved in primary data collection over the several years of this study. At least two served as interviewers in each of

Table 2.5   Overview of CLS measures

Measures	Occasion	Source	Characteristics of measures	Areas of assessment
Social networks	A	Peers, self	Composite maps of social organization	Peer influence, friendship, social reciprocity
Risk control	I	Schools	Nominations by teachers, administrators	Antisocial acts, aggressive behaviors
Interview	A*	Self, parents	Personal interview with subjects, parents	Cognitions on family and peer social relations
Observations	I*	Investigators, self	Direct behavioral observation of interactions	Aggressive escalation, friendships, prosocial
ICS-T	A*	Teachers, parents	Ratings by teachers, parents	Social competence (e.g. popularity, aggression)
ICS-S	A	Self	Self-evaluations by subjects on ICS	Social competence (e.g. popularity, aggression)
Nominations	A	Peers	Assessments of conflicts, friendship	Social patterns (e.g. popularity, aggression)
Maturation	A*	Investigators, self	Maturational status on physical dimensions	Rate of maturation, age of menarche
Academic	A*	Schools, self	Academic progress and performance	Cognitive achievement and school failure and dropout
Delinquency	A*	Courts, self, parent	Arrests, adjudication, and self-reports	Antisocial and criminal, delinquent behaviors
Marriage, births	A*	Self, parent, records	Marriages, divorce, and parenthood of subjects	Teenage parenthood and teenage marriage, divorce
Family status	A	Parents, self	Changes in families structure and influence	Effects of family disintegration and changes in family
Employment	A*	Self, parents	Jobs and career aspirations, lifecourse changes	Lifecourse changes, developmental constraints
Health, accidents	A*	Self, records, parent	Mortality and morbidity information	Health status related to development and generational changes

"Occasion" abbreviations: A = annual; I = initial year; * = not all measured are employed annually.

the years, and typically four individuals were involved. However, one of us (Beverley D. Cairns) was one of the interviewers in the first several years of the study. This ensured continuity in contact with parents, schools, and subjects. Interviewers were rotated to different participants from year to year so that potential biases could be eliminated. This rule was modified only in unusual circumstances.[15] In addition, appropriate safeguards were instituted to ensure that the observers, interviewers, raters, and coders were blind with respect to the participants' standing on the relevant variables and information gathered from other sources. Each year, different teachers were enlisted as raters, and participants, peers, and parents were never given feedback with respect to their performance. When appropriate, fresh investigators were introduced into the study to safeguard the objectivity of the measures and the coding.

After the data were collected, a staff member was in charge of monitoring data quality at the succeeding steps of transcription, coding, and computer entry. Cross-checking the materials prior to computer entry was critical, so that repeated checks were made with original records. Analyses were conducted at several levels, from direct assessment of the raw protocols to the fitting of structural equations and cluster models. Since several people were involved in the research task, it was possible to have reliability checks by independent observers at every stage of data collection, coding, and analysis. In addition, ready access to the raw materials and intermediate codes permitted an immediate check of the primary protocols if questions arose in the analysis. The availability of several years within a single cohort, two independent cohorts, and a separate preliminary longitudinal study permitted cross-validation of all main findings.

One issue of data quality should be mentioned, namely, our decision to include observations and semi-structured interviews in adition to a brief standardized annual inventory. The integration strengthened the research design on the following counts:

1. Self-report measures (whether called tests, surveys, or interviews) are seriously constrained by the perceptions of those who are providing the information. Hence, lengthy assessments by overlapping inventories that purport to measure a given quality tend to provide correlated information. On this score, they provide an overload for the subjects without a redeeming increase in information.
2. Longitudinal assessments conducted on an annual basis yield information about stability and change, and thereby enhance the reliability of any given measure. For example, brief assessments can become robust by permitting the investigator to contrast, construct, or combine over adjacent years.

3. It is an illusion to view measures with constrained response categories for subjects to be more "objective" than measures which permit individual response variation. The objectivity arises in the scoring and interpretation process, not in the way information is recorded at the first stage.

4. This investigation gave priority to the concrete realities of the individual's life and his/her perceptions rather than the tracking of psychological constructs as defined by tests currently in vogue. We felt that the more concrete measures we obtained could in any generation be translated by cross-validation into the results of comparable tests and surveys.

5. Perhaps most importantly, we felt that many of the standardized survey procedures currently available tended to obscure real developmental changes by a focus upon between-individual differences rather than upon the concrete adaptations of individuals. A measurement tug-of-war exists between the use of objective tests of individual differences and less standard measures of developmental change. We hoped to preserve information about both phenomena in our measurement strategy. This meant that we needed to conduct additional assessments to ensure that our procedures showed an expected network of relationships with other commonly employed measures, in addition to our demonstration of their ability to predict real-life outcomes.

The "average child" and other myths of aggregation

In a prescient essay that appeared in the first *Handbook of Child Psychology*, Kurt Lewin outlined the need to study the dynamic relations between the individual and the environment in the concrete particularity of the total situation.[16] Lewin challenged the dominant methodology of psychological inquiry on two counts: (1) its reliance on aggregation for description and statistical analysis to describe the mythical "average child" or "average family", and (2) its focus on psychological "variables" independent of the context in which they occurred. On the first matter, Lewin argued that the "average child" was a statistical invention. It was worse than a benign illusion; it was a productive mischief. For Lewin, clumping together children who were similar with respect to salient extrinsic or demographic characteristics but different with respect to psychological dynamics was guaranteed to mislead.

More than a half century has passed since Lewin's seminal contributions. Some of his ideas on the need to establish ecological validity have been incorporated into the mainstream of the field, and they are no longer identified as distinctively Lewinian. But one nuclear issue, namely, the need to understand the behavior of specific individuals in specific settings, remains to be resolved by developmental psychologists. At first, the problem of when or whether to group participants may seem to be an important though technical issue, one that should be decided by statistical and methodological journeymen. But choice of the unit of analysis, the person, the variable, or the group, is what all subsequent decisions of research strategy necessarily rest upon. An issue so central to understanding science is too important to leave to the experts.

In a cogent analysis of the issues, David Magnusson has outlined a framework for developmental research that has radical implications for how the scientific enterprise should proceed.[17] In brief, Magnusson argues that the field should make a commitment to understand the processes of human behavior, and that technological goals (i.e. prediction and control) should be secondary. Moreover, the configuration of factors that operate in each individual's life requires that attention be given to the behavior of each person as an "integrated totality". The action patterns of every person represent a unique mosaic of biological-interactional-situational factors. To the extent that these configurations are distinctive and individual over time, the person's status on a single variable (or set of variables, independent of context) is a fallible guide for understanding.

Developmental researchers are usually confronted with networks of relationships, not single antecedent–consequent linkages. This state of affairs has yielded many positive findings and interpretations. The abundance of "significant" findings in contemporary developmental research has also had a negative side, in that it shifts responsibility for understanding phenomena away from the data. The findings have often become projective tests for the field, where the burden for interpretation shifts from data to *a priori* beliefs.

It has been widely assumed that because social phenomena are multi-determined and complex, the statistical analyses employed to study them should be equally complex. We believe that the assumption is misguided. When the complexity within the phenomenon is permitted to breed complexity in the analysis and interpretation, it often means that there has been a failure in theory or a lack of creativity in design. To clarify complicated issues, the simpler the statistic, the better. Parsimony in analysis may be permitted because the major analytic problems have been solved in the design created, in the methods adopted, and in the precision of the hypotheses (Cairns, 1986).

Beyond the usual challenges that face social science investigators confronted with complex data sets, developmental researchers have special problems. Virtually all "lifecourse" and "developmental" hypotheses presuppose that fresh influences and new opportunities arise from within the individual or in the social context. Most theoretical statistical models assume, however, that there is nothing new under the sun.

How might categories and dimensions that permit novelty be introduced, without presupposing that the same pattern of latent variables is expressed at all developmental stages or in all people? The factor or dimensional stability question has been investigated in our research by employing concrete categories at the first level of data collection. Whenever feasible, the initial coding distinctions are qualitative not quantitative. We adopted measures which preserved the concrete characteristics, functions, and features of the behaviors of participants. This technique of data recording was followed in direct behavioral observations, in interview reports, and in community reports. The use of qualitative categorical classifications permitted us to determine whether some concrete behaviors would rise and others would fall across time, and still others would emerge or disappear. In addition, the information permitted the use of multivariate statistical techniques to determine whether new dimensions appeared over time. This strategy permitted us to conclude, for example, that a new dimension of "social aggression" appeared in girls in early adolescence that co-existed with confrontational "aggression" (Cairns *et al.*, 1989).

A second issue concerns the appropriate unit or dimension of analysis. Magnusson and Bergman (1984; 1990b) observe that most analyses of behavior are "variable-oriented" rather than "person-oriented". An alternative to multivariate analysis would be a multi-person analysis, where the task is to identify the patterns of problem behaviors that occur across individuals – the "packages" of deviance. The second step in this strategy would be to determine why delinquent characteristics covary in particular combinations. The proposal may be subsumed by the more radical proposition that certain developmental phenomena require analysis at the individual, configural level rather than at the sample, population level. Generalizations may then be reached on the basis of the lawfulness of processes within persons over time, as opposed to the lawfulness of associations within populations (see Allport, 1937). The unit of study becomes the individual, not populations. One enduring problem in behavioral study concerns the issue of how to translate ephemeral processes about individual adaptation into quantifiable generalizations.

One strategy that we have adopted has been to identify configurations of boys and girls who have common behavioral and demographic profiles in childhood. This person-orientated strategy is based on the assumption that developmental trajectories of behavior reflect the operation of both personal and social factors over time. Hence the simultaneous employment of internal and external characteristics should be the key to isolating commonalities in developmental pathways. Such a strategy directs as much attention to the failures of prediction as to the successes. The hazard with conventional models has been that developmental phenomena may themselves become distorted by the very operations designed to make them accessible to empirical analysis. The problem is magnified when standard multivariate analyses treat distinctive trajectories of individual development as error variance.

The pitfalls in understanding are more often logical than mathematical. On this score, it is a minor irony that many of the statistical procedures introduced to study children of different ages have served to reduce or eliminate the impact of maturation and developmental change; for example, the workhorse of longitudinal research, the familiar correlation coefficient, as it is typically employed, eliminates real differences in performance associated with maturation. Similarly, statistical transformations that underlie the IQ ratio get rid of age-related differences in cognitive functioning. Modern refinements of scaling have achieved the same outcome through standard scores, where same-age peers provide the reference group. These scaling techniques are not limited to the study of intelligence. They have become the strategies of choice for measures of aggressiveness, deviance, and unconventional behavior.[18]

To sum up, the chapters have been prepared so that advanced training in statistics is not a prerequisite to understand the main points. When it looks as if reference to technical statistical information is necessary to clarify questions for specialists, it is included in the chapter notes.

Concluding comment

Measures reflect both the art of design and the objectivity of science. Systematic theory, when combined with appropriate methods and analyses, is a necessary springboard to extend our understanding beyond common sense as well as to understand common sense. But precise methods and advanced analyses do not guarantee progress. On the contrary, misleading findings may arise when there is a gap between the ideas that gave rise to the work and the empirical operations adopted to define and analyze those ideas. The ways that you attempt to clarify phenomena in large measure determine the worth of the solution. So it is a danger signal when the procedures seem irrelevant to outcome of research, or when they are viewed as optional appendages. To summarize the research in four points:

1. The aim of this investigation was to track personality and social development, including the risks and the lifelines of adolescence. The 695 participants were representative in race, socioeconomic status, and likelihood of achievement and/or getting into difficulty.
2. These individuals were seen individually, on an annual basis. We also saw the peers in their social networks and their teachers and counselors. The aim was to understand their lives in the context of their families and their communities. The assessment procedures were at multiple levels. Other information sources included the schools, the courts, and various state agencies, from Motor Vehicles to the State Medical Examiner.
3. Follow up was a high priority. We maintained contact with 100% of the 695 participants, and interviewed 99% of the living participants in the last year of high school. Our aim was to track each participant from the time he/she began in the study in the 4th or 7th grade until the cohort completed high school. This recovery rate was particularly important, because there was a relationship between risky and problem behaviors, on the one hand, and the difficulty of relocation and recovery, on the other.
4. To determine the generality and applicability of the findings, systematic comparisons have been made with other national and international longitudinal studies prior to, during, and following our investigation. There is no substitute for precise replication and the analysis of similarities and differences across studies and populations.

We turn now to the trajectories of social development and patterns in individual lives to see what they reveal about lifelines and risks in adolescence.

THREE

Growth and aggression

In many respects man is the most ruthlessly ferocious of beasts. As with all gregarious animals, "two souls", as Faust says, "dwell within his breast", the one of sociability and helpfulness, the other of jealousy and antagonism to his mates.

William James (1890)

Each year in the Carolina Longitudinal Study, participants were asked to describe two conflicts: one conflict with a person of the same sex, and another conflict with a person of the opposite sex. These interviews were audiotaped for subsequent detailed analysis. The following excerpt is from Donna's interview in the 10th grade when she was 16 years old.

I: Has anybody caused you trouble lately or bothered you?
D: Let's see, well, I hate to say it, but I did. I got in a fight at school . . . she kept bothering me. I got sick and tired of it, and I told her – I said I mean I was not gonna fight the girl. I said, "Listen, Linda, I said I wanna be your friend". I said, "We need to talk". Because she – I heard her calling me something. I mean I read her lips and it was horrible, and I knew that we needed to talk. The girl followed me, and then she, oh, she slapped, and, Oh Lord. Everybody was there. It was in the hallway, by the girls' lavatory. Everybody in the whole school, and she slapped me, and I – I just stood there, and I was surprised and I know I wasn't gonna walk away after she slapped me in front of all those people and I went off. I mean I left the girl laying. She was crying. I had – I had banged her head up against the tile wall. They thought she had a concussion. I mean I really – I went crazy, and I don't do stuff like that. I don't. I get along with everybody, and she just didn't act right, and she didn't

45

wanna get along, and anything anybody said. She didn't get along with anybody.

I: How did the fight stop?

D: Her head was bleeding. She had a black eye. Her mouth was bleeding. I mean her elbow was bleeding. Her knees were bleeding. She was bleeding all over, and I just got up and I wouldn't – there wasn't a scratch on me, except for – she did scratch me with her fingernail on my neck.

I: How did you feel about the fight?

D: I felt – I felt – I thought I just let myself as low as she let herself. I mean – I just put myself down to her standards, and I just – I was sorry on my part, but everybody makes mistakes. You learn from your mistakes.

I: How did she feel?

D: Well, when she got up she was crying and holding her head and bleeding and all this stuff and she just – I turned around and I said – I said "I gotta go", and she said, "Ah, you're just walking away 'cause you don't want no more of this". I mean everybody knew that I'd kicked her butt. She was laying there crying and bleeding and she said – I mean still – she always runs her mouth, so I just walked away. I didn't wanna mess with her anymore. . . . She's real moody. I can't stand being around moody people because they're just a bother. I mean I could have walked away. But after she slapped me, you know how hard it would be for me to walk away, and all your friends are behind you and I don't know. It was just a bunch of junk, and I'm glad it's over.

No one who knows Donna would describe her as violent. Nor does she see herself as aggressive. She was one of the most popular girls in her high-school class, a cheerleader, Homecoming Queen, and the envy of many. Yet she beat Linda almost senseless and left her crying and bleeding in the hallway. Although modestly embarrassed, she showed little remorse in talking about the incident. There was some veiled satisfaction that she had banged the other girl's head into the tile wall, and "kicked her butt" as well.

This was not the most severe conflict we have observed. More serious incidents in which our female participants have been involved have led to hospitalization and imprisonment. There have also been homicides and suicides. Beyond the modern redefinition of gender behaviors, Donna's account underscores that bloody physical conflicts occurred in the lives of many normal teenagers we studied, both male and female.

Violence calls forth mixed emotions. For many, it can provoke both terror and attraction. As the mass media have long understood, violence sells. For societies, it can stimulate nationalism or generate internal chaos. National violence is also seen as a hallmark of leadership. Most of the revered presidents of the United States – such as Lincoln and Roosevelt – served when the nation was engaged in a major internal or external war. This lesson has not been lost on contemporary presidents who discovered the salubrious effects of successful "little" wars on national polls and popularity.

But violence in the 1990s is also a national tragedy. It is the leading cause of death among young African-American men and women from 15 to 44 years of age, and it is the second leading cause of death of all teenagers across the United States.[1] According to a recent report from the Surgeon General of the United States, violence prevention in youth is one of the top health priorities for the country.[2] The problem of violence as a health risk has reached epidemic proportions among both European and North American youth. Moreover, the violent child is as much a victim as a perpetrator. Aggression has now been linked in the lifetime of individuals to a host of problems of living (see Chapters 5, 7, and 10).

Concrete answers to some issues of human aggression may be provided by tracking the development of aggression, and determining if there are stepping stones from childhood disputes to adolescent violence. We were also concerned with the functions aggressive behaviors serve in the everyday adaptations of children and teenagers and the differences between males and females. We address the problem of aggressive development in two parts. This chapter reviews the development of aggressive behavior in normal youth; Chapter 4 focuses upon children and adolescents who are at special risk.

The national picture

The relationship between age and arrests yields a dramatic picture, describing a profile like the face and back slope of the Matterhorn (Figure 3.1). This relationship between age and violence might be the most important single fact about delinquency.[3] The abrupt rise in arrests for violence begins at about age 11, rises sharply, and peaks at ages 17 and 18. Seventeen- and 18-year old males constitute the age group that is most likely to be arrested for crimes of violence. The drop-off in arrests for violence begins in the early 20s, and decreases steadily until senescence. Females are less likely to be arrested for violence than males, and older males are less likely to be arrested than teenage males. There is a rise in female arrests for violence at adolescence, but the increase is modest compared to that of males. Other national data –

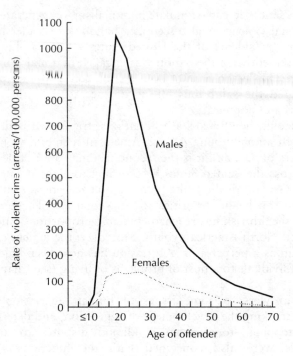

Figure 3.1   Arrest rates for violent crime by males and females as a function of age, with rape excluded due to bias in statistical reporting. (Sources: Crime in the United States (1992) and US Census Report (1990))

including murder and victimization information – yield parallel outcomes.

Fifteen years ago we published a parallel graph which showed approximately one-half of all arrests for violence in the United States involved persons 21 years of age and younger.[4] Although the data in Figure 3.1 are newer, the age course of the phenomenon is the same. Only the height of the curves – the severity of the problem – has changed. While there are temporal changes in the frequency and severity of violence, the age-sex-arrest pattern has remained consistent across time and space. A virtually identical curve may be drawn from the arrests for crimes in England and Wales in 1842.[5] Three aspects of the graphs should be noted. First, these data are based on number of arrests, not the number of persons. The difference is significant. For example, it may be the case that violent older teenagers are likely to be arrested on two or more occasions each year, while younger ones are likely to be arrested only once each year.

Second, the information is cross-sectional not longitudinal. These data do not represent composite growth curves for individuals. From the FBI annual compilation of local arrest statistics, it is unclear whether there is an increase in the number of people who become violent as they reach teenage, then decrease as they enter adulthood, or there is no increase in the number of persons who are violent, but there is an increase in the severity of their violence. The two possibilities – increasing numbers of violent people at adolescence, or increases in violence by a small number of people – call for different strategies of prevention and intervention. A similar problem holds for interpretation of the severe drop in the curve with age. It is unclear from annual arrest data whether becoming an older adult is therapeutic, or whether the data were merely incomplete and misleading. It would be misleading if the "age-out" effect is due to the removal from society of the most serious offenders by prison, injury, or death.

Third, there is a large difference between males and females in arrests for violence, particularly in late adolescence. This difference is greatest in magnitude in late adolescence, given the less steep slope in the rise of arrests for females relative to males. Gender differences in arrests for assaults are age-relative, with the largest differences appearing between the mid-teenage period and adulthood. In addition, even though there is a fourfold to tenfold gender difference in violence, a large number of females are arrested for violence. Lastly, the male and female curves show similar developmental points of age-related increase and similar points of age-related decrease. This suggests that at least some and perhaps most processes related to aggression are common to males and females.

It should be noted that arrest statistics from the FBI provide only part of the picture. The national picture should also include information about morbidity and mortality, since violence is a major health risk for youths. As we observe in Chapter 9, homicide is the leading cause of death in minority youths in America, and it is the primary cause of trauma injury among youth in the inner city.[6] Moreover, highly aggressive teenagers are more likely to become involved in other health-threatening problems than are nonaggressive teenagers. They are also over-represented in accidents, suicide attempts, and mortality statistics (Chapter 9).

Aggression through time

It does not require research to tell us that there are enormous differences between the inadvertent injuries produced by toddlers, the angers of childhood, and the lethal violence of adolescence.[7] But do any linkages exist among these behaviors over time in the individual? Is the child who throws a box of crayons at another kid across the room in the 1st grade likely to be the adolescent who draws a knife in a fight in the 9th grade and becomes imprisoned for homicide as a young adult? And if there are links across time and space, what accounts for the continuity? Are the effects in the genes, in the child's personality and early experience, in the family coercion, in the peer relations, in the neighborhood, or in a combination of the above? These questions about individuals and how they differ can be answered only by an intensive study of the same persons over this time in their lives.

One goal of our research plan was to track the developmental pathways for aggression and violence from childhood through adolescence, into adulthood, and into the next generation. Our aim was to clarify how the characteristics that have been implicated in aggression – gender, race, socioeconomic status, size and morphological development – were linked to subsequent problems of living, including problems with aggressive behavior. After identifying the main pathways, we hoped to clarify how the lives of people at risk could be diverted or modified to produce more benign outcomes.

Different longitudinal sampling procedures allow investigators to plot trajectories forward from childhood to adulthood. One is to take a large, representative group of children and track their lives from childhood through adolescence to adulthood. This procedure can yield invaluable information about what is normal and what is not. It may be the case that tantrums and nasty behaviors that are troublesome at one stage are, in fact, unrelated to later problems. For example, colic is a common transient digestive condition of infancy, hence a colicky, crying baby is not more likely than other infants to become a whining adolescent.

Yet other conditions of childhood may be less common and indicative of more enduring characteristics. On this score, longitudinal work is required to determine which characteristics are false-positive predictors and which are true-positive predictors of later adaptation. In the case of serious but infrequent problems of living, the sample must be large enough to identify a reasonable number of problem youth to learn, whether they could be identified by early predictors. In addition, normative studies over time are essential to understand some basic questions of age-related changes, including gender differences and when they arise. Are boys more confrontational, hostile, and aggressive than girls at all developmental stages? Or do they merely seem that way? Finally, normative studies are required to clarify how the child's thoughts of herself/himself shift and change over time, or whether they shift over ontogeny and over generations.

A second strategy would be to identify children who are at high risk for subsequent violence, match them to a control group, and track the development of children in both groups to adulthood. One reason for studying children at risk is that a smaller research investment is likely to pay larger immediate dividends in laying plans for prevention. Rather than distribute research resources across an unselected population, the majority of whom are unlikely to experience or perpetrate violence, attention is focused upon those who are at greatest risk. The information yielded by this search could clarify when and if it is possible to intervene in the course of living. There are advantages and disadvantages to this matched control design. One advantage is selectivity and focus, in that restricting attention only to normal development might create a flood of information that washes over the rare but critical cases of violence. A single extreme act of violence could, simultaneously, eliminate one life and doom another, and those people and those acts require special attention. One disadvantage of a narrow focus is the possible misinterpretation of what is normal and what is pathological. Focus upon the distinctive characteristics of risk groups and clinical samples cannot provide information about children who have these characteristics, yet develop in normal or meritorious ways.

Each method (normative samples and risk-control comparisons) has proved to be informative in recent investigations. Our research combined the two designs into a single study. We hoped to zoom out to study development in normal youths, and zoom in upon particular individuals who were at high risk. There were two interlocked designs, one embedded within the other.

First, we selected a sample of 695 children who attended elementary and middle schools in representative communities. That group provided information on the normal development of persons who would come of age in the late 1980s and early 1990s.

Second, we identified subgroups of boys and girls within that representative sample who were extremely aggressive. Each person was paired for subsequent comparative purposes to a child who was not aggressive. No one – not teachers, parents, principals, children, and even members of our research team – knew the identity of these at-risk children and their matched controls. That was important both to protect confidentiality and ensure that the child would not be singled out for extra help, or special stigma.

This two-in-one design strategy permitted us to avoid reliance solely upon clinical cases to construct models of normal and pathological behavior. This was a pitfall of psychoanalysis, and it continues to present problems for the science. We hoped to track people in a clinically relevant sample over a significant proportion of their lifetimes but not divorce them from the contexts of everyday life. At the same time, we wanted to track normal development in the lives of ordinary people. This chapter provides an overview of the processes of normal development; Chapter 4 introduces children at risk.

Why aggression?

Sigmund Freud, William James, and Goethe agree that aggression is universal and immanent for the species. Both the shadows of aggression and the synchrony of interdependence seem ubiquitous in the human condition. Both seem woven into the fabric of social interactions. Perhaps the question should not be "Why aggression?" but "Why not aggression?" Developmental science takes up where philosophical speculations and biological concepts of instinct leave off. The developmental assignment is to clarify how the behavior pattern becomes established in the normal course of growth. To understand the events involved in shaping and controlling the direction of aggressive expression over development, we had to plot the year-to-year changes in the "normal" course of the behavior in the contexts of everyday life. And the concern must not merely be with the external expression but with the beliefs and attitudes about aggressive acts.

Aggression has been viewed as a prototypic American problem, and somehow exaggerated by youths in North America. This belief has been fueled by the unhappy fact that there is no contest in comparisons between the homicide rates of the United States and those of all other industrialized countries. Yet there is now cause for alarm on both sides of the Atlantic. Close examination of developmental information suggests that there are few differences in the normative incidence and severity of aggressive behavior among children and adolescents, if firearm violence is omitted. In addition, current demographic and epidemiological data suggest that the rest of the world is about to experience an epidemic of violence among its youths that parallels the one currently underway in America. It remains to be determined whether the epidemic is preventable.

Before examining what is normal and what is pathological in aggressive development, it is important to understand what gives rise to aggressive behavior in the lives of ordinary children and adolescents. To begin, three fundamental questions on the nature of aggression must be addressed:

1. Does aggressive behavior increase, decrease, or remain the same in form and function from childhood through adolescence?
2. Compared to other people, and to oneself, is there a continuity in aggressive expression over time?
3. Do females and males differ in the likelihood that they will behave aggressively?

At a glance, the answers to these questions may seem self-evident. But be wary. There are good empirical reasons to distrust one's common sense on most "simple" questions about aggression. Consider the first question, on the "growth" of aggression. Paradoxically, all three possibilities, increase, decrease, and no change, can be supported by findings in the empirical literature. On the possible increase with age, there is a sharp rise in arrests for assaults and violent crimes from 10 through 19 years, with a gradual drop-off through later maturity.[8] Leonard Eron and his colleagues at the University of Illinois show a developmental increase in peer nominations for aggression.[9] On a possible decrease with increasing age, Rolf Loeber at the Western Psychiatric Institute of Pittsburgh has indicated that most longitudinal studies of children typically show decrements in ratings of aggressive behavior as they enter adolescence.[10] Still other reports have found no significant age-related shifts in global ratings of aggressive behavior in children.[11] It was our hope that the ambiguities in these findings could be resolved by longitudinal work that took each perspective into account.

The second question asks whether there are discernable relationships between aggressiveness in childhood and aggression-related outcomes in adulthood. In the course of growing up, aggressive expression is modified by multiple factors, including the changing effects of family influences, peer involvement, social norms, and social context.[12] This should lead to only low or moderate levels of prediction from childhood to maturity. However, Dan Olweus of the University of Bergen has claimed that individual differences in the aggressive behaviors of boys are virtually as stable as those of intelligence.[13] Such outcomes raise questions on how stabilities arise despite continuing developmental modifications from within and without.[14] Again, it was our hope that fresh longitudinal information could resolve this question of individual difference prediction.

The question of whether men and women differ in basic cognitive and social functions remains controversial in psychology. On the one hand, social psychological experiments of young adult men and women in controlled studies of aggression typically show only modest differences between the sexes.[15] On the other hand, epidemiological, health, and court records consistently show large sex-related differences in suicide, homicide, and arrests for violence.[16] One problem in these comparisons has been that development has often been ignored. The apparent assumption seems to be that significant gender differences in behavior should be stable and present throughout the life span, regardless of age. Such an assumption is uninformed with respect to the developmental emergence of biological gender differences.

Accordingly, one of our goals was to provide some fresh information on these issues from a normative, developmental perspective. Since the measurement technique employed can color the answers, we have been especially sensitive to the properties of the assessment procedures employed. On this count, all participants provided detailed self-reports of conflicts and feelings each year in tape-recorded interviews. Finally, information was obtained from teachers and the individual annually with respect to the participants' acting out aggressive behaviors.

As we indicated in Chapter 2, a multi-method approach was adopted in order to address these issues. In this chapter, we will summarize the answers that can be obtained from a representative sample of people by self-reports of conflicts and from reports of others, including teachers, peers, and direct observations.

Conflicts, sex, and audiotapes

Each year we asked all participants about recent conflicts that they had with other people. Donna's response at the beginning of the chapter was to the annual set of questions beginning with, "Has anybody caused you any trouble lately or bothered you?" The question was asked more than 8,000 times over the nine years the 695 participants were in school. Participants described two conflicts: one with a person of the same sex, and the other of the opposite sex. All of these interviews were audiotaped for subsequent detailed analysis.

Eyewitness reports are fallible, particularly when they concern emotionally charged events in which people themselves are involved. When we asked children and adolescents to tell us about their recent conflicts, we anticipated that they would provide subjective reconstructions of personal memories rather than objective video-recall accounts. To be sure, some public and salient aspects of the incidents should conform to those of objective observers (e.g. whether or not an incident occurred, the identity of the participants, the degree to which physical force and injury were involved). But other aspects were expected to be projective. The projective information would be reported in accounts of personal responsibility and attributions of feeling and expressions of empathy. The follow-up probes were modeled after the Thematic Apperception Test, and the aim was to obtain subjective accounts of the participants' feelings and attributions of guilt, shame, control, and dominance.

Many of the reports on conflicts were, like Donna's, rich in detail and emotion. We encouraged participants to be as specific as possible, and gave a standard series of follow-up questions to clarify events, interpretations, and feelings that might have been omitted.[17] The coding was objective, and dealt with issues of initiation, emotion, escalation, intensity, and termination. At this point, we switch from the individual case histories to a summary of the trends that can be abstracted from the reports.

First, we found that few children or adolescents see themselves as causing a conflict. The proportion of participants who reported that they initiated the conflict ranged from 5 to 10%. In the other 90% of the cases, the other person was responsible. While this bias toward external blame may be partly a function of the interview and the way questions were asked, it seems more likely that this represents a genuine attribution of responsibility. In our own eyes, we tend to see ourselves as victims rather than perpetrators, regardless of the conflict.

Second, there were strong age-related differences in the kinds of conflicts that the children and adolescents reported. The normative differences observed were, however, highly gender dependent. Boys and girls reported conflicts, but they differed in terms of types and consequences with age. Through the 5th grade (age 11) girls and boys reported similar themes of conflict. Strong sex-related differences emerged at 11–12 years of age, when girls began to report increasingly that their conflicts involved matters of relationship alienation and untrustworthy actions. Accordingly, adolescent female conflicts often involved a triangle of relationships, accompanied by feelings of jealously and alienation. Yet traditional conceptions of romance lost ground, in that it was rare to find instances where two boys fought each other over a girl. Girls, however, often had conflicts over who stole whose boyfriend or girlfriend. The broader picture was that the conflicts females reported were more often about the loss of relationships, and those that boys reported were more often about the loss of dominance.

Males and females also showed differences in persons with whom conflicts were reported (i.e. objects of the conflicts). As they grew into adolescence, boys were more reluctant than girls to report conflicts with girls. Prior to puberty (at 10 years of age), there were no reliable sex differences (i.e. 31% denial by girls, 42% denial by boys). At 13 years of age, there was roughly twice as much denial in male → female conflicts as female → female conflicts (i.e. 51–60% of the boys denied having conflicts with girls, while only 20–24% of the girls denied having conflicts with girls). At 16 years of age, two-thirds of the boys denied having a recent conflict with females. By contrast, roughly equal proportions of boys and girls reported conflicts with males, and this effect was observed at all ages.

There are a couple of possible interpretations of this gender-age difference. The age shift could mean that male → female conflicts became less frequent with age because there were fewer opportunities. In support of this interpretation, both behavioral observations and social network analyses indicated that most social interactions of childhood and adolescence are with members of the same sex. And boys may have provided more opportunities than girls for overt conflicts because of their confrontational interactional style.

An alternative explanation of the infrequency of male-reported conflicts with girls is that they may reflect the stereotypic self-attributions of boys more than interchanges in reality. Adolescent boys simply may have been unable, or unwilling, to report peer conflicts with girls. Teenage girls seemed less handicapped by such image problems, in that girls reported more conflicts with boys than vice versa. Specifically, the rate of denial of cross-sex conflicts for males was consistently twice the rate of denial of cross-sex conflicts for females. Furthermore, adolescent girls reported roughly similar numbers of female → male conflicts as adolescent boys reported male → male conflicts. Support can be claimed for both interpretations of the gender relativity of conflicts; namely, that there are different opportunities for conflict and boys and girls have different self-images to maintain. These interpretations are not mutually exclusive, and both processes seem to be at work.

The third finding concerned the emergent gender differences in forms of aggressive expression. Direct confrontation and physical aggression represents a theme carried forward by boys and men from childhood through adolescence and maturity. Nonconfrontational aggressive behaviors emerge among girls at the threshold of adolescence, and continue with force into late adolescence and early adulthood.

The direct confrontation-physical aggression infects conflicts that boys have with both sexes. As shown in Figure 3.2, physical aggression was a dominant theme in conflicts involving young males. One trend in Figure 3.2 deserves special attention; namely, the greater amount of male involvement in conflicts, the more the likelihood of physical aggression. In all cross-sex comparisons, male → male reports of conflicts had three to four times greater likelihood of physical aggression than female → female conflicts. Cross-sex conflicts (i.e male

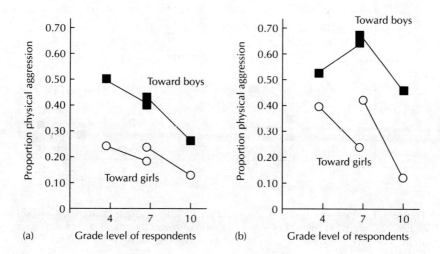

Figure 3.2 Reports of conflicts involving physical aggression in (a) females and (b) males, shown as a function of sex and grade of respondent and sex of the other individual involved in the conflict (data shown separately for Cohort I and Cohort II).

→ female and female → male) were intermediate, and girls consistently reported more physical aggression in their cross-sex conflicts than boys did. Further, the gender difference becomes greater as a function of age. From the 4th grade to the 7th grade, the proportion of boys involved in physical aggression with other boys shows a progressive increase to two-thirds of the conflicts. Unlike girls, boys did not quickly outgrow direct confrontation and physical coercion in their conflicts.

By contrast, conflicts among girls tended to involve indirect aggressive expression. In adolescence, social aggression, including rumor spreading, social ostracism, and group alienation, became the preferred technique of aggressive expression in girls. From the 4th grade to the 10th grade, the percent of female → female conflicts involving themes of alienation, ostracism, or character defamation rose from 14 to 56%. The developmental trends are unambiguous no matter how the data are analyzed (Figure 3.3). It also shows up in other parts of the interview, including the following response from Bonnie, an 8th grader:

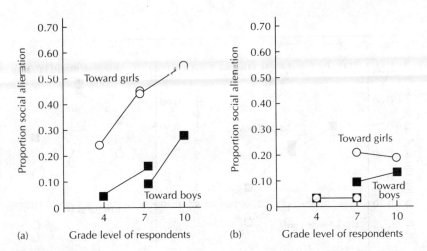

Figure 3.3 Reports of conflicts involving social alienation in (a) females and (b) males, shown as a function of sex and grade of respondent and sex of the other individual involved in the conflict (data shown separately for Cohort I and Cohort II).

I: What do you do when you get mad at another girl?

B: I talk to my other friends about it. I don't really talk about them behind their back – I have to tell someone. Or else I just explode. You have to tell someone about your problems.

Boys may be described as "socially retarded" in the use of indirect forms of aggressive expression. They rarely reported them in conflicts with males or females, whatever the grade.[18] There is an emergent dual standard in adolescence in the tendency among boys to deny conflicts in cross-sex relationships as participants grew older. More boys denied having conflicts with girls in the 7th grade (60%) than had denied them in the 4th grade (42%). This difference in conflict strategies, whereby girls develop indirect techniques in addition to direct ones, emerged clearly at 10–11 years of age. Factor analytic analyses indicate that the gender difference was not present at younger ages, and it appeared at subsequent ages.[19]

In sum, the findings from the reported conflicts reveal unambiguous normative developmental patterns in the kinds of conflicts children and adolescents report. In adolescence, these patterns differ markedly for males and females. One upshot is that the findings indicate no single curve for the growth of aggression can be plotted which parallels the growth curves for height and weight. At 10 years of age, girls and boys report similar patterns of aggressive expression. By 13 years of age, girls develop indirect strategies of anger expression that coexist with direct expressions. Adolescent boys continue to be limited to direct confrontations and physical aggressive patterns of earlier childhood. These strategies are closely correlated with differences in themes of conflicts, in that the conflicts of girls increasingly involve troubles about relationship loss or engagement. These strategies, themes, and objects, as we will show later, are not mere inventions of the participants or their sex; they are constrained and supported by the person's network of relationships.

It is important to remember that we are dealing with group trends, not individual behaviors. The report at the beginning of this chapter reminds us of the difference between the two and suggests that times are changing. If the provocations are sufficiently public and severe, some adolescent girls like Donna are fully capable of a Rambo-like attack.

In the eyes of others

The problem of determining what reports of conflicts really mean brings us to the subjectivity of self-reports; are they projective tests for social images or do they reflect actual behaviors? Is the self that we construct the same as that seen by others? On this score, there are good reasons to think the constructed self is not necessarily the same as the person viewed by others.

To obtain information from outside the self, we obtained ratings from teachers on dimensions of aggressive behavior, along with nominations from peers. The interpersonal competence scale (ICS), a brief teacher rating procedure, yielded an aggressive factor score based on three items. Exactly the same items were used for the teacher's descriptions as for the participants' self-descriptions. Both teachers and participants completed the eighteen-item scale. The ICS procedure struck a good balance between practicality and validity. Although the test is quite short, it is sufficient to identify characteristics of the participant that are stable, reliable, and predictive.

These evaluative ratings suggest the "growth" of aggression is regressive, not progressive (see Figure 3.4). Children and adolescents were rated by teachers as becoming progressively better in their behaviors. When the participants were adolescents, they were rated as being less aggressive than they had been in middle childhood, and when they were in high school, they were rated as being even less aggressive. Although this finding may defy the judgments of parents, police, and

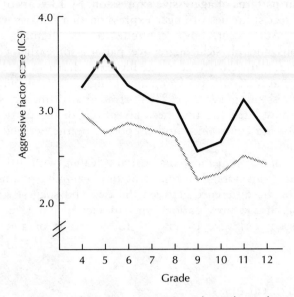

Figure 3.4   Teacher evaluations on aggressive factor by males (solid line) and females (shaded line) as a function of grade. (Cohort I and Cohort II combined, and data shown only for subjects who did not drop out of school. Parallel findings were obtained among those who dropped out of school.)

the courts, the decrease was highly reliable. Nor was it simply measurement error or a fluke of sampling. The same results were independently obtained in both genders in both cohorts, and it was unchanged when school dropouts were eliminated from the analysis. The latter correction was required because dropouts may be both more aggressive and unrepresented by teacher ratings in the higher grades.

How do these ratings from teachers match the judgments that participants render of themselves over the same age period? To answer this question, we employed the same ICS ratings, but participants, not teachers, made the evaluations. The self-evaluations taken from the participants show the same decline in aggression observed by teachers (see Figure 3.5). In general, both boys and girls believed themselves to be getting more and more agreeable as they grew from childhood to adolescence and early adulthood. These age-related trends were highly significant by multivariate regression analyses.

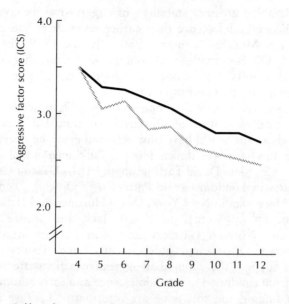

Figure 3.5 Self-evaluations on aggressive factor by males (solid line) and females (shaded line) as a function of grade. Cohort I and Cohort II combined, and data shown only for subjects who did not drop out of school. Parallel findings were obtained among those who dropped out of school.

Two empirical generalizations on stability

In a discussion of personality development fifteen years ago, we cited two empirical generalizations on longitudinal prediction that had been derived from studies of individual differences in height, weight, and IQ.[20] They read:

1. The shorter the interval between two assessments, the more likely it is that the individual's relative position in the distributions of score will be similar.
2. The older the children are at the time of the initial assessment, the less likely it is that their positions relative to each other will change over a given interval of time between assessments.

At that time, sufficient information was not available to answer the questions on whether these generalizations applied to aggressive behavior. That state of affairs has been corrected in the intervening years, due to the longitudinal studies completed throughout the world. The reviews based on incomplete data sets strongly suggested that there was considerably greater stability of aggressive behavior from childhood through adolescence than earlier researchers had previously recognized (e.g. Moss & Susman, 1980; Olweus, 1979). In his early review, Dan Olweus made the courageous claim that individual differences in aggressive behavior were almost as stable as individual differences in intellectual performance.

The longitudinal research completed over the past fifteen years permits a critical evaluation of Olweus's assertion. Different research teams throughout the world have now reported evidence relevant to the issue. The groups have been directed by Lea Pulkkinen in Finland, David Magnusson in Sweden, David Farrington and D. J. West in Cambridge, Michael Rutter in London, Gerald Patterson in Oregon, Leonard Eron and Rowell Huessman in New York, David Huizinga and Delbert Elliott in Colorado, Emmy Werner in Kauai, Jack and Jeanne Block in California, and Norman Garmezy and Ann Masten in Minnesota, among others.[21] Operating independently, the results of these investigators support the claim that aggressive actions are reasonably predictable from childhood to late adolescence and early adulthood.

Our own findings on this issue are informative because they both illustrate the issues and clarify the limitations. Given the two sources of ratings – the self and others – there are two potential trajectories of stability. Because the trajectories differ in significant ways, the results of the two domains will be presented separately.

o *Teacher ratings.* The median one-year stability correlation for the aggressive factor was $r = 0.51$. This figure was obtained by computing all of the one-year stabilities (4th–5th grade, 5th–6th grade, etc.), then computing the median (see Table 3.1). Two surprising features of these results concern the limited extent to which they conform to the empirical generalizations on stability. First, the median eight-year stability correlation ($r = 0.44$) is not unlike the median one-year stability correlation ($r = 0.51$), suggesting only modest decay over time. Second, there does not appear to be much gain in the stability of teacher ratings as a function of age at first assessment. On both counts, the matrices of stability correlations for aggression look to be remarkably similar for boys and girls.[22]

These results on the stability of "teacher" ratings are especially striking because the present design was biased against finding stability for evaluations in ratings by multiple "others". The students were assigned to new classes each year.

o *Self-ratings.* How well do self-ratings perform in terms of year-to-year and long-term stability? On *a priori* grounds, it would seem for three reasons that self-ratings should be more stable than the teacher ratings. First, while the same individual is involved in the self-ratings each year, different people are involved in the outside the self-assessments over time. Second is an unlikely, although possible, methodological confounding of memory and recall of self-evaluations from year to year. Third, the individuals have the longest acquaintance with themselves and should know themselves better than anyone. Any one of these three factors may heighten self-stability.

In the light of these considerations, it was hardly surprising to find that the median one-year stabilities of the self-ratings of aggression were high and positive (see Table 3.2). The median one-year stability for self-ratings of aggression was $r = 0.53$. What was surprising, given the fact that the same person (the participant) generated these ratings each of the nine years, was the sharp decay in long-term self-stability. On this score, the stability of the self-ratings was barely above chance ($r = 0.16$ overall, and $r = 0.18$ for females and $r = 0.14$ for males). In addition, there is a reasonable indication in the data that the older the participants at the time of first self-ratings, the higher the stability. Both of these self-stability findings for aggression

Table 3.1 Teacher ratings of aggression: median stability coefficients as a function of years between ratings

	Years between ratings							
	+1	+2	+3	+4	+5	+6	+7	+8
Females	0.48[a]	0.44	0.41	0.29	0.34	0.35	0.20	0.30
Males	0.48	0.40	0.34	0.34	0.34	0.44	0.34	0.46
Combined	0.48	0.42	0.38	0.32	0.34	0.40	0.27	0.38

[a] The median stability coefficient across all one-year intervals (4th to 5th grade, 5th to 6th grade, . . . , 11th to 12th grade). Data were combined across Cohort I and Cohort II.

Table 3.2 Self-ratings of aggression: median stability coefficients as a function of years between ratings

	Years between ratings							
	+1	+2	+3	+4	+5	+6	+7	+8
Females	0.50[a]	0.41	0.40	0.27	0.21	0.18	0.25	0.18
Males	0.56	0.47	0.37	0.34	0.35	0.27	0.28	0.14
Combined	0.53	0.44	0.38	0.31	0.28	0.23	0.27	0.16

[a] The median stability coefficient across all one-year intervals (4th to 5th grade, 5th to 6th grade, . . . , 11th to 12th grade). Data were combined across Cohort I and Cohort II.

are in accord with the two empirical generalizations on intelligence and nonbehavioral domains.

Recall the Olweus speculation that aggressive behavior was virtually as stable as intelligence. Do our findings support or refute that claim? The problem in evaluating this assertion is that the assessments of intelligence and aggression differ markedly in measurement properties and goals.[23] In general, tests of intelligence have superior psychometric properties, hence bias the procedures toward higher levels of stability. To create a level playing field, it would be desirable to assess the two factors by the same method. In the present work, it is possible directly to evaluate the proposition by the same method (i.e. teacher ratings and self-ratings of academic competence and of aggressive behavior). While such a comparison has some limitations, it is a rather good approximation of the stability of two characteristics when the methods are roughly similar. The remarkable finding is that two characteristics yield parallel stability curves, with the self-ratings of academic competence decaying more rapidly than the "other" ratings.

Are the self-ratings and others' ratings measuring the same characteristic from different perspectives? Or have the different perspectives identified qualitatively different characteristics? With regard to this question, it may be noted that the self-ratings and others' ratings of aggressive behavior were only modestly correlated. In Cohort I, the median correspondence correlation for the aggressive factor was $r = 0.32$ for girls and $r = 0.34$ for boys. The parallel self-other relations were even lower in Cohort II ($r = 0.21$ for girls; $r = 0.28$ for boys). Although these correspondence correlations are statistically reliable, they suggest there is a problem with assuming that the two kinds of assessments are measuring the same thing. It looks as if the constructions of the self are qualitatively different from the judgments of other people. We discuss this matter and its implications in more detail in Chapter 7.

In different voices?

Are girls different from boys in the development of aggressive behaviors, and, if so, does aggression in the two genders require different explanations? In answer to the first question, the information now available indicates that the similarities in developmental processes clearly outweigh the differences.[24] There are similarities in levels of prediction, and parallel trends over time in the direction of both self and other evaluations. There remain, however, two gender differences that should be underscored. One concerns the gender difference in employing direct confrontation as the major mechanism of aggressive expression. Between the ages of 10 and 13, girls develop alternative, nonconfrontational techniques of social aggression in the expression of anger, which are used along with direct confrontation.[25] Boys, however, persist in direct confrontation as a primary strategy. The second gender difference is that there is a higher likelihood of injury among the conflicts of males as they become older, stronger, and gain access to weapons. This outcome follows from the higher likelihood that boys persist in direct confrontation.

To be sure, females are not necessarily limited to indirect methods: girls and women retain the capacity directly to confront antagonists. The Donna–Linda episode illustrates as much. With increasing age, however, a diminishing proportion of girls are identified as extremely and chronically assaultive. As we observe in Chapter 4, roughly the same proportion of girls (15%) as boys (17%) were identified in this investigation as highly aggressive at 10 years of age. But at 13 years of age, however, twice the proportion of boys as the proportion of girls were identified as highly aggressive (i.e. 19% males versus 8% females). These outcomes are consistent with the proposal that girls anticipate boys in the development of new and nonconfrontational strategies in development.

Concluding comments

We can now bring together some of the findings on the three questions on normal development of aggression raised at the beginning of the chapter. As it turns out, the three "separate" questions do not permit separate answers.

Consider the growth of aggression. It looks as if growth and aggression cannot be described by a single trajectory or psychometric function. Different curves are required because they depend on which measures are adopted. Whether there is growth or shrinkage depends upon what is measured, and how. Global ratings by the self and others indicate a general trend over time toward reduction in overt aggressive expression. In-depth analyses of conflicts, however, indicate a sharp increase in some forms of aggressive expression. These increases are sex-specific for both the perpetrators and the victims. If these distinctions are kept in mind, we find virtually unanimous agreement across contemporary studies, including our own. Seemingly contradictory findings fall into place. Although there may be fewer instances of overt physical aggression, they become more serious when they occur, and they may be life threatening.

On the important point of continuity, all major longitudinal studies now agree that there is reasonably high stability from childhood across adolescence in the use of direct confrontational, aggressive techniques. Males and females who used them at the beginning of adolescence tend to use them at the end. This is the story told by Olweus' short-term longitudinal studies.[26] It has since been confirmed by the Swedish investigation of David Magnusson and the American work of Leonard Eron and his colleagues. Our studies tell the same story, but with some twists. First, although the correlations are significant, there is plenty of room for individual change over a five to six year period. This is true for both boys and girls. Second, focusing only upon "stability" draws attention away from change in other aspects of aggressive expression. From childhood through adolescence, stability is superimposed on a shift downward in frequency and an increase in intensity. In brief, persons were predictable over time, and the stabilities were only marginally higher for boys than for girls.[27] Moreover, the results underscore the sheer efficiency and economy of the teacher ratings and nominations which required only 2–3 minutes per child to complete. These ratings correspond with other "external" evaluations, including peer nominations and behavioral observations.[28]

There is a problem in framing the issue in terms of the personal continuity of aggression because the construct itself becomes expanded in development. Evidence for the expansion was obtained from self-reports. Social manipulation and ostracism – alienation, rumors, and social rejection – emerge as a major property of aggressive behavior in early adolescence, especially for girls.[29] Affiliation-romance-alienation themes recur in the conflicts reported by girls in early adolescence. The strategy adopted seemed to be consonant with the form of perceived injury; alienation of relationships leads to counteralienation. Rather than report everyday offenses of peers to adults as they did in childhood, adolescent girls report to each other. In the early teenage years, boys persist in their reliance upon direct confrontations and/or physical aggression if the conflict cannot be otherwise ignored or avoided. But it would be incorrect to conclude that girls did not retain the ability for direct aggressive confrontation. Conflicts among girls can involve either direct confrontation or social manipulation.[30]

In adolescence, a new set of aggressive strategies emerge that are, by nature, indirect and concealed. These fresh techniques are seen most clearly in the conflicts of girls. Such "hidden" assaults are superior to direct confrontations on several counts, not the least of which is the inability of a victim to identify the antagonist, and to reciprocate. But what is hidden to the victim may also be hidden to the researcher. The conflicts of adolescence provide a window into the raw politics of everyday life, and their complexity cannot be overestimated.[31]

It is tempting to fall into the trap of answering "yes" or "no" to the question of whether there are gender differences in aggression. Yet it is the wrong question, and a categorical response would be misleading. Surely sex differences are present, but these are highly dependent upon age and measure. As we will see in Chapter 4, sex differences in aggression are not absolute; they depend upon temporal change in the society, the subculture in which the observation occurs, and the age-developmental status of the females and males.

Stepping stones to violence

Developmental roots

I'm popular in some ways and fightin'. I don't want to be popular in fightin', but that's how I'm known around here.

Julian, 13 years old

Ah, made me mad? Yeah, my girlfriend accused me of taking her money. I pushed her, and she shot at me you know so I'm – I'm going off. You know, don't shoot at me unless you're gonna kill me, you know. We've worked it out now. It's all worked out. I quit drinking for awhile, except for last Monday when I got pretty tight for the first time in two weeks.

Julian, 20 years old

These excerpts illustrate three issues that we touched in the last chapter – the longitudinal continuity of aggression, the escalatory nature of violence, and the blurring of perpetrator and victim in the eyes of the reporter. It also illustrates comorbidity; namely, the interrelations among substance abuse, aggression, and other problems of living.

In Chapter 3, we observed that we hoped to close the gap between the conflicts of everyday life and the violence of national crime reports by identifying children and adolescents who were strong candidates for later violence, either as perpetrators or as victims. Following identification, our aim was to track their lives forward, in tandem with nonaggressive people individually matched to them. This strategy would enable us to compare "at-risk" children with those who developed normally. The aim was to clarify why some children and youths become and remain vulnerable, and why some succeed despite serious constraints in their lives. In addition, we sought to track those at risk because of where they lived rather than because of their own behavior. To this end, we conducted additional observations in one of the poorest sections of one of America's most violent cities.

Who is at risk for the development of violence?

The first task that had to be addressed was to identify children and adolescents who, at maturity, are likely to be violent. Our attempts to identify such youths in an ordinary population were simple and straightforward. We assumed, all things equal, that the best predictor of future violent behavior would be aggressive behavior in the person's childhood.

Since all of the children in this study were required to attend school, we felt that school personnel, including teachers, principals, assistant principals, and counselors, could provide information on children with severe acting-out problems. Stated simply, we assumed that the people in the best position to identify extremely aggressive children should be those who have to deal with the problems that they provoke. Accordingly, we asked such school personnel in the school grade under investigation to nominate students who showed "the most serious problems of aggression" in the school in that grade. Children must have been named by two or more independent sources to be kept in the pool of potentially highly aggressive children. This list of highly aggressive participants was kept confidential from the schools, parents, children, and even our research staff. They were intentionally hidden by the research design in the group of 695 participants. This seemed to be the safest way to conceal their identity.

Through the process of school nominations, some 40 highly aggressive subjects were identified at the beginning of the study, along with 40 matched comparison subjects. There were 20 male and 20 female aggressive subjects, half of whom were in the 4th grade and half in the 7th grade at the beginning. For each aggressive subject, another person from the same classroom was chosen for comparison purposes. These control subjects were individually matched to the aggressive ones in sex, classroom attended, race, physical size, and socioeconomic status. The control subjects had not been nominated for the highly aggressive group.[1] All of the measures, interviews, and reports that we obtained on the full sample of 695 were available for this embedded sample of extremely aggressive youth and their matched controls.

The independent measures that were taken at the time of initial selection indicated that the nominations for risk-yielded groups that were in fact different. At-risk participants differed from the matched control group on the primary aggression variables. These included independently secured peer nominations for aggression and teacher ratings of aggression. In addition, the groups differed in judgments of popularity (see Table 4.1). In brief, the youths identified as being at risk for aggressive behavior were at risk on multiple dimensions.

The control group itself could be seen as at risk, since they had been individually matched to the risk group on several sociodemographic, maturational, and school variables. One nonobvious consequence of the matching was that the control participants in Cohort II were as a group more aggressive and less academically competent than members of the general Cohort II sample. On this score, the CLS control participants could be classified as being at risk themselves because of their

Table 4.1 Characteristics of risk and control subjects at onset of CLS

	Measures external to self				Self-measures		
	ICS-T[a] Aggress	Peer aggress	ICS-T popular	ICS-T academic	ICS-S[b] aggress	ICS-S popular	ICS-S academic
Cohort I							
Risk females	5.17	2.80	3.60	4.00	4.53	5.20	5.25
Risk males	5.83	4.10	3.90	3.40	3.90	5.67	5.85
Control females	2.53	0.80	5.07	4.50	3.33	5.74	5.33
Control males	3.50	1.20	5.27	4.25	3.77	5.67	4.85
ANOVA							
Significance[c]	Risk***	Risk***	Risk**	–	–	–	–
Cohort II							
Risk females	5.50	1.90	3.47	3.55	4.03	5.23	5.20
Risk males	5.17	1.90	3.77	3.64	4.13	4.67	3.80
Control females	3.03	0.50	4.87	4.05	2.97	5.70	5.15
Control males	3.80	0.70	4.27	3.56	3.50	4.77	4.80
ANOVA							
Significance[c]	Risk***	Risk*	Risk*	–	Risk*	Gender*	Gender*

[a] ICS-T refers to teacher ratings on the interpersonal competence scale; "aggress" refers to the ICS-T aggression factor, "popular" refers to the ICS-T popularity factor, and "academic" refers to the ICS-T academic competence factor. The ICS scales range from 1 (low) to 7 (high). "Peer aggress" refers to the mean frequency of being nominated by peers for initiating conflicts.
[b] ICS-S refers to the self-ratings on the interpersonal competence scale.
[c] Analyses of variance were computed separately for each cohort. "Risk" indicates that the risk and control groups differed significantly, while "Gender" indicates that boys and girls differed. *** = $p < 0.001$; ** = $p < 0.01$; * = $p < 0.05$; – = nonsignificant. No two-way interactions between risk and gender were significant.

socioeconomic, ethnic, and school status. As a result, this investigation errs toward conservatism in identifying differences between the risk and matched control groups.

Two other features of Table 4.1 deserve attention. One is that the gender differences between risk groups on the aggression variables were generally modest and insignificant. The only main gender effects appeared in the 13 year olds in self-ratings of popularity and academic competence; 7th grade girls saw themselves as smarter and more popular than boys. In addition, the control group females were consistently rated by teachers and peers as less aggressive than males. The second noteworthy finding is that the self-ratings generally failed to discriminate between the risk and control groups. However, measures taken by others (i.e. teachers, peers) saw the two groups as markedly different in aggressive behavior. This information-source difference (i.e., self vs. others) is no fluke: it shows up in all years of the study.

Behavioral realities: observations in context

Beyond the procedures that involved all participants, at-risk participants and their matched controls participated in a series of behavioral observations that were completed over the first three years of this investigation. The observational technique, synchronized observations of behavior and context (SOBAC), was unusual in its completeness. The goal was to obtain simultaneous and detailed accounts of both social behavior and social context. Accordingly, microanalyses were made of the social actions of the participant, the social actions directed toward the participant, and the dynamic context and background in which the behavior occurred.

The procedure required the participation of two independent observers who operated in synchrony. One observer made a continuous record of the participant's social behavior, recording details every 5 seconds. Simultaneously, a second observer recorded the classroom activities, teacher behaviors, and social disturbances every 60 seconds. Each 5 minutes, the two switched roles. This continued through the duration of the observation series, in at least two settings each day, and ensured that the participant and control were observed in the same contexts. The subject–control pairs were observed on four consecutive days in a variety of classroom settings.

According to previous investigators, aggressive behaviors are infrequent events, accounting for a mere 3–6% of all interactions. Accordingly, a large investment of time must be spent in order to find instances of negative actions. Yet they did occur, and we anticipated that our preselection of participants for aggression would heighten the rate of occurrence. The following excerpt is a representative account of one of the incidents that we observed with Cindy, one of the girls nominated in the 7th grade as being at risk for violence. This account is derived from a recoding of the information available from the two protocols after they were integrated. It was mid-winter, just after the beginning of the second semester. Cindy is in Mrs. Stewart's 7th grade math class. The class period is almost over, and the students continue to work on their assigned math problems. At the beginning of this 5 minute observation period, Cindy is sitting by Katherine, steadily talking to her. Katherine does not seem comfortable with the arrangement, but she talks back softly.

The focal observer recorded the following events:

Minute 1: Five seconds into the first minute of observation, Cindy calls out, "Mrs. Stewart!". Mrs. Stewart looks at Cindy and says, "Go back to your seat, Cindy". Cindy just sits there, and does not move. At 30 seconds, she talks to Katherine. At 45 seconds, she pulls on the handle of Katherine's pocketbook that is on the table in front of Katherine. She looks at Katherine.

Minute 2: At five seconds into the second minute, Cindy pulls on the handle of Katherine's pocketbook again and Katherine says, "Stop it!". Cindy continues to talk to Katherine. Twenty-five seconds into Minute 2 she shows Katherine her "E.T." button. At 35 seconds, Cindy stands up and then sits back down and stabs Katherine with the sharp pin of the button. Katherine yells, "Ow!" in pain. At 50 seconds into the second minute, she shows the button again to Katherine and continues talking to her.

Minute 3: Cindy continues talking to Katherine. At 30 seconds, she stabs Katherine with the pin again, and Katherine yells, "Stop it!" and holds up her hand to block Cindy's attempt to stab her again. At 45 seconds, Cindy attempts again to continue to engage Katherine in conversation. At 55 seconds, she looks over at Douglas.

Minute 4: Cindy looks back at Katherine. At 15 seconds, she pulls on the handle of Katherine's pocketbook, and begins to talk to Katherine. At 25 seconds, she turns around to look at Roger sitting behind her. At 30 seconds, she leans over the table and vigorously stabs Katherine twice with the pin. Katherine tries to block Cindy with her hands, and Katherine yells, "Better stop!". Mrs. Stewart looks over at Cindy and says harshly, "Cynthia, I thought I told you to go back to your seat". Cindy initially ignores her, but at 45 seconds she gets up and walks slowly over toward her desk. At 50 seconds, she returns to Katherine and stabs her again with the pin, and Katherine yells, "Cindy, go on!".

Minute 5: Cindy arrives at her desk, but does not sit down. From 10 to 30 seconds, she leans over her desk, staring down at the floor. At 30 seconds, she continues to lean over the desk and look around the room, and then down at the floor again. At 45 seconds, she stands up and walks over to Katherine when it is time to change classes. At 50 seconds, she stabs Katherine with the pin very hard. Katherine becomes visibly angry and yells, "Better go on!". She then hits Cindy with her fists. Cindy laughs, and walks out of the room.

Other classroom incidents are even less concealed. For example, in the 7th grade math class of another middle school, a physically handicapped child was dumped out of his wheelchair by a couple of male classmates. Since he could not defend himself, the victim laughed at the "prank". In the same class, another participant threatened classmates with a switch-blade knife. In another middle school, the two research observers themselves were harassed when they were left as the sole adults in a "study hall" consisting of a difficult to handle mix of 7th, 8th, and 9th grade students.

Classroom exchanges sometimes erupted into full-scale fights outside the classroom, in the lavatory, and in the hallways. The upshot of the behavioral observations was to confirm that the school nomination process was accurate in identifying subjects who were highly aggressive. The aggressive subjects were more likely to insult classmates, ridicule each other, defy the teacher, and provoke fights.

It should also be noted that the direct observations of aggressive behavior were reliably associated with peer nominations for aggressive conflicts, teacher ratings of aggression (see Cairns & Cairns, 1984; Green *et al.*, 1980) and subsequent problems of living (see below). However, the self-ratings were inconsistently related to the direct observations. An insignificant correlation was obtained between the ICS-S factor of aggression and direct observations of aggressive episodes in Cohort I ($r = 0.17$). In Cohort II, however, the behavior–self-judgment correlation was reliable ($r = 0.56$, $p < 0.01$).

The anatomy and meaning of aggressive interactions

With a cursory glance, the conflicts of everyday life, including those described in this chapter, may seem interesting, but trivial when contrasted with acts of extreme violence. But when these developmental incidents are viewed in terms of what they reveal about interactional processes, and when these processes are in turn linked to longitudinal outcomes, they take on fresh meaning.

Context bound

Vast differences occur among classes in the rate of hostile–aggressive behaviors. The range is twentyfold: from 1% of the interactions being hostile–aggressive in some classes to 20% in others. There is clearly enormous variation according to context, activity, and instructor. Conflicts, albeit a minority of the interactions even in the most disorganized settings, play a big role in social reorganization. They are also very salient and long remembered by the participants.

Hostility begets hostility: contagion and clustering

Regardless of context, whenever an instance of hostile behavior was observed between two people, it was likely to have been part of a negative chain reaction. Tracing backward, we found that at least half of aggressive, negative episodes were precipitated by prior negative, aggressive acts. But not all instances of unkindness are likely to bring about counteracts of the same sort. Tracing forward, we find that children and adolescents ignored or otherwise tolerated insults and rudeness, up to a point. Overall, only 25% of the aggressive, negative acts precipitated counteracts of the same type. But when a given threshold is reached, negative acts beget more negative ones, in an escalating cycle (Toch, 1969). The problem here is to escape from the constraints and synchrony of hostile actions.

Does aggression beget aggression? Often, but not always. There were clearly clusters of hostile–aggressive acts during the course of the interchanges that we observed and in a summary of the sequential analyses. Essentially the same pattern of interpersonal facilitation of aggression appears in boys and girls, 4th and 7th grade, and highly aggressive and matched control subjects. These effects are shown in a cluster map of hostile interchanges (Figure 4.1). Aggressive acts by the subjects (R1) heighten the likelihood of counter-aggression by the "other" person at the next social turn (R2). This process continues when the subject responds in her/his turn at R3, and the counter-response is given by the other (R4). The typical classroom conflict ends after about five turns. This process holds for conflicts in which both risk and control subjects are involved, with the exception that risk subjects were involved in more aggressive conflicts. Essentially the same effects may be described by the correlational relation between aggressive acts across all observation sequences ($r = 0.70$), and in the conditional probability of a specific aggressive–hostile act being preceded by one of the same type ($P = 0.50$).

The reason for the qualification "not always" is simply that hostile acts do not usually lead to immediate hostile responses, even among

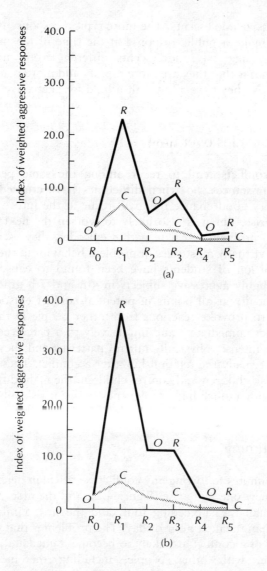

Figure 4.1   Sequences of aggressive acts as a function of the preceding act among (a) 4th grade and (b) 7th grade girls. The interchanges of at-risk subjects (*R*) is shown in the solid line, and interactions of matched control subjects (*C*) is shown in the shaded line. *R* refers to actions in turn-taking sequences, and intensity of aggressive response shown on the ordinate. *O* is the other people in the episode.

highly aggressive adolescents. The more typical response is to ignore or at least not make a public response at the time of the incident. What makes highly aggressive adolescents different from more normally aggressive ones is that they are more rapidly and more readily triggered. In other words, they have a lower threshold for aggressive responding.

Aggressive cycles over time

Aggressive conflicts tend to recur among the same persons and in similar circumstances. So when difficulties have erupted in the past, there is a very good chance they will recur in the future when similar conditions arise. But it is also likely to worsen the next time around. Not only do problems escalate within episodes, they escalate between episodes. In virtually all studies of problem behavior in the classroom, a small proportion of students have been found to cause most of the problems. Highly aggressive subjects in 4th and 7th grade classrooms get into difficulty at all points in potential conflict episodes. They are more likely to provoke reactions from other people in the class, more likely to react immediately and impulsively to a perceived insult, more likely to use intense, physically hurtful patterns, and they rarely try to make up or remedy the relationship after a conflict. These stages occur in both at-risk children and control children; the main difference is that they occur with a much higher frequency in the at-risk subjects.

Time and timing

The first 5 minutes following any conflict is critical in determining when and how a new one will arise (Figure 4.2), and the first minute is more important than the succeeding four, and the first 5 minutes is more important than the next hour or day. The problem is that those who are in the midst of a conflict are likely to become immediately embroiled in a new one, with other people, including the mediator. Early intervention seems to be a key, but it can be hazardous.

Antisocial and prosocial actions

The idea that antisocial and prosocial behaviors are at opposite ends of the same dimension is embedded in many intervention programs that are designed to reduce the level of violence in the inner city, hence the

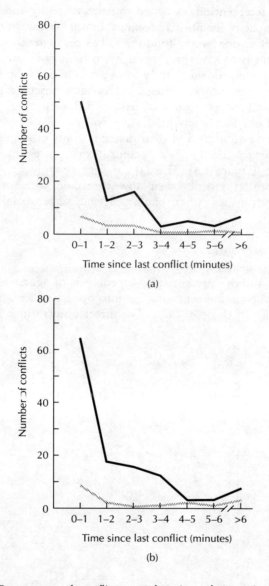

Figure 4.2 Recurrence of conflict as a function of time since last conflict (shown separately for females in Cohort I and Cohort II). (a) is 4th grade girls and (b) is 7th grade girls. Solid line represents at-risk subjects and shaded line represents matched control subjects.

popularity of interventions designed to teach empathy and increase the individual's capacity for positive feelings. In our observations, however, aggressive behaviors were found to be orthogonal to prosocial behaviors. That is to say, the propensity to be hostile and impulsive is independent of the propensity to be kindly and friendly. Specifically, the correlation between observed negative acts and observed positive acts was $r = 0.06$ and $r = -0.19$ in Cohorts I and II, respectively. Moreover, the likelihood of friendly and kindly acts was not distinguished between highly aggressive subjects and their matched controls (Figure 4.3). This is in contrast to the large risk-control differences in hostile and aggressive acts (Figure 4.4). These data suggest that a primary problem of these youth at risk is their low threshold for hostile, hurtful interpersonal strategies rather than a deficiency of prosocial strategies.

When girls are bad

Fewer girls than boys present serious problems of aggression in middle school. But when adolescent girls get into open conflicts, the processes are very similar to those of boys. The direct observations indicated no

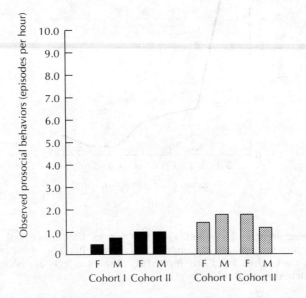

Figure 4.3 Prosocial behavior observed in risk (solid bar) and control (shaded bar) subjects in terms of episodes per hour (F = female, M = male).

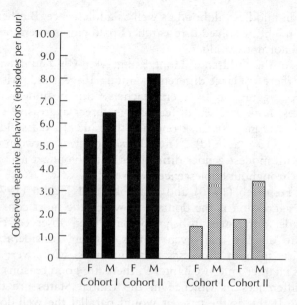

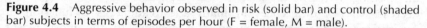

Figure 4.4 Aggressive behavior observed in risk (solid bar) and control (shaded bar) subjects in terms of episodes per hour (F = female, M = male).

gender differences among the risk groups in terms of the frequency or severity of hostile exchanges. The rate of aggressive–hostile behaviors in both the risk males and risk females significantly exceeded their respective matched control groups. No differences were observed between the aggressive risk groups of males and females in the observations of hostile–aggressive behaviors.

How does this finding fit with the broadly replicated finding that males and females differ in aggressive behavior? First, it points to the need to consider the age-developmental stage in which sex differences are observed. Recall that twice as many 7th grade boys as girls qualified for the "high-risk" classification, while an almost equivalent proportion of boys and girls qualified in the 4th grade. The "risk" group of boys and girls were highly selected, with a smaller proportion of older girls qualifying. But when girls are hostile, at whatever age, the observation data suggest that they can be as hostile and hurtful as boys.

Second, the expected sex differences in aggression appeared in the observations of control groups of boys and girls (see Figure 4.4). These reliable differences are consistent with the gender effect in teacher ratings of aggression in both grades. The fact that a gender difference appeared in the 4th and 7th grades indicates that normative differences are present in middle childhood as well as adolescence. But herein lies a puzzle that might be solved if researchers paid closer attention to social context and normative values.

In studies of the children of Hong Kong, Man-Chi Leung has recently shown that there are large differences among 10 year old girls and boys in ratings of aggression by their teachers.[2] In the inner city of the United States, however, sex differences in direct aggressive expression were modest and inconsistent from the 4th grade (10 years old) through the 7th grade (13 years old).[3] The CLS sample was between these two extremes, with modest gender differences in the younger ages and large differences throughout adolescence.

As both Feshbach (1970) and Maccoby and Jacklin (1974) earlier concluded, aggression is the domain in which the most consistent and reliable gender differences in behavior have been observed. Hence it is important to observe that, even in this domain, considerable gender overlap exists in both processes and outcomes. Moreover, as shown later in this chapter and in Chapter 9, there are good reasons to believe that sex differences in violence in the United States are themselves diminishing. If this is the case, it would parallel the well-documented decrease in sex differences in math and reading as a function of generations and temporal changes in society. In the most recent assessments, gender differences in scholastic potential and performance that were highly reliable three decades ago are now trivial.[4]

Long-term predictions

There are good reasons why one might expect behavioral observations to be inadequate for long-term prediction. Prior to the beginning of this study, we outlined several reasons to have modest expectations.[5] The gist of our concern was that behavioral observations may be too precise to be useful in prediction. They focus on the precise controls of behavior. To read the fine print of the Compact Edition of the Oxford English Dictionary, a magnifying glass works better than a high-power microscope. So it is with "reading" behavior patterns; if an observational technique is too detailed and precise, the broader form of the behavior and its meaning may be lost.

In this regard, less costly methods such as teacher ratings and peer nominations have typically been shown to be superior to detailed behavioral observations in the longitudinal prediction of individual differences. Why? Observations are designed to capture precise information about momentary contextual and relational information on every action of the individual being observed. The very precision of the observations may work against their being effective in prediction equations. That is to say, precise second-by-second behavioral observations in context focus attention to the details of interaction and the precise conditions that immediately surround them. Such detail is required to analyze the fine structure of interactions and the processes by which they operate. But it can be a poor gauge for predictions.

Hostility is determined not only by personality, but by the level and extent of the provocation, the person who provokes, and the setting in which it occurs. The same remark from a peer might yield different consequences for a teenage boy depending on whether it occurred in a Sunday School class, at a party on Friday night, or in a football game. Behavior is regulated simultaneously by the syntax of situations and distinctive individual patterns. Ratings are easy to make, presumably because such judgments take into account the rater's understanding of the situation and the appropriateness of a whole range of responses. The ability to arrive at social consensus in such ratings doubtless taps into the same processes that permit individuals to make instant decisions on whether a remark is a joke, a tease, or an insult. The ability to make subtle distinctions between hostile and appropriate acts has been shaped over a lifetime. Such social perceptions are essential for survival.

We also argued that we could beat the odds by making extensive observations so that contextual factors would cancel each other in aggregation, and distill information about individual differences. In our case, each at-risk child and each matched control were observed by two people over four days and in multiple settings. These observations were recorded every 5 seconds, and it was possible to reconstruct the details of each exchange, along with the members of the relationship. That is the reason we employed an observational schedule that required three years to complete.

The investment paid off. The linkages between the direct observations and composite scores of adult adjustment proved to be strong overall. The composite score, discussed further in Chapter 10, included instances of criminal arrest (excluding trivial traffic violations), school dropout, instances of serious violence, teenage parenthood, residential psychiatric treatment, and drug rehabilitation. Further analysis indicated that the most robust predictions between direct observations and adult outcomes occurred in the cohort of participants that were an average of 13 years of age at the time of the observations. The linkages between behavior and later outcomes were modest in the case of the 10-year old cohort. These findings were replicated for both boys and girls.

Specifically, we found highly significant correlations between the rate of aggressive behavior observed in both boys ($r = 0.59$) and girls

(r = 0.50) of Cohort II with the composite index of adult mal-adjustment. But the parallel correlations among the males and females of the younger cohort were modest and unreliable (r = 0.09 and r = 0.22, respectively). These findings were confirmed by a family of multivariate regression and logistic multiple regression analyses. The prediction equations include the several positive and negative behaviors as predictors, and both composite measures and specific indices of adaptation as outcomes. The specific measures included, for example, the dichotomous criteria of school dropout and teenage parenthood, and the composite measure involved a linear combination of the several domains. The consistent finding was that hostile, negative behaviors emerged as significant predictors in the standard regression and logistic regression models. To illustrate, the composite outcome regression equation retained only the negative behaviors as predictors, and the multiple regression coefficients were identical to the bivariate correlations. When the cohorts were separated for analysis, the aggressive behaviors were significant predictors only in the older cohort (13-year-old group).

While the aggressive behavior categories were robust in the predictive equations, so were other independent indices of aggressive behavior. In this regard, the only significant factor to emerge as a predictor of adult maladjustment among the younger cohort of boys was their classification as being at risk for subsequent violence and assaults. The multiple correlation, again, was high and positive (multiple R = 0.58). The same findings held for both boys and girls in the older cohort when measures in addition to the direct observations were included as predictors. For the boys in Cohort II, the first and only predictor of the composite measure of adult maladjustment to emerge was aggressive risk (multiple R = 0.63). For girls in the older cohort, the only predictor to emerge was teacher ratings of aggressive behavior (multiple R = 0.67). Of course these measures of aggressive risk, behavioral observations of aggressive behavior, and teacher ratings of aggressive behavior were themselves intercorrelated, and it was something of a coin-flip as to which predictor would emerge as the winner in the building of the predictive equation. They referred to correlated characteristics. The only possible exception to this rule is that unpopularity emerged as the predictor of adult maladjustment among 10-year old girls (multiple R = 0.57). Again, the difference may be more apparent than real, because unpopularity in this group was correlated with high aggressiveness.

To sum up, the multivariate analyses of behavioral observations, ratings, and school nominations converged toward the same outcomes. Hostile behaviors in school, whether assessed by observation or reputation, emerged as primary risk factors. These effects outweighed the effects of the demographic variables of race and social class, and the positive characteristics of prosocial behaviors.

Comparisons and contrasts

We have observed that most of the stuff of behavior including aggression depends upon the context in which it occurs. Does this mean that generalization is impossible, and that we need to have a different set of principles for London, Stockholm, and Los Angeles? Not any more than, say, we need to have a different set of meteorological principles to forecast the weather in those three locations despite large differences in the snowfall in December. Yet, local conditions must be considered in predicting the weather, and in predicting behavior. Contextual conditions may play a large part in determining the weight that should be given to any set of variables or configuration of variables. In this regard, it seems important to comment on the extent to which the findings that we have discussed in this chapter must be adjusted to take into account the local conditions in which the information was gathered. Since comparable procedures have been used in other settings in the inner city, in other places in the United States and Europe, and in earlier eras, we can comment on the scope and limits of our observations.

The inner city and an epidemic of violence

Recently we were invited to take part in a call-in television program in a large inner-city school system to address the problems of violence among youths. Christmas vacation was upcoming, and this was an attempt by the school system to reduce injury and prevent harm. As it turns out, Christmas is a period of heightened violence within and outside the home. The program was interactive, in that students were permitted to call-in questions.

It is enlightening to learn what is on the minds of these young people. Here is a sample of the 18 questions that we were asked:

> I'm from (T) High School and I wanted to make a comment that crime prevention programs are not enough. Violence has been magnified and glamorized so greatly that you are not going to find many people that are willing to clean up their act. Violence sells. And I wanted to ask a question: How can we glamorize nonviolence?
>
> My name is Lynneta Grant and I attend (X) Middle School. I'm in the seventh grade and I want to know: How come when a black

person gets hurt in a black neighborhood and they call the police it takes them around an hour to get there? But on the other hand, if a white person gets hurt in a white neighborhood, they'll be there before they can hang up the phone?

Hi, my name is Tommy Scott and I'm from (Y) Middle School and I'm in the sixth grade. I want to know: How do children bring guns into the school when someone has already checked them for guns?

I'm Veronica Wilson and I'm from (Z) Middle School. I would like to ask: Are the police and the adults afraid of the gangs?

My name is David Gimbel and I'm a seventh grader at (X) Middle School. My question is: What do you do when you know someone has a gun in school?

Despite the public nature of the interchanges, the questions seemed to capture real concerns of these young people. Indeed, they were not unlike those we had been asked in the individual interviews that we had conducted in the same inner city. Violence was not a trivial concern in their lives. Within the span of a single month, one 12 year old student of the school had been killed in a drug-related incident, and a former student (currently an 11th grader) was assassinated by three other teenagers.

In our interviews and analyses of over 500 African-American children from 10 to 14 years of age who resided in this inner city, we found only marginally higher levels of aggressive behavior rated by the teachers and the participants themselves relative to the findings from suburban and rural samples. The youths who grow up in this risky environment share more similarities to than differences from youths who grow up beyond the inner city. The youths we saw in the inner city have similar aspirations, similar views on how to avoid conflicts, and similar concepts of friendship and trust to those outside the inner city.[6] The upshot is that the individual difference processes in this inner-city sample of African-American youths closely parallel those of young people in the CLS sample.

We also found salient differences in the community. Virtually all of the 13 year olds listed gangs which operated at the school and in their neighborhoods, as we describe later in this book (Chapter 6). Why then the higher levels of violence in the inner city, if the developmental processes of individual children are similar to those observed elsewhere? The answer here is speculative, given the limited amount of information available from the inner city. What seems different across settings is the sheer risk of living from day to day. While the gangs contributed to the higher rates of violent injury and death, detailed accounts of injury patterns indicate that most of the violence is *not* the result of gang activities. Rather, the violence represents conflicts in the home and among acquaintances that have gone awry, and the homicide rate is linked to the frequent use of firearms in the conflicts. There appears to have been a shift in the acceptability by adolescents of extreme violence as a means of settling disputes. These values are illustrated in gang violence, which itself contributes to the new normative standard that becomes increasingly applied in individual relationships. In some communities, entire neighborhoods become at risk because of the epidemic of violence that rules in the absence of other authority. To be sure, the dispositions of the individual make a difference, in that individuals who join gangs are those who demonstrate early-on high levels of aggressive behavior.[7]

It would seem that the solutions required are more akin to those employed in public health than in individual treatment (Earls, Cairns, & Mercy, 1993). Accordingly, efforts to reduce violence effectively among youths in the inner city call for programs which address community-level risk factors, including the correction of deficiencies in the basic community services (i.e. sanitation, police, fire), creating safer neighborhoods and schools, and reducing the prevalence of young gangs which establish government by default and terrorism. In an epidemic, all people are at risk.

Are girls becoming more violent?

In "Problem Girls", social historian Steven Schlossman compared our longitudinal data of the 1980s with the information obtained from an analysis of the Los Angeles county juvenile records from 1910 to 1950.[8] Today, as in the past, no research tradition has emerged to advance knowledge of girls who seriously misbehave and/or are adjudged formally delinquent. As a result, few data have been regularly collected that are related to the participant. The absence of systematic and serious interest in problem girls by historians, social workers, developmental psychologists, psychiatrists, sociologists, criminologists, or educationists highlights the wider neglect and marginality of girls *per se* in social science scholarship. Only when boys act out and/or become formally delinquent has the scholarly community, and society at large, shown sustained interest in them and recognized a need to develop appropriate and remedial responses.[9] Profound shifts have occurred during this century in both the social expectations and the legal machinery that society uses to encourage conforming behaviors by girls, and to punish nonconforming ones. In the first half of this century, juvenile court was the arena of first resort for dealing with acting-out youth. The philosophy and machinery of the juvenile justice system were geared toward nipping behavioral nonconformity in the bud, in large part by facilitating access to the courts by parents, neighbors, private agencies, school officials, and other less formal monitors of youth. This philosophy applied with special stringency to girls under the legal doctrine of *parens patriae*, where the state legitimately steps in as guardian or superparent for children at risk, the behavior of girls was subjected to especially rigorous scrutiny and disapprobation (particularly with regard to sexual behavior).[10] A similar dual standard, where sons are provided greater freedom of movement and activity than daughters, has been broadly observed in developmental studies of families.[11]

We noted earlier in this chapter that there has been a more rapid increase in arrests for violent crimes among girls than among boys over the past thirty years, although a large gender gap remains. The combined data from the national arrest statistics, the Los Angeles county juvenile records, the state records, and our current longitudinal study seem consistent with the hypothesis that there has been a generational increase in the occurrence of assaultive behaviors by adolescent girls outside the home. Three aspects of the data relevant to this matter require comment as well as caution. First, it appears that arrests for physical assault have increased for girls from the 1940s to the 1980s. Along with the arrest information, our direct observations and the annual self-reports indicated that brutal fights with other girls were not uncommon events for many adolescent girls in the 1980s. The reported physical assaults extended beyond the "at-risk" girls to include many girls within the general population. In addition, some of the more serious acts of violence – stabbing a brother or sister, stabbing a stepfather, suicide, suspected infant abuse – occurred in the home and arrests were not made.

Second, it seems likely that physical attacks within the home were also under-reported in Los Angeles in the 1940s, and elsewhere in the country if Los Angeles is assumed to be representative of an era rather than merely a region. Embedded in the available court records are reports of family violence where the adolescent girls seem to have played active instigating roles. Hence it would be inaccurate to assume that physical assaults did not occur in the 1940s, although arrests were made for other violations. All this is to say that some adolescent girls were physically assaultive in the 1940s, although that behavior tended to be concealed in the home and/or by the courts. But in the 1980s, physically aggressive behaviors which involved adolescent girls seem more frequent, more public, and more often adjudicated. Generational changes are occurring in both female behavior and criminal justice policies. Public confrontation and "male-typical" assertive responses appear to have become more acceptable for female conflicts in the 1980s than in the 1940s. This shift in behavioral standards for girls seems to have been correlated with and perhaps helped to provoke counter-responses by the institutions of society (including schools and the courts).

Third, sexual misconduct was, from the 1920s to the 1940s, the primary cause for delinquency among girls in Los Angeles and, presumably, in other areas of the United States. Arrests for violence were infrequent for girls. The statistics have now been reversed. In the 1920s and 1940s, girls were most often arrested for sexual promiscuity and incorrigibility. In the 1980s, arrests for such status offenses were rare. In the contemporary period, adolescent girls tend to be arrested for behaviors that used to be crimes for adolescent boys. Although national statistics indicate that there are residual differences in the kinds of offenses which lead to arrests in boys and girls, the longitudinal data suggest that these differences will continue to diminish.

Available evidence indicates that arrests of girls for "status offense" has diminished sharply. But teenage running away, unwed motherhood, and difficulties at home seem to have increased in the 1980s relative to the 1920s and 1940s. Why then fewer arrests and complaints about these behaviors in girls? One hypothesis is that the standards of the community, including those of the courts and police, have shifted and these behaviors are no longer considered to be sufficiently deviant to warrant legal prosecution in and of themselves. Following World War II the prevalence of one or all of these behaviors expanded so rapidly among adolescent females that law enforcement had little practical choice but to "decriminalize" them in order to concentrate resources on the increasingly criminal and gang-related activities of both male and female delinquents.

Across time and place

The present outcomes are consistent with other reports which have focused on individual differences in the continuity of problem behaviors from childhood to adolescence and early adulthood.[12] In overview, we can conclude from these investigations that acting-out aggressive behavior in childhood is a significant antecedent for a full range of problem behaviors at maturity, including violent behaviors and criminal assaults. This relationship between early social acting-out difficulties and later problems holds for both males and females. This generalization is supported regardless of the methodology employed, whether prospective longitudinal designs or retrospective interviews.[13] The levels of prediction are impressive, given the earlier dismal track record of psychology to predict features of behavior other than intelligence. It must be noted, however, that there is still plenty of room for error in early assessment, given that the hit rate of adult maladjustment (i.e. true positives) on the basis of high aggressive behavior in childhood is about 50%. Moreover, these summary statistics are static rather than dynamic, and they conceal the fact that most of the participants who experience problems in living also experience successes. We will turn to a more precise analysis of these lives in progress in Chapter 10.

Three other new lessons of the work of the past decade should be underlined. First, the traditional psychological focus on the prediction of pathology by identifying withdrawn, shy children seems to have been misplaced. Given the predictive significance of acting-out behavior patterns, greater attention should be given to the co-occurrence of problem behaviors in childhood, including the combination of withdrawn and aggressive children (see Ledingham *et al.*, 1982; Dolan *et al.*, 1993). Externalizing and internalizing behaviors are not independent in childhood or at maturity. Individuals who are violent are also at risk for suicide and depression, a point which we return to in Chapter 9.

Second, the prediction of aggression and violence is not just an individual affair. One of the lessons of our own work and other investigators is that the context directly modifies the frequency and intensity of aggression and violence. So does the time. This generalization holds true whether time is measured in terms of minutes after an aggressive episode, in terms of years between childhood and adulthood, or in terms of decades of social change. Absolute statements about gender differences in aggression are likely to fail if they are not also accompanied by the conditions under which these generalizations are appropriate.

Third, convergent results have emerged in longitudinal studies on aggressive behavior that have been conducted in several disciplines and in several societies. The longitudinal findings show that there is considerable order in the development of deviant behavior, despite individuality and diversity. Agreement across investigations becomes sharpened when attention is given to the context and details of measurement. For instance, brief behavioral observations of hostile behaviors are unlikely to pay off in longitudinal predictions but extended behaviour observations are effective for prediction in adolescent girls and boys. The convergence across studies that emerges when careful attention is given to context and measurement confirms that a developmental science of human behavior is possible.

Concluding comment

Problems of aggression come in packages, not as single variables. The effects of biology, family, peers, and culture can simultaneously support aggressive and violent behavior. Indeed, hurtful actions may simply be a marker of a pervasive set of circumstances and multiple behavior problems. When there is redundancy with failures in school, affiliations with other deviant peers, and few social and community supports, youth become at very high risk for subsequent problems of living, regardless of their sex.

Societies change in the standards of their acceptability of violence over time, just as individuals change over development. In the past forty years in the United States, there has been an increasing acceptance of violence in both males and females. The effects are clearly seen in the rising incidence of violent behaviors of girls. This broader social acceptance appears at multiple levels, from live entertainment and movies to national arrest statistics and incidence of teenage gang wars. Beyond differences across generations, there are equally large differences among areas of residence in our generation. On this score, the lesson from observations of the inner city indicate that some neighborhoods are in the midst of an epidemic of violence. Hence efforts effectively to reduce violence among youths in the inner city call for programs which address community-level risk factors. Aggression is contagious, whether in the neighborhood, classroom, or family.

Implicit in the above developmental conclusions are some ideas about the nature of aggressive regulation. Aggressive behaviors, in the short run, can be extraordinarily effective in human affairs. Unfortunately, the short-term effectiveness can obscure the long-term problems created for people who adopt them. Once hostility and aggression become significant components in the life style of individuals or become woven into the coercive interchanges of a family or group, it can gain a stranglehold on relationships. Once opportunities are lost due to the problems created by hostility, including grade failure, school suspension, and expulsion, further constraints are created for future choices and opportunities. Any effective intervention/prevention program must attend not only to the characteristics of the person but also the characteristics of the social context. Support for aggressive violent behavior beyond the person in the social ecology must be changed in addition to whatever changes are effected in the person. One ominous trend for society is the increase in aggression and violence among girls. This trend is of special concern when we look beyond individual development and consider who will become the mothers of the children of the next generation.

FIVE

Social networks and the functions of friendships

The development of the child's personality could not go on at all without the constant modification of his sense of himself by suggestions from others. So he himself, at every stage, is really in part someone else, even in his own thought of himself.

James M. Baldwin (1897)

Peer influence gets little respect. It is commonplace to blame peers for deviance, delinquency, drugs, dropout, and other developmental disasters. Yet peer influence is rarely credited for good things, including the transmission of moral values, academic excellence, and courageous acts.

James Youniss has recently tried to rescue the reputation of peers. In his book, *Peers and Families*, Youniss insightfully discussed the several roles of friendships as children enter adolescence and adulthood. He found that there is a sharing of values and aspirations among peers that proved important in successfully negotiating the transition from adolescence to adulthood. This transition involves both changes without (in the social context in which these relationships occur) and changes within, in cognitive and biological functions. Mature levels of cognition are reached in adolescence, and the individual in the relationship gains the ability to generate abstract perspectives on the self, society, and moral values and ethics. Following James M. Baldwin (1897) and Jean Piaget (1926), the intimate sharing of perspectives with peers and parents provides the substrate for the self-concept; thoughts of oneself (Youniss, 1980).[1]

This framework can be extended to provide a broader view of peer social influences, one which can accommodate both positive and

90

negative outcomes. Friendships that synchronize and integrate persons in relationships can also produce shadows (Cairns, Cairns, & Neckerman, 1989). The forces that operate to bring individuals together in intimate relations are effective in part because others are kept out. The boundaries that identify friendships and groups imply barriers for entry and penalties for exit. In informal social groups, distinctions between who is "in" and who is "out" can be reinforced by gossip, innuendo, and rumor, for one type of group, or by beatings and mortal threats, for another type. There are also barriers designed to keep members in line and within the group. Defectors risk being punished. These processes are not limited to children and teenagers, though they may be most salient at this stage of living due to the fluidity of social affiliations.[2]

One truly dark side of synchrony arises when the values and actions of peer groups come into direct conflict with conventional institutions. This shadow of synchrony is age graded. Groups of 9–10-year old children rarely gain the coherence and control that permits a *Lord of the Flies* outcome, and if they do, the event can draw international attention. By contrast, groups of adolescent peers 15–17 years old can seize power through terror and coercion when there has been an abdication of local authority. In some high schools and neighborhoods in the inner city, such gangs routinely fill the vacuum of authority.[3]

More generally, subgroups of youths tend to be granted increasing levels of hegemony in the establishment of social norms and values as they enter adolescence. Bradford Brown and his colleagues have recently described the characteristics and properties of "crowds" typically found in American high schools.[4] Given the diversity of students who attend public high schools, students tend to become labeled by the company they keep. Common labels in the 1980s included "jocks" (athletes), "druggies" (counterculture dropouts), and "nerds" (serious students). This analysis of the crowds of youth is a refinement of Coleman's concept of a monolithic "adolescent culture".[5] As Brown's analysis implies, being affiliated with a group or crowd can be a buffer against problems or it can be an invitation to serious difficulties.

Segregating peer groups and family systems also runs the hazard of treating these forms as if they were independent, when in fact they impinge upon one another. In this regard, recent studies have shown how the child's parents contribute to the formation and dissolution of friendships and social groups.[6] But it is not simply parents who are responsible for the monitoring. In an insightful analysis of how the community operates to maintain itself, Lawrence Steinberg, Ann Fletcher, and their colleagues have shown how the parents of the children's friends actively participate in the monitoring of children. The division of social networks into a "peer group" and a "family system" invites the error of viewing these social influences as if they operated independently. That is an illusion which has been fostered by the narrowness of our conceptions of how these units operate.

Because of the fluid nature of peer groups and the shortcomings of methods for tracking them, there have been few systematic attempts to follow peer groups over time. Tracking peer relationships is inherently more difficult than tracking individuals and families, because peer groups constantly change in structure and composition. They are not only moving targets, but also changing targets. The upshot is that an information gap exists on the basic issues of childhood and adolescent social networks, including the nature of group stability and the mechanisms by which peers influence behaviors and values with respect to time. To make this information accessible, the CLS project had to devise new procedures for the assessment of social networks.

Looking ahead, we will address the dual questions of how relationships can serve as lifelines, and how they function to magnify risks. In Chapters 5 and 6, we examine friendships and groups, and how they wax and wane over time. Despite changing faces, there can be a continuity of influence.

To begin, we provide an illustration of the need to go beyond the simple concept of "peer influence", whether for good or ill.

The cheerleaders

One incident that we encountered two years ago illustrates the benefits and perils of cheerleading, peer networks, and their linkage to families and communities. At Van Ness High School, we identified a closely knit group of six girls, all cheerleaders, in our routine social network analyses. These girls were the social leaders in the school.[7] The girls could typically be seen walking together to classes, gathering at the same lunch table, and simply "hanging around" together.[8]

> One common bond was that all six girls were attractive and popular at school, and membership in the group seemed to confirm and support their attractiveness and popularity. But there were some differences among the girls, and group membership cut across socioeconomic lines. Together, the "gang of six" formed the nucleus of girls who were chosen as cheerleaders and elected as class officers.

This changed in the middle of the fall semester. A school counselor who had been greatly concerned about the growing problem of substance abuse established a drug-awareness and drug-prevention program at the high school. As part of the program, the state Drug Enforcement Office was authorized to conduct random searches of students' cars in the school parking lot whenever there was suspicion of drug use and drug sales. In one such search, 10 grams of crack cocaine were found in the two cars that the girls drove to school.

Close relationships can have either positive or negative consequences for individual development, and sometimes both. Membership in a group carries with it constraints on behavior. In this regard, it was not surprising to find that substance abuse was shared by members of a close-knit peer group. Recent work strongly suggests that the best predictor of illicit drug use in adolescence is whether the individual's friends use illicit drugs.[9]

A second point further illustrates the nature of social clusters of youth; namely, that "peer group influence" is not just kid stuff, and it is not independent of family and school influence.

> All six girls were arrested, suspended from school, and faced trial for the possession and sale of illegal substances. The charges were abruptly dismissed by the presiding magistrate and the high-school counselor who was in charge of monitoring drug awareness was accused of having created the whole affair to bring attention to her efforts.

Peer groups provide a mechanism for the translation of the values of parents and society to the next generation. As such, they are not the sole invention of youth. Peer groups are typically supported by forces within and without, including the support of parents and schools. The structure in which the groups are embedded is typically implicit and in the background, but it can be thrust into the foreground by open challenges. Day-to-day monitoring of the conventional groups may occur at the individual family level, or in schools by teachers and in churches by youth leaders, for example. Complete freedom in the selection of companions is an illusion for most children and adolescents. A third point was illustrated in the longitudinal tracking of this same cluster. Social groups are typically fluid in their composition over time, yet they can exercise a continuing and influential effect upon individual development.

> The next semester four of the girls resumed their roles of school leadership, but not as a single group. The girls became reorganized into different subgroups and networks over the final years of high school. But the original cluster was not totally dissolved: in the 12th grade two of the

original group members remained friends, though affiliated in separate groups.

The social cluster formed by the six girls and transformed over time was unique in its outcome, but general in its structure, dynamics, and course. Some of the most powerful effects of groups have been overlooked because they seem so commonplace. For example, embedded in the account was the fact that the group was comprised exclusively of girls. This same-sex organization is ubiquitous in youth groups across societies, and continues from early childhood through adulthood.

What's important in a friend?

Each year we asked CLS participants, "What's important in a friend?" Since we saw them every year, it was possible to determine year to year changes in what they viewed as the essential qualities of friendship. Adelaide's responses over the years illustrate some universal age changes, in addition to some stable ways of expressing herself. This is what she said when she was interviewed as a 10 year old in the 4th grade:

I: What's important in a friend?
A: I think that they're nice, um, they's-they keep your, you keep your friends a long time. Ah, (tongue-click) some friends are just, you know, mean and they go tell other people. But these friends, friends that are friends to you don't do stuff.

As a child, she identified three elements of friendship: being "nice" rather than being mean, constancy ("friends a long time") rather than fickle, and confidentiality (don't "go tell other people") rather than tattle.

As an adolescent, she was still concerned about faithfulness and caring. But what had been mentioned as one of several qualities had now become the dominant feature of friendship. Here is how Adelaide responded in the 9th grade at 15 years of age:

I: What's important in a friend?
A: (tongue-click) Uh, being able to be there when you need help or so – And to um, care for you and not go out and tell everybody, you know, everything, hey, hey, this you know, if you've got a secret or something, you know, somethin' bothers you, and you don't want to tell everybody else, you know. I want 'em to keep it to (laughs),

you know, between me and them or so.

Although Adelaide's response at 10 years of age was somewhat precocious, she was otherwise representative. We found a systematic shift in the attributes of friends from the immediate service of providing help and getting involved in common activities to the more abstract functions of trust, honesty, and loyalty.

This progression is virtually the same as found in other, cross-sectional studies over the same age range.[10] The shift is toward the increased importance of friends as sources of support, advice, and sharing. There is also a concern about possible betrayal of confidence, particularly among girls in discussing their intimate relationships. The emphasis on honesty and loyalty in adolescence may be more than an increase in the cognitive ability of individuals to think abstractly and recognize the relevance of these virtues. This age change is gender related, in that the qualities of trust and honesty figure more prominently in the descriptions of friendship of girls than of boys.

Age-related changes in social organization suggest that this emphasis upon loyalty may become increasingly important for self-protection. On this count, recall the increasing use of social alienation and manipulation, especially among girls. It seems that self-disclosure and confidence is an important characteristic of human relations, from youth to maturity. It is also hazardous, given the instability of most friendships in childhood and adolescence.

Relationship fluidity

Another concrete aspect of friendship is stability, as Adelaide indicated in the 4th grade when she said, "you keep your friends a long time". That raises the simple question of how long children do keep their friends. To obtain this information, each year the participants were asked the following questions: Some people have a number of close friends, but others have just one "best friend"; still others don't have a best friend. What about you? Who are they? Does this person go to this school? What about when you are not at school? Do you have a different set of friends then? Who?

The answers to these questions could be compared across several years to determine when, and if, persons tended to recur as best friends. Contrary to what most people recall about their own friendships, there is a very short half-life for most relationships.

When we plotted the year-to-year stability of friendships, we found that the friendships of childhood and youth were remarkably fluid. It was very unusual for participants to name the same best-friend from one year to the next (see Figure 5.1). At 11 years of age, roughly one in five kids named anew any person they had considered to be one of their best friends the previous year. After a two-year interval, from 10 to 12 years, the probability shifted downward to approximately one out of ten (but see Berndt & Hoyle, 1985). In the light of these empirical findings, it is ironic that constancy and stability in the relationship is typically viewed as a primary feature of friendship.

But are these group statistics representative of individual experience? A great deal of individual information gets lost in the computation of averages, and it may be the case that some kids switch friendships willy-nilly, while others place a higher value on constancy and faithfulness. In the light of Adelaide's self-reported emphasis on friendship constancy as a 10 year old, she would seem to be a good candidate for the latter category. An analysis of what Adelaide reported the next eight years showed otherwise. Over nine annual interviews, there was not a single recurrence of any of the four persons whom she had indicated were her best friends at 10 years of age. This is not to say that there were no repetitions of persons who were first named in subsequent years (i.e. at

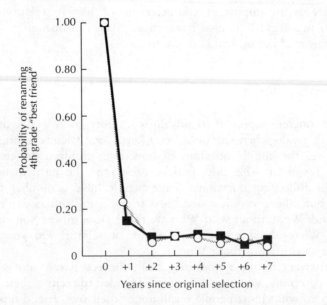

Figure 5.1 Probability for renaming in each of the succeeding years through the 11th grade an individual who had been named as a "best friend" in the 4th grade ($N = 50$ girls and $N = 50$ boys). Solid line represents boys, shaded line represents girls.

ages 11–17). Over these eight consecutive years, the conditional probability of renaming friends if they had been named the immediately preceding year was $P = 0.32$. For Adelaide, the conditional probability dropped to $P = 0.15$, $P = 0.05$, and $P = 0$ after lags of two, three, and four or more years, respectively. To be sure, there were some streaks of stability. Beginning at age 12, one girl was named four years in a row then dropped out; at age 13, another girl was named two years in a row; at age 15, a third girl was named three years in a row; and at age 17, a boy was named two years in a row. Her friendship history, like that of many participants in this investigation, is consistent with Henry Adams' (1918) autobiographic reflection that: "one friend in a lifetime is much; two are many; three are hardly possible" (p. 312).

In a separate investigation, we plotted friendship stability over shorter periods in order to establish the short-term stability (or reliability) of the assessment.[11] It was reassuring to find a moderately high level of stability in the short-term, with over half (54%) of the people named as best friend by 10 year olds still being named as a best friend three weeks later. In the 7th grade, there was a higher probability (i.e. 74%) of renaming the best friend after three weeks. These effects match up with what Berndt has discovered in his careful analysis of the literature on children's friends.[12] Moreover, if the assessment is limited to people who reciprocate their best-friend choices on the first occasion, the probability of being renamed as a friend was even higher.

But why the large shifts over the course of a year? Part of the answer seems to be that the opportunities for friendship maintenance tend to shift during that time. When children move, when they are assigned to a new class, or when they take up new activities, opportunities for new friendships arise. We speculated that there would be a shift in the direction of greater relationship continuity as persons develop the ability to control their lives.

The data were consistent with that expectation. As our participants grew from 10 to 18 years of age, there was a systematic shift in the direction of greater year-to-year stability (see Figure 5.2). This trend is found in both boys and girls. To be sure, plenty of change remains even among 18 year olds. The probability of maintaining the same best friend from one year to the next in high school was less ($P = 0.50$). Friendship stability was clearly higher than in earlier childhood, but it was surely not guaranteed. This conclusion matches earlier reports in the literature.[13] It is also in accord with the experience of individuals in the CLS. Adelaide, for instance, had more stable friendships in the last three years of high school ($P = 0.60$ overall) than in the two years of elementary school ($P = 0.13$).

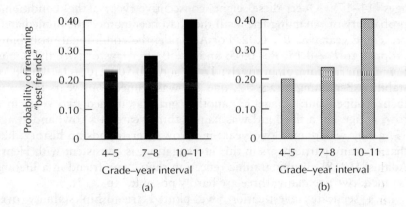

Figure 5.2 Conditioned probability for renaming an individual as a "best friend" after one year, shown for the same people in the 4th, 7th, and 10th grades. (a) $N = 50$ girls and (b) $N = 50$ boys.

The functions of fickleness

Why are some friendships long lasting, or, alternatively, why are most friendships short term in childhood and adolescence? Although our answer to these questions must be speculative, three propositions seem to be in line with prior considerations and the empirical findings:

1. Close, intense relationships serve, at different phases in development, to support and consolidate behavioral organization, as well as contribute to self-attributions and personal goals. Depending on the age and status of the people in the relationship, different functions may be served. Relationships also promote social and interpersonal support and buffer individuals from harm.
2. When one or both individuals' goals or needs change, the relationship necessarily undergoes changes. The direction in which the relationship is altered depends upon whether the interests and behaviors of the people become realigned and synchronized, or diverted and disengaged.
3. Since there are inevitable changes during adolescence, within people and in social circumstances, multiple shifts may be expected in relationships that have been established among peers. Constraints that may stabilize interactions include such factors as kinship, economic dependence, or social mores.

As the needs and goals of adolescents change, so should their relationships. On this count, changes in "best friends" may, for many people, be adaptive in the course of growing up. The problem, of course, is that changes can be disruptive in the short term, even if they are adaptive in the long term. From the reports of our teenage subjects, there are few satisfying ways in which relationships may be broken up or modified without distress to one or both individuals.

Adolescent friendships are dynamic and predictably unreliable. As we report later in this chapter, the shifts are not willy-nilly, and they occur within a framework which is itself predictable. This instability of friendships does not diminish their importance in personal development. In point of fact, the unreliability can ensure variability of influences and the evolution over adolescence of relationships consistent with other features of the individual's preferences and life. The broader issues raised by fickleness concern the utility of interpersonal constancy. In these adolescent experiences, it would appear that it is usually more functional to switch than stay. Indeed, failure to switch friendships when the interests, goals, and beliefs of the members diverge may lead to chronic conflicts in the relationship and in the self.

What are those conditions that make continued commitment between two people adaptive and functional despite developmental changes? Enduring relationships are likely to occur when individuals change together, and adopt the goals which may be integrated with those of the other person. The foregoing suggests a developmental proposal on adolescent relationships; namely, a stable friendship in adolescence is not a passive thing, but a dynamic process that requires active changes by both members of the relationship. Hence friendships between adolescents must change in order to remain stable, and the changes must somehow be coordinated. To the extent that the people involved share similar social backgrounds, athletic or musical talents, and interpersonal skills, the changes that each undergo are themselves likely to be coordinated. But if the friendship is based on characteristics that are ephemeral or likely to be sharply modified in development, the foundation for mutual support may become eroded.

In this regard, best friends among teenagers and the intense emotional commitment associated with them are not likely to endure, despite the hopes of the people involved. Nor, over the long run of development, may it be functional for such adolescent relationships to remain constant. Their immediate service could be to facilitate social and personal growth by providing avenues for change in each person through the support of fresh adaptations in behaviors and beliefs. In order for this function to be served, the relationship must be intense, involve high levels of mutual trust, and each individual should believe that the relationship is highly durable. The last requirement appears, in most instances, to represent a necessary fiction so the other criteria may be met. In the course of development, there may be a selective evolution across relationships in order to arrive at behavior patterns and beliefs distinctive for each person.

"Hanging around" and social cognitive maps

Despite insightful contributions about the nature of social influence and the embeddedness of personality over the past century beginning with the insights of James M. Baldwin, there has been a large gap between concepts and methods. There have been few successful attempts to identify social networks in the natural environments of adolescents, notwithstanding the important early contributions of Frederick Thrasher (1928) and J. L. Moreno (1934). Accordingly, we made a large investment at the outset of this longitudinal investigation in the establishment of an effective way to track people in social context. Once the problem was solved, it provided a method to investigate the social dynamics and social control of relationships in adolescence.[14]

It is a minor irony that the richness of the theoretical speculations about peer groups and their influence has been matched by the poverty of the empirical data available. The scientific assessment of peer groups has been retarded by a gap in methods available for social network analysis. A problem has been that the better quantitative techniques for describing social networks demand near-universal cooperation among members of those networks.[15] This limitation handicaps researchers who hope to employ the procedures in natural settings.

One such procedure, sociometry, involves the use of the social organization descriptive procedures of J. L. Moreno in his volume, *Who Shall Survive?*.[16] Each member of the unit provides an account of their own friends and enemies in specific, real-life settings. Various early attempts were made to quantify this information and to develop inferential statistics in order to determine the reliability of the structures and the adequacy of descriptive structures in summarizing a given data set.[17] It was recognized early on that the quantitative matrices generated in this procedure had distinctive mathematical properties. Paradoxically, the more advanced the mathematics became, the less recognizable were the solutions to the practical issues of social group identification. Moreno's own primitive placement of individuals in a social organization permits him to summarize information obtained from all or nearly all members of a social unit. The procedure has been effectively employed in school settings and in various social organizations, but at a cost of generality.[18]

Social clusters could be of great importance in understanding social development, but the standard methods of sociometry and social network analysis would contribute little. In the United States, explicit signed consent for participation was required from the parents or guardians, as well as consent from the children themselves. This requirement effectively limits the applicability of most methods of social analysis which require near 100% cooperation, since, for many classes, only 50% or less of the subjects are available for assessment. For the network analysis to succeed, we need to know not only whether the individual is fitted into the social network, but with whom. It would be useful to have a method for describing the network in terms of identifiable clusters of children.

Our solution was based on a simple assumption; namely, that children observe and understand more in their social world than they directly experience. When given the opportunity, we found that every child in the class was capable of describing much of the basic information about the social structures of his/her classroom.[19] After a preliminary study we found a set of questions that were understandable by virtually all children and easy to answer. They were asked: Are there people in school who hang around together a lot? Who are they? (If only same-sex groups are named, subjects were asked:) Are there any groups of boys/girls? (If the subject herself/himself was not included, she/he was asked:) What about yourself? Do you have a group you hang around with in school? What about outside of school, do you have a group that you hang around with? On the basis of these questions, the subjects typically generated clusters of people and differentiated among the social clusters within and outside school. This procedure permitted the generation of a social cognitive map (SCM) for every respondent. In doing so we captured the placement of most persons who were seen as actively participating in the social system.

Consider the people who were typically left out by this procedure. Were they the ones who were disliked, shunned, or ignored? To determine whether people were actively shunned, we asked the further question: Are there any people here in school who do not have a group?

Children found the questions on social networks nonthreatening and easy to answer. This was because virtually all of them have a keen awareness of the social structure, even when they themselves might be minor players or on the periphery. Most subjects typically reeled off names effortlessly, as if they were consulting a social map that was cognitively imprinted. The procedure allowed subjects to provide information about the entire network; they were not limited to a description of their own circle of friends or enemies.

This task seems to have had some of the properties of a free-association procedure that made few demands on the subject. By late adolescence and early maturity, the "maps" are less elaborate and seemingly more difficult to generate. The robustness of these cognitive social maps probably accounts for why, despite the potential limitations of this free-recall procedure (e.g. forgetting, selective ignoring, unawareness), high levels of agreement among independent respondents have been obtained.[20]

The results from a small classroom of 7th graders 12–13 years of age illustrate how the associations can be analyzed into quantifiable social clusters. The construction of Table 5.1 proceeded in three steps. First, each respondent's social map was summarized independently, preserving both the order in which groups were recalled and the order of individual nominations within groups (i.e. each group identified by a given respondent was assigned a letter, A, B, C, etc., ascending the alphabet in the order of recall). Second, a "recall matrix" (Subject (row) by respondent (column)) was constructed. Third, a square "co-occurrence matrix" was constructed directly from the recall matrix in order to represent the number of occasions any two persons co-occurred in the same group. The diagonal of the co-occurrence matrix summarizes the sheer number of times the individual was named in any group. This measure of social salience has proved to be key in identifying the status of individuals and their groups in the social network.

Certain natural groups rapidly emerged in the tabulation of the data. As shown in Table 5.1, there was reasonably good agreement among respondents that the first seven girls, Amy to Gay, are members of the same group. Two other groups are evident among the girls, namely, a group of four, composed of Ida, Joy, Kim and Lyn and a group of three formed by Mia, Nia, and Ola. Hea, the eighth subject on the list was sometimes named with the largest group, and on some occasions, with the group of three. Note that Pam was not placed in the social structure by any of the respondents. When asked the question, Are there any people in the class who do not have a group?, ten of the eleven female respondents (91%) named Pam. No other girls were named as being isolated.

The above solution can be further quantified by the application of appropriate multivariate statistical models to a co-occurrence matrix derived from Table 5.2.[21] Table 5.2 was constructed by tabulating for every two individuals the number of occasions that they had been named in the same group by one of the respondents. For example, Amy

Table 5.1 Recall matrix of social clusters in 7th grade

		Female respondents											Male respondents					
		Amy	Bea	Cam	Edi	Fay	Gay	Hea	Joy	Lyn	Nia	Ola	Cal	Gig	Hal	Ian	Jan	Ken
Girls	Amy	A	B	A	A	B	D	A	A	B	–	–	C	C	D	–	–	B
	Bea	B	**B**	A	A	B	D	A	A	B	A	–	C	–	D	–	–	B
	Cam	A	A	**A**	–	B	D	A	A	B	A	–	C	C	D	–	–	–
	Di	–	B	–	A	–	D	A	A	B	A	–	C	C	D	–	A	–
	Edi	A	B	A	A	B	D	A	A	B	A	–	C	C	–	–	A	C
	Fay	A	–	A	A	**B**	D	A	A	B	A	–	C	C	D	C	D	C
	Gay	A	–	A	A	A	**D**	A	A	C	A	–	–	–	E	–	D	–
	Hea	A	B	B	A	A	–	A	A	A	B	C	E	D	E	C	–	–
	Ida	B	C	B	B	A	–	E	B	A	B	C	E	D	C	C	–	–
	Joy	B	C	B	B	A	–	E	**B**	A	B	C	E	D	C	C	D	–
	Kim	B	C	B	B	A	–	E	B	A	B	C	E	D	C	C	–	–
	Lyn	B	C	B	C	C	–	E	B	A	B	C	D	D	D	C	D	–
	Mia	A	–	C	–	A	A	–	–	A	A	A	D	–	E	–	–	–
	Nia	–	–	C	–	–	A	B	–	C	A	A	D	–	E	–	D	–
	Ola	–	–	C	–	C	A	B	–	C	A	A	D	–	–	–	–	–
	Pam	–	–	–	–	–	–	–	–	–	–	–	–	–	–	–	–	–
Boys	Arn	A	A	A	C	E	B	C	–	–	A	A	A	A	A	A	C	A
	Bil	A	A	A	C	E	B	C	–	–	A	A	A	A	A	A	–	A
	Cal	A	A	A	C	E	B	C	–	–	A	A	A	A	–	A	C	–
	Dan	A	A	A	–	E	B	C	–	–	A	A	A	A	A	A	–	–
	Edd	–	–	–	–	E	–	C	–	–	–	–	–	A	A	A	–	–
	Foz	–	A	A	D	D	–	–	–	D	–	B	B	B	–	B	–	–
	Gig	–	–	D	D	C	–	D	–	D	B	B	**B**	**B**	**B**	B	B	–
	Hal	–	–	D	D	C	–	D	–	D	B	B	B	B	**B**	B	B	–
	Ian	–	–	–	D	D	–	D	–	D	B	B	B	B	B	B	B	–
	Jan	–	–	D	D	D	–	D	–	D	A	B	B	B/A	B	–	–	–
	Ken	–	A	–	–	–	–	–	–	–	A	A	B	B	B	B	–	–

Cell entries (A, B, . . .) refer to the clusters that were generated by the respondent, where each respondent's social cognitive map is shown in the column below her/his name. The "A" cluster was recalled first, "B" second, and so on. A dash (–) indicates that the person's name was not generated by the respondent. The entry "B/A" indicates that "Jan" was assigned to both the "B" and "A" clusters by respondent "Gig". From Cairns, Perrin and Cairns (1985).

and Bea had been placed together in a group on eleven occasions (see intersection of Amy and Bea). Similarly, Amy and Di had been simultaneously placed in the same group on seven occasions, and Amy and Ida were never mentioned as being in the same group. The diagonal (e g Amy–Amy) is simply the number of occasions (13) that Amy had been nominated for any group. The same goes for Bea (i e she had been nominated on twelve occasions).

The degree of similarity between each person's relationship with every other person in the school can be further expressed as a profile similarity index. This index is derived by correlating the profile of relationships of Amy with Bea, Amy with Di, Bea with Di, etc. Subjects were assumed to be in the same cluster if their profiles are correlation $r = 0.40$ or higher. It is then only a matter of bringing together the individuals who meet this criterion in order to construct the social network. The social cognitive map (SCM) provides a simple procedure for integrating the social perceptions of an entire classroom or school in order to construct a composite map of independent views of the social world in which they live. It works primarily because of the logic of the method and the robust nature of the phenomena under investigation, not because of the mathematics. A topographic map of the social linkages in the classroom can also be drawn (see Figure 5.3). The lines between girls represent significant pair associations.

Two assumptions key to the SCM procedure should be noted. First, the procedure assumes that respondents have only a limited knowledge of the classroom, but that the information they provide will be replicated by other respondents. That is, there are frequent errors of omission in naming people and groups, but there should be very few errors of commission. Respondents often err by leaving people out of the network who actually belong in it, but they rarely include people in a group when they do not belong. The second assumption is that respondents can provide information about the composition of groups, even though they themselves are not members. Although this seems to be a simple and self-evident proposal, it has rarely been built into systematic analyses of peer social networks. Once adopted, it significantly extends the amount of information that may be derived from one respondent. As a byproduct, it makes feasible the application of social network methods in the classroom, the workplace, and the community.

Could we get exactly the same information from the children and youths themselves simply by asking them who they hung around with? This question taps into one of the hotly debated methodological issues in the discipline on the accuracy of self-reports. We will take up this matter in the context of self-concepts in Chapter 7. For here, the simple

Table 5.2 Co-occurrence matrix for the females in Table 5.2[a] (from Cairns, Gariépy and Kindermann, 1990).

	Amy	Bea	Cam	Di	Edi	Fay	Gay	Hea	Ida	Joy	Kim	Lyn	Mia	Nia	Ola
Amy	**13**[b]	11[c]	12	7	12	10	5	4	–	–	–	–	2	–	–
Bea	11	**12**	11	6	11	8	5	4	–	–	–	–	3	1	1
Cam	12	11	**13**	7	13	10	5	4	–	–	–	–	3	1	1
Di	7	6	7	**8**	8	5	3	2	–	–	–	–	–	–	–
Edi	12	11	13	8	**14**	10	5	4	–	–	–	–	3	1	1
Fay	10	8	10	5	10	**12**	6	5	–	–	–	–	2	–	–
Gay	5	5	5	3	5	6	**6**	3	–	–	–	–	4	–	–
Hea	4	4	4	2	4	5	3	**9**	–	–	–	–	4	4	4
Ida	–	–	–	–	–	–	–	–	**14**	14	14	14	–	–	–
Joy	–	–	–	–	–	–	–	–	14	**14**	14	14	–	–	–
Kim	–	–	–	–	–	–	–	–	14	14	**14**	14	–	–	–
Lyn	–	–	–	–	–	–	–	–	14	14	14	**14**	–	–	–
Mia	2	3	3	–	3	2	–	4	–	–	–	–	**9**	7	7
Nia	–	1	1	–	1	–	–	4	–	–	–	–	7	**8**	8
Ola	–	1	1	–	1	–	–	4	–	–	–	–	7	8	**8**

[a] The table frequencies represent the nominations made by all (17) respondents; note that the person "Pam" was omitted from the co-occurrence matrix because she had zero nominations.

[b] Diagonals indicate the number of times the individual was named to any group.

[c] Off-diagonal numbers indicate the number of times respondents named the two people (designated by the row and column) to the same group.

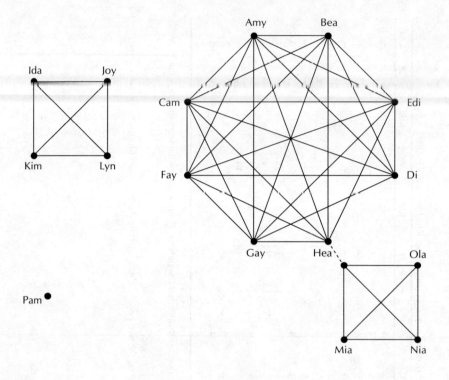

Figure 5.3 Network linkage analysis of female social network in Table 5.3. Example of social cognitive map of girls in 7th grade. Note dual group membership (Hea) and presence of isolate (Pam). From Cairns, Gariépy and Kindermann (1990).

answer is that self-reports, though useful for many purposes, have two major drawbacks. One is that they are biased toward accentuating the positive and eliminating the negative. Well-behaving acquaintances are more likely to be included in self-reports, and poorly behaving friends more likely to be excluded.[22] A second drawback is that many subjects give incomplete information or omit their self-groups. For these subjects, an advantage of combining self-reports with information beyond the self is the greater efficiency, completeness, and accuracy of the combination. Most people in a social network have valid information about the network as a whole, that they are willing to share if asked.

Do the cognitions correspond to behavior? The validity of the subgroups derived through the social cognitive procedure was then confirmed by the direct observation of social interactions among the children of the same cluster.[23] It has been found, for instance, that children and adolescents are more likely to interact with members of their own subgroup than with members of other clusters, they formed same-sex clusters in early adolescence, and the clusters were recognizable after a one-year period when the assessments were made in the same school. One further point should be anticipated in the light of the problems that we will raise later on the "objective" accuracy of self-reports (see Chapter 7). In their descriptions of social groups of peers, respondents showed high levels of agreement, with fewer than 4% errors of commission.

International maps

To determine the generalizability of the SCM technique across social and cultural boundaries, colleagues in several countries in Europe and Asia have employed the procedure. Its applicability is not bounded by language and geography. Children in Hong Kong and Taipei can generate the social structure in their schools as readily and easily as Icelandic or Portuguese children.[24] Nor are the effects limited to a particular social segment. Children in the bowels of the inner city are able to generate the social structure of their peers as readily as children enrolled in exclusive private schools.

Across these different countries and contexts, children and youths have in common an awareness of the extant social structure in the "personal computer" of their minds. In any case, with these techniques available and readily applicable to social networks from childhood through adulthood, it became possible to investigate whether James M. Baldwin was correct when he asserted that each of us was one of another, even in our own "thoughts of oneself". It was also possible to determine directly whether the technique and the information it generated were limited to local and American concerns, or whether they were general and international in scope.

Propinquity, friendships, and making love: the dynamics of groups

One of the best-established findings in the study of social development is that emotional attractions are powerfully influenced by physical closeness. This phenomenon has been nicely established by research attempts to "make love", that is, to create new and intense emotional attractions. Experiments on this phenomenon of synthetic attraction have tended to focus on the very early years. The results indicate two noteworthy findings: one concerning social bias and the other concerning propinquity. First, there is a strong bias toward social attachment in infancy. Human infants (and most other mammalian young) become rapidly and strongly attached to specific others, with the age range of very high susceptibility in babies falling between 8 and 30 months of age. Second, human infants tend to become strongly attached with whoever they interact, whether male or female, young or old. Caretaking facilitates the attachment, but it is not necessary. Propinquity is the necessary factor. Paradoxically, mammalian infants – monkeys, puppies, lambs – become attached emotionally even to individuals who are punitive if they are kept in close proximity to them. By controlling propinquity, it is possible not only to create the conditions for affection and friendship, but also to manufacture it in the hospital, nursery, and preschool (Cairns, 1979).

The effects of propinquity are not limited to infancy in humans and animals. Beyond childhood, close relationships tend to become established when people are brought into proximity to each other, whether the constraints are by employment, training, or geography. Friendships and groups are formed by people who attend the same college, become assigned to the same military installation, attend the same church, or work together in the same factory (Homans, 1950).

It might be expected that school-age friendships and groups are formed by children and adolescents primarily among the pool of people assigned to the same classroom. The facts bear out the expectation. Regardless of how we sought information about group affiliations, there was a strong tendency for friendships and groups to be forged among the relationships available in the classroom. When classrooms were reshuffled, so were the friendships and groups. The net result of this constraint was that relationships within the school were rather stable within a given year when classrooms, teachers, and students were kept intact, but this stability was lost when the elements of the system were reshuffled. Space and time are critical elements in any equation that seeks to explain the fluidity and stability of groups and group influence.

When Holly Neckerman (1992) analyzed the effects of propinquity on social groups in the CLS in her recent doctoral dissertation, the profound effects of proximity were identified in two ways. First, comparisons were made between schools which kept students in the same classroom configurations from year to year while changing teachers, as opposed to schools where both teachers and students were shuffled. Unity in classroom configurations was associated with stability of social groups. The probability of identifying stable groups in the schools where classes moved as a unit was $P = 0.67$, while the probability of identifying stable groups where the classes were shuffled was $P = 0.16$. This was essentially the difference between complete turnover in social groups *versus* a reasonably stable structure.

The second technique was to compare the effects of propinquity in all schools, regardless of policy for shifting classes. Here the comparison was made among students who were friends/group members in the first year who were kept together the following year or who were placed in different classes. Again, the probability of the relationship persisting into the second year was dependent upon propinquity. Among those in the same class the second year, the probability of a stable relationship was $P = 0.57$. Among those in a different class the second year, the probability was $P = 0.12$.

"Birds of a feather"

Children and adolescents do not cluster together at random after propinquity is controlled. Gender continues to be a factor in group affiliation. In addition, groups tend to be homogeneous with respect to age and, in the United States, race. We expected that the weight assigned to these factors in group formation would shift over time, with greater weight given to race and less weight given to age as people grow older. The basis for this expectation is that there is greater awareness of differences, greater pressure toward similarity, and more opportunities to achieve similarity as a function of development. In addition, we expected that the child's and adolescent's deviant behaviors would be important above and beyond the "social address" variables of gender, race, and age. This last effect takes on importance in any account of deviance or risk, and whether it is a cause or a consequence.

Sex, age, and race

One of the more obvious properties of the social clusters of kindergarten, elementary and middle schools is the assortment by gender. Boys hang around with boys, and girls with girls. As the subjects get older, grouping with respect to gender diminishes, though it remains strong, even in college. Race is also a potent variable. Observations in elementary school, middle school, high school, and college indicate that the role of race follows a developmental trajectory opposite to that of gender. Tracking social clusters from the 4th grade through high school indicates that resegregation is intensified among girls as they enter adolescence. The emergent racial propensity occurs, even though most of the schools in which we made the initial observations were in the Southeastern United States. These schools were strictly integrated and kept under close judicial supervision over the past twenty years. Thanks to this supervision, they are among the most thoroughly integrated schools in America. Similarly, social class appears to take on greater importance in peer groups in mid-adolescence, though its influence can be seen earlier. All of these effects are, of course, overlaid on propinquity.

Recent investigators have proposed that the ubiquitous tendency for males and females to affiliate in same-sex groups is of great importance for gender role development (e.g., Cairns & Kroll, 1994; Maccoby, 1990; Strayer & Noel, 1986). The phenomenon of same-sex social affiliation tends to overwhelm other demographic, behavioral, and racial factors. The effect is not limited to Western societies; it is as prominent in Taiwan and Hong-Kong as it is in the United States and Iceland (Cairns, Gariépy, & Kindermann, 1990).

These influences on gender role identification and sex-typing are ubiquitous, powerful, and broadly accepted, but they have tended to be ignored by researchers. The age-grading of peer group affiliations ensures that the nature of "gender-appropriate" interchanges shift and remain sex- and age-appropriate, from preschool to college. In this light, the conclusion of Lytton & Romney (1991) that parental socialization has only a modest direct effect on gender typing may not be far-fetched. In this behavioral realm, the effects of peer groups may overwhelm those of parents.

Evidence for these effects and age trends were found in various aspects of the longitudinal data set. The intraclass correlation (r') is a statistic that detects the degree of within-group similarity. This measure is derived from standard analysis of variance, and reflects the magnitude of within-group similarity on specific characteristics. It can be interpreted as a measure of internal similarity where $r' = 0$ represents no within-group similarity and $r' = 1.00$ perfect similarity.[25]

We find reliable intraclass correlations are obtained with respect to gender, race, and social class, with an intensification of the effects of race and class as the children enter junior high (Table 5.3). The effects of race and social class are usually confounded, but they have unique contributions when the other factor is held constant statistically. The experiences of Melanie unhappily illustrate how the role of socioeconomic factors and family background seem to take on increasing importance with entry into junior high and high school.

Table 5.3 "Birds of a Feather": within cluster similarities in demographic and physical characteristics

Domain	Gender	Age	Cohort	Intraclass correlation
Ethnic status	Males	10	I	0.65***
		13	II	0.48***
	Females	10	I	0.67***
		13	II	0.87***
Socioeconomic status	Males	10	I	0.14
		13	II	0.09
	Females	10	I	0.17*
		13	II	0.16**
Chronological age	Males	10	I	0.10
		13	II	0.37***
	Females	10	I	0.23**
		13	II	0.22***
Maturational status	Males	10	I	0.34**
		13	II	0.39***
	Females	10	I	0.27*
		13	II	0.17**

* $p < 0.05$.
** $p < 0.01$.
*** $p < 0.001$.

In the 4th, 5th, and 6th grades at Porter City, Melanie was one of the most popular and admired girls in her class. She was pretty, friendly, and selected for the GT (Gifted and Talented) class for academic acceleration. Toward the end of the 7th grade at junior high, her status went into a tailspin. In the course of the annual interviews across the school, it came out that her primary rival for popularity, Bonnie, had begun to talk liberally about Melanie's problems at home. She was ostracized by her former group, and fell entirely from favor in the peer social structure at school. The next year, she transferred to Westwood Junior High, and she began to reconstruct a new pattern of friendships. Through the year, she remained pretty, friendly, and bright, but her social status continued its downward spiral. In the 11th grade, Melanie dropped out of school.

There is a developmental reshuffling of social relationships and clusters to bring members into line with their racial and economic characteristics especially among groups of girls.

Similarity in behaviors and interests

Within-group similarities are not limited to exogenous characteristics. Behaviors, interests, and values also figure importantly, and may supersede demographic factors in determining social clusters. To investigate the role of behavioral properties such as the individual's aggressiveness, popularity, and academic talent, separate intraclass correlations were determined for the various clusters in elementary and junior high school. Separate, gender-specific analyses were conducted, with the primary results of this analysis shown in Table 5.4.

Aggressive behavior. The strongest behavioral pattern of within-group similarity in childhood and adolescence is on the general domain labeled "aggressive behavior". As noted in Chapter 4, however, aggression is a composite variable associated with a number of other characteristics, including behaviors that are aggressive and/or deviant. In any case, the clusters of both boys and girls are characterized by moderately high levels of similarity on this dimension.

Popularity. We had anticipated that popularity with peers would be

Table 5.4 "Birds of a Feather": within cluster similarities in social and behavioral characteristics

Domain	Gender	Sample	Intraclass correlation	p
Aggression	Males	10 year old (Cohort I)	0.47	< 0.000
		13 year old (Cohort II)	0.28	< 0.001
	Females	10 year old (Cohort I)	0.38	< 0.000
		13 year old (Cohort II)	0.41	< 0.000
Popularity	Males	10 year old (Cohort I)	0.14	ns[a]
		13 year old (Cohort II)	0.02	ns
	Females	10 year old (Cohort I)	0.47	< 0.000
		13 year old (Cohort II)	0.35	< 0.000
Academic	Males	10 year old (Cohort I)	0.16	ns
		13 year old (Cohort II)	0.11	ns
	Females	10 year old (Cohort I)	0.32	< 0.01
		13 year old (Cohort II)	0.26	< 0.000
Attractiveness	Males	10 year old (Cohort I)	0.16	ns
		13 year old (Cohort II)	0.44	< 0.000
	Females	10 year old (Cohort I)	0.28	< 0.001
		13 year old (Cohort II)	0.36	< 0.000

[a] ns indicates that the intraclass correlation is not statistically significant.

another primary domain of similarity. The data indicate that it was a factor for girls in both childhood and early adolescence, but it is inconsistently represented across the different age levels in the social groups of boys.

Leadership. The term "leader" implies that one individual is outstanding in a group, and that there would be scant basis for a group of leaders to form. The data indicate that even leaders form groups, like the six cheerleaders who temporarily went awry. C. A. Edwards (1990), in another recent dissertation which involved the study of girl scouts at summer camp, found a reasonably strong tendency for leadership groups to form over a period as short as two weeks.

Academic achievement. Do smart kids hang around together? There is a reasonably strong tendency for academic achievement to be a factor in group affiliation and relationships among adolescents of both genders, but not among elementary school children.

Maturation. Are youths who hang around together similar in terms of physical maturation? Physical maturation, independent of age, tends to be associated with selective affiliation in social clusters. This is supported by the linkage between ratings of physical maturity and affiliation in the 7th grade for both boys and girls. As we note later, there is also some evidence that younger girls affiliate selectively on the basis of their sexual maturity (i.e. onset of menarche).

Age. Even within the same grade, people tend to hang around with others who are similar in age. It is possibly mediated by similarity in not only years of age, but also whether the person has failed a grade or was otherwise held back in school, since that is the primary basis by which children older than peers would be in the same school grade. By middle school, the effect of age on social affiliation is quite strong for males.

Athletics. Because of the powerful effects of propinquity, virtually any activity that requires people to spend significant periods of time together can provide the basis for social clustering through recurrent associations. This includes participation in sports.

Attractiveness. Beautiful people do tend to hang around together, particularly in adolescence. It makes little difference how attractiveness is measured, whether by the judgments of teachers, researchers, or the subjects themselves. There is a propensity for individuals who are rated as attractive, or unattractive, to be associated with others who are rated similarly on the dimensions of appearance.

Research participation. Beyond similarities on various dimensions of salient activities in their lives, there are also similarities with respect to seemingly trivial matters. One of these is the decision to participate in extracurricular activities in which they have a choice, including participation in research studies. While this is an inconsequential decision for the subjects, it is a matter of vital importance to all researchers who are attempting to understand their behaviors. On this score, in all three experiments that we have conducted, we find that children, adolescents, and their parents who chose to participate in the research tend to be members of the same clusters, and those who do not choose to participate also tend to share cluster membership. Because of the high rate of participation in these investigations, the bias was modest, but consistent. Nonetheless, the data strongly suggest that *all* research studies which require individual consent are likely to be influenced by group bias and the attitudes which prevail in the clusters of which the individuals are members. Volunteering is itself influenced by group coaction, a matter that could have significant implications for statistical analysis and generalization.

The upshot is that groups tend to form along any salient characteristic where similarity can be defined. This holds for sex, age, race, smoking, failing a grade, aggression, doing well in class, playing football, or being a cheerleader. Once clustered, contagious reciprocity in behaviors and actions appears, creating new types of similarities among cluster members. Accordingly, some level of within-group commonalities may be found with respect to virtually all dimensions capable of identification. Perhaps as a result of these provoked similarities, members of clusters tend to share plans about major changes in the lifecourse, such as the decision to join the Marines, become engaged, or select a particular college. All this is to say that similarity is a pervasive phenomenon that transcends ongoing behavior, and includes plans for transitions in their lives.

Predictive associations: teenage parenthood and early school dropout

Does group membership in childhood provide any clue as to what may happen later in life? Although we are jumping ahead of the story, proceeding forward in time to five to ten years after original data collection, it should be noted that people with whom the subjects affiliated in elementary school and middle school tended to have similar outcomes in whether they became teenage parents and whether they dropped out of school. These findings are summarized in Table 5.5, which shows the links between the group membership in the 4th or 7th grades and outcomes several years later. The two outcomes shown are teenage parenthood and early school dropout. This may reflect a "sleeper effect", a long-term outcome of early experience that was dormant until late adolescence or early adulthood, or it may reflect the dynamic regeneration of social influences from year to year in ways consistent with the early group formation. The evidence suggests that it may be both. The early affiliations can place constraints on which pathways are chosen by (or for) the child, and the subsequent affiliations serve continually to regenerate in new ways and new forms the directions that have been established in early years. But the facts are firm. We can predict outcomes not merely on the basis of early behaviors, but on the basis of early associates.

Homophilies and similarities: causation or correlation?

Is an ordering of similar characteristics possible, such that one property can be consistently shown to be more important than others in leading the way for group formation? For example, the single decision to cooperate with a group of visiting researchers would seem to be the consequence rather than a cause of group involvement. Which of the several characteristics – from aggression and dropout to popularity and school achievement – are causes and which are correlates of group formation? There is no single method to sort out the answer to this question, although some related techniques (i.e. MANOVA, ANOCA) seem to provide reasonably adequate solutions.

Using these procedures, we have found generality across studies, ages, and cohorts in what are the basic dimensions of similarity. Once

Table 5.5 "Birds of a Feather": early cluster membership and subsequent teen parenthood and school dropout

Domain	Gender	Sample	Intraclass correlation	p
Teenage parenthood	Males	10 year old (Cohort I)	0.26	< 0.05
		13 year old (Cohort II)	0.36	< 0.000
	Females	10 year old (Cohort I)	0.31	< 0.01
		13 year old (Cohort II)	0.36	< 0.000
School dropout	Males	10 year old (Cohort I)	0.03	ns
		13 year old (Cohort II)	0.26	< 0.01
	Females	10 year old (Cohort I)	0.28	< 0.01
		13 year old (Cohort II)	0.35	< 0.05

propinquity is removed as a factor, sex and race prove to be consistently important. The importance of race tends to increase in later adolescence. Similarity in social class seems to be more important for girls than for boys, and similarity in academic achievement is a bigger factor for females than males in social cluster formation. Interestingly, aggressive behavior, including the tendency to get into trouble at school and in fights with other kids, was the primary behavioral characteristic implicated in group formation across ages. Regardless of the statistical solution employed, it appeared at the head of the class relative to other behavioral variables.

How groups form

The CLS investigation provided the opportunity to go beyond cross-sectional surveys in order to address matters that seemed critical for understanding how such groups came about and what were their impacts upon individual development. Accordingly, we were concerned with three issues:

1. How do similarities within the groups of childhood and adolescence come about?
2. What are the conditions for movement in and out of clusters?
3. What are the linkages among social clusters, including those among peer groups and between peer groups and family groups?

Consider first the generation of similarity. One possible process is selection, where similarity comes about through an initial sorting process by individuals, by groups, or by forces beyond the individuals or groups. Biselection refers to cases where there is selective affiliation by persons on the basis of similarities with respect to some salient dimensions of behavior or status. Biselection emphasizes that affiliation is a two-way street, where individuals who select are simultaneously being selected. The simple idea that youngsters or children "join" a particular group fails to recognize that groups themselves have boundaries and often highly restrictive conditions for affiliation.

First, while the process of biselection tends to make sense when the only players in the game are peers, it might be too restrictive in a world where other forces are involved. For example, consider the simple case of academic tracking, the state of affairs where children of similar achievement are kept together in school classes. Such a constraint on propinquity constitutes an institutional technique to manufacture friendships. Academic segregation is also a way to ensure that better-behaving kids hang around together. On the flipside, such separation also promotes gang formation through propinquity, and invites classroom chaos by promoting coalitions among problem children. On this score, probation officers that we have known believe that juvenile detention facilities provide an excellent opportunity for gangs to propagate across the city by providing new contacts and making new converts. On a lesser scale, epidemics of problem behaviors are promoted by the clustering of problem children and adolescents in school settings.

Second, reciprocal socialization refers to the tendency for people to adopt behaviors, attitudes, and values that are similar to those with whom they have had recurrent interactions. Increased similarity thus emerges in the course of the relationship. The reciprocity comes about because social interactions necessarily provide mutual support. The behavior of one person in an interchange provides constraints on the freedom of action of the other person, and vice versa. To the extent that two people remain in an interchange, their behaviors are reciprocally shaped. Hence increased levels of similarity over time should evolve if interactions are maintained. But if one person should fail to support the actions of the other, and the second resists modification, a strain on the relationship may emerge, along with increased conflict and, possibly, diminished interactions.

Third, when a time dimension is considered, biselection and reciprocation may be seen as operating together, not as opposed processes. On this score, similarity attracts because of the promise that the individuals who are alike on key dimensions will also have an adequate basis for interaction. The rejection of dissimilarities may be functional, in that some key characteristics in common are required for successful interactions to begin. But once the joint selection occurs, a new process is set into motion to ensure conjoint growth and further similarities, without which the embryonic relationship will dissolve. According to this third possibility, selection and socialization are mutually supportive.[26]

There is strong support for the idea that selection and socialization cooperate over time, as far as our own observations are concerned. There is clearly a selection process, where children and adolescents affiliate on the basis of sex, race, and socioeconomic class. There is also a contagion effect, such that once the groups are formed, the "selected" behaviors are escalated for good or ill. The constraints on escalation typically operate from without, in the case of younger children and adolescents. Equally interesting, however, is the creation of novel behaviors within groups, and their transmission across members. This is a particular problem in the case of deviant groups.[27]

In the examination of the dynamics responsible for creating the similarity in delinquency, three explanatory processes have been proposed: differential selection (where delinquent adolescents chose other delinquent adolescents for friends), reciprocal socialization (where adolescents adopt the attitudes and behaviors of the other group members, therefore creating similarity over time), and selective elimination (where the most disparate members of a group leave, either voluntarily or because they are rejected).[28] In the latter case, adolescents who do not share the norms and behaviors of the group may not be tolerated; they can choose to leave or be kicked out. Moreover, these processes are not mutually exclusive. They may operate simultaneously or at different points in the history of the peer group.

Denise Kandel conducted a classic study of friendships to assess both selection and socialization processes.[29] Data were collected at the beginning and end of the school year. First the subjects were asked to name their best friend in school. Second, all of the subjects were asked to report on the frequency of marijuana use in the previous month. Subjects were also asked to report on their participation in a variety of deviant activities. After the second data collection session, she analyzed the dynamics of the friendship dyads to determine if they remained stable or changed over the course of the year. The friendships were further categorized as reciprocated or nonreciprocated. She classified the friendship dyads as one of three categories: stable over time, new friendship pairs, and pairs that had broken up over the course of the year. Kandel concluded that stable pairs of friends were, at the outset, more similar than the soon-to-be unstable pairs; that coresemblance or similarity increases over time, if the pairs remain together, and similarity among former friends is lower than among new friendship pairs.

Kandel proposed that selection and socialization processes were jointly responsible for the observed similarity in friendship dyads. She argued that if the significant behaviors or attitudes of two friends are in a state of disequilibrium, then one of two responses may take place. Either the pair will break up or they will change their behaviors in order to create equilibrium where it was lacking. Kandel's methodology provides a notable advance, in that she obtained information about both parties in the friendship dyad at two points in time.

Extending the above work, Richard Udry and his colleagues investigated how individuals chose friends on the basis of demographic/classification characteristics (e.g. grade, sex, race) and salient behaviors (e.g. smoking, sexual intercourse, drinking, underage driving, cheating in an examination). These researchers anticipated that the analysis would illustrate the process by which people select their friends on the basis of similarities. They examined the selection process by first controlling for the personal characteristics of race, sex, and age. Given that there are many potential choices for friends, adolescents were expected to assign a priority with respect to those characteristics most important to them. It was expected that participants would first eliminate those who did not fit their preferred demographic/ classification characteristics, then choose potential friends on the basis of salient behavioral variables.[30]

The subjects were supplied with a list of all students in the school and were asked to name their three best male and female friends. From these data, friendship dyads were constructed. The data analysis was conducted on the reciprocated pairs (where two people selected each other as "best friend"). Each subject was also asked whether or not they had ever participated in the various behaviors. The investigators found that both males and females selected friends by grade, race, and behavior. For example, white males considered smoking as a salient factor when making a selection of friends, while females had friends who were similar on a configuration of behavioral variables (i.e. smoking, drinking, sexual promiscuity). A parsimonious interpretation of these findings is that the selected behaviors simply index a broader lifestyle, and it is similarity with respect to deviant lifestyles that is the actual basis for selective affiliation.[31]

In an assessment of the processes responsible for homogeneous peer groups, Cohen analyzed high-school data from the school year 1958–9.[32] He concluded that "most group uniformity comes from initial homophilic selection, conformity pressures contribute something to uniformity on selected items, and the ostracism of deviates adds little to group uniformity" (1977, pp. 237–8). So initial selection is seen to be the critical process. But there is a problem. It is unclear whether the initial "homophilic selection"[33] is due to the positive attraction for peers like oneself, or to social forces that reduce the individuals' freedom of movement in the social network, and predetermine the clusters to which any person may belong.

Lord of the Flies and similarities in deviance

Of the various concerns about social clusters, the one that has received the greatest attention by society has been the peer influences among adolescents in deviant behaviors. The nature of the deviance ranges from "gangs" that support hard drug use and violence, on the one hand, to "groups" of school dropouts, on the other. From the above discussion of similarity, it would appear that similarities with respect to such negative behaviors reflect the operation of the same principles as do similarities on other, more benign dimensions.

The group of 10th grade girls described at the beginning of this chapter got our attention because of the problems they created for themselves, their parents, and their schools. Another example, taken from the same class, illustrates a different kind of problem.

> In the 9th grade at Walnut Valley Junior High School, a group of five boys – Perry, Jesse, Ben, Jimmy, and Rob – were identified as a peer cluster in the social network analysis. Individually, they had been judged to be among the biggest problems in their middle school in terms of troublesome behavior, including fighting. Together, they presented extraordinary discipline problems. The group maintained its cohesion for the next year, getting arrested for shooting out the lights on a special fourth of July display on the Main Street of Walnut Valley, and other acts of vandalism. Within one year, all five boys had dropped out of school. After the first year out, they began to develop separate alliances with people in their jobs or in the community. They followed different paths in adaptation, with one of them being sentenced to prison for theft and drug violations and another getting married and buying a house.

The evidence on similarity from our longitudinal samples is consistent with the findings of Suzanne Zank on the role of social groups in the support of drugs and violence. She studied adolescents in West Berlin who were seriously addicted to glue sniffing. To her surprise, she discovered that former patients would return to their earlier associates for help and support, even after they had suffered irreversible neurological damage because of the addiction.[34] The physiological addiction thus became coupled with behavioral support, with the perpetuation of this self-destructive habit. Similarly, we found few instances of profound substance addiction that could be described as "individual". The group involvement of the six cheerleaders is a case in point. In this case, the peer cluster did not endure the publicity and court hearings stimulated by the charges. Shortly after the charges were dismissed, the members of the group went in separate directions. The reassortment of relationships was within the expected range, except that there were only two strong residual immediate linkages among the girls in the group. Note, as well, that the gang of five boys described in the preceding paragraph tended to break up within one year after they dropped out of school.

Consistent with similarities on antisocial behavior and drug usage, within group similarities were obtained in dropping out of school. There was a strong tendency for people who were eventually to drop out of school to cluster together several years prior to the actual dropout. For example, the intraclass correlation for dropout in clusters of 4th grade girls was highly significant, as was the intraclass correlation for 7th grade boys. In both instances, the dropout did not occur for two to five years following the observation of mutual similarities. How can this effect be explained? It seems reasonable to interpret the selective affiliation to be due, in some measure, to the mediational effects of age/grade failure. That is, children who have been held back a grade, whether in the 4th grade or the 7th grade, tend to hang around together. And since school failure is directly linked to school dropout, the circle may be completed by an enhanced predictability of dropout by earlier group associations.

But those are unusual instances. Most social clusters are not involved with self-abuse, deviance, and otherwise deviant behaviors. Typically such groups are in the background of the social organization of the class and the school, unnoticed because they constitute the ubiquitous substructure for everyday interactions. Although social clusters are in the background, they may easily be brought into the foreground by bringing the individual's attention to them. Yet their lack of salience should not be equated with their lack of importance in everyday living and normal personal development. The roots for childhood groups such as the one described in the *Lord of the Flies* seem ubiquitous in development. The direction taken by the groups, whether for good or for ill, reflects the particular contexts in which they are formed.

Social cliques over time

Peer social networks do not emerge from nowhere in adolescence. They are alive and well in the 4th grade and before. Some of the primary findings on development of social clusters concern their emergence in childhood, behavioral and non-behavioral dimensions critical for biselection, continuity of roles and groups over time, and developmental changes in group composition and dynamics. Only after these features of social organization are understood will it be possible to have an informed appreciation of peer group influences on aggressive and deviant behaviors. As it turns out, it is not necessary to invent special principles for the "bad" effects of peer groups; the same operations appear to operate for the positive effects.

Social clusters were as easily identified in the 4th grade as in the 8th grade. Not only can members of the social networks identify the various cliques that exist in that network, they can reliably name members of clusters beyond the one they are in. The average size of social groups identified in the SCMs of children at the two age levels is similar for boys and girls. Fred Strayer's observations of younger subjects indicate that peer subgroups form even among preschool children.[35]

As subjects get older, they become more reluctant to list multiple peer clusters. The sizes of the groups they describe are similar to earlier years, but they identify fewer clusters. This may mean one of at least three things: (1) the peer clusters are beginning to lose their salience in the advanced grades of high school, but the groups tend to be as cohesive as in earlier years, (2) there is a loss of importance and coherence of peer groups in later adolescence, compared to childhood and early adolescence, and (3) the clusters are just as pervasive and cohesive in late adolescence, but older subjects are reluctant to describe group membership beyond the self.

Beyond the bare bones of quantitative descriptions, a question may be asked about the social dynamics of peer groups and their effects upon the lives of children who are members. Our impression is that this clustering of children and adolescents is extraordinarily important, not only in their own lives but in the lives of people who deal with them. This holds even though there are frequent changes in how groups are made up.

Reshuffling, reorganization, and stability

Across development, social cliques are not in a state of equilibrium. From week to week, month to month, and year to year, there are shifts in alliances, support, and clique membership. Given the year-to-year fickleness of best friendships, these changes in social cluster composition may be expected. It is unlikely that a cluster will maintain its cohesiveness in the face of sharply diminished opportunities for interaction among its members, in the light of the powerful effects of propinquity. There are, however, circumstances when some groups are more likely to remain stable. These include conditions where the class membership remains intact from year to year, and when there is little pressure for reorganization. But that state of affairs is unusual. As the subjects enter junior high and high school, diffusion is increased, not decreased. Accordingly, group membership tends to be reshuffled from year to year. Nonetheless, despite reshuffling, the intraclass correlations on behavioral and demographic characteristics remain constant.

How can high levels of within group similarity be maintained even when the identities of the members of the group change? According to the preliminary studies of Holly Neckerman, the reconstitution of adolescent social groups is not a random affair. To the contrary, clusters are reformed each year by reconstitution of members who are drawn from a common pool of candidates, not from people in the school network as a whole. In the younger ages, the most salient properties that define the larger pools are gender (male or female) and behavior (acting out or quiet). As the individuals enter adolescence and early adulthood, race and social class factors take on increasing importance in defining the pool, with a diminished importance of gender. In any case, the process of biselection may be likened to the game of "musical chairs", where there is an exchange of membership in clusters depending upon similarities in some common domains.

According to Neckerman's findings, a constraint on the reshuffling of affiliations occurs in the heterosexual relations of adolescents exactly parallel to the same-sex relations. The romantic and sexual affiliations of teenagers are as unstable as same-sex best friends. But in fresh biselection of boyfriends and girlfriends, the resampling occurs from the same pool as the original selection process. New boyfriends tend to be from the same social clusters as ex-boyfriends. The same holds for girls. There is thus constancy in the midst of change, in both the same-sex and opposite-sex relations of adolescence.

Given the dynamics of the changes that are constantly underway, there is scant wonder that various coalitions arise within clusters and that difficulties arise between clusters. More generally, peer social clusters can serve as "attack groups" as well as "support groups". This employment of social clusters seems to be especially important for girls. Norma Feshbach has shown that girls in early adolescence tend to employ indirect techniques of aggressive expression, including social exclusion, character defamation, and ostracism, as opposed to direct confrontational techniques.[36] In this form of social attack, the manipulation of the opinions and attitudes of peers can be essential, and necessary for self-defense. It may be partly for this reason that the characteristics of trust and honesty figure importantly in the criteria for friendship in early adolescence.[37] On the nature of social networks and social conflicts in adolescence, we earlier concluded that "the conflicts of adolescence provide a window into the raw politics of everyday life, and their complexity cannot be overestimated". Nor can their subtlety.[38]

The general picture is that children and adolescents in the social networks generated within schools tend to find some basis for affiliation. Not surprisingly, universal categories – gender and age – constitute two of the earliest and most powerful bases for commonality. It is of interest that behavioral categories are also employed, including aggression. Although there is considerable reshuffling of companions in social clusters, some of the basic similarities remain, even though there is a change in the identity of the members. The year-to-year reshuffling may be necessary to permit removal of people who fail to meet new criteria that emerge in development, and to include people who earlier did not.

One other point on social rank consistency should be noted. Even though clusters change and associates are modified, the relative standing of people in the social network remains relatively stable from year to year. Four levels of cluster membership can be identified in all networks. The individual's status within the cluster depended on the proportion of occasions that she/he was named to be in a cluster. A practical rule was to consider a person to be identified as a nuclear member if she/he was named on most of the occasions that the cluster was named ($\geq 80\%$), a secondary if sometimes named (30–80%), and peripheral if rarely named (10–30%). The person was considered isolated/rejected if they were named to no group by people other than themselves. Similarly, the cluster itself could be identified as being high, low, or medium status in the network, following the same rule. When the two classifications are considered, jointly, the person's status in the social network can be specified.

People rarely shift upward from the isolated or peripheral status to become nuclear members of the social network, and vice versa (see Figure 5.4). Why the inertia? It seems likely that this relative placement of people in the social network reflects the operation of personal attributes, such as skill in relationships as well as motivation, in addition to enduring demographic and cognitive characteristics. Although people shift from relationship to relationship, there is reasonable consistency in the dynamics of their status.

Peers and parents

The final point concerns the roles of parents and families, and how they can contribute to the formation, continuity, and breakup of peer relationships. Discussions of the influences of parents and families traditionally focus on their roles in socialization and the establishment of status among peers in early childhood. Specifically, the findings of Steinberg and his colleagues[39] are consistent with our own findings that parental strategies for regulating peer relationships and peer groups may be hidden or manifest (Table 5.6).

Some of the most important influences operate indirectly, as does institutional school policy. Given that propinquity is a key principle of affiliation, the nature of peer group opportunities may be clearly established by which neighborhoods the families live in and which

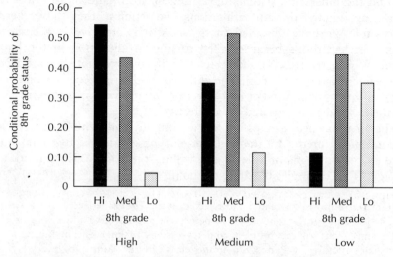

Figure 5.4 Stability of status in social networks over a one-year period: conditional probability of 8th grade status given 7th grade status. Chi square (4) = 60.98 $p < 0.001$. Gamma = 0.51.

Table 5.6 Links between peers and families

The "invisible hand" of parental influence:
SES status
Neighborhoods in which families live
Schools attended
Activities and organizations engaged (e.g. sports, music, church)
The "iron glove" of parents in direct regulation:
In hazardous contexts (e.g. inner city and potential gang involvement)
In crisis problems (e.g. high deviant involvement)
Inconsistently in coercive families
Works in short run, and potentially alienate in long run

schools the children attend. Parental influence extends to the settings or contexts that are optional, including sports activities, church groups, and recreational choices. But we have also observed the operation of the iron glove that on occasion seems successful. Among the inner-city youths we have followed, we find authoritarian parental constraints on where kids can go outside and when, and the more threatening the context, and tighter the constraints, the more successful the outcome.

Beyond the inner city, parents have used an iron hand in an effort to break up highly deviant affiliations. Sometimes, they have been successful. We have observed cases where it is effective in the short term, but hazardous because it led to mutual alienation in the long term. Which strategy is likely to be effective cannot be specified independent of context. For some children, both are needed. A balance is called for in commitment and affection, along with an ability to use whatever strategy is required to be effective.

The idea that peer groups are formed only by children for children is a convenient myth. In the longitudinal observations, teachers and parents played a major role in controlling the composition of social clusters. Two examples illustrate the point.

> Pam was uniformly isolated and rejected in the 7th grade (see Table 5.1). The principal of the school, a very perceptive and effective administrator, became aware of the problem and took steps to intervene in the peer social structure of Pam's 8th grade class. In the course of everyday instruction, Pam was singled out for special attention and praise by the teacher. In addition, the principal and the 8th grade teacher together instituted a "personality day" in which every class member became the focus of positive attention by the teacher and other members of the class. This concrete step, among others, was engineered by the school to create new friends and opportunities for Pam. The social cluster analysis made of the same class at the end of the next year indicated that the efforts were highly successful. On longitudinal reassessment, Pam was clearly accepted as a secondary member of one of the two reconstituted social clusters in her classroom.

> Camilla was the nuclear member of the high-ranked group in the class (see Table 5.1). In the course of the 7th grade interviews, it became clear that rumors had begun to circulate about the morals and promiscuity of Cam's older sister and, by association, Cam herself. One of the girl's reported that "my Mom and Bea's Mom said that neither of us could go over to Cam's house anymore". Similar sentiments were expressed by other girls in the class about their parent's disapproval of Cam and her sister. In the next year follow up, Cam had been removed from the high status cluster and had been assigned, instead, to peripheral status in a secondary cluster. Her appearance had changed as well as her social status in the classroom. Once impeccably dressed in the 7th grade, she was considerably less careful about her looks.

The realignment of social clusters throughout adolescence suggests that parents play an active role in filtering friendships as the adolescents near maturity. But this active role is not an invention of adolescence. The same process occurred when the parents chose to live in a particular section of the community, sent their toddler to particular preschools, enrolled their child in particular schools, and helped the child become involved in particular kinds of sports, musical, and educational activities. Each step contributed to the development of the child's special interests and talents, and exposed her/him to a particular set of potential friends. But it would be hazardous to identify Cam's change in status with a single factor, including parental disapproval of promiscuity in a 13-year old. It is more likely that multiple forces operated, including peer interchanges and Cam's own behavior as well as parental sanctions, to provoke changes in her social status.

Pam's story is a happier one. Insightful teachers can play a role in the person's status in the social network, even among adolescents in junior and senior high school. By implication, it suggests that Pam's ostracism in the first place may have been tolerated if not actively supported by the teachers involved in the 7th grade. In any case, the turnaround in Pam's social life was dramatic and powerful. Although her behavior changed, the shift was a consequence of the social manipulation rather than its cause. The limits of such manipulation remain to be determined, but work from various sources, including our longitudinal data set, yields outcomes consistent with Pam's experience.[40]

The more important point is that selection for cluster membership and interaction is not merely a peer process. It is interwoven with familial values and influences, along with the not-so-invisible hand of adults in the school.[41] These influences, together with emerging choices and values of adolescent subjects, serve to realign groups, so that they are consistent with personal as well as familial norms. The social affiliations of adolescence may be dissected into discrete units, but the process is more like a stream where there is a continuous melding of influences. Although the identity of particular peers may shift in the course of movement over time, there are usually sharp constraints on who qualifies for durable relationships, and why. By the end of adolescence, these constraints help produce some basic similarities in values, beliefs, and aspirations. Those who do not fit are simply shifted to another pool.

The development of social clusters

Taken in overview, the data suggest that there is sufficient commonality across investigations to propose the following outline on how social networks develop and function:

1. There is a strong bias toward social synchrony at all developmental stages, in that actions and attitudes of other people are readily

enmeshed with the behavioral organization of the self. One byproduct of this reciprocal integration is mutual similarity. Beginning in late childhood and early adolescence, there is a sharp developmental increase in the ability to reciprocate behaviors beyond the dyad in unstructured relationships with peers. The resultant peer clusters develop norms and behavioral similarities which can support – or compete with – those of other social units, including the family and the school.

2. Peer social clusters not only provide for intimacy and personal identity, they are tools to express individual aggression and control. Aggressive expression includes ostracism and character defamation, which are especially effective because they are "hidden" forms of attack and conceal the aggressor from possible counter-responses by the victims. Because the peer clusters of early adolescence are not in a state of equilibrium, due in part to shifting alliances and jealousies from within and without, safeguards must be established for the maintenance of synchronized, reciprocal intragroup relations.

3. There are norms for initial acceptance into the cluster that serve to promote internal synchrony. Such "gatekeeping" criteria help to heighten the likelihood of initial similarity of cluster members with regard to key characteristics. These criteria shift as a function of age, context, and the goals and needs of the members. In childhood, gender membership is universally important and most childhood clusters are unisex. What is valued (or devalued) reflects parental standards and expectations, as well as the age–gender status of the individual. In one society, it may be sexual maturation; in another, it may be appearance and beauty. With the onset of adolescence, cluster boundaries become increasingly rigid, and the conditions for selection and entry become more clearly delineated in terms of behaviors and values.

4. Within the clusters of adolescence, strong reciprocal forces operate on all members toward conformity with respect to salient attitudes and behaviors. An extension of influence across persons within the cluster leads to the establishment of generalized patterns of deviance, beyond the index behavior that may have been required for initial group entry. But a common standard for deviance is only one of the outcomes of the reciprocal exchanges within groups. Once in a social group, there is conformity with respect to a broad spectrum of behaviors and attitudes, including shared linguistic and communication patterns, areas of worry and concern, and "lifestyle" characteristics. For many youth, the problem is to escape from synchrony with deviant or escalating values. Hence the finding that social isolation is often a buffer from delinquency.

5. A systematic account of social clusters and friendships must take into account the powerful effects of reciprocal influence demonstrated in experimental studies and observational analyses.[42] The message from these investigations is that reciprocal interactions lead to high levels of behavioral and attitudinal similarity, regardless of the initial status of the people involved. The evidence on adolescent group dynamics strongly points to the operation of both differential selection factors and reciprocal influences.

6. The social clusters of adolescence are unstable, due to developmental changes in their members and to dynamic social forces within clusters. Among other things, suballiances shift among members and continuously challenge the integrity of the social organization itself. With the developmental breakdown of old clusters and the formation of new ones through renegotiated alliances, the cycle of differential selection and reciprocal similarity is repeated in a stepping-stone process across time. At every stage, individuals are changed by their associations, and they carry to the next set of relationships the behavioral residue of the recent past. These changes provide the basis for new alliances and a fresh network of supporting relationships.

Concluding comment

Relationships are likely to endure when individuals change together, and each adopts the goals, values, and behaviors which may be integrated with those of the other person. Friendship and group affiliation in childhood and adolescence are not passive, but a dynamic process that requires active changes by all members of the relationship. Hence friendships with peers and relationships in the family must change in order to remain stable, and the changes must somehow be coordinated. To the extent that the people involved share similar values, social backgrounds, and talents, the changes are likely to be coordinated.

SIX

Shadows of synchrony

The things I worry about – my Old Man getting busted – going to jail or anyone – you know, the guys that live here. You know we're all one family there. I'm afraid something'll happen to them.

Heidi (age 18)

Chapter 5 demonstrated how the longitudinal study of social groups and social networks can provide the essential information to explain the stability of peer group influence, despite the instability of the groups. This chapter illustrates how this information can solve some beguiling puzzles on relationships between peers and problem behaviors.

One puzzle concerns the role of social rejection, and whether aggressive children are inevitably rejected. Or is social isolation actually a buffer against delinquency for some children? A second puzzle concerns the link between "normal" group affiliation and gang involvement. Do groups and gangs reflect similar processes in terms of social support and social control, or are gangs without any redeeming features? The third puzzle concerns the role played by biology in group formation and deviant affiliations. Is early sexual maturation a biological ticket for entry by girls into deviant social groups, or is the link carried by some more salient features of attractiveness and appearance? The chapter closes with some conclusions on the development and function of social networks and social relationships in the lifecourse of people in our time.

Aggression and delinquency: deficits or adaptations?

Any discussion of friends and social networks brings attention to the contrasting condition of the friendless and rejected. How do socially

130

isolated or rejected children survive adolescence? At the outset, it may be observed that attempts have been made to distinguish between "rejection" and "neglect". Neglect refers to the state of affairs where the individual has few if any contacts with peers, whether good or bad. Rejection refers to the active dislike and shunning of the individual by peers.

While these social concepts seem intuitively clear, their operational definition is another matter. In one measurement scheme, rejection is determined by the individual's winning a class vote on who is most unpopular; for another analysis, it means that the individual is avoided and without any close friends and associates. Problems arise because these two measurement operations do not always identify the same persons. One set of researchers discovered that being isolated from peers is a protective factor against delinquency and drug use (Elliott, Huizinga, & Menard, 1989), while another set of researchers discovered that rejection and isolation are correlated with delinquency and school dropout (Asher & Coie, 1990). Which conclusion is correct? To make sense of these competing findings and the educational implications associated with them, it is necessary to step back and analyze what rejection means in the lives of individuals and their social networks.

Rejection and social deficits

There has been a strong tendency to assign responsibility for rejection to the individual being rejected. Presumably the rejected child cannot make it in a social group because of personal deficiencies, either emotional or cognitive. Once rejected, this provides a stepping stone to a wide range of problems in late adolescence and early adulthood. This view on the social alienation of delinquents is captured in Yablonsky's (1962) account of gang relationships:

> Today's violent delinquent is a displaced person – suspicious, fearful, and not willing or able to establish a concrete human relationship. The formation of the violent gang, with its impermanence, its possibilities for hollow glory, its limited expectations of any responsibility on the part of its members, is all-inviting to youths who have difficulty fitting into a more integrated and clearly defined world. . . .Violent gang organization is ideally suited to the defective personality and limited social ability of these disturbed youths . . . they join gangs because they lack the social ability to relate to others, not because the gang gives them a 'feeling of belonging' (pp. 3–4).

Following this line of reasoning, delinquent and aggressive youths are described as socially incapable of relating to members of a nondeviant or even a deviant peer group. Rejected by conventional society and peers, delinquent youths are forced to join with other social deviants. The adolescent delinquent gang is presumed to be comprised of social rejects or outcasts.[1] In this regard, Travis Hirschi writes, "the idea that delinquents have comparatively warm, intimate social relations with each other (or with anyone) is a romantic myth".[2]

This view that aggression and psychopathology are rooted in the failure of basic social and emotional ties may be traced directly to object relations theory and derivative social learning statements. In *Wayward Youth*, psychoanalyst August Aichhorn describes the basic problem of aggressive adolescents as being an inability to form adequate bonds with others. Accordingly, therapy must be directed toward the establishment of this capacity through the reduction of anxiety associated with close personal relationships.[3] A similar position is offered by John Bowlby in *Forty-four Juvenile Thieves*, an argument that captures the core of subsequent object relationship statements of attachment theory.[4]

Following the lead of neoanalytic theorists, Albert Bandura and Richard Walters reframed essentially the same hypothesis in modern social learning theory terms. Bandura and Walters (1959) proposed that their group of highly aggressive boys between the ages of 14 and 18 were:

> . . . markedly distrustful; they feared and avoided situations in which they might have become emotionally dependent on others. . . . Their behavior, moreover, was apparently self-defeating, because it alienated them from the affection of which they already felt deprived and brought them under the more direct control of the authority figures whom they distrusted and resented (pp. 312–313).

These authors go on to describe the treatment implications of the dependency–anxiety model for these "undersocialized aggressive" adolescents. Accordingly, it is assumed that "the establishment of a close dependency relationship of the patient to the therapist, similar to that of a child to his parents, is a necessary condition for the development of internalized controls".[5] To sum up, this statement of social learning theory presupposed that the essential problem of aggressive behavior and acting-out was a basic inability to form close and effective social relationships with others. The inability stemmed from serious disturbances in basic familial relationships.

A similar theme characterizes contemporary social learning views, albeit with a shift toward the primacy in deficiencies in social cognition rather than social affiliations. This shift in emphasis follows the recognition in the 1960s and 1970s of the role of cognitive factors in some of the presumably basic processes of social learning, including modeling, social reinforcement, and social motivation.[6] The shift in emphasis was in line with the Piagetian cognitive revolution in developmental theory and with the introduction of information processing constructs in experimental psychology.[7]

Does aggression reflect social support or social failure?

There has been a cyclic, self-fulfilling relationship between broadly held beliefs about deviant children and the apparent weight of the scientific evidence on them. The present beliefs about the social and cognitive deficits of aggressive children are a case in point.

A good amount of scientific energy has been expended to demonstrate that aggressive children are deficient in their relationship capacities and their social perceptions.[8] Within this model, distortions in information processing predetermine problems of social interchange. These distortions lead in turn to aggressive behaviors by the child and subsequent social rejection and/or isolation. Once rejected by peers, the individual becomes the target for further aggression. So the cycle goes. The upshot is that the aggressive adolescent is seen as being rejected or controversial in his or her social status, unpopular with peers, and marginally competent in social settings.[9]

In our analysis of social clusters, we consistently found that some people were more central to the organization of the group, defining its identity and status, and others were peripheral and dispensable. Furthermore, the clusters could be ranked in terms of salience and apparent dominance in the social network. Taken as a whole, these clusters, and the ranking among them, provided a basis for identifying the social network.

Is it the case that adolescents on the fringe of the social network are most likely to present problems for themselves and for the network as a whole? The answer depends, in part, on how "being on the fringe" is defined (Cairns, 1983a). For our purposes, it made sense to use information from the network analysis to tell who was central in the network, and who was rejected or isolated from the social system. The latter category was of special interest in the light of the belief that people who are left out of the social network are at special risk for current and later psychopathology. Only a small proportion, 2–10%, were isolated or rejected at any given age level (Figure 6.1). There is an interesting discrepancy between boys and girls in the likelihood of their

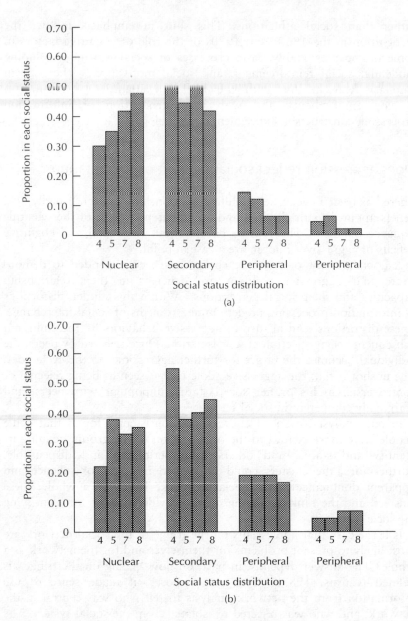

Figure 6.1   Social network status of (a) girls and (b) boys in grades 4, 5, 7, and 8.

being identified as isolated within the social network as they enter adolescence. One possibility is that this gender difference is an artifact of the method, in that girls tend to name, on the average, slightly more groups than do boys. This tendency of girls to name more and larger groups of girls makes it less likely that anyone will be left out entirely. But some are left out, such as Pam.

Are the isolated and rejected children most likely to be the aggressive and disrupted ones? In our longitudinal cohorts, we find scant evidence for the belief that the most disruptive people are the rejected ones. As shown in Figure 6.2, there were virtually no differences between the individual's centrality in clusters and the salience of his/her clusters and the sheer level of his/her aggressiveness and disruptiveness. To the contrary, some of the most troublesome kids were dominant in their clusters and in their classrooms. Nor, as it turns out, were the peripheral and isolated/rejected people more likely to be aggressive. Relative to other subjects who were less obnoxious, aggressive subjects tended not to be as well liked as their classmates in general. But they were apparently respected, feared, or both, and they had as many reciprocated close friends as nonaggressive control subjects.

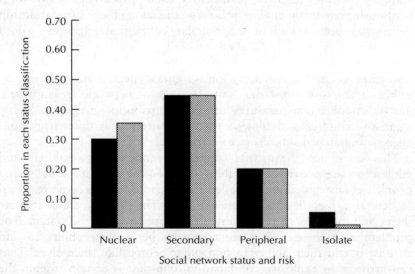

Figure 6.2 Proportion of risk (solid bar) and matched control (shaded bar) subjects who were classified as nuclear, secondary, peripheral, and isolate in SCM social network analysis (combined across gender and cohorts). (From data reported in Cairns et al., 1989.)

Is deviance and aggressive behavior necessarily linked to social alienation and rejection? It depends upon what is measured and how. The difference lies in the kinds of behaviors that they support. Aggressive children and adolescents are feared and not liked by most teachers, administrators, and police, and these attitudes are shared by many of their peers. However, even bullies have friends. In our analysis of the social networks and friendships of aggressive children, we find that they enjoy, on the average, as many reciprocated friendships as do matched nonaggressive children. And they are as likely to be members of social groups, even nuclear members of those groups. That is to say, there is similarity in aggression just as there is similarity in other characteristics of friendships among less deviant groups. There is also the possibility of escalation of this characteristic, so it becomes the primary one by which this group becomes identified.

In view of findings that aggressive people associate with each other, why do claims that the "violent delinquent is . . . not willing or able to establish a concrete human relationship" so broadly accepted? It may be due to the projections generated by the leaders themselves. These youths behave badly, and they have major problems in their relationships with teachers and counselors, therefore the youths must be incapable of forming relationships. Otherwise, it would be due to the inability of the teachers, counselors, and psychologists to form relationships with them. The proof for this assignment of relationship deficit has been found in the popular belief that aggressive youth misattribute responsibility and are generally feared and disliked by their peers. Unfortunately, such proof of peer rejection and cognitive distortion is itself flawed by measurement peculiarities. When an unbiased assessment of friendships and social networks is employed, and when objective measures of social attribution are used, highly aggressive children and adolescents do not necessarily differ from non-aggressive matched subjects (see Chapter 7).

This does not mean that aggressive and unruly children and adolescents are not rejected by the system. To the contrary, these young people get suspended and expelled from school, and become removed to detention facilities and training camps. The system cannot tolerate them, and they cannot be permitted to create havoc in the system. The problem with these youths seems not to be in their ability to find friends, but in their ability to find other people like themselves. That can provide an explosive combination, one that is certain to gain the attention of those entrusted to keep the system in order.

In this regard, sociological analyses of delinquency in the 1950s and 1960s emphasized the role of group cohesion and mutual support for antisocial activities.[10] Albert Cohen reported that gang members established and maintained close relations with each other. He observed, "relations with gang members tend to be intensely solitary and imperious . . . the gang is a separate, distinct and often irresistible focus of attraction, loyalty, and solidarity".[11] Recently, Peggy Giordano and her colleagues reported the self-reports of friendships from youths representing the full range of delinquency involvement. Deviant youths have friends who are of a similar deviant status.[12]

We now return to the claim that deviant adolescents are incapable of close personal relationships. The evidence from the CLS is clear. This finding shows up not only in the quantitative analysis of group structures, it appears in the detailed individual analysis of people over time.

Heidi: "We're all one family"

When we first became acquainted with Heidi, she was an above-average 7th grader living in a middle-class home in a small mid-south town near the Atlantic coast. She hung around with a group of three other girls who shared a lot in common; worries about home, fantasies about boys, and a concern with grades. After the 7th grade, Heidi's relationships at home with her stepmother deteriorated. She moved across the country to live in a Seattle suburb with her mother and her mother's new husband. Over the next fourteen months she bounced back and forth across the continent. On a return trip to Washington state, she ran away to join a group of migrant farm workers in the San Joaquin Valley of central California. She soon left them and, at 14 years of age, she became "homeless" on the streets of a Southern California community.

H: . . . it was an awful place, but you know I found a few friends on one street – it was called Broadway. It's awful. It was the slums. There were a few good people there. It was all right. They wouldn't let nothing happen to me 'cause I was the baby on the street."

When we next located her at 18 years of age, she was living in a small community on the California coast in a small house with her boyfriend and other members of the "family" in a communal arrangement.

For Heidi, the progression from an average middle-school adolescent to a homeless street person to a "family" member is not merely a story of her rejection of society and conventional norms as much as vice versa – it also has elements of acceptance. The bonds formed by Heidi at these stages were perceived by her to be strong and protective. They were also critical for survival.

Was Heidi distrustful and incapable of forming relationships? There was no indication of any shallowness in our relationships with her; nor did our tracking of her relationships with peers in middle school fit a harsh description of shallow and brittle relationships. If anything, she has been too vulnerable and trusting. Her beliefs that "we're all one family" may reflect her projections of unity as much as the reality that exists. But even the projections reflect her goals and hopes, which are themselves rooted in a desire for continuity, belongingness, and being cared for.

Groups and gangs: lessons for the inner city

A related controversy concerns the roles and functions of gangs. Concerns about teenage gangs are of course not limited to the inner city of America. Parallel issues have been raised about today's homeless street gangs of Mexico City, about Latino gangs in East Los Angeles in the 1940s, and the Hell's Angels motorcycle gangs that first emerged in Southern California after World War II and persist through the 1990s.

In the CLS, gang activities were not highly visible in the communities in which the work was begun. The gang members that we tracked typically had moved in mid-adolescence to the inner cities of New York, Washington, DC, and Los Angeles. In tracking these young people, we found that most were, as younger adolescents, quite similar to aggressive peers who did not move and did not become involved in gang activities.

To explore the links between groups and gangs, we needed to extend our analyses to an equally large group of children and adolescents who lived in the inner city. Then an opportunity came to investigate children in one of the large metropolitan areas of the United States. Using the same interview and assessment techniques that we employed in the CLS, we asked what were the characteristics of children/adolescents recruited into gangs? And could "embryonic" gangs be identified in elementary and middle schools? The difference between the studies is that the inner-city sample was comprised exclusively of disadvantaged minority children, and we had reason to believe that the areas where the work was conducted was controlled in large measure by competing organized gangs.

It did not take long to find out who the gangs were. Seventh grade students in the inner-city schools found it as easy to name the gangs in their neighborhoods as it was to name social clusters in the classrooms. In some cases, the clusters and the gangs were one and the same!

One goal was to determine whether the social network methods worked with some of the most difficult situations in the inner city (Gaines, Cairns, & Cairns, 1994). We began with the 7th grade in very high-risk neighborhoods. We found excellent cooperation with the superintendent, assistant superintendent, principals, and teachers. The middle schools to which we were given access were among the most violent in the city. There was a murder in an adjacent high school the day before we began, and there was a red alert for a gang shootout in our school the day after we began, possibly in retaliation for the murder. The week we left, a 6th grade boy was killed, reportedly because of a drug dispute.

We used our standard network interview, along with two additional questions: one on weapon use, the other on gangs. We find that social networks and groups are readily plotted within the school. Students generated names, nicknames, and group names both in school and out of school. They also generated an impressive list of gangs operating in and out of school. In the course of the investigation, we recognized that both boys and girls generated these gangs. A few even named gang members in the school, and others named their brothers, cousins, and brothers-in-law. We were careful to not ask for gang membership directly, since it could be dangerous to the participants.

The gangs were not merely social clubs; rather, they referred to organized groups that supported a rule of tyranny which pervaded all aspects of life at school and in the community. The reports from ninety 7th grade students in one inner-city middle school illustrate the point. In response to the question, "Do you know of any gangs in the neighborhood or the school?" a large majority of the boys (87%) and half of the girls (50%) listed gangs. Of those who answered the question, the students listed an average of four gangs. As indicated in Figure 6.3, there was high agreement among boys and girls on which gangs were most prominent in their community. The product–moment correlation between the two lists was $r = 0.96$ ($p < 0.001$).

Student reports were consistent with police information that Crips controlled the section of the city in which the school was located. But apparently the control was not absolute, given the frequency of listing other prominent gangs. There were three levels in the frequency of occurrence of gang activity. The top four gangs mentioned for this inner-city community were the Crips, Disciples, Blood, and Folk. An immediate level included the Vice-Lords and various code names, such as the TYG (The Young Gangsters), IGD (Insane Gang Disciples), and GP (Gangster Pack). The names and codes seem designed to stimulate

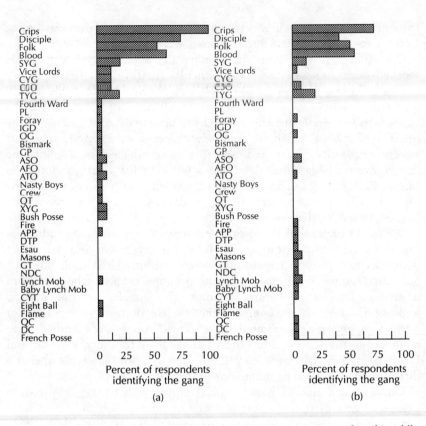

Figure 6.3 Reports of gangs identified in an inner-city sample of middle-school students (7th grade respondents). (*n* = 90; *n* = 38 males and *n* = 52 females.) (a) Male respondents, (b) female respondents.

risk, danger, criminality, and fear, about in equal measure. Then there were the infrequently mentioned gangs, such as Lynch Mob, Baby Lynch Mob, South Town Posse, and SYG (Sophisticated Young Gents). These are colorful names, and they were associated with distinctive colors, signs, symbols, clothing, and secret handshakes.[13]

In comparisons of the CLS findings with the inner-city results, the major difference between those involved with deviant companions outside the inner city and those gang members in the inner city appears to be a function of context and opportunity, not psychological makeup. In both contexts, the deviant clusters are individuals who have the ability to cooperate and collaborate toward deviant goals. As children, they showed virtually the same range of social competence as found among those who did not become involved in deviant groups or gangs.

But they do differ in terms of a propensity toward aggressive, acting-out behaviors. In the teenage years, the likelihood of belonging to a truly deviant group or gang seems to depend upon as much the structure of the community and the opportunities that it affords as the individual characteristics of the youths. Gang membership in the inner city appears as accessible for male teenagers as fraternity membership in college is for male undergraduates. The processes are similar although the outcomes are different.

Biology and deviance: "early for her age"

One of the more important developmental proposals in recent years concerns the role of biology as a determinant of social affiliations. David Magnusson and his colleagues have discovered that very early maturing girls (i.e. those who achieved menarche at 10–11 years of age) tended to show a strong bias in their social affiliations (e.g. Magnusson, 1988; Stattin & Magnusson, 1990). At age 13, they differed from less physiologically mature females in that they joined groups of peers, both females and males, older than themselves. As may be expected, their social and sexual behavior patterns were more characteristic of their older peers than other, physically immature members of their cohort. In terms of alcohol consumption and sexual behavior, both the early maturing females and the older boys with whom they associated differed markedly from the rest of the sample.

Magnusson (1988) hypothesized that the rate of biological maturation does not act upon behavior directly; rather, its effects are mediated by a differential selection of friends and the values that they endorse. Since Stattin and Magnusson's (1990) work was longitudinal, it was possible to obtain follow-up information on both the early maturing females and those who developed at a normal (or slower than normal) pace. When subsequent assessments were made at age 16, virtually all girls had attained menarche. Furthermore, the behavioral differences between the early and later maturing girls had also been eliminated by mid-adolescence. Drinking patterns and sexual activities at age 16, and other measures of social behavior, were no longer related to maturation rate. It appears that the "advanced" standards for the early maturing girls at age 13 had become the norm for the entire sample by age 16. One other aspect of this research deserves notice. Although the differences in social behavior were eliminated in follow up, differences in school achievement proved to be residual. The very early maturing sample married earlier, had more children, and did not attend university.

The broader point is that, in the Swedish sample, the very early onset of sexual maturity did not directly produce deviance. On the contrary, a key mediational variable appears to be social affiliations promoted by the pace at which normal biological changes occur. When other girls reached menarche at the normative age, there was no difference in female deviance as a function of the rate of maturation. The behavioral differences have been eliminated, in part, by similarities in levels of sexual maturation mediated by similarities in social interchange. Early biological maturation is not the only route to differential association and deviance; it merely provides a biasing condition.

Essential features of these findings have been replicated in other settings and with other samples. For instance, Caspi and Moffitt (1991) find the same early maturation-deviance phenomenon in the longitudinal study of a sample of New Zealand girls. The effect was obtained, however, only if the girls were enrolled in a coeducational school. Presumably the opportunities for deviance by differential association were greater in the coeducational setting than in all-girl schools.

This is intriguing, and it signals a new way of thinking about the relationships between biological characteristics, on the one hand, and social adaptations, on the other. The idea that there is a straight line between biology and behavior is rejected. Rather, biological influences must be filtered through a social system which has values and pathways of its own, as the following indicates:

early maturation → deviant social network → deviant behavior

This also implies that different societies could have different pathways for the same biological influence.

We had high hopes of replicating these findings in a US population. But hopes are no substitute for hard data. We found little in our data set to support the specific prediction of higher levels of deviance in early maturing girls. We did find, however, strong support for the basic proposition underlying Magnusson's (1988) proposition; namely, social processes must be understood in social context.

As shown in Figure 6.4, the mean age of menarche was 12.56 years in both cohorts. The age of onset was amazingly consistent in the two cohorts of girls, and it was virtually the same as reported by Stattin and Magnusson for their Swedish sample (Stattin & Magnusson, 1990). There was support for the first link in the equation: namely, girls in the 4th grade tended to affiliate with other girls who were similar in terms of very early maturation. This is another instance of the ubiquity of homophily.

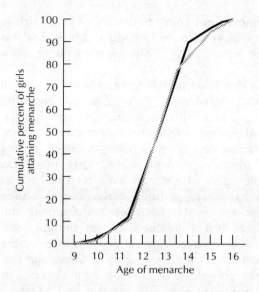

Figure 6.4 Age of menarche in two longitudinal cohorts. Cohort I (*n* = 104, shaded line) and Cohort II (*n* = 214, solid line).

There was not, however, much evidence to indicate that early maturing girls showed higher levels of aggression, difficult behaviors, or lower levels of school performance at age 13 or 16. Nor were there differences between early and late maturing girls in the subsequent school dropout or teenage pregnancy.

The one reliable relationship between menarcheal age and later psychological or biological states to emerge was a slight but consistent relationship between menarche and attractiveness. Judgments of attractiveness, whether by the girls themselves or by teachers, indicated a negative correlation between age of menarche and attractiveness as measured in late adolescence. Girls who matured early tended to judge themselves as being less attractive. They were also judged by others to be less attractive than girls who matured on time or late. The appearance effects emerged in late adolescence when the girls were 15–18 years of age rather than at the actual age of menarche. These outcomes are consistent with Tanner's (1962) report that girls who mature very early tend to be shorter and heavier at maturity than girls who are on time.

Why the failure to replicate the maturation–deviance phenomenon across studies and across national boundaries? It is not obvious why very early maturation is not linked to deviance among girls in American schools in the same ways as in the Swedish and New Zealand schools.[14] No answer can be offered at this time, but a couple of speculations are relevant.

One problem is that there may be greater heterogeneity in American schools than either Sweden or New Zealand (in terms of race, socioeconomic status, and living circumstances), and these factors could overwhelm the subtle effects of maturational rate. Such factors could account for the strong continuity between deviance in preadolescence and deviance in adolescence found among girls in American society. Even in US samples, girls who mature early tend to hang around with other girls who have also matured early. But this propensity for differential affiliation on the basis of maturational status is not necessarily translated into promiscuous sex and deviant behavior.

There may be some broader cultural explanations for the difference in findings. The conditions for growing up in Sweden in the 1960s and 1970s are different from those of growing up in America in the 1980s and 1990s. In considering this issue, Stattin and Magnusson (1990) concluded that a primary difference between the two societies lies in the more permissive climate for adolescent sex in Sweden when compared to the United States. How different are the societies in sexual mores? According to a national Swedish probability sample, the percentage of girls who report sexual intercourse was 33% at 15 years of age, and 82% at 18 years of age (Stattin & Magnusson, 1990). While getting accurate data on sexual activity in the United States is not an easy matter, the most reliable figures indicate considerably lower percentages of sexual intercourse among girls at age 15. In addition, the dual gender standards are reversed in the two countries. Fifteen-year-old Swedish girls (Stattin & Magnusson, 1990) were more likely than boys to report intercourse (i.e. 39% *versus* 30%), while 15-year-old American boys are more likely than girls to report having had sex.

Given these national differences, the effects of early pubertal maturation must be viewed in light of the practices and beliefs of the society. On this score, early physical maturation may in fact be more directly linked to early sex for girls in Sweden than for girls in the United States. The more permissive climate for adolescent sex in Sweden could make physical maturation of girls a more salient gateway for deviance than in the United States. Sexual permissiveness is not the only difference; there has been a temporal difference in the identification of attractiveness. The standards for feminine beauty and maturity have not been static in our time, including the period as short as the thirty years from 1960 to 1990. If female models and mass advertising are any indication, the most beautiful women in the 1980s were considered to be those who showed few signs of traditional femininity (in terms of bust growth, body fat distribution, height, bodily configurations). Paradoxically, normal sexual maturation may have become equated with diminished attractiveness among girls.

The heterogeneity of American schools suggests that several background factors (socioeconomic, racial, educational) may success-fully compete with differences in maturational status in determining social associations and behaviors. In Swedish schools, classes are kept together as a unit throughout elementary and middle school. This means that the onset of differences in maturation may be more readily recognized by peers and teachers in Sweden than the United States. The physical effects and their implications could also be accentuated in Sweden, and diminished in America.

Given the relatively greater homogeneity of Swedish schools compared to the diversity of American ones, it seems likely to expect that there are ways to categorize social group and social availability other than in terms of maturation. Ethnic group membership, socioeconomic class status, and acting-out tendencies appear to be more important than sexual maturation in determining social affiliations in American adolescents. Moreover, there are other biological factors beyond the onset of menarche in American girls that have proved highly relevant for social adaptation and deviance. Consider, for example, physical attractiveness. Physical attractiveness was a ubiquitous antecedent of social and school success in the CLS sample, particularly in girls. Girls judged to be unattractive by others were less popular in middle school, received lower grades, and, five years later, were more likely to drop out of school and become teenage mothers (see also Elder, 1974). There is an intriguing hint in some research that very early pubertal onset is marginally associated with unattractiveness in girls (e.g. Simmons & Blyth, 1987). It is also the case that attractiveness is less important for boys than for girls in our US data.

To sum up, the Stattin and Magnusson (1990) work provides an elegant illustration of both the complexity and the simplicity of developmental social systems. Plasticity in the individual and in the social system underscores the need to be careful about the point in ontogeny when "outcomes" are identified. Lives in progress are moving targets, and so are societies. Biology makes a difference in which social networks girls are found and in their status within the networks. It is instructive that the relations between biology and social behavior are dynamic and capable of modification across time and place.

Concluding comment

It appears as if the difficulties of adolescence can be as much a problem
of social acceptance by peers as social rejection. The outcome depends
upon which group is rejecting and which is accepting. Group membership potentially offers personal benefits for the individual, along with
the potential hazards. This seems to hold whether the gang operates on
the streets of Mexico City or the inner city of Los Angeles. There are
clearly some links between psychobiological factors and group
membership, particularly among females. But understanding how these
factors operate demands as much attention to the social context as to
biological change.

SEVEN

The self and the other

Low self-esteem is believed by many to be an important predictor of problem behavior. The literature, however, does not support that hypothesis. Measures of self-esteem and locus of control rarely reach significance levels in multiple variable analysis.

Joy G. Dryfoos (1990, p. 96)

On a stroll down the boardwalk at Venice Beach, reliving happy childhood memories of body surfing and penny arcades, a passing T-shirt brought us back to the 1990s. It read:

> It's not who you are
> It's what you wear
> I mean who really cares who you are anyway?

Beyond the sand and the satire, issues of personal identity and relationships seem alive and well these days. They are as relevant for youths in the beach communities of Southern California as for their counterparts in Walnut Valley, Pleasantown, Stockholm, and the rural villages of Nepal. Concepts of self-efficacy and self-esteem have won new life in accounts of resilience and explanations of why some people succeed despite the odds stacked against them.

Up to this point in the book, social cognitions and concepts of the self have been in the background. Now it is time to bring these issues to the foreground. They are important for methodological and theoretical reasons. Whenever our subjects described themselves and their lives in an interview, their accounts reflected their personal constructions of the reality they experienced. The same holds for their "objective" self-reports in surveys and questionnaires. Those responses reflect the person's personal frame of reference and constructions of reality.

147

Due in part to these problems of scientific method, there are large gaps in the discipline's understanding of self-esteem and how it develops. For example, teenagers who act badly and present problems for themselves and the community are commonly viewed as lacking in self-esteem. Accordingly, it has been broadly assumed that they will behave better if they are encouraged to have higher opinions of themselves and their talents. This line of reasoning has led to intervention programs throughout the United States concerned with raising the self-esteem of inner-city children, chronic delinquents, and school dropouts. Despite twenty years of experience with these programs, the research evidence on the link between deviance and low self-esteem is not compelling, as Dryfoos (1990) observed.

These uncertainties underscore the need to complete a longitudinal analysis of self-concepts and beliefs. It seems to be a key component in any developmental study that deals with the integration of social, biological, and cognitive processes. We hope to clarify how social cognitions become interwoven with behavioral adaptations to promote resilience. Accordingly, we open this chapter with an illustration of some of the issues and comments on the nature and development of self-esteem. We then turn to longitudinal results on the development of self-thoughts and self-efficacy.

Invulnerability and life satisfaction

If a woman is poor, elderly, widowed, African American, and living alone in the abject circumstances of a Washington, DC inner-city ghetto, how satisfied should she be with life? On a scale of one to ten – where the lowest score is the "least satisfied" and the highest score is the "most satisfied" – it would seem reasonable to expect that her life satisfaction score should be near the bottom of the scale. That expectation was wrong.

Women in this highly disadvantaged sample achieved life satisfaction scores that were high and positive. They were uniformly near the top of the "Cantril Ladder" scale (mean = 9.05, given a possible range from 1 to 10). This was not just another case of inflation inside the Washington beltway. To the contrary, parallel results were obtained among similar samples of elderly poor African-American women who lived in a small town in South Carolina and in another upscale suburban community in North Carolina that has been described as having the highest average level of academic achievement in the United States.[1] In all three circumstances, the mean scores were near the top of the scale, as shown in Figure 7.1.

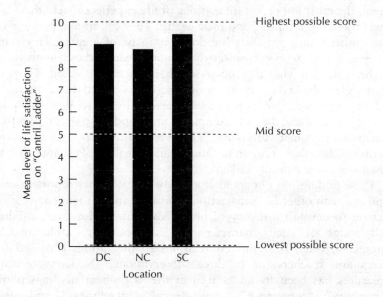

Figure 7.1 Mean level of life satisfaction obtained from widowed elderly African-American women living in poverty in three locations (DC = urban Washington, DC; NC = suburban North Carolina; SC = rural South Carolina).

Why should these women have such a high opinion of themselves when their lives appear miserable on objective grounds? Was it denial and unawareness, or did the women simply fail to understand the scale? Their own answers suggest that it was none of the above. In the interview, as in the scale, it became clear that their evaluations were based on dimensions and values different from objective accounts. They acknowledged the dismal concrete details of their lives, including concerns about having their apartments broken into, their purses stolen while waiting for the bus, and the problems of living next door to a group of prostitutes. They also talked about their disappointment at being neglected by a government that cuts programs vital to them, including the "meals-on-wheels" program which provided a daily meal for nonambulatory elderly poor.

These women did not deny such problems of living; rather, they relegated less weight to them in judgments of personal life satisfaction. If you feel powerless to change your circumstances, why create additional stress by focusing on the discrepancies between need and reality? When constraints appear unalterable, stress can be reduced by heightening your evaluation of what is available and accessible. For them, the most important dimensions of life experience were their faith, their friends and family, and their health. They calibrated, perhaps with each other's support, their life domains to be of greatest importance. They did not overlook objective economic facts; they simply placed higher value on what they possessed than what they lacked. They were seemingly unbowed by adversity or selectively ignored disadvantage.

The expressions of personal satisfaction by these women had an ironic twist. They did not complain, and modern politics pays scant attention to quiet survivors. Their resilience and lack of power permitted further economic abuse and neglect. Perhaps the two phenomena are causally linked.

These findings do not stand alone. Michael Ross has reported similar findings with other life satisfaction measures, and the tendency for each person to develop a theory of his/her own life.[2] Moreover, children's self-ratings of such characteristics as popularity, affiliation, and aggression often bear modest relations to the ratings obtained from peers and teachers, or to direct observations.[3] Nonconvergence of measures has been found as well in the assessment of "masculinity–femininity", "conscience", "dependency", "attachment", and various other personality/social dispositions.[4]

These observations speak to the question of who or what determines levels of self-esteem. First, consider concepts of the self, then the special issue of the self-esteem of problem youth. These proposals have implications for both resilience and vulnerability.

Dual masters

There exists an ongoing tension between beliefs that serve to enhance personal well being and integration on the one hand, and beliefs that capture and precisely reflect external circumstances and social evaluations, on the other.[5] Moreover, developmental changes are inevitable. For instance, beliefs in their omnipotence by 3-year-old children may enhance feelings of personal control, and reduce the child's fear. But if the same ideas are retained in 16 year olds, they provide the makings of paranoia. Old beliefs and processes must be revised in development. While the cognitive bias in dealing with the social world should be toward accuracy and efficiency in assessing other people and social circumstances, cognitions about the self must be biased toward maintaining integration and reducing stress. On this score, self-attributions should be reasonably adaptable, but biased toward self-integrating concepts of freedom, social acceptance, and competence.

Correspondence between thoughts of the self, behavior, and the perceptions of others does not seem to be a given in nature. Rather, it appears to be a compromise renegotiated throughout development. Regardless of age, the more public and salient a phenomenon, the more compelling its constraints upon social cognitions of the self and others. Of the several components of the organismic system that may be modified, one's personal thoughts of oneself might seem to be most vulnerable to rapid reconstruction. One advantage of self-cognition over behavior is that thoughts appear more susceptible than actions to rapid transformation and manipulation. To reduce tension within and without, self-systems can incorporate, ignore, rationalize, reconstruct, eliminate, and accentuate information and feelings. One of the lessons of modern cognitive science is that memory is a dynamic, continuing process and recall can be rerecorded. Memories of yesterday and plans for tomorrow are constantly updated to bring them into alignment with the constraints of today.

Which has priority in self-concepts: the inside drive toward harmony, or the outside drive toward veridicality? As philosopher W.V. Quine suggests, every person has a right to create his/her own ontology. Even if old and anxious and poor, there should be a reason to get out of bed in the morning. In the tug of war from without and within, the self and its integrity must be preserved first, and the social consensus second. Accordingly, self-cognitions do not have to be veridical in order to be functional. Close correspondence across all internal and external domains is not inevitable for the individual, nor necessarily healthful.

One strategy to achieve alignment would be for the person to assign different weights to activities that are designed to assess his/her own worth and esteem – such as the elderly women in Washington, DC. But this may not just be a function for the elderly. For example a major difference between some aggressive and nonaggressive children seems to lie in the relative weight they assign to violence as a determinant of their self-esteem.[6]

To illustrate the point, consider what the aggressive adolescent studied by Bandura and Walters had to say about what makes him proud of himself (Bandura & Walters, 1959, pp. 121–2):

I: Are there things about yourself that you're proud of, and wouldn't want to change?

S: Motorcycle riding.

I: Is there anything else?

S: Say, something like you're proud of? You probably won't understand, but "stomping". I'm proud of it because, I don't know, all the guys I hang around with do that. Do you know what "stomping" is?

I: No, I don't.
S: Fighting with two feet without using your hands, see. I'm not trying to be conceited or anything, but I know I can use my feet better than all the guys I hang around with, so I wouldn't want to change that. Like my Dad, he said, "If you know how to fight with your feet, it's in your hands, you got it made", or something like that. "You never need be afraid of anybody."

Similar responses were obtained in the CLS thirty years later. Billy, when he was asked in the 7th grade about a best friend, replied:

B::   Well, I got friends. I got people that know me, and I don't know them, so I'm popular in some ways and fighting. I don't want to be popular in fighting, but that's how I'm known around here, and I've got a few friends.
I: What makes a boy popular?
B::   In this school? Fighting, rich, I reckon looking good. I don't know.

These self-assessments are not particularly healthy, if the association to later violence is a criterion of adjustment. Nonetheless, it should also be noted that one of the most admired athletes of this century won fame for fighting.[7] Then there are the modern movie heroes, from James Bond to Rambo and the Terminator.

More generally, synchronous and effective self-concepts seem to be accessible to all individuals, not merely the best and brightest. In this regard, self-evaluations and expectations that are too high can be harmful, because they contribute to heightened stress and internal dysynchrony. Self-evaluations and expectations that are too low may be harmful because they promote feelings of unworthiness, lack of planning, and depression. Accordingly, it has been proposed that a moderately positive bias in self-conceptions should be optimal for most people most of the time, regardless of an individual's actual level of competence and achievement.[8]

In addition, five points on development should be stressed because of their implications regarding the adaptability and flexibility of self-concepts:

1. There are age-related increases in the cognitive ability of individuals to extend their concepts beyond the self, to perceive and to empathize with the motives and actions of other persons. A byproduct of cognitive development is an advance in the skills of adolescents and adults to invent convincing theories of themselves and self-serving explanations for their acts. At all ages, rationalizations provide distance between the here and now concrete features of existence and individuals' conceptions of themselves. Depending

on the domain, self-other discrepancies could be the norm for health rather than the exception.

2. Biophysical, cognitive, and social changes are universal, but variations in the rate and content of the changes are distinctive to the individual. These changes lead to inevitable modifications in the organism and concepts of the self. Age-related changes necessarily occur in morphology, cognition, and social role. These transitions take place from early childhood and adolescence to maturity, and pose new challenges to self-organization. Accordingly, organisms and self-concepts are stable only in a relative, dynamic, and ever-changing sense.

3. There are age-related differences in communication processes and content. In the face-to-face interactions of everyday life, positive, kindly evaluations are more frequent than negative, hurtful ones, in accordance with the Pollyanna Law.[9] Specifically, stable social interactions are inherently biased toward positive information and actions and against negative confrontations and direct hostility.[10] In accord with interactional theory, the Pollyanna bias should apply when the other individual is physically or vicariously present in the interaction, and able to reciprocate. According to this model, strong negative attitudes can be more safely expressed behind the individual's back through gossip and through the social network. Hence the opinions and evaluations of others could reflect different content and sources than the opinions and evaluations of the self.

4. Two sets of information about the self typically coexist in the social system: public, where others share information about the people with each other and with the person; and private, where others share with each other but not with the individual. Although there are developmental advances in the ability of people to understand and employ this two-level process, there are also advances in the ability of social groups to conceal private information. There may be a balance between these processes in development, and little change in the congruence between self-reports and the attributions of others.

5. Self-reports can be synchronized with respect to the social consensus, or with the needs of the self. Whether self–other congruence is observed depends upon the domain in which self-reports are obtained, the context, the form of the inquiry, and the costs and consequences of "accuracy" or "inaccuracy". There is also a need to understand the functions of the self in a cultural and temporal context.

Recent observations of how rapid cultural changes affect concepts of the self among young women in Nepal illustrate the last point. In ethnographic observations conducted for several years in a Nepalese village, Dorothy Holland and Debra Skinner (Holland & Skinner, in press) tracked the self-concepts of girls and young women through their "songs of sadness" and qualitative interviews. These investigators found that as the cultural view of women changed, so have their songs and their concepts of themselves. The concepts that people form of themselves are dynamically bound by context, relationships, and time.

Relevant longitudinal findings

Understanding self-evaluations and their functions requires more than snap-shots of a person's life. However, research on self-concepts and the concepts of others has been limited, for the most part, to here-and-now correlational analyses. On this count, longitudinal study provides a fresh tool for tracking the emergence, continuity, and change in self-concepts.

Self-concept measurement has presented a difficult problem for the field. A number of scales purport to assess beliefs about the self (i.e. "self-concept"), the values placed on the self in general (i.e. "self-worth" or "self-esteem"), or beliefs about the capability to master events, whether within or without (i.e. "self-efficacy" or "self-mastery"). There are also self-doubts, and questions on whether the concept of the self in any of the above forms provides useful information for understanding normal or pathological functioning.

The term "self-report" refers to the results of a family of methods used to collect information from individuals in which they describe themselves. One of the methods in the CLS is the semi-structured interview conducted annually over a six to nine year period. Another method – the one upon which we rely heavily in this chapter – is the ICS, administered to subjects each year. The ICS instrument contains eighteen brief items in the original version, and is very economical in time and expense. We use the same instrument for children and adults, so words are kept simple and judgments concrete. It is geared to accommodate a 3rd grade, 8-year old reading level. The modest reading skill requirement of the procedure makes the test accessible to virtually everyone, although the items are read to the younger children as a safeguard. The midpoint of each ICS item and factor is 4.0, and the scales are constructed according to rigorous psychometric standards (e.g. bipolar, single dimension items, reversal of positive and negative poles, use of filler items). Subsequent statistical analyses indicated that the scale is robust with respect to the classical psychometric criteria of internal coherence, test–retest reliability, construct validity, concurrent validity, and predictive validity.[11]

To be sure, there are trade-offs between the use of standard and standardized measures such as the ICS and more flexible, in-depth procedures provided by interviews. There is no question that greater richness and depth is provided by interview procedures. The ICS procedure has its own distinctive advantages. It permits us to draw exact self–other comparisons, since exactly the same items are used by participants to describe themselves and by others to describe participants. This comparison is available every year. It permitted systematic analyses of self-other enhancement, age-related changes, and the developmental trajectories of self-concepts relative to the developmental trajectories of the "other".

A comment is in order on who the "other" should be: peers, parents, teachers, or researchers?[12] Teachers proved to provide some of the most consistent and reliable information as the "other"; over the years, teacher ratings have provided robust and powerful predictions. In addition, there is the advantage of diversity and heterogeneity. Social change is built into most American schools. Unlike some places in Europe, public schools in the United States typically reassign children to different groups, different teachers, and different classrooms each year. The "other", defined as the teacher who knows the child well, represents many different persons for each subject across the years. Hence this particular "other" source became, over nine years, many different people who shared a similar role with respect to the participants. Teachers also have standard frames of reference for making judgments about participants each year relative to other children.[13]

Six on a scale of ten

The "Lake Wobegone Effect" is the phenomenon whereby most children tend to be somewhat above average, at least in their own eyes.[14] The qualification "most" is important, because not everyone overestimates their competence and potential. To the contrary, the range "somewhat above average" implies that a significant proportion of children – including those who are above average or better – tends to underestimate their potential.

To determine whether or not people see themselves as above average in their self-reports, it is necessary to specify what being above average means in terms of measurement.[15] One measure can be assessed directly from the raw score on the test, and it does not require a comparison sample. Hence self-scale enhancement occurs when an individual's self-report score is beyond the midpoint of the relevant item. The raw score is almost "absolute" because it does not require comparison to a standardization sample or population to be interpreted. But it is "semi-absolute", because there is indeed a comparison frame that defines the scale, implicit in the mind of the self completing the rating.

Self–other enhancement occurs when self-rating scores exceed the scores rated by "others". This enhancement can be expressed either as individual self–other difference scores, or as the difference between the means of the self-ratings and the means of the ratings of the "other". How does one know whether a given self–other discrepancy is an instance of enhancement, modesty, or debasement? For most social and cognitive factors, this question seems moot. There is little reason to doubt that those who describe themselves as brighter, more popular, better athletes, and better looking than others describe them are giving a positive account of themselves.

But what about rating oneself as stronger, tougher, and more challenging than other people? Being assertive and "masculine" can have either positive or negative connotations, depending upon age, authority, gender, and frame of reference. For most parents and teachers (though not all) aggressiveness is not particularly desirable. But for some youths, such as Billy, "taking no bull" is something to be proud of.

With these distinctions in mind, we now turn to see how subjects actually described themselves from childhood to adulthood.

Self-scale enhancement. In the CLS, a strong self-enhancement bias appeared across development. There were 105 mean ICS factor scores for the self-ratings of males and females (i.e. 210 overall). The factors were computed over the period from 4th grade (10 years old) through the 12th grade (18 years old). The means for the male sample were above midpoint for all "unambiguous" factors (i.e. omitting aggression). Nor was it only boys who had a high opinion of themselves and their competence. Self-scale enhancement held for the 105 female comparisons on the unambiguous factors, save for one. The exception was the "olympian" factor which contained the girls' self-evaluation of attractiveness. Throughout early and mid-adolescence, girls described themselves as average or significantly below average in appearance.[16]

The proportion of research participants who described themselves above the midpoint of the scale differed systematically over the domains assessed. For example, only 52–60% of the girls judged themselves above mid-point on the attractiveness factor ("good looking") while 90–95% of the sample judged themselves above the midpoint on the affiliation factor ("friendly").

Self-other enhancement. In the unambiguous domains of popularity and academic competence, the self–other enhancement results are consistent and reliable across genders and across ages (see Figure 7.2). The mean scores that subjects assigned to themselves were more positive than the mean scores assigned to them by teachers. A large proportion of the sample, however, did not obtain a positive enhancement score. Depending upon domain of assessment, 10–40% of the subjects underestimated their competence (they rated themselves below the level they were judged by teachers). People who underestimated themselves included participants who, in their ratings, were viewed as extremely popular and above average.

Importantly, there is less spread or range among self-ratings than among teacher ratings. Accordingly, the standard deviations of the subject's distributions of scores typically were smaller than the standard deviations of the teacher's distributions. This was consistent with the proposition that participants regressed to a common mean in their self-evaluations, while teachers continued to discriminate among participants.[17]

As in self-scale enhancement, self–other enhancement did not hold across the board for all characteristics. The two exceptions, the same as in the self-scale enhancement, help unravel a broader story. One exception concerned self-ratings of aggressive behavior among girls; the other involved self-ratings of attractiveness for both genders, but principally among girls.

First, consider aggressiveness. For females, there is a reversal of enhancement, in that girls tend to describe themselves as being *more* aggressive than do their teachers. This "reversal" was observed from 10 to 13 years of age for girls. Boys show only nonsignificant self–other discrepancies, in that their self-ratings on the aggressive factor fluctuated around the teacher ratings.

How might the girls' reversal in aggressiveness be explained, or was it a reversal? It is known that subjects in this age range place a high value on being assertive and aggressive, within limits (the "brutalization norm" of adolescence in Ferguson & Rule, 1980; Cairns, Perrin, & Cairns, 1985). For early adolescents, being argumentative and assertive may not be seen by them as being all bad, particularly when the target is a parent, teacher, or male peer. Seeing themselves as being more assertive than they are seen by teachers may be self-enhancement for the girls. In this regard, the girls' mean self-scale ratings on aggressiveness were significantly below the mid-point. This means that they did not describe themselves as being above average in aggression, they simply described themselves as being not as nonassertive and nonaggressive as their teachers had described them.

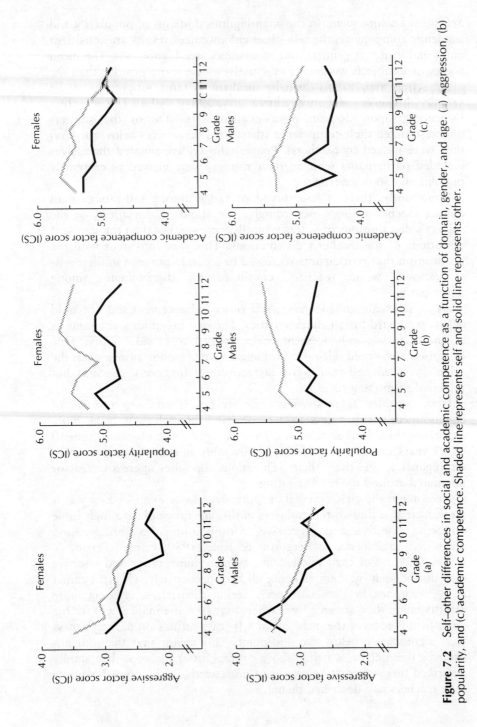

Figure 7.2 Self–other differences in social and academic competence as a function of domain, gender, and age. (a) Aggression, (b) popularity, and (c) academic competence. Shaded line represents self and solid line represents other.

The other domain where normative self-enhancement was not found was in ratings of attractiveness (i.e. "very good looking"). Although both girls and boys saw themselves as being less attractive than their teachers did, the differences appeared in different age ranges and possibly for different reasons (see Figure 7.3). For boys, the self–other difference where they judged themselves as less "good looking" than teachers and researchers saw them was in the 10–13-year-old age range. Self–other differences in attractiveness for boys were modest and/or unreliable through the rest of adolescence.

For girls, it is a different story. Girls throughout childhood and adolescence were hard on themselves, and they were particularly harsh from 10 to 16 years of age.[18] Why was there a reversal from self-enhancement to self-diminution in evaluations of appearance? And why did the effect appear more strongly for girls than boys? This may be another instance where the scale was calibrated according to a different standard by the two groups of respondents. Specifically, young teenage girls employed a harsher standard for their appearance than their teachers did.

The participants self-evaluations and the evaluations of others show normative changes over time, in that most people on most dimensions

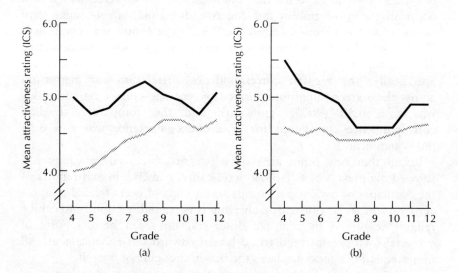

Figure 7.3 Mean attractiveness ratings by the CLS participants (shaded line, self-ratings) and by their teachers (solid lined, teacher ratings) each school year, shown separately by (a) girls and (b) boys (Cohort I and Cohort II combined).

see themselves getting better and better with age. Modest improvement in the self-assessments continue at a gradual rate up to 18 years of age. The age-related increases are seen in measures of higher popularity, lower aggression, and greater friendliness. Even self-ratings of attractiveness improve with age, with the largest gains shown among girls. By the end of high school, girls finally saw themselves to be as attractive as boys.

Except in the attractiveness ratings, there was no general trend for the ratings of the self and the ratings of others to converge as a function of age. Although the subjects and teachers are presumably moving closer to common standards as the subjects themselves become adults, and although the subjects have a greater capability to make abstract judgments about themselves and the social world, the mean self–other discrepancies on the abstract categories of personality were as large at 18 years of age as they were at 10.

Public people, private selves

There was only modest agreement between self-ratings and the ratings of others. We had expected that the highest levels of agreement would occur in the most public and concrete domains, namely, aggressive behavior and academic competence. That expectation was confirmed. The higher self–other relations occurred in the aggression and academic dimensions, but the relationships were modest in magnitude. Specifically, the median correspondence correlation for aggression across the sixteen subgroups formed by sex–age–cohort classifications was $r = 0.30$ (90% significant), and the comparable median correspondence correlation for academic competence was $r = 0.29$ (80% significant).

Recall that one other area of self-report discussed in Chapter 5 showed high levels of self–other veridicality; namely, the self-reports of the participants' own social groups and groups of peers tended to agree across informants. Cluster membership is presumably public and can be reliably identified by multiple observers. But even here, reports of subjects' own groups tend to be biased toward self-enhancement. All things equal, the good displaces the bad in thoughts of oneself.

The remainder of the correspondence correlations were lower, as expected. In other words, the median self–other correspondence correlations accounted for about 9% of the explained variance in the aggression and academic competence factors, 3–6% in the popularity, affiliation, Olympian, and sum social competence factors, and 0.6% in attractiveness. These modest correspondence effects were replicated in both genders and in both cohorts.

Two alternative explanations for the low self–other correspondence could be tested in the present data set. The magnitude of the correlation across information sources is affected by the reliability of each measure (see Block, 1977; Epstein, 1973). Hence one possibility is that the factors themselves were not very stable, depending each year upon a single set of ratings of the child and a single set by the teacher. The greater the number of items used to assess a characteristic, the more reliable the measure and the higher resultant relationships (Gulliksen, 1950; Magnusson, 1966). On psychometric grounds, it would be expected that higher correspondence correlations would be obtained by aggregation within each domain across adjacent years, or across the entire school-age period (nine years in Cohort I and six years in Cohort II). However, even when the self and other ratings were aggregated over nine years of observation in Cohort I, there were only modest gains in the level of correspondence between "inside" (self) and "outside" (other) sources.

A second possibility was that children and adults were not marching to the same drummer. As they grow older, the subjects may become more capable of abstract thinking, become more self-aware, and/or become more likely to calibrate their ratings with the standards employed by adults. Again, the results do not support the argument. The level of correspondence failed to change systematically, regardless of dimension or gender. The same low levels of correspondence were found in the first assessments as were at different ages, and continued throughout high school. Poor correspondence cannot be attributed to one set of poorly informed teachers or to the lack of contact between students and instructors. Despite a new cast of raters each year (students were exposed to a variety of teachers over the nine years), the low correspondence relationships look remarkably similar each year.

The assessments of attractiveness illustrate the point. Every year, three separate measures of attractiveness were obtained, from the subjects themselves, from their teachers, and from the researchers' evaluations at the end of the interview. Again, the pattern of relationships was consistent with the rule that information outside the self was intercorrelated, but information from the self was not (see Table 7.1). The median correlation between teacher's assessments of attractiveness and the researcher's assessments across eight years was $r = 0.37$, and all of these concurrent validity correlations were statistically significant. However, the median correlation over eight years between the self-assessment of attractiveness and the researcher's

Table 7.1   Intercorrelations for appearance: self, other, and real

Gender	Age	Self/other	Self/researcher	Other/researcher
Females	11	0.05	0.03	0.40**
	12	0.17	−0.04	0.20*
	13	0.00	0.07	0.06**
	14	0.01	0.18**	0.28**
	15	0.16*	0.25**	0.36**
	16	−0.02	0.11*	0.43**
	17	0.04	0.10	0.51**
	18	0.11	0.17**	0.33**
Males	11	0.01	0.05	0.36**
	12	0.22*	0.18	0.44**
	13	0.06	0.10	0.15**
	14	0.09	0.11*	0.40**
	15	0.14*	0.11	0.33**
	16	0.14*	0.23**	0.31**
	17	−0.02	0.12*	0.23**
	18	0.09	0.14*	0.32**

* $p < 0.05$.
** $p < 0.01$.

assessment taken the same day was only $r = 0.11$. This outcome matches the result found earlier on low levels of teacher–self correspondence on attractiveness.

Both female and male self-ratings on attractiveness ($r = 0.51$ and $r = 0.49$) were slightly more stable after a one-year interval than the researcher ratings of attractiveness (i.e. $r = 0.47$ for both girls and boys). All one-year stability correlations were highly significant ($p < 0.001$), regardless of agent. However, the slight advantage in self-stability ratings was erased after two years, and became reversed over longer intervals. Among girls, for example, the self-stability was not reliable after a seven-year interval ($r = 0.07$). By contrast, the stability correlations for teacher ($r = 0.39$) and researcher ($r = 0.47$) ratings of attractiveness remained robust ($p < 0.001$) over the same seven-year period.

Parallel findings on the stability of aggression in the eyes of the self and others were described in Chapter 3. Taken together with the findings of the stability of other self–other comparisons in personality and social characteristics, these data suggest the empirical generalization that, beyond a one-year interval, ratings on personal characteristics of the person from informed sources outside the self are at least as stable as judgments rendered by the self. A corollary of that proposition is the slope of the decay of prediction for self-evaluations is steeper than the evaluations of others. The slope cross-over appears to occur in the present data after a one to three year interval. After a year, the "outside the self" ratings are at least as stable as the self-ratings.

In the light of these findings, how might we account for the deeply held belief cherished by many of us on the stability of our own lives? To be sure, additional analyses are called for on whether this generalization holds beyond the early age of onset. The human mind and memory may continuously make dynamic adjustments to bring past judgments into alignment with the present. Over a one to three year period, an adolescent's thoughts may change more dramatically than his/her actions.

The self-esteem of aggressive youth

At the beginning of the chapter, questions on the relations between self-esteem and difficulties of living were raised. It was observed that the objective circumstances of life do not necessarily have a great deal to do with circumstances and life satisfaction. In the same introductory section we also raised questions about the possible linkages between an individual's self-concept and deviant, aggressive behavior. The present study is in a unique position to address this question, because we have tracked a group of highly aggressive people from childhood to early adulthood.

Did problem adolescents have low self-esteem when they were children? To address this question, we contrasted the self-report measures of the highly aggressive boys and girls with their control counterparts. In accord with previous findings, both boys and girls who were at risk for problem behavior tended to judge themselves happily with respect to meritorious characteristics (i.e. popularity, academics). Even on the dimension of aggression, high-risk subjects saw themselves only modestly more aggressive than the matched controls.

In Chapter 4, we observed that these data suggest at-risk children do not necessarily devalue their own social and cognitive skills (see Table 4.1). If teacher and peer judgments are taken as the criterion, at-risk subjects provide an overly positive view of their competence and skills, even in the domain of aggressive behavior. They see themselves in a highly positive light, particularly compared to how teachers and peers evaluate them. They described themselves as less aggressive, more popular, smarter, more friendly, and more socially competent overall than others saw them. This outcome does not make much sense if self-concepts provide a "looking glass" reflection of prevailing public opinion. But they are wholly consistent with the proposal that self-ideas reflect an adaptive process where veridicality is not the sole or even the most important criterion. This freedom to construct positive evaluations of themselves might be particularly important for problem youth and elderly, poor women.

But are aggressive, deviant adolescents more prone to distort their self-descriptions of aggressive behavior than control or normal adolescents? To investigate this possibility, absolute – as opposed to algebraic – difference scores for aggression were determined. Self–other deviations, regardless of whether they were in a self-enhancing or a self-debasing direction, were determined without respect to the difference sign. We anticipated that this absolute measure would reveal the extent to which subjects tended to distort their self-descriptions of aggressive behavior relative to opinions and attributions outside the self.

The results fail to show a tendency by any subgroup to demonstrate reliable differences in the propensity to distort (Figure 7.4). Though few reliable differences were found, it appeared that the at-risk, deviant subgroup showed a tendency toward less self-devaluation and less distortion than their control counterparts.[19]

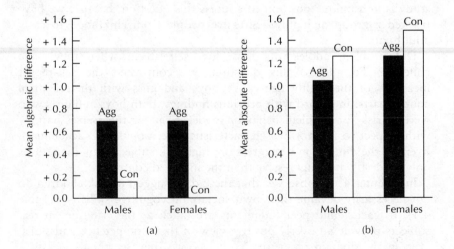

Figure 7.4 (a) Self–other discrepancy expressed as a mean algebraic difference score. (b) Self–other discrepancy expressed as a mean absolute difference score. Agg = Aggressive risk group; con = matched control group.

To sum up:

1. At-risk children and adolescents provide marginally lower levels of self-evaluation than nondeviant subjects.
2. At-risk children had greatly inflated views of their own capabilities, behaviors, and skills relative to the evaluations of others.
3. At-risk, control, and normal groups showed similar absolute levels of self-other distortion.

These outcomes are consistent with the repeated failure of interventions that attempt to reduce antisocial behavior by raising the child's self-esteem. The problem may be that many deviant children already think too highly of their skills.

The State of California, along with other states, has enacted programs designed to raise the self-esteem of children, presumably with the hope that it will enhance the welfare of children and decrease crime and violence. Perhaps this program will achieve its goals, but the present analyses and information from other investigations provide scant support for this basic proposition.[20] Why has it been so attractive for society to accept the dual propositions that problem children have low self-esteem and that self-devaluation and social–cognitive deficits lie at the root of deviant and delinquent behaviors? A possible answer may be that most people in conventional society have low regard for antisocial adolescents. This low esteem is projected to the antisocial youths, on the assumption that anyone who behaves so despicably must have little or no self-respect. The present data strongly suggest that deviant children's self-esteem is not as low as the esteem in which they are held by others.

Concluding comments

Cognitive constructions of the self must serve multiple masters for developing humans. Not only do youths create personal theories of themselves, other people create theories about them. Longitudinal analysis indicates that the two levels of theory often show a poor match. In this regard, the concept of the "looking glass" self seems to require re-examination. If the contents of our self-system only reflected the evaluations of significant others, we could expect a closer match between the self and others. Rather than a single looking glass, subjects and observers may live in a house of mirrors. If that is the case, small wonder that the study of self-concepts has been handicapped by distortions of conceptual and measurement issues.

The "gift of time" embedded in longitudinal study provides a fresh perspective on both self-reflections and other-projections. The results indicate that at least two coherent sets of beliefs about the self exist. One set is constructed by the person, and a second set of beliefs and expectations is generated by others. These two sets of beliefs coexist, yet they track separate trajectories. The two "selves" differ in how information is enhanced and weighted in the present, and in how closely they are linked to outcomes in the future. Self-constructions appear to be at least as susceptible to change over development as actions.

Finally, self-concept is at once a scientific abstraction and a set of intimate personal beliefs on identity. In the latter role, they constitute a key to the future and a sense of well-being. Accordingly, the functions, stability, and correspondence to the reality of self-concepts are ordinarily hidden from exposure, by science or common sense. Perhaps that is why some of the proposals and findings of this chapter may seem counterintuitive.

EIGHT

Dropouts, throwouts and runaways

I got throwed out, mainly.

Arnie (former 10th grade student)

In *Kids As Capital*, Jonathan Rauch observes that the elderly in all societies depend on the next generation to take care of their needs.[1] Historically, this meant that children were committed to taking care of their parents as well as themselves. Nowadays in America that is changing, with the responsibility for the elderly being shifted from their children to pension funds, medicare, and social security. This modern solution does not escape dependence upon offspring, however. It serves to enlarge the scope. Dependence shifts from your own children to other people's children.

Pension funds, medicare, and social security will work only if the economy itself is healthy. A major problem is looming because a significant proportion of the members of the next generation in the United States may be ill-educated and otherwise unwilling or unable to fulfill the needs of the society for a modern workforce. Where this is the case, the whole society will suffer, not merely the forsaken elderly or the beleaguered young. It is in this sense that the young must be valued as capital. On this count, children are as important as other raw materials of the society. To reverse the squandering of this critical resource may be the most important economic challenge for our generation.

Then there are the individual costs. Picture the bleak stereotype of school dropouts in the United States in the 1980s.[2] Male dropouts are often portrayed as destined for a lifetime of unemployment or underemployment, resident members of the underclass whose legitimate economic needs are frustrated or met through the illegal drug industry

167

and violence. Female dropouts are pictured as even less likely than their male counterparts to escape the stigma of poverty, welfare, and underclass. They are expected to become the welfare child-mothers of a new generation of equally ill-educated, unskilled children who will be prone toward crime and violence.

How accurate is this picture for the society or for the individual? Is it possible that the stereotype captures too much too simply? Michelle Fine has argued persuasively that people who leave school early are as differentiated – and sometimes more adaptable – than those who stay.[3] Depending on the options and opportunities available, dropouts may perform quite differently in adapting to the nonschool, community environment.

A second possibility is that correlation has been confused with causation. Dropping out of school may be the factor that leads to subsequent social and economic failure, or a correlated outcome of basic deficiencies of the person or system that lead both to failure in the school and failure in the community.[4] Adolescents who do not have the resources to get along at school may be the same ones who cannot get along at work and in the community. School completion and graduation may not be so much a cause as a diagnosis. The person's failures in school may index and predict subsequent economic and/or relational problems, but may not produce them. Dropout must be understood in context. We should consider not only what environments individuals are leaving, but what environments they are entering.

To bring these images into focus requires information about the developmental events that lead to dropping out of school. It also demands knowledge of what happens to the individual after dropout, in contrast to those who are comparable but remain in school. Accordingly, we made a major investment in tracking the people who left school, those who remained, and what happened in their lives.

The national picture

Estimating school dropout rates is surprisingly difficult. Reporting standards are not uniform from state to state, and rarely have students been followed individually to determine whether or not they eventually graduate.[5] Virtually all major reports, such as the Current Population Survey, rely upon cross-sectional data and/or retrospective questions (e.g. "Were you enrolled in school last October?"). Of 10,331,000 people who said they had been enrolled in the 9th, 10th, or 11th grades during the previous year, 535,000 reported that they were no longer in school in 1983.[6] Taking into account grade-specific rates, it has been estimated that for a given group of new 10th grade students in 1983, about 15% did not graduate.

Other estimates indicate much higher dropout rates for inner-city high schools. Michelle Fine concluded that 66% of the 9th grade students who entered one New York City comprehensive high school in 1978–79 did not graduate within five years.[7] Fine's detailed tracking of individuals yielded a higher dropout rate for the school (80%) than had appeared in official reports. Even some of the official reports are dismal, when they are examined closely. In this regard, William Julius Wilson found that the most disadvantaged neighborhoods of inner-city Chicago had higher dropout rates than the city as a whole (along with crime, unemployment, and teenage births).[8] In these Chicago high schools, the dropout rate was 67%.[9] There was a gender difference, in that 57% of the boys did not graduate while 45% of the girls did not complete high school according to school records.

Studies of school dropout have identified a variety of factors associated with the phenomenon. These include sex, socioeconomic class, race, scholastic shortcomings, and behavioral problems.[10] A close examination of one of these trends shows a counterintuitive result that has escaped the attention of most people, including professionals in education and social science. It is a twofold finding. Contrary to general belief, the ten-year trend from 1973 to 1983 indicates that a diminishing number of students dropped out of high school in the United States. Even more contrary to stereotypic beliefs, the biggest dip in dropout rates occurred among African-American males.[11] It is not clear why these findings have not been given wider coverage, but the trends are unmistakable.[12] They demand to be understood in the context of study which provides a better picture of the circumstances, motives, and consequences of dropout.

In this regard, the writers of the *Current Population Reports, School Enrollment* observed, "Ideally, one would need a longitudinal survey in order to see how many of the people who were in school at some beginning date were still enrolled at a later date".[13] That was, in brief, our strategy in order to obtain a picture of the individuals behind the statistics.

A significant proportion of our sample either dropped out of high school or were expelled. We analyzed the data to find out who was likely to leave school early, and what happened after they dropped out. We believed that the phenomenon of school dropout and its consequences should not be divorced from the cultural, social, and personal contexts in which they are embedded. Specifically, we anticipated that there would be a strong association between dropping out and the convergence of poor school performance and disruptive behavior early in the school years. Either failure of academics or disruptiveness in behavior taken alone, could probably be tolerated by school personnel if there were redeeming features to the individual. When these difficulties co-occur and converge into a single configuration, the problems in school escalate as kids grow older. Unruly kids who are poor students and troublemakers in elementary school are at high risk for school detention and suspension in middle school, and removal and expulsion early in high school. Nonetheless, even this linkage is modulated by the temporal-ecological factors of generation, region, neighborhood, socioeconomic status, and race.[14]

Defining school dropout

At first, there seems to be no problem in determining dropout. The student is either enrolled in school or is not. But precisely what is "enrollment"? The criteria for legal withdrawal differs from state to state, and dropout itself is not an all-or-none phenomenon. On the first point, states differ as to what age is acceptable for withdrawing from school. In North Carolina, school attendance is compulsory by statute until age 16. The individual can then withdraw from school, on their own volition and without penalty. In other locations, the minimum age is higher. For example, in 1990 students could quit school in the neighboring state of Tennessee before attaining the age of 17 only with parental approval and if they convince the court that their reasons are justifiable. This is not a simple matter, and serves to keep many enrolled in school. Regions also differ in policies on grade retention. If students had been held back two or three years prior to entry into high school, it would be impossible for them to graduate from high school before their 21st or 22nd birthday. Dropping out of school at 15 or 16 years of age has quite a different meaning from dropping out at 19 or 20 years of age, regardless of state.

Are individuals who leave school involuntarily, because they are suspended or expelled, the same as those who leave school of their own volition? The distinction between "pushout" and "dropout" becomes muddied when the individual's actions that led to suspension or expulsion are examined. The nature of the incidents that led to the adolescent's removal from the school system suggest that many were designed by the student to provoke suspension or expulsion. More broadly, the overlap between dropout and expulsion underscores that dropout is a two-way street, and that adolescents are not the only ones to make decisions about whether or not school attendance is continued. Then there are the gray areas of full-time, part-time, and evening school attendance. After leaving school full-time, students may participate in half-day programs where attendance requirements are liberal and progress is at one's own pace. In the absence of clear criteria on whether or not the individual is in attendance, it is ambiguous as to whether the person is in or out of school.

Given these problems of definition, we held to a straightforward standard. School dropout was defined for individual subjects by the judgment of the school administration as to whether or not the student was currently enrolled in full-time attendance and making progress toward a high-school diploma. Dropout did not preclude the student's readmission at some future date, or enrollment in an alternative program of schooling. The time at which the subjects dropped out was determined by dividing the academic year into quarters. The decision to terminate school attendance could be made by the subjects and/or their parents (e.g. self-removal) or by the school administration (e.g. suspension and/or expulsion). In a few special cases, decisions were required on whether or not dropout had occurred. For instance, where individuals were imprisoned, academic courses might be offered. Because of the coercion, we did not consider prison-related involvement in school to be full-time attendance or re-entry. But in other instances, where the persons were chronically ill and permitted to attend the hospital school, they counted as having continued in school.

Who drops out?

The summary statistics on who dropped out in our own investigation are in line with comparable statistics that have been obtained nation-wide (Table 8.1).[15] Of the 692 CLS living participants, we found:

o One-sixth (16.6%) of the participants left high school before they completed the 11th grade.
o White males had the highest proportion of school dropout – 19% by the 11th grade – while 18% of the white females dropped out. For African-American males and females, the proportions were 10% and 12%, respectively, by the 11th grade.
o Younger white students – 16 years old or younger – were especially vulnerable to early dropout. Thirteen percent of the white males and 9% of the white females left school when they were 16 years old or younger. In contrast, significantly fewer young African-American males and females dropped out. Only 2% of the African-American males dropped out before they were 17 years old, as did 3% of the African-American females.

Table 8.1   School dropout rate as a function of sex and race (*N* = 692)

Race	Sex	Proportion dropout		Proportion remain		Total N
		P	(N)	P	(N)	
White	Males	0.19	(49)	0.81	(207)	256
	Females	0.18	(47)	0.82	(216)	263
African-American	Males	0.10	(7)	0.90	(67)	74
	Females	0.12	(12)	0.88	(87)	99
Total		0.17	(115)	0.83	(577)	692

o African-American males were more likely than white males to have been retained one or more grades by the time they entered the study in the 7th grade. A larger proportion of African-American males (56%) than white males (28%) were behind one or more grades by the 7th grade. African-American and white females did not differ on retention by the 7th grade: 22% of African-American females and 14% of white females were at least one year behind. More boys than girls had been retained, regardless of race.[16]

These results are in line with recent national statistics. There is one apparent shift, having to do with race differences. The stereotyped African-American–white difference in dropout rate is reversed in our data, in that younger African-American males are *less* prone to drop out than young white males. This was found in both cohorts. The difference may be due to the difference in residence and whether or not the African-American youth live in racially isolated pockets of the inner city or rural south. In such nonintegrated areas, dropout rates for African-American youth appear to be radically higher than where integration has been successful, as in the present data. But this is only one possible interpretation, and we return to this matter later in the chapter.

One other significant outcome should be noted. There was a close relationship between the likelihood of an individual's dropping out and his/her age in the 7th grade (Figure 8.1). One-half (50%) of the white females who were a year older than peers in the 7th grade left school before the end of the 11th grade, while about one-fourth (26%) of white males who had been behind a year in the 7th grade dropped out. Retention of one year had a negligible effect upon the dropout rate in African-American subjects, regardless of sex. It appears that the category of subjects most vulnerable to being retained – African-American males – were buffered from the retain and dropout effect at

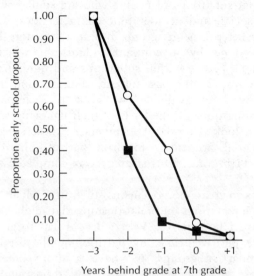

Figure 8.1 Percentage dropout as a function of grades failed at the 7th grade plotted separately for African-American (■–■) and white (○–○) subjects (males and females combined).

ιιιι γeαι Kιιι ιhere αre limits. Uf the subjects who weιι 3 yeaιs ulder than their peers by the time they reached the 7th grade, none completed the 11th grade year. This outcome held regardless of race or sex.

Identifying vulnerability by a person-oriented analysis

We expected that certain subjects would be more vulnerable to early school dropout than others. In line with our expectation that school dropout is as much a symptom as it is a cause, we anticipated that students who simultaneously had performed poorly in the classroom and presented serious problems because of their aggressive behaviors would be most susceptible to dropout. Moreover, we felt that a high proportion of these vulnerable ones who were "at risk" for failure could be identified by the 7th grade.[17]

This task seemed particularly suited for a person-oriented analysis. Our results are straightforward, but they require a word on how we approached the task. "Cluster analysis" is a statistical procedure for creating coherent subgroups of people who are similar with respect to key personal, social, and demographic characteristics. The procedure divides a large heterogeneous group into smaller, more homogeneous ones. This is done by a computer algorithm which maximizes similarities among people within subgroups and minimizes similarities between subgroups. On the basis of early findings and the number of subjects that we had available, we split the sample into seven homogeneous subgroups on the basis of their characteristics in the 7th grade. We then looked to see if members of these subgroups would have a differential propensity to drop out of school before they completed the 11th grade. This strategy was completed separately for boys and girls.

One goal was to create homogeneous subgroups which would permit the analysis of interactions and relationships that might be obscured in standard multivariate analyses. A second goal was to generate a basis for tracking people over time. By partitioning the total sample into reasonably similar subgroups, we have a more precise basis for identifying those who "beat the odds" and those who fail, despite having multiple advantages.

What do these profile clusters look like? The technical findings have been summarized in detail elsewhere (Cairns, Cairns, & Neckerman, 1989), so we can provide an overview of the characteristics of the subgroups and their links to dropout.

The results of the cluster analysis for school dropout were striking. The subgroup of adolescents who were extreme in their disruptive school behavior (getting into conflicts with peers and teachers) and who performed poorly in school in the 7th grade were very likely to drop out of school. Eighty-two percent of males who fitted the configuration failed to complete the 11th grade (Figure 8.2). Low socioeconomic status was neither necessary nor sufficient for dropout in males, nor was being "rejected" or isolated from the peer social network. Unpopularity by itself is not a significant factor in predicting subsequent school dropout.

For girls, the high dropout configuration is similar (high aggression, low school performance). Few girls in the upper half of the socioeconomic status distribution, as judged by parental occupation, tended to drop out of school early. It is important to emphasize that it is a configuration of problems, not conflicts nor scholastic incompetence taken alone (Figure 8.3).

Using a more conventional strategy, logistic multiple regression analysis, we find the same story is told via a different avenue. As shown in Figure 8.4, high aggressiveness in the 7th grade is not, in itself, the key for anticipating dropout in the 11th grade. Nor is lack of

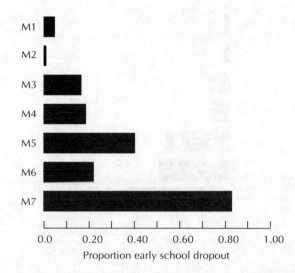

Figure 8.2 Homogeneous subgroups of boys were identified on the basis of behavioral and demographic characteristics in the 7th grade. The figure indicates the proportion of each subgroup which dropped out of school beyond completing the 11th grade. Characteristics of subgroups: M1 = "stars"; M2 = high SES; M3 = low SES; M4 = unpopular; M5 = aggressive; M6 = low academic; M7 = high aggressive plus low academic.

achievement in school. The two variables are linked in a staircase fashion, with increments in likelihood of dropping out associated both with behavior and academic performance.

Despite the robust cross-sex similarities, one gender difference should be noted. Socioeconomic status played a modulating role for dropout in females but not for males. Only 4% of the females in the upper half of the SES classification dropped out of school while 13% of the females in the lower half dropped out. The dropout rates for males in the upper and lower halves of the SES distribution were 11 and 20%, a non-significant difference.

It should be noted that other social characteristics in the 7th grade contributed to differences in the subsequent dropout rates. It has been generally presumed that adolescents who drop out of school had been earlier alienated from the peer social system, and had suffered peer rejection or isolation. The present data indicated, however, that the boys who dropped out appeared to occupy the same peer social status as those who did not. Furthermore, they had the same proportion of "best friend" reciprocated nominations. It seems likely that boys who

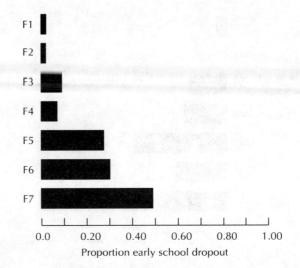

Figure 8.3 Homogeneous subgroups of girls were identified on the basis of behavioral and demographic characteristics in the 7th grade. The figure indicates the proportion of each subgroup which dropped out of school beyond completing the 11th grade. Characteristics of subgroups: F1 = "stars"; F2 = high SES; F3 = low SES; F4 = early mature, high academic; F5 = older, low SES; F6 = low academic, low popular, low SES; F7 = high aggressive plus low academic.

dropped out were not friendless; rather, they probably developed affiliations with other people who, like themselves, were vulnerable to dropping out.

There was some support for the view that females who dropped out had only second-class citizenship in the social network of the school. An analysis of the 7th grade social structures indicate that girls who subsequently dropped out were less likely to be nuclear members of social clusters than girls who did not. There were no differences, however, in whether they had close, reciprocated friendships. It should be remembered that these assessments of aggression, performance, and relationships were made several years before the subjects actually dropped out.

Peer groups and dropout

In Chapter 5, we described the powerful effects of peer groups upon individual behavior and decisions. We anticipated that peers would play

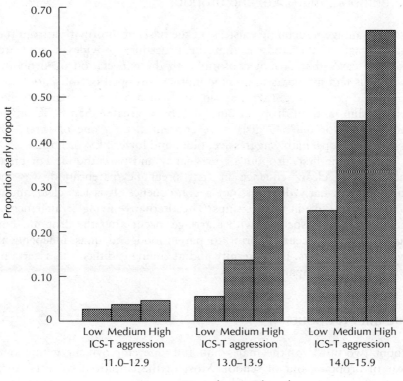

Figure 8.4 Outcomes of early school dropout as a function of the subjects' prior school adaptation (i.e. teachers' ICS ratings of aggression and age of student in the 7th grade). (Source: Cairns, Cairns, & Neckerman, 1989.)

a big role in determining whether a given person will remain in school, or leave early. The SCM procedure for identifying social groups was described in Chapter 5. Once identified, the social groups would provide a means to determine whether particular groups were more likely than other groups to have members who would drop out three to four years later. The results indicate a statistically significant relationship between peer associations in the 7th grade and dropout before the 11th grade. Even in the 4th grade, girls who will eventually drop out tend to affiliate with other girls who will also prematurely terminate their schooling.[18] After the individual has left school, his/her closest peer associations tend to be with others who have dropped out.

Parenthood, marriage, and dropout

One advantage in defining clusters on the basis of information from the initial stage of the study is that the procedure provides a guide to examine cases that do not conform with the expectation on dropout. Nine girls had infants, and all nine mothers dropped out of school. Six additional girls had gotten married or formed a live-in, marriage-like relationship, and all dropped out. Moreover, greater than 80% of the mothers and/or married girls were concentrated in one of three 7th grade subgroups: highly aggressive, older and lower SES, or both.

Which came first, dropout or pregnancy and parenthood? For girls, there was a clear sequence in that pregnancy/parenthood was an antecedent of early dropout, not a consequence. It is less clear about marriages and live-in relationships. The alternative living arrangements, including those associated with marriage, occur after the dropout. For males, dropout occurred prior to parenthood and quasi-independent living arrangements. But paternity and its timing is difficult to ascertain, even for the participants.

Life after dropout

About two-thirds of the males had full-time employment within one year of dropping out of school. Most of the employed subjects were factory workers in local mills, construction workers, and laborers. Fewer girls than boys were employed; only one-fourth of the females were employed full-time within the year. They tended to hold factory or service jobs.

The remaining third of the dropouts had made a marginal community adjustment, and some extremely marginal. Two males and two females were paroled, and two males were currently "on the run" and would be returned to prison if apprehended. Three of the four boys were located in the "aggressive" subgroup when they were in the 7th grade. Other female and male dropouts have had episodic court convictions, and they experienced trouble finding work and/or holding jobs. The assertive–aggressive behavior identified in the 7th grade continues to limit adjustment to life outside school. It should also be noted that the court can be a factor in *not* dropping out. In two cases, probation was contingent upon remaining in school. Nonetheless, at the termination of probation, the individuals immediately left school.

Despite multiple academic and interpersonal shortcomings while in school, the majority of the dropout males within two years held jobs like other members of their family. After testing the extra-school world for one to two years, these subjects found they could adapt to jobs as well as they could to the school environment. In terms of work and social adaptation, the majority of the dropouts seem indistinguishable from other young adults of their socioeconomic status in the community.

Plans for continued education may be viewed at three levels: professed desire to complete a GED, high-school diploma, or college; actual re-enrollment in a high school or alternative school program; and completion of a GED certificate. Notably, a higher proportion of the girls (31%) than boys (15%) have completed the GED or are in the process of completing it within two years of drop-out. Of the remainder, virtually all of the dropout subjects who are not attending some alternative school express their plans to do so in the future. But with few exceptions, the expressions of intent are open-ended and without conviction. Typically the "plans" are vague, and no concrete steps have been taken to enroll.

The problems with authority and lack of conformity that got many dropouts into trouble when they were in school continued to plague them outside school. On the average, the dropout group differed from the nondropout group in arrests for serious automobile violations (e.g. drunk and reckless driving) to felonies (e.g. possession of drugs with intent to sell, criminal assault, breaking and entering).

Problems in organizing themselves and meeting responsibilities are not restricted to crime. It showed up in several aspects of their lives, and our research relationship was no exception. Not surprisingly, dropouts encountered special difficulties in fulfilling appointments for the annual interviews. The reasons that school dropouts are typically not followed after leaving school are that they are usually difficult to locate, they are sometimes uncooperative, resistant, and suspicious, and they frequently fail to keep appointments, even after they have agreed to cooperate.

Self-reflections: reasons and rationalizations

When asked about why they dropped out of school, the subjects came up with reasons that were acceptable to themselves. These include failure, repeated suspension, and concerns that they would never graduate anyway. Among boys, the theme of expulsion was coupled with the attractions of leaving school. Here is a sample of what they have had to say in response to the inquiry, "Why did you drop out of school?"

They made me mad, so I just quit. . . . He was going to expel me for two weeks, I believe, for smoking in the bathroom. I just told him, "I quit" and walked out. (Albert)

I'll tell ya. Well, I just got tired of going, and. . . . Feel like I wasn't accomplishing nothing, learning, and then I just stopped going. (Bob)

No real reason . . . it was boring, I felt like I knew all I had to know . . . was going to go back . . ., but I figure I was making $6 an hour and nothing in school, so . . . (Chuck)

Just cause I didn't want to take it anymore . . . anymore coming home, listening to my mom and dad arguing and then going back to school and don't have my homework. Just got tired of it. (Dan)

I didn't do my work. I didn't particularly like school, so I just quit and got a job. (Ed)

All of the above boys were identified in the cluster of males who, on the basis of their performance and failures in the 7th grade, were at very high risk for dropout. Over 80% in that subgroup dropped out.

It is of interest to find a boy who dropped out early but who was not in the "at risk" category. The 8th grade comments of one of the boys in the "average" subgroup were prophetic. He was the only boy in this "nonrisk" subgroup who dropped out of school. This interview was conducted one week prior to his leaving:

I'd like to get rid of all the schools. I hate school. All my brothers and sisters got to quit in the 6th grade. Before that my father didn't even make it – my father went to the 8th grade and then his parents made him quit. I wish they'd make me quit . . . I like to wish I was better in school then I wouldn't wanna quit . . . I'd like to graduate. I doubt I make it. I'll be 62 years old before I do graduate . . . I wish some of the teachers would like me. (Gerry)

On objective grounds Gerry seemed to have both the skills and the prior achievement to graduate. But he was constrained by familial tradition and, quite likely, under implicit familial pressures to leave school.

Overall, the boys who dropped out expressed considerable frustration at their inability to continue to fit into the program and restrictions of the school, and/or the expectation that life outside school would offer immediate advantages. Some of them did not have to rationalize their decision; the blame was placed on the school administration for having suspended them.

With one exception, the reasons girls offered were similar to those cited by males. The exception had to do with motherhood and marriage. It is of interest that, at dropout, almost as many boys claimed to be fathers as girls were mothers, but family responsibilities were never mentioned by males as the reason for dropping out. Here is what the girls said:

> I just hate it. I said well if I could go to school 8 hours a day, I could get me a job 8 hours a day, 5 days a week. I said I'm going to school 40 hours a week and I said I'm not getting paid for it and I said well I'm gonna go get me a job and get paid. (Amy)

> Well, one was because I was not very good in math, and it sort of kept me back some years. And plus school was kind of – had lots of pressures with it. And, um, if I – probably if I'd have stayed, I'd have prob'ly been held back because of my math. And so all my friends were going ahead of me, and that, that didn't set too well with me because I wanted to be with them. (Betty)

> When I got pregnant with Melissa, I quit then. (Carole)

> I didn't like the teachers or any of the students, I didn't get along with none of 'em, and they all acted like they were better than everybody else and I just didn't get along with 'em . . . Don't like school. I don't want to go back . . . I know how to read and add . . . I get by. (Diane)

How can we interpret these self-descriptions and perceptions? About the same way that we can interpret other self-reports. They are constructions of actions that serve several purposes, not the least of which is self-justification. Beyond the reasons that are offered, we know that conflicts with school personnel and with other students were a big part of the pattern, and that neither the student nor the institution was likely to give. It seems also the case that improvement in either area – behavior or academics – would have been a key for maintaining the person in school.

Re-entry and burnout

Simply because a student drops out, or is expelled, does not mean that he or she cannot re-enter at some future time. Most of our subjects, in fact, believe that the dropout decision is reversible. Consider Jerry, a member of the high-risk configuration of males:

> I'll tell you why. Well I just got tired of going and – uh – I got – when I kept going and I don't know. I felt like I wasn't accomplishing nothin' – learning – and then I just stopped going. Then once I got out I quit – and then I found out how hard it is to find jobs without a diploma and I

decided to go back next year. That's my reason. I'll be registering again next year. (Jerry)

The most common reason for dropping out is reflected in Jerry's explanation; "I just wasn't accomplishing nothin'". In truth, he was accomplishing something, but not at the same rate as his peers. He had failed two grades, and he was on the verge of flunking again. He had also been identified in the 7th grade as being highly aggressive. The brightest parts of his school day in the 8th grade were in after-school sports; he is a large boy and a talented athlete. But that did not outweigh his recurrent difficulties inside and outside the classroom. When he became old enough to quit legally, reaching his 16th birthday, he ended formal schooling. His explanation of why he dropped school seemed accurate, as far as it went. But did he return or did he not? No, he did not by the end of an additional year. He told us:

I was gonna go to Camelback Tech and get my GED, but I'm still thinking about doing that. I don't know. When I talked to them down there they said it takes as long – however – as long as you want it to take. It depends on you. (Jerry)

Whatever the reason for leaving school, few of the males returned within two years, despite the strength of their original statements of intent. For instance, Jerry initially said, "I'll be registering next year". Two years later, he had not registered for any program. He lives at home and works at on-again, off-again low-level jobs.

Overcoming dropout

As we indicated above, the majority of the boys who dropped out became employed. In some instances, they seem to be doing considerably better outside of school than they ever did inside, but not without difficulties and detours. By way of example, Ralph had been held back in school for two years before he finally dropped out. His first full-time job was in a factory, in a low-level starting position. It was enough for him to buy a new car, get married, and purchase a home, a sure instance of precocious and successful maturity. It would have been if our data had stopped at that point. But things began to unravel when his wife left him, and he had bills he could not handle alone. Ralph returned to live at home. With family help to pay a $4,000 tuition bill, Ralph enrolled in a reputable technical school for welding. On our last interview, he had just completed the course and was about to accept a job in the area.

It is too soon to offer generalizations about how school dropouts will fare in the long term, relative to the earnings and stability of comparable subjects who remained in school. Other reports indicate that the effects will begin to emerge at age 25 or older.

Recall the problem of confounding correlation with causation. To evaluate the effects of dropout *per se*, as opposed to factors that led to dropout, it seems unreasonable to offer comparisons other than those in the general population of graduates. For rigor, comparisons should contrast members of the high-risk subgroup who remained in school and those who dropped out. Both would have been aggressive and would have had problems in the classroom in the 7th grade. The more general point is that long-term comparisons between dropouts and nondropouts on economics and job stability need to take into account levels of prior adaptation and current opportunities, if the unique effects of dropout are going to be understood. For males, however, this reasonable strategy will not be possible in this study. The problem was that virtually all males in the highest risk subgroup dropped out, and no adequate contrast can be made with those who graduated. A comparison will be possible for the subgroup of high-risk girls, since only half of them left school early.[19]

Comparisons and comment

Early school dropout is reasonably predictable. Not many American investigations have tracked a representative sample of youths from elementary school to high school, but recently completed investigations are consistent with the above findings. In this regard, the Chicago Woodlawn project directed by Sheppard Kellam and Margaret Ensminger has recently reported the follow up of children from the 1st grade through the end of high school (Ensminger & Slusarcick, 1992; see also Kellam *et al.*, 1983).[20] Data collection began in the 1st grade, and comparisons were made between dropout and nondropout at the end of high school. The findings indicate that low grades and aggressive behavior in 1st grade were associated with later dropout for males. First grade behavior and performance were less important for girls. Girls in the Chicago investigation seemed less influenced by earlier grades and aggressive behavior than boys. In both males and females, the links between early school performance and later high-school graduation were not as strong for those whose families had incomes below the poverty level as for those who were not poor.[21] It is as if poverty had a steamroller effect on dropout, subsequently flattening the effects of individual differences in early behavior and performance.

The Chicago Woodlawn results raise the question of how well we could predict dropout from the 4th grade information available in Cohort I, when participants were 10 years old. Although Cohort I was a smaller sample than Cohort II (i.e. $N = 220$ *versus* $N = 475$ for Cohort I and Cohort II), the outcomes help fill the gap.[22] As it turns out, virtually the same set of predictor variables operate for younger boys in the 4th grade as for those in the 7th grade: aggression and grade failure. For the girls, however, only poor academic performance (as indexed by teacher ratings and failure) was a strong predictor. Unlike the inner-city Chicago results, these effects held regardless of socioeconomic class and parental employment. These results suggest that the steamroller may not be poverty *per se*, but the combination of being poor and living in the chaos of a truly disadvantaged inner-city neighborhood.

One diagnostic aspect of our overall results should be stressed. As important as aggressive behavior is in predicting school dropout, its key role is derived in configuration with other problems of adaptation. Even though there is a significant correlation, the relationship is carried by only a portion of the sample. Two clusters of highly aggressive and/or rejected boys did *not* differ from the base rate in early school dropout. For these males, aggressive behavior was not accompanied by other problems of adaptation, notably failure at school. This finding is consistent with Magnusson's contention that developmental correlations with "aggression" are likely to be misleading because the variable serves, for some children, as an index of multiple problems of adaptation. But for other people, aggression is not associated with multiple problems.[23]

Some findings do not fit preconceptions. For example, being "unpopular" and/or rejected by peers was not a major determinant of dropping out of school, either separately or in combination with other factors. Nor did SES enter independently as a predictor in either the regression analysis or the cluster analyses. The variance associated with these characteristics appears to be captured by more fundamental factors.

One most curious outcome concerns differences in dropout rates as a function of race. Compared to white males and females, African-American adolescents are not more likely to terminate school early in this population.[24] This difference defies the common expectation that African-American students, particularly African-American males, are inevitably more likely to drop out than white students. Why were these students so different? We speculate that the region in which they live is a major factor. Although the African-American subjects were economically disadvantaged, none of them lived in an inner-city environment at the time the investigation began. There is clearly a higher rate of dropout in urban and/or racially isolated communities. In this regard, our African-American subjects were products of school integration. By that we mean that each of the three communities was located in a region where school integration had been sharply enforced throughout their school careers. All schools in these districts were required by the courts to have the same proportion of African-American-to-white students, with only a small percentage variance. It seems reasonable to expect that both these factors contributed to the difference in dropout rates among the African-American students, from 15% in this study to estimates of 50–75% in the inner-city schools of Chicago and New York.

A related matter concerns the modulating factors in African-American students that make them less vulnerable to the retention–dropout relationship. Three explanations seem worthy of further analysis:

1. There may be less stigma attached to school retention among African-American than white students, in part because it is more common.
2. Jobs may be seen as less available to African-American than white dropouts, so leaving school early is a less attractive alternative.
3. There may be ethnic differences in the perception of education as a route for economic and social advance (i.e. with school integration, new advantages have arisen for this generation of African-American youth).

This effect may help explain why the major change in dropout rates from 1973 to 1983 was observed primarily by a decrease in the rate of dropout by African-American males (from 32 to 20%).[25] Further research could productively explore the generality of the retention–dropout effect and why it is ameliorated in the case of African-American students.[26]

A noteworthy finding concerns actual post-dropout community adjustment. According to Steinberg, Blinde, and Chan (1984, p. 113), "failure to complete high school is associated with limited occupational and economic prospects, disenfranchisement from society and its institutions, and substantial loss of personal income over his/her lifetime". In the light of such expectations, the employment status of the male dropouts is noteworthy. To determine the disadvantages of failing to complete high school, future comparisons on economic, marital, and social status should be made with other members of their cluster who remained in school. Most people who drop out are already in disadvantaged groups prior to leaving school.

Three comments are in order on the implications of these findings for dropout prevention and educational policy. Clusters of students most likely to drop out may be determined at least four to seven years prior to their leaving school. Efforts to reduce dropout rates might productively focus on the very high-risk clusters while they are still in school. But these are also the adolescents which schools find most troublesome if they remain. It seems reasonable to suspect that schools contribute, unwittingly or intentionally, to their departure. The dropout rate seems to be promoted by the institutional attitude that "school is not for everyone".

So what can be done? The first task should be to determine what kinds of education and training would be appropriate for all young people, appropriate in terms of enhancing their ability to live productive lives within this society. It is of interest that some of the successful dropouts designed their own curriculum: they enrolled in a training program for mechanics, got on-the-job training in supervising others, took a full-time job in a hosiery mill, but found time to complete a GED. For these subjects, the "school" they created for themselves could tolerate them and they could tolerate the intellectual and attitudinal discipline. One challenge is for schools to create opportunities within the context of the standard curriculum. Such programs could extend the options for adult productivity in a concrete fashion for at-risk adolescents who did not have the resources that are available to the dropouts who made it.

The second and related comment concerns the school and behavioral problems cited by the dropouts themselves. They typically attribute leaving school to specific difficulties they had with the standard curriculum and/or school restrictions. Those dropouts who eventually complete high school or an equivalent course usually have taken advantage of programs offered by alternative schools or community colleges. To ameliorate the long-term effects of dropping out, further efforts should be made to coordinate access to these programs among people who have left school or who are planning to drop out.

Once out of school, dropouts are no longer adolescents. They become merged with the rest of society and most of them begin to function as adults, for good or for ill. This is where the dropout stereotype fails; it is a mistake to lump them together into a single group. Within this sample, about one-third conform to the dismal image of continued failure in the community. Another third are functioning at an acceptable though modest level. The remainder are doing better in the "real world" of work and living than they ever had in school. For them, further training through employers or continuing education programs may serve the same economic functions as remaining in school. Several who dropped out have begun or completed technical training, including the equivalent of a high-school diploma. The realities of the job market seem to have demanded it. With the support of spouses, boy/girlfriends, or employers, they have begun to create their own stepping stones toward economic and social independence.

But the stepping stones to adaptation are slippery. The new relationships formed with spouses and boy/girlfriends which provide valuable support are also, unfortunately, the relationships most vulnerable to disruption and dissolution. Those who drop out must be resilient not only to failure in school and in jobs, but in the stability of intimate relationships. It remains to be seen how they will fare in the long term, when their peers enter the adult world alongside them.[27]

Perhaps we should not have been surprised that a majority of the dropouts in this study are in the process of creating lives for themselves in the community, with the usual number of problems of early adjustment. They also tend to defy the stereotype. But the other third of the school dropouts constitute a major drain on social resources, both legal and welfare. They are the ones arrested for the most serious crimes, and they are parents when they are least competent for the role.

Runaways and throwaways

In the course of this longitudinal work, we were struck by the large number of participants who, as young adolescents, talked about running away, and/or left home. In this context, "runaway" is defined as children who leave home without permission and stay away overnight or longer.

Table 8.2 shows that 22% of the subjects in the first cohort ran away from home. Boys rarely stayed away for more than a week, but girls often remained for an extended period or permanently. Equally surprising to us was the high proportion who said they "thought a lot" about running away, and had made plans to do so. When ideation is added to action, most of our sample indicate that they want to get away, regardless of parental consent. Over half of the girls (53%) and boys (62%) have run away before they are 18 years old or seriously contemplate it. About twice as many boys think about running away as do it, while the proportion of girls who act is about the same as those who have thought seriously about it. When they leave, boys stay away shorter periods than girls. In general, boys seem less willing to take responsibility for managing their lives and their actions.

Our results on runaways are generally in line with previous analyses, including the studies of the Colorado group (Brennan, Huizinga, & Elliott, 1978). The exception is that our incidence rate is higher.

Table 8.2   Runaway behavior: ideation and occurrence (CLS Cohort I)

	Females		Males	
	Number	Percent	Number	Percent
Runaway occurrence				
Overnight	2/99	2.0%	6/81	7.4%
One week	8/99	8.0%	8/81	9.9%
Extended	4/99	4.0%	1/81	1.2%
Permanent	9/99	9.0%	2/81	2.5%
Sum Occurrence	23/99	23.0%	17/81	21.0%
Runaway ideation or occurrence				
A. Serious ideation	29/99	29.3%	33/81	40.7%
B. Prior occurrence	23/99	23.2%	17/81	20.9%
Sum (A + B)	52/99	52.5%	50/81	61.6%

Whether this difference reflects variation due to decade – 1970s *versus* 1980s – or to region – Rocky Mountains *versus* Southeast – remains to be determined.

Emancipation or abdication?

Children who are emancipated by judicial order become independent of their parents, and they assume adult responsibility for their own personal and financial affairs. Parents, in turn, no longer have legal or financial responsibility for their emancipated children. The minimum age for judicial emancipation differs across states; for example, in North Carolina, emancipation by judicial order is limited to children 16–17 years of age, while in California, children 14–17 years old may qualify. Questions have been raised recently on whether emancipation is in the best interest of the child, or whether adults employ the statute to abdicate parental responsibilities (see Friedrich-Cofer, 1989; Willemsen & Sanger, 1991).

   Tied to the issue of statutory emancipation is "functional emancipation", where, without the benefit of legal maneuvering minors, live outside the family. This may occur by running away and staying away from home (i.e. moving in with a boyfriend, girlfriend, or another family). The incidence and causes of such legal and extra-legal arrangements have rarely been studied, although it appears to be a matter of increasing significance in the United States. The matter first arose in our work when we discovered that a significant proportion of the adolescent subjects did not live with their families, for one reason or another. Another large proportion had run away from home, or had given it a great deal of serious thought. Since our work is longitudinal, we have been able to focus on the nature of those children and families who sought emancipation in one form or another.

In most states, statutory emancipation can occur for minors in three ways: by judicial order, by joining the military, or by marriage. None of our group achieved emancipation by judicial order or by joining the military. Marriage was the route for statutory emancipation in this group, but only by girls: 4% of the girls and none of the boys got married before age 18.

There is another issue here for our adolescent subjects and their families, that of functional emancipation. This occurs when minors have removed themselves or have been removed from their original family setting. In some cases, removal was not so much emancipation as it was parental abdication.

Four categories of functional emancipation may be identified, based primarily upon the living arrangements that these people formed outside their original families. This first group consists of those who move in with a boyfriend or girlfriend. A smaller group live alone, or with a same-age friend and try to make it on their own. A few are placed in foster homes, or in county homes for children. Members of the largest group move in with another relative, such as a grandparent, an aunt or uncle, or a brother or sister. Included in this last group are those who leave the custodial parent to live with the other parent, or a stepparent. All in all, about 12% of the subjects in our sample were emancipated in one form or another before 18 years of age.

The question is whether these emancipated youths were better prepared for living on their own, more mature and responsible than their peers? Our findings strongly indicate that they were less prepared. Follow-up results bear this out. Over half of the emancipated girls left school before completing the 11th grade, and nearly half of the boys left school before graduating. The differences from base rate were highly reliable. If employed, they held menial "entry-level" jobs. Virtually all of them indicated major financial problems.

Did the problems of adjustment arise because of the abdication/emancipation, or were serious problems already present in the child's behavior prior to changing families? We compared school and social adjustment when all of these people were in the 7th grade and prior to them leaving their families. The logistic regression results indicate that emancipated and unemancipated boys differed in the 7th grade, but the differences were slight. There was a modest elevation of teacher ratings of aggression in prospective emancipated boys, but that was all.[28]

Greater differences were found in the girls, and the findings were in the same direction as the boys. As a group, emancipated girls tended to be in the lower half of the socioeconomic classification, they tended to be white rather than African American, and they were more aggressive than other subjects in the 7th grade. The last effect tells the same story as the boys' data. In any case, these girls seemed to be no better prepared for independence than their peers. In terms of aggressive behaviors, they were clearly worse prepared.

The realities of living extend beyond the numerical tabulations. In examining the family situations of children who leave home, we found that this representative sample of youths shows a diversity of living conditions as they grow up. Here are reasons offered by two different girls. Kathy, reflects hurt and longing:

K: Um, well, me and my mom don't really get along. I moved back home for about two weeks. And mama told me she didn't want me there. And when she told me that I just, I left again. I mean, it's so hard. I mean, it hurts so bad when your mama tells you she doesn't want you there. I mean, your own mama. And so when she told me that I couldn't take it. I couldn't stay there. See, deep down inside I'd say she cares. She just don't show it.

For another girl, Louise, the changes in family context were chaotic from childhood to early maturity.

I: Who lives at your house?
L: (Louise, 10 years old) I'm living at the Martin's right now. . . . (Three wishes?) I wish that maybe if my mother would come back and I'd know where she is, then maybe I could go back home with her, 'cause I want to go back home and live with her.

After a couple of years, Louise was granted her wish. She, her brother, and her mother were reunited, and they lived together with her mother's new husband and his children. That arrangement lasted for one unhappy year. Then Louise was rejected again by her mother. She was sent to live with her maternal great-aunt. At 16 years of age, Louise became functionally emancipated, and she won a "freedom" that she did not seek.

How are these and the other functionally emancipated adolescents in our sample making it in early adulthood? So far, it has been difficult. Few have completed high school, and most are living in dismal economic and social conditions. There are some exceptions, but the overall picture is bleak for the present and the future. The jobs they hold are typically transitory or menial.

Even if the adolescents do not seek emancipation or run away, we have observed the granting to adolescents the appearance of independence without providing concrete lessons in economic adaptation. Overall, the 16–17 year olds in our general sample in high school who work are employed for an average of 20 hours per week. A substantial proportion (15%) work a full 40 hours per week while attending high school. This can set the stage for problems, even when they are living at home. For those already on their own, the difficulties are multiplied in impact and in number. They become locked out of educational opportunities and locked into the economic underclass.

Remedies and recommendations

Given the state of affairs that currently exists with runaway and throwaway youth across the nation, certain recommendations seem called for:

1. There is a need for broader recognition that the achievement of educational and social potential is not just an individual affair. It also involves the constraints of the peer groups in which the youths are embedded, and the constraints of the schools they attend. When schools segregate or cluster individuals who share low standards of accomplishment (or expectations for school dropout), they explicitly help bring about those outcomes. To keep educational opportunities open, there should not only be challenges for achievement, but ample assistance and support to ensure that each student will reach adequate standards. This means that middle schools and high schools must expect reasonable levels of performance in subjects such as algebra and biology for all students, not merely those who have been identified as being the best and the brightest by standardized test scores. "Ability" scores, like the individual's self-beliefs, are themselves open to change and modification over development. The responsibility for academic achievement must become at least as great for teachers as for students.
2. The curriculum should include information that is not only preparatory for subsequent accomplishments; it should place the information in the context of living. For example, Stanford University has recently developed a biology curriculum for middle schools and high schools that does not "water down" genetic and microbiological principles, but it does make them attainable and teachable. Moreover, the curriculum involves information about the realities of living, including the mechanisms of HIV transmission, and how it might be prevented. Similarly, issues of substance abuse

are placed both in the context of physiology and the realities of personal experience and addiction. Science and literature need not be divorced from the issues of living, while simultaneously preparing students for further work and providing reasons why the work may be rewarding. Again, the lessons should be prepared for the full spectrum of students, not merely the best and brightest.

3. In plans to prevent serious problems of behavior, at-risk youths should be kept in the conventional system, not excluded from it. Exclusion serves to exacerbate problem behavior by the selective isolation of the individuals from the rules and standards of conventional society. But how to keep youths who seem to be constrained by forces within and without that seem designed to exclude them from the system? Here is where fresh programs are called for to emphasize what the at-risk students can accomplish rather than underscore what they cannot. What programs might be introduced for the students if suspension was not an option?

Consider, for example, the use of poorly performing students to help tutor those students below them. In the course of learning to tutor and in tutoring, there is a "bootstrap effect" where the "teachers" themselves become motivated learners. Rather than select only the brightest students for tutoring, the opportunity for teaching can be opened to poorly performing students. Learning becomes a cooperative, productive experience rather than an individual hurdle. Another example from San Francisco involves the close monitoring by faculty and principals of all students in the school. Despite being located in one of the high crime-rate areas of the city, the Dr Martin Luther King, Jr. Academic Middle School maintains an open-door policy, so students can work by choice until 5:00 p.m. each weekday and Saturday. Principal James M. Taylor has a peer mutual help program, and thereby helps establish a network of positive support for school success among disadvantaged youths. But there is also structure along with support. Students need to learn how to behave and perform responsibly. Schools need to build this instruction into the curriculum, since many students do not arrive expert in this skill.

In another example, a school-based program of the Dispute Settlement Center of Durham, NC involves the use of peer mediation. Executive Director of the Center, Michael Wendt, indicates that one-third of the school-aged mediators were themselves at high risk. Enlisting troubled adolescents into the program may assist them even more than the peers who are in conflict.

4. In the inner city and elsewhere, schools and the values they represent constitute safe havens for many students. In cases of children of

privilege, the school is more typically an extension of the rest of the individual's life experience. For seriously disadvantaged youths, the haven might serve a unique function. This function must not be compromised, and society must ensure that access to schools remains open and safe, including zones around schools and places within it. This speaks to the need for a major social investment to be made in the educational system, no matter what might be perceived as its shortcomings or costs. A Brooklyn high-school counsellor remarked to us that the "society that devalues its children devalues itself". There is a direct correlation between the social esteem assigned to an institution and its willingness to support, maintain, and extend that institution.

5. The national investment in Headstart and other early intervention programs, while laudatory, constitutes only a first step in the solution. The bulk of the information available on Headstart effects indicate that they are most clearly and strongly represented in the here and now, not in the future of the children it serves. That is excellent, but only the beginning. If the basic arguments of this book are correct, development is a dynamic process, and adaptations and thoughts of self shift over time, as a function of context and opportunity. So it is with the effects of Headstart. Given what we now know about the dynamics of development, it would be unrealistic to assume that positive effects are frozen into place in the early preschool years. While such effects are important at five years of age, so are the effects that occur at 10 and 20 years of age. As we found in Chapter 7, ideas of the self at age 10 are barely predictable of ideas of the self at age 20. The changes in self-concept are continuously aligned with contemporary circumstances and ongoing events.

In the light of these findings, the implications for educational enhancement are clear. Programs to ensure equal educational opportunities for disadvantaged youth and children at risk should not be restricted to the short time span of infancy and preschool. That is only the beginning. If such programs are to succeed in opening opportunities for a lifetime, they should begin early and continue throughout elementary and secondary school. Kids are not merely economic capital; they are also human beings whose skills for good or for ill are developed throughout childhood and adolescence.

NINE

Life and death

I got real depressed after I broke up with my girl friend – and my parents were fussing and fighting a lot and my father's throat was acting up and he wouldn't stop smoking. And that bothered me and stuff – so I got real depressed and I tried to kill myself and I had to go to the hospital for three months.

Marvin (10th grade)

Investigators trained in the behavioral sciences ordinarily think of the risks and lifelines of adolescence in terms of psychological issues, not as a matter of life and death. Yet a brief study of actuarial tables informs us otherwise. Though the mortality rate in adolescence is low, deaths do occur, and they should be expected in a sample of almost 700 teenagers. The national statistics on death and survival indicated that we should have observed two to three deaths over the period of the study until the completion of high school. This was an underestimate. As it turns out, there were eight adolescent deaths. Five subjects died and two deaths were caused by or closely associated with the behavior of our subjects. The major causes of death in adolescence – auto accidents, homicides, suicides – were all observed in the course of this longitudinal observation. When each death occurred – all were sudden and unanticipated – it was a shock to members of the research team. After all, these were people who had become known to different members of the research staff since they were children. Beyond the deaths recorded, there were more near-misses, where the subjects survived by luck or their youth.

When the severity of the health problems became clear, we enlisted the collaboration of physicians who specialized in problems of adolescent health, including internal medicine and adolescent psychiatry. This led to some modifications in research design and research emphasis, including an inquiry into the nature and determinants of injury and death in our population. Because the issue was of the highest importance and because it was so basic, we wanted to make sure that the accounts we provided were accurate and complete. Since the number of adolescent deaths associated with the sample was small in a relative sense, we had to extend our study of serious assaults and suicide to encompass a larger, state-wide sample to ensure accuracy and replication.

Still, this chapter was almost omitted from the volume. A visit by Tore Bjerke of the University of Trondheim to our laboratory in late 1989 made the difference. Dr. Bjerke is the Norwegian director of the World Health Organization cross-national study of suicide monitoring and prevention. In Norway, suicide is increasing at an alarming rate, and most of the increase is due to a rise in suicide rate in adolescents and young adults. After a week of discussion with Bjerke, he convinced us that the information that we have available on the matter should not be left out.

The national problem

Behavior is the primary factor in the morbidity (illness) and the mortality (death) of adolescents. The causes of death and disability in the young in any era typically differ from the causes for death and disability in the middle aged and elderly. They differ in physiological status, on the one hand, and in the likelihood of getting involved in behavioral risks, on the other.

The difference in the risks associated with age are seen in the mortality tables for people of different ages. Among adults of 50–59 years of age, the risks are greatest for heart disease, cancer, and accidents. But in adolescence, the risks are greatest for the behaviors associated with accidents, homicide, and suicide. The rates for the three most important causes of death in 15–19 year olds in the United States in 1986 are shown in Figure 9.1 by sex and race. Accidents, specifically automobile accidents, constituted the primary cause of death, with suicide second and homicide third overall. In African-American adolescents, homicide plays a larger role, and it was the leading cause of death in both males and females between the ages of 15 and 34. Accidents and suicide were the second and third most frequent cause of death. As we look across countries, we find a similar picture, except

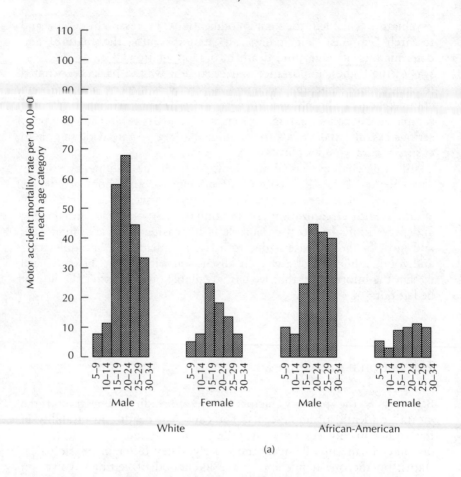

(a)

Figure 9.1 Mortality in the United States due to (a) vehicular accidents, (b) homicide, and (c) suicide among people 5–34 years old. (Source: National Center for Health Statistics, 1993).

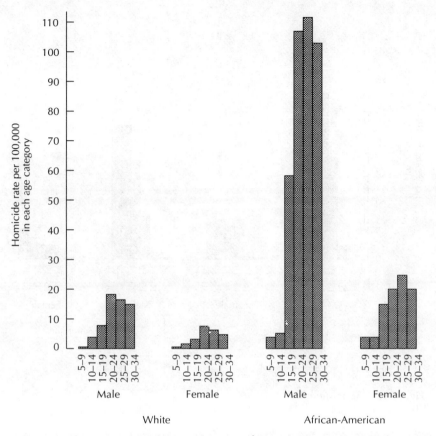

(b)

Figure 9.1 (continued)

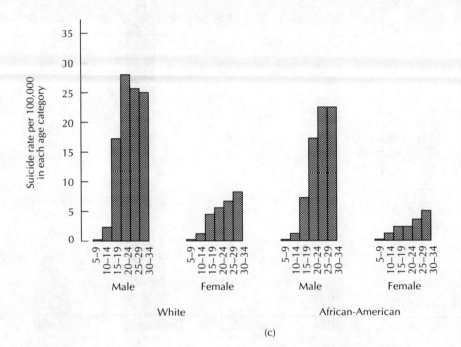

Figure 9.1   (continued)

that auto accidents may play a less critical role in societies with fewer automobiles accessible to adolescents.

One of the most serious health problems in this past decade for adolescents was the increasing proportions of adolescents who were victims of violence, either self-inflicted (suicide) or inflicted by others (homicide). Although the death rate has been relatively constant, the proportion of adolescents who are suicidal and victims of violence has shown a sharp increase relative to accidents. In America, death due to homicide in youths is a national tragedy. As shown in Figure 9.2, the United States is by far the leader in homicidal deaths among industrialized nations. The overall difference is accentuated by the extremely high rate of homicide among African-American youths. But a parallel effect is observed among American white youths who, as a group, exceeded the homicide rate of all other industrialized countries. As we document below, this difference in mortality rates parallels a difference in morbidity rates and trauma.

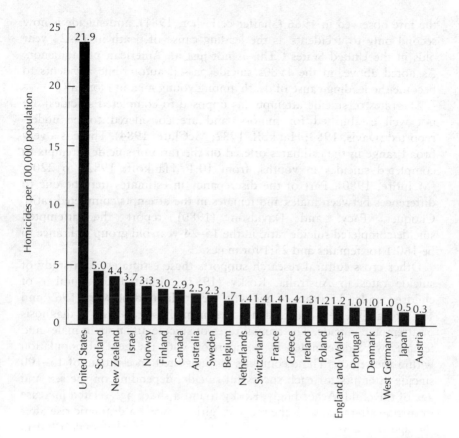

Figure 9.2 International variation in homicide rate for males 15–24 years of age in 1986 or 1987. Data sources: National Center for Health Statistics, World Health Organization, and country reports (Source: drawn from Fingerhut & Kleinman, 1990).

The rate of suicide among adolescents in the United States has increased dramatically over the past thirty years. According to the National Center for Health Statistics, the nation-wide suicide rate in 1986 was 4.6 per 100,000 population for 15–19 year olds. In that year, white adolescent males 15–19 years of age had almost twice the rate (16.4) as African-American males in the same age range (9.1). Similarly, white adolescent females (15–19 years of age) had twice the suicide rate as African-American adolescent females (4.1 *versus* 2.1, respectively). The rate of suicide in the 15–19-year category in 1986 is about double the rate observed in 1966 (Shaffer & Fisher, 1981), and suicide is now second only to accidents as the leading cause of death in 15–24 year olds in the United States.[1] This is not just an American phenomenon. As noted above, in the 1980s suicide passed automobile accidents to become the leading cause of death among young men in Norway.[2]

The rates of suicide attempts (as opposed to completed suicides) are not well established for minors, and are considered to be under-reported (Davis, 1983; Hankoff, 1982; McClure, 1984). There is a very broad range in the estimates offered on the ratio of suicide attempts to completed suicides in youths, from 10:1 (Hankoff, 1982) to 220:1 (McIntire, 1980). Part of the discrepancy in estimates may be due to differences between males and females in the attempts/completed ratio. Choquet, Facy, and Davidson (1980) report the attempted suicide/completed suicide ratio in the 15–24-year-old group in France to be 160:1 for females and 25:1 for males.

Other cross-cultural research supports these estimates. In a study of suicide rates in Australia, Kosky (1982) tabulated the number of children under 15 years of age who were admitted between 1969 and 1978 to all Western Australian government hospitals with a diagnosis of attempted suicide. The annual rates of suicide attempts in males and females were determined by comparison with the general population within the region. These comparisons suggested an estimate of 15–100 suicide attempts for each successful suicide, depending on the sex and age of the child. Accordingly, Kosky found a sharp age-related increase in suicide attempts, with the rates for girls showing a dramatic rise after the age of 12 years. He also found that that the male:female ratio in rate of suicide attempts for children under 15 years of age was 1:3.6, but the male:female ratio in rate of completed suicides was 3:1. The sex discrepancy between attempted suicide and completed suicide was attributed by the investigator to the use of more violent, or lethal, suicidal actions among boys than among girls.[3]

Finally, it is useful to place these findings on mortality in the context of development. Figure 9.1 summarizes the age–sex–race trends for the three most likely causes of death among people from childhood through early adulthood. Note the difference between males and females, beginning at adolescence, in mortality rates of all types which are related to behavior, and the rate of mortality due to homicide among African-American males, beginning in adolescence. By contrast, the "number 1 killer" of Americans, cardiovascular disease, does not qualify as a major cause of death among the young (Figure 9.3). The traditional focus of medicine is upon diseases of later adulthood. However, the immediate hazards of life and death in youth have more

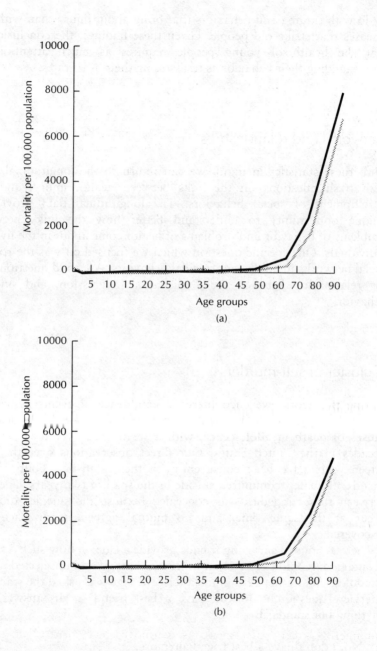

Figure 9.3 Mortality due to heart disease over the life span as a function of gender and ethnic status. (a) US white; (b) US African-American; males = solid line; females = shaded line (Source: National Center for Health Statistics, 1993).

to do with trauma and behaviors that bring about injury than with the diseases that strike old people. Given these findings, the conclusion is that the health of young people requires as much attention to understanding their behavior as to assessing their heart rates.

Networks and relationships

With these statistics in mind, we can return to the longitudinal data with fresh questions on the links between health, injury, and the development of social behaviors. The longitudinal data provide a unique opportunity to understand better how the links between problems of behavior and problems of health come about in the lives of individuals. One specific question which we focused on was the role of social networks in adolescent suicidal behaviors. A second question was the relationship between social alienation, aggression, and suicidal behavior.

A cluster of self-murders

During this work, we encountered a confluence of events associated with suicide. It should be recalled that suicide is one of the leading causes of death in adolescence, with a steady rise over the past two decades in the United States. Our direct observations over the past fifteen years have been consistent with these statistics. Four of five friends, all males, committed suicide in the span of two years. The link between these tragedies was concealed because the suicides did not occur at the same time, and no mutual agreement or pact was discovered.

The reactions of surviving friends provide a clue on how such a tragic "contagion" could evolve in an otherwise normal and unselected group of adolescents. In the 12th grade interview, Pete was asked the standard interview question, "Do you have a best friend?". His answer was anything but standard:

P: No, I don't have a best friend anymore.
I: Used to?
P: Yeah, but he's dead now. It was Jeff.

I: Sorry. Friends now?

P: Tommy, ah, I got a bunch of 'em up there. Wade, Benny, Sammy, ah, Kenny, Jay – that's about all I hang around.

I: Any others?

P: Pat? Well, he–he just committed suicide about a month ago. And then a week after that, another one of my friends killed himself by "OD-ing" (overdose of drugs). First it was Jeff, and you remember Ned?

I: Sure.

P: He–he killed himself and then Pat and then Tim.

I: Why did Pat kill himself?

P: He was just depressed.

The suicidal cluster suggests that certain elements can produce an explosive mix. One factor is the adoption of adolescents of risk-taking "games" with life-threatening activities or substances. Teenage males – including the participants in our research (see below in this chapter) – are especially vulnerable to such involvement. Direct challenges are a part of the male role stereotype that becomes intensified in mid-adolescence. It appears in direct aggressive confrontations as well as in serious risk activities (e.g., playing "chicken" on the highway to see who is the first to swerve from a high-speed, head-on collision; challenging for the ultimate "high" with rock cocaine; playing "Russian roulette"). A second factor is the reciprocation process that operates in all social clusters. In the special case of suicidal activities, the effects can lead to a seeming contagion of self-destruction. These activities seem to be an extension of the reciprocal processes of mutual challenge, matching, and escalation. The third factor is the relative isolation of the cluster from external curbs on the escalation process. Inhibitions might arise from other close peers or from parents and other adults in the community.

An additional perspective on the context in which suicides occur was provided by Clark. In explaining why he had gotten arrested for driving while intoxicated (DWI), Clark said:

C: It was that friend of mine that died. He shot himself. He was playing with a gun. And everybody was up there drinkin'. And this is when I was a lot wilder. I didn't have any girlfriend and I was, hung around my friends, and did everything they did. 'Cause, you know, I didn't care. I just wanted to party and have fun. So, let me see, he was up there and he, that happened. Then he went to the hospital. One night later, everybody went over to his house to see his little brother and everybody was over there. Just about the whole school. And they were, they were drinking over there in the back. So we started drinkin' with 'em, sitting' out in the back. And this one guy, I was, I reckon I was drunk, I can't remember. But I wasn't gonna drive home. I was thinkin' in my mind, I wasn't gonna drive home. So this guy was throwin' up and he, he looked awful. He was sick and he started walkin' home. He's name is Bob. But, uh, he started walkin' home and just about got hit by a car. I said "whoa . . . come here". So I got him in my car and I said, "Will somebody drive?" you know. And nobody would so I just started drivin' him home. It was pourin' down raining and my wipers half-way worked . . . and I turned left real quick and hit a tree . . . head on. Bob got out of the car and started running. That's when I knew to stop hangin' around this crowd. It ain't worth it.

Following from this analysis is the expectation that males will be susceptible in mid-adolescence and early maturity to life-threatening violence of all sorts, whether it is classified as an accident, suicide, or homicide. Because the separate components and the mix are more likely to occur in males than in females, boys as a class should be at greater risk than girls. A large difference appears between white and African-American males, to the extent that the deaths of young African-Americans are more likely to be due to homicide than motor accidents.

The provocative and protective nature of relationships

Why do some adolescents choose to take their own lives and others do not? The studies available are too preliminary to permit anything other than speculative answers and the issues are too important for guesswork. A host of factors have been implicated, from personal depression and social alienation to social contagion and the loss of family members. One problem is that exceptions to any of the presumed "causes" are easy to find. In this regard, the flux of friendships and relationships in adolescence indicates that the breakup of intense relationships is typically within a year and is the rule, not the exception. Similarly, family disruption through separation, divorce, or death is common during the adolescent years. Yet most adolescents survive. What then makes for differences among those adolescents who attempt to take their lives and those who do not?

One impression that we gain from the analysis of the prospective, longitudinal records of suicidal subjects is that intense personal relationships are important in both the provocation of and protection from suicide. Among the people who spontaneously described suicide attempts and suicidal ideas, the rupture of a close relationship is often depicted as a pivotal trigger. Not only is an important relationship disrupted or severed, there is little else to take its place. Below are some excerpts of interviews taken from subjects when they made suicide attempts or became obsessed with suicidal thoughts.

When Marvin M. was in the 9th grade (15 years old), he reported the following:

M: I got real depressed after I broke up with my girlfriend – and my parents were fussing and fighting a lot and my father's throat was acting up and he wouldn't stop smoking.

Kathy K. in the 10th grade (16 years old) told her concern through song:

K: Can I sing a song?
I: Sure. What's it about?
K: It's called "Hear Me Cry. . . . (singing)
"I cry to be heard, but you were too busy with your life
And now it is too late."

A common feature of these interviews, when the subject is brought up by the subjects themselves, is the feeling of separation, rejection, and alienation (i.e. "nobody would pay attention", "no one wanted me"). Yet alienation, separation, and rejection is not unusual in this period.

In the course of this study we discovered there was an additional element in the behavior and background of many of our teenage subjects who completed suicide or made the most serious attempts at it (as judged by hospitalization). Their history was characterized by a pattern that has not been broadly understood as a risk factor in suicide; namely, the occurrence of prior acting-out, impulsive, and aggressive behaviors. Since the most serious suicidal behaviors were also linked to drug or alcohol episodes, it is unclear whether the effect between impulsive action and suicide is direct or indirect. For example, one pathway could be:

acting out behavior → substance abuse → suicidal actions

However the link may be explained, the association between

aggressive/acting-out behavior and suicide was surprising and important enough to investigate in a separate investigation of a state-wide group of extremely aggressive youths. Our question was whether the essential aggression–suicide association would be replicated in a highly assaultive population of adolescents.

Suicidal behavior in extremely assaultive youth

The depiction of suicidal adolescents as withdrawn and inward turning individuals has been broadly accepted. This stereotype fails to capture most of the suicidal adolescents. Recent studies indicate that suicidal children are in fact mainly characterized by aggressive, acting-out disorders, rather than introverted, withdrawn problems. In this regard, psychiatrist David Shaffer analyzed all suicides that occurred among children aged 16 years and younger in England and Wales between 1958 and 1970. Approximately two-thirds of the suicides that Shaffer identified involved adolescents characterized by acting-out problems.

To explore this curious relationship between suicide and aggression in adolescence in the 1980s, we extended our analysis to include the most violent boys and girls throughout the state. This extension was possible because, at the time we began our longitudinal work, North Carolina launched the state-wide Willie M. program for the identification and treatment of extremely aggressive and assaultive youths less than 18 years of age. Willie M. et al. refers to a class action lawsuit filed in 1979 against the State of North Carolina. A group of concerned attorneys, judges, and parents joined to initiate a class-action suit against state officials on behalf of four children (one of whom was named Willie M.). The suit claimed that appropriate treatment and educational services had been repeatedly denied these children because of their emotional and behavioral handicaps. Each had a history of violent behavior, and the state did not have adequate programs for their needs. In an out-of-court settlement, North Carolina agreed to provide appropriate services for children who face similar obstacles. The ensuing services provided to these children have become known as the Willie M. Program. It has since become a model for the nation. Dr. David Langmeyer, Chief of Research and Evaluation in the State Department of Mental Health, and his associate, Gustavo Fernandez, gave us permission to analyze the behaviors and backgrounds of this special group that constituted most aggressive youths in the state (i.e. less than two people out of 1,000). The subjects were the first 800 children identified as qualifying for the class of violent and aggressive youths. They ranged from 4 to 18 years of age. To qualify for the Willie M. program, candidates must be deemed to be violent or assaultive, as well as have behavioral, emotional, or neurological problems. Candidates were nominated by private individuals or, more usually, service agencies such as schools, social service, mental health centers, or juvenile courts. Applications were screened and potential class members were evaluated by designated psychiatrists or psychologists. The psychological/psychiatric evaluation included the following procedures: familial, medical, educational, legal history, standardized psycho-logical tests including an individual intelligence scale, educational achievement tests, and various personality measures. The report of a recent physical examination was also included in the diagnostic protocol.[4]

We anticipated that children identified as extremely assaultive to show sex, age, intelligence, and race differences from the general population. Each expectation was confirmed. Compared to an unselected group of youths, the 800 assaultive subjects were mostly male, dull in tested intelligence, and adolescent. In addition, minority subjects were over-represented. Specifically, 80% were male and 20% were female; the mean IQ was in the low normal range (i.e. mean IQ = 80); equal numbers of African-American and white subjects were identified, even though the African-American/white ratio in this age group in the state population was 1:4; and the mean age of the aggressive sample was 14 years. These differences from the general population of under 18-year-old youths are wholly consistent with the national statistics on violence.

Suicide attempts were reported for 13.2% of these 800 extremely aggressive adolescents. The percentages of males and females who were judged to have a history of suicidal behavior increased as a function of age. Selected subgroups differed markedly in the probability of suicidal behavior. Robust trends were observed as a function of age, sex, race, and their interactions. Accordingly, an analysis was made of the frequency of attempts relative to these developmental–demographic characteristics. Table 9.1 shows the age–sex–race trends in the first study of the 800 violent and assaultive youths.

Older adolescents are more likely to have recently attempted suicide than children and younger adolescents, females are more likely to have tried to kill themselves than males, and white adolescents are more likely to demonstrate suicidal behavior than African-American adolescents. Certain subgroups were considerably more vulnerable than others. Among white females in the 14–15 age group, an astounding two-fifths (39%) had attempted to kill themselves. In the 16–17-year range, the reported suicide attempts were virtually the same in white

Table 9.1   Subjects with history of attempted suicide: Study 1 (proportions as a function of age, sex, and race* (from Cairns, Peterson and Neckerman, 1988)

	Age of subjects				
	<12	12–13	14–15	16–17	Sum
Females					
White	0.18	0.25	0.39	0.24	0.29
	(2/11)	(3/12)	(12/31)	(5/21)	(22/75)
African-American	0.00	0.00	0.17	0.27	0.15
	(0/10)	(0/12)	(7/41)	(6/22)	(13/85)
Males					
White	0.11	0.13	0.12	0.29	0.17
	(8/70)	(6/47)	(13/106)	(24/82)	(51/305)
African-American	0.05	0.02	0.07	0.06	0.05
	(2/44)	(1/45)	(8/121)	(5/87)	(16/297)

* Thirty-eight of the total 800 were other (3.3%, predominantly Oriental or Indian), or were not classified as to race (1.4%).

females (24%), African-American females (27%), and white males (29%). But African-American males in that age range (16–17 years) had a markedly lower proportion of suicide attempts (6%). It should be noted that African-American males showed a low frequency of suicide attempts overall, and African-American males showed only modest age-related increases in the proportion who showed suicidal behavior. The 2%–7% incidence for African-American males remained stable over the age range covered in this sample.

We conducted a second study with a fresh sample of 520 Willie M. subjects to see whether the findings could be replicated and extended. A history of suicidal behavior was found for 10.5% (44/420) of the males, 24% (24/100) of the females, and 13.1% (68/520) of the combined sample in Study 2. The male:female sex ratio of 1:2.3 is statistically reliable. Although the definition of suicidal behavior was different than that employed in the first study – based on an evaluation of the details of the reported behavior instead of the clinician's judgment – the incidence of suicidal behavior was remarkably similar across the two samples of these assaultive youth.

To determine whether the violent subjects with a history of suicide attempts differed from the nonsuicidal subjects in terms of the intensity and seriousness of their aggressive activity, the individually matched subjects were compared on an aggressive severity scale. The overall mean indicated that the average aggressive-act intensity involved serious injury, including broken bones and/or knife wounds, and cuts that required emergency medical attention. There were, however, no reliable differences as a function of the subject's suicide history, gender, or the statistical interaction of these variables.

The results also indicated that only one of the suicidal subjects in a matched suicidal/nonsuicidal comparison sample had not produced significant physical harm to others (2%; 1/57). (This boy had attacked a teacher's aide with a broken bottle on one occasion, and attempted to stab a staff adult on a second occasion, but no actual physical injury occurred before he was subdued. His actions thus qualified for a rating of 1.0 on the aggressive intensity scale because no one was hurt in the incident.) The individually matched nonsuicidal sample had four subjects whose aggressive acts had not produced physical injury to others (7%; 4/57). It thus does not appear that the subjects qualified for certification as violent and aggressive because of their history of suicidal behavior. The common factor appears to be intense aggressive acts directed toward others.

There was a high degree of similarity in parental victimization between the individually matched suicidal and nonsuicidal groups. Parents or parent substitutes were among the attack victims in 61% (35/57) of the suicidal cases, and 56% (32/57) of the nonsuicidal cases. Girls were somewhat more likely to attack parent/parent substitutes than boys (74% *versus* 53%, respectively). The sex difference in the likelihood of parental victimization was statistically reliable. The injuries ranged from repeated attacks and physical beatings to the use of guns, axes, poison, and knives (e.g. one mother was stabbed to death by her son).

One curious outcome of the ratings of the severity of the suicidal behavior was the failure of males and females to show a reliable difference on this dimension. That is, the literature indicates that women show a higher frequency of suicide attempts, but men show a higher mortality from suicide. The present results demonstrate adolescent sex differences in frequency of suicide attempts (i.e. over twice the occurrence for females than for males). But the severity levels were approximately equal for the two suicidal groups (mean = 4.93 for males and mean = 4.75 for females). In both boys and girls, the average rating indicated the acts were typically life-threatening and required medical attention. A further analysis was made of the suicidal attempts to determine whether the actions favored by boys may have differed from those of girls, in the likelihood of producing immediate and mortal outcomes. The males in this sample were more likely to hang themselves than were females. Girls, on the other hand, tended to overdose on various drugs and medications. These differences are in accord with prior reports on sex differences and are consistent with the expectation that males on the average would be less likely to survive subsequent attempts.

These two studies of suicide yielded basically consistent findings on the high incidence of suicidal behavior in a population of juveniles selected primarily for their history of violent, aggressive behaviors. The suicidal and nonsuicidal subjects were virtually identical on the severity of outward violence and uncontrolled aggressive behavior. The predominate diagnosis of "conduct disorder, aggressive" in both the male and female suicidal groups indicates that the basic behavioral problem was judged to involve extreme aggressive behavior.

Why the adolescent suicide–aggression link?

Why is there an association between extreme aggression and suicidal behavior? One proposal would be that suicidal behavior and aggression are both manifestations of poor impulse control. The current context, circumstances, and mood of the subject would determine whether destructive dyscontrol is self-directed or other-directed. Aggression towards others and aggression towards oneself may not be opposite and compensatory forms of aggressive expression. Rather, both outward aggression and self-injury may reflect difficulties in impulse control. To the extent that subjects impulsively react in an aggressive fashion towards others, they may elicit punitive counter-reactions, and, in turn, higher levels of personal stress for themselves. Dysphoria and impulsive self-injury could follow when the subjects discover they are closed-off from social support and adaptive solutions. Girls in late childhood and early adolescence would be especially subject to alienation and depression following aggressive actions for two reasons. It has been shown that adolescent girls are more likely than boys to be victims of ostracism by peers, and aggressive behaviors are less likely to be tolerated in adolescent girls than boys (Cairns & Cairns, 1986).

A related proposal is that aggressive juveniles or those with conduct disorders in general are no more likely to become depressed than are their nonaggressive counterparts, but aggressive juveniles are more likely to act out their impulses when depressed, frustrated, or fearful. Accordingly, the essential problem concerns the threshold for impulsive action, with the highly aggressive child being less able to inhibit self-destructive actions. More generally, a neglected characteristic in juveniles who qualify for the Conduct Disorder diagnoses may be the propensity toward self-destructive acts.

A third possibility is that the manifest aggressive behavior may be a reflection of irritability accompanying an agitated depressive disorder.

However, only 2% of the subjects in Study 2 had a Primary Affective Disorder diagnosis. The affective disorders may have been omitted because the aggressive features were more salient, thus given priority in diagnosis, or the subject was not clinically depressed at the time of the evaluation. On the first point, the signs and symptoms of depression may not have been thoroughly explored by the clinician who, after all, was evaluating people who had been referred for violent and assaultive behaviors. On the second point, it has been observed in clinical practice that it is usual for adolescents hospitalized with no diagnosis of affective disorder subsequently to manifest depressive signs and symptoms in therapy.

Recent studies of behavioral neurobiology, strangely enough, promise to permit us eventually to select among the preceding interpretations. Studies of the brain neurochemistry in animals and humans are now providing convergent information on the nature of brain functions that are associated with violent and aggressive behavior. In particular, recent teams at the National Institutes of Health in Bethesda, Maryland, Karolinska Institute in Stockholm, and the University of Helsinki in Finland have reported a strong relationship between impulsive, violent behaviors among males in late adolescence – both suicidal and assaultive – aggressive – and high levels of the brain neurotransmitter serotonin in cerebrospinal fluid.[5] In addition, parallel studies of nonhuman species that differ in aggressive behavior show large differences in the same brain centers. Equally important, the differences in aggressive behavior are like those observed among violent human males.[6] To the extent that these findings are further studied, the biological biases toward impulsive behavior may be systematically plotted from the genetic biases to the behavioral and social exchanges. In some circumstances, the lower thresholds for impulsive behavior are translated into violent aggressive actions.

To sum up, violent acts and suicidal behavior are not mutually exclusive; on the contrary, they covary in a significant number of adolescents. This relationship is not limited by sex or race; a robust association has been identified in males and females, African-American and white. An exception to the above empirical generalization may be found for adolescent African-American males, in that their suicidal behavior was consistently below that of white males and both African-American and white females. Nonetheless, the proportion of highly aggressive African-American males who attempted suicide, although low relative to other subgroups, exceeds the expectation for an unselected population of African-American youths. In conclusion, our findings support Shaffer's (1974, 1985) contention that there exists a significant cluster of adolescents prone to both violence and suicidal behaviors.

More unhealthy behaviors

Our concern with issues of health led us to undertake collaborative studies of our subjects with colleagues in medicine and nursing (Cobb, Cairns, Miles, & Cairns, 1994). Three of these substudies are especially relevant to the issues of this chapter. One study examined risk-taking behaviors in youth, a second addressed youth violence in terms of emergency department admissions, and a third concerned gun ownership in the CLS.

Testing the limits

In the analysis of risk-taking behavior, a subgroup of the total sample ($N = 271$) participated when they were 15–18 years old. The sample was unbiased with respect to school dropout, since subjects were enrolled in the study prior to dropout, and all of the subjects were seen, even if they had dropped out of school by the time of this collection wave (27% dropout (73/271); 73% in-school (198/271)). If they had not dropped out of school, subjects were enrolled in the 9th–11th grades. As part of one of the annual individual interviews, subjects reported on whether they had been "hurt or injured" within the past year. If one or more injuries were reported, subjects were asked to provide the details of the incidents, treatments, and aftermath. They were also asked to report on "close calls or near accidents", along with a follow-up request to provide details.

The findings indicated that boys (55%) were more likely than girls (45%) to report they had been recently physically injured ($p < 0.05$). Detailed accounts of reported injury incidents indicated that adolescent males were more likely than females to be involved in "testing the limits" (i.e. showing risk-taking behaviors), and the injuries of males were more likely than females to be the outcome of carelessness. Children who had been nominated four to five years earlier to be highly aggressive were, as adolescents, more likely than nonaggressive males and females to report that they had recently been injured. Compared to people who did not leave school, adolescents who dropped out were judged to be testing the limits.

In Chapter 8, we showed that youths who are at high risk for aggressive behavior are vulnerable to multiple problems of social behavior, including adolescent parenthood and school failure. The present results add physical injury to this list (see Jessor, 1982). Although males are more vulnerable in general than females, the early aggression/subsequent injury relationship was observed in both sexes.

Trauma injury and violence

As the longitudinal investigation unfolded, we became increasingly concerned about the incidence of serious injury and death in our sample. We were also concerned as to whether our sample was an aberrant, more injury and violence prone group than others in the United States. When we looked for relevant statistics and comparison groups, we found there was a great deal of information on mortality, and only modest information on trauma and morbidity. Our aim in this substudy was to examine the incidence and severity of injuries due to violence or nonviolence among children and adolescents who were admitted as trauma patients. A special concern was to assess the incidence of violence as a function of the age, race, and sex of the patient, and the mechanism of injury. In accord with the mortality statistics, we anticipated males would be over-represented relative to females as victims of violence, and that African-American youths would be over-represented relative to white youths as victims of violence in an urban hospital. We also expected that firearm-related injury would be a significant mechanism of injury for all male youths, regardless of ethnic status.

In collaboration with attending physicians in the Emergency Department of the Harbor–UCLA Medical Center, we assisted in the study of all trauma patients admitted over three months in 1990. We analyzed these patients with respect to age, sex, race, mechanism of injury, and mortality. A total of 353 cases were available for analysis after selection for age (≤35 years) and high severity of trauma. The results indicated an unhappy confirmation of our expectations on the special risks of youth. Among other things, we discovered that violence was the leading cause of serious trauma for males and females 15–19 years of age, accounting for 63% of the admissions in that age group (Figure 9.4). This is the only age group where violence was the most frequent cause for admission; motor vehicle accidents were the primary mechanism of injury in all other age groups. Recall this was Los Angeles, one of the few truly large cities in the world that has no subways and whose public transportation system was gutted fifty years ago. So the incidence of motor vehicle accidents was no surprise, but the high frequency of violence in adolescence was.

A closer look at the rest of the data tells an equally dismal tale. Considering only violent injuries, gunshot wounds were the most frequent mechanism (62%), followed by knife wounds (27%), and blunt instrument wounds (12%). Those with gunshot injuries had a higher incidence of death prior to hospital discharge than those with knife or motor vehicle injuries. Finally, although males were more likely

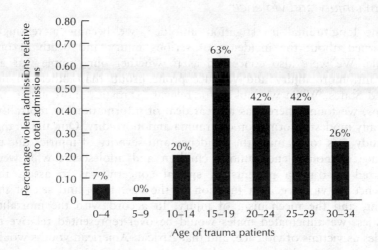

Figure 9.4 Proportion of trauma admissions for violence to UCLA–Harbor Medical Center for three months of 1990 (percentage violent admission computed separately for each age category) (Source: Cairns *et al.*, 1991).

than females to be trauma patients – approximately 3:1 – males and females in the same age–ethnic category showed similar injury profiles. One of the most ominous features of these findings was the high representation of females in the gunshot wound category in late adolescence; firearm injury accounted for 80% of the serious trauma admissions among African-American girls 15–19 years of age in this sample.

Our findings on the injuries of youthful trauma patients in this Los Angeles sample show the severity and cultural relativity of these injuries. In comparison, recent studies of emergency departments in the United Kingdom show few instances of gunshot wounds. For example, in a recent southeast London study, 15% of the attacks involved knives, but these attacks accounted for 47% of the admissions and virtually all (90%) of the serious injuries due to violence.[7] The investigator Hocking (1989) observed that:

> The results support the view that it is becoming common for youths to be armed. Assault victims, particularly those with knife wounds, place a considerable burden on hospital resources. Accident and emergency departments are ideal places to monitor the epidemiology of assaults (p. 281).

The urgency of the problem is shown by the present finding that gunshot wounds are more prevalent than knife wounds as a mechanism of serious injury in this Los Angeles sample. They are also more lethal. Firearm injuries appear in all age groups and are especially high among adolescents. The difference between the United States and other industrialized nations in homicide rates appears to be largely due to the accessibility and ownership of firearms by youths in America, not the differential prevalence of violence (Cook, 1991).[8]

Guns and violence

In 1985 there were 2,475 firearm deaths among 15–19 year olds in America, and the firearm fatality rate among older adolescents has steadily increased since 1960. The mortality rate for unintentional or "accidental" firearm deaths is highest among 15–19 year olds, and firearms are involved in the majority of teenage suicides and homicides.[9] Since the mortality rates for males significantly exceeds females in all accidents involving firearms, we were curious as to how this pattern developed in a normal population. We were surprised to find an astounding number of households have firearms accessible to the teenagers in our sample. Depending on whether the respondent was male or female, firearms were available in 69–81% of the households (Table 9.2).

Perhaps even more surprising was the proportion of our subjects who claimed firearm ownership themselves. Before they were 16 years of age, approximately half of the boys indicated that they owned a gun themselves. These were in addition to the standard BB and airguns. The more frequent firearms were rifles and shotguns, although three of the subjects indicated that they owned illegal automatic rifles (i.e. machine guns) and automatic handguns. In contrast, few girls claimed gun ownership of any kind (5%), and they tended to be vague about the nature of the weapons available in the home.

Table 9.2 Availability of firearms in the households of CLS teenagers

Sociodemographic characteristics		Firearm availability (%)	Handgun availability (%)
Sex:	Female	69	31
	Male	81	36
Race:	African-American	63	22
	White	79	37
SES:	Lower	71	22
	Higher	79	38

Some of the characteristics of firearm owners are shown in Table 9.3. There seems to be little difference among owners in social class, even though some of the rifles and shotguns owned by these subjects were expensive (*ca.* $150–$450). There was no effect of age; as many subjects younger than 16 years claimed gun ownership as those older than 16 years. More school dropouts indicated that they owned handguns than nondropouts, a somewhat ominous statistic.

As might be expected from these sharp differences in gun ownership, there were differences between the sexes in gunshot injuries. Serious firearm injuries were observed in four of the males. Three of the incidents were fatal: one suicide and two manslaughters. In the nonfatal assault, one subject became involved in a fight and was shot in the leg. No girls were involved in firearm injuries.

How did the boys get the guns in the first place? Their first firearms were typically gifts, and these were given to the boys at 12.5 years of age, on the average. The primary giver was the father or some other male relative. Mothers rarely were identified as the agent who gave the child the firearm.

Our data are consistent with the idea that firearm ownership was, for our population, part of the modern initiation rite which signaled that the boy had entered a new, "manly", stage of development where he was responsible for the ownership of deadly weapons. That the injury and death rate is high in this age suggests that many boys are grossly unprepared for this responsibility. Recall that firearms are involved in the majority of suicides and homicides among 15–19 year olds in the United States, and firearm-related injuries are the second leading cause of death among persons in this age range. Teenagers appear to be at special risk, in that mortality rate for unintentional or "accidental" firearm deaths is highest among 15–19 year olds.

Correlates of firearm ownership

We made a further analysis to determine whether firearm ownership was related to personality and social behavior patterns. For males, there

Table 9.3 Ownership of firearms among the CLS teenagers

Sociodemographic characteristics		Firearm ownership (%)	Handgun ownership (%)
Sex:	Female	5	1
	Male	52	11
Race:	African-American	11	3
	White	33	7
SES:	Lower	27	5
	Higher	28	6

was no strong relationship between social and personality characteristics and gun ownership. Other measures – popularity, maturation, peer nominations for conflicts – failed to show a direct association with gun ownership in males. It was a different story for girls. Ownership among females, though infrequent, was clearly associated with a complex of personality and social characteristics. Girls who owned guns tended to have higher ratings of aggression and lower levels of popularity than those who did not.

There was no reliable association between overall firearm ownership and school dropout, for either sex. But boys who dropped out were more likely to own handguns than those who did not. The general finding seems to be that non-normative firearm ownership – handguns for boys and any type of gun for girls – was associated with behavioral and personality patterns. The normative pattern of firearm ownership, namely rifles and shotguns for teenage boys, is not related to any distinctive personality configuration. But it is strongly related to whether or not the boy said he liked to hunt.

In 1985 there were 2,475 firearm deaths among 15–19 year olds in the United States (Fingerhut & Kleinman, 1990), and the firearm fatality rate among older adolescents has steadily increased since 1960. Previous research has suggested an association between firearm availability and firearm-related deaths (Cook, 1991).

The findings indicate that males were more likely to claim gun ownership than females, and that these guns were provided by adult males. Even in single-parent households, the mothers arranged to have other males provide the gifts, so that there was only modest differences as a function of the structure of the household. Mothers, while not direct agents, served indirectly to support the transmission of values and gifts.

In the light of the magnitude and pervasiveness of gender differences found here, the focus of contemporary father–child research upon infants and young children may be a case of asking the right questions at the wrong time. Insofar as fathers are involved, their greatest differential effect in sex typing may be at the developmental stage when secondary gender differences emerge full-blown. Although we focused upon a single masculine activity (guns and hunting), it seems reasonable to expect that similar differences would occur in other prototypic male behaviors. By the same token, it seems likely that mothers would be most closely involved in prototypic feminine activities of daughters. As new sex-typed interests, values, and activities emerge in development, so might the socialization roles of fathers who are "experts" in these activities. Hidden paternal skills become manifest in their children's adolescence rather than infancy.

The failure to find strong relations between firearm ownership and various measures of personality requires comment. The results indicate that highly aggressive boys are no more likely to claim gun ownership than nonaggressive adolescents. This outcome is moderately reassuring, given the social consequences of a strong positive relationship between the two variables. A likely explanation for the failure to find a correlation is that, among white males in this population, firearm ownership is normative and found in the majority of teenagers, and is associated with recreational preferences rather than enduring personality patterns. Such a pattern of ownership obviously does not preclude a relationship between firearm injury and personality characteristics, including aggression. The finding of personality and social behavior correlations between gun ownership among girls is consistent with the idea that the ownership in females is a non-normative for the gender. Girls who differ with respect to firearm ownership tend also to differ with respect to behavior. It appears that a similar pattern may hold for handgun ownership among males.

Given the linkage between guns and adolescent health (firearms are the first or second cause of death and injury in teenagers, depending on race and region in which the data are collected) the matter is one in which both developmental psychology and the health sciences should have a compelling interest. Firearm ownership and usage is strongly gender typed, and this gender typing appears in late childhood and early adolescence, and perhaps earlier (through toy guns). The attitudes of the children and adolescents appear to be formed not merely in early childhood, but in late childhood and adolescence as well. Moreover, the agents involved in the transmission of primary attitudes and values about actual firearms differ at the two developmental stages. Whereas mothers may be involved in the purchase of toys (including toy guns), fathers seem to be almost exclusively involved in the purchase of firearms. The attitudes of children about firearms may themselves be stage- and context-specific, and these attitudes may be revised as young males enter a new developmental stage. The lessons of childhood do not suffice for adolescence.

Concluding comment

The findings of this chapter suggest certain specific conclusions:

1. Suicidal patterns cannot be divorced from the social context and social networks in which adolescents live. Focus upon the traditional psychological measures of depression and withdrawal is likely to

miss some of the most important immediate factors in the events that lead up to and account for the occurrence of suicide attempts.

2. There is a close relationship between aggressive behaviors and suicidal actions. But it seems likely that the link is not merely due to individual differences in "aggression". Instead, the variable captures a number of influences, including the greater involvement with drugs and alcohol, deviant peer groups, and habituation to life-threatening activities. Not everyone is tempted to play "Russian roulette", and the events and conditions associated with such activities are linked to a configuration of personal and social factors. Recent neurobiological studies have strongly implicated specific brain transmitter substances and brain nuclei associated with the occurrence of impulsive behaviors, including violence and suicide. This development in neurobiology promises to clarify one of the genetic-biological biases toward impulsive actions, whether suicidal, aggressive, or alcoholic.

3. Social relations can protect adolescents against self-destructive behaviors, or can promote them. Even though the loss and dissolution of close relationships are often seen as a trigger for adolescent suicide, this interpretation requires caution. Such problems are extremely common in adolescence. If social loss is the factor, then the question must be asked why suicide attempts are not even more frequent. The findings suggest that additional factors in the social context and in the individual contribute significantly to suicidal behavior.

4. Gun availability and ownership is startlingly high among the teenage males. This gender difference in ownership and availability helps account for the gender differences in firearm injuries and death. The adolescents more likely to have guns available to them are also more likely to use them and become injured by them. The fact that the guns are transmitted from fathers to sons in early adolescence suggests an important consideration on the relativity of gender typing by fathers to the age and sex of their children. Personality factors are not correlated with gun ownership in boys, but individual differences in aggressive expression and popularity are linked to gun ownership in girls. The non-normative aspect of the behavior in girls is probably the reason that this gender difference is related to personality.

When the findings of this chapter are considered in conjunction with the rest of this volume, they suggest an explanation for some of the large gender differences in morbidity in adolescence. Boys continue through the teenage years to be more direct and "immature" than girls in their social and personal confrontations (see Chapter 4). If these norms for interpersonal behavior are coupled with differential support from parents and peers for involvement in activities that are harmful, a higher incidence of injury and death in males seems predetermined.

We remarked that developmental psychologists think in terms of behavior patterns rather than life and death. An opposite criticism can be made of the health disciplines whose focus is upon morbidity and mortality rather than behavior. In the light of the critical links between behavior and health in this age group, the study of development and social interchanges seems to be as essential for pediatrics and adolescent medicine as, say, the study of physiology and immunology. Yet time is rarely set aside for training in the first domain at any level of medical preparation. It appears to be high time to bring the two worlds together.

TEN

Risks and lifelines

The opportunities of a lifetime

Well, I had some trouble. Yeah, it's been about half the year. Me and Tom, we got in a fight in the bathroom and he pulled a knife on me and I kicked the knife out of his hand and he left me alone and we haven't fought since. Yeah, well, it really wasn't a fight or nothing but it wasn't too tight so I wouldn't call that a fight but we have been friends ever since.

Sean (13 years old)

I knew there was gonna be trouble so I took a bed spring. I put it in my hand you know. I knew it was gonna be more than one, and here they come. Sure enough, it was about four of 'em, and they're sitting there shaking. I wasn't gonna do nothing 'til they started it. When they swung, I started swinging and that's more or less all of it. The officer comes in and gives me a write-up and everybody else one 'cause I defended myself. Nothing come of it because they shipped them back to another prison.

Sean (20 years old)

Lives in progress are moving targets. Endpoints other than death reflect the interests and choices of outside observers, not of nature. So it is with simple judgments of success and failure in living. This chapter examines the developmental trajectories of youths who had been identified as children as being at risk. In our sample of 695 subjects, a subset of 40 boys and 40 girls were identified in matched pairs of highly aggressive and nonaggressive subjects. They were individually tracked from childhood through early maturity. At the time of the last follow-up interview, they were in their early 20s (20–22 years of age). They had been seen annually since the 4th grade or the 7th grade through high school. We begin this chapter with an example that illustrates the folly of categorizing the outcomes of lives into separate bins. We then examine the statistical record, and return to an evaluation of what these findings reveal about the lifelines.

The fluidity of risk

Mary showed serious problems of aggressive behavior as a child, with difficulties that continued into adulthood. Depending upon when her life is frozen for analysis, she may be claimed a "success" for statistical prediction. Yet her life has been anything but static and unchanging. The potentials for change were clearly present, and her behavior actually underwent periodic beneficial changes. These modifications, though real, were short-lived in the broad timeframe of development. The shifts were not sufficient to disengage her from constraints within and without, and to lock her into a different, more conventional trajectory of life. But some changes did occur and persist.

The broader concerns raised by Mary's coming of age involve those pathways that might have been followed, but were not. Other girls in Mary's class were at risk in youth as well. Yet some of them were able to enter the framework of conventional society. When their lives are examined closely, we find that each of them, including Mary's, have hidden competencies in dealing with serious problems of living. In the case of Mary, the strengths may be overlooked by the deviant and unconventional nature of her adaptations. But they are strengths nonetheless.

When we first became acquainted with her, she was 11 years old in a 4th grade classroom at Walnut Valley Elementary School. She was one of the only girls in her grade who had been held back one year. If she had been a different sex and race, she would have been in the majority. Over half of the African-American boys in her school district – 58% to be exact – had been held back at least one year by the end of the 6th grade. She had been in the class since September, having moved to the school district in the fall. In the individual interview at mid-year, she was asked, "Do you have a best friend in school?" She began to cry.

Something truly beneficial happened the next year. She moved to a new school and a new class with a superb and sensitive teacher in charge. Mary responded splendidly; she was no longer considered a problem in school, and she had friends and accomplishments. She looked attractive, behaved confidently, and talked easily, a real change in trajectory. The school was pleased with her, concerned only that her attendance record could be improved. Mary did well throughout the year and was promoted to middle school. Mary clearly had competencies, but they had been previously concealed by other factors.

Her "wishes" for the future – becoming an actress and becoming rich – were not especially realistic nor original, but most are not at this stage of development. More important was that she had at least looked ahead, beyond the here and now. All in all, this year could have been a major turning point in her life.

But when we saw Mary the next year, her relationships and school status had gone downhill. The cycle of rejection, isolation, depression, and failure reappeared. She got into fights with both girls and boys almost daily. There were several attempts at intervention during the year – by school personnel who were sensitive to her needs – but the constraints on her life resisted change.

More generally, Mary's life and the lives of her contemporaries challenge the assumption that problems of living can be lifted out of context. For her, many of the difficulties she encountered were linked together. One led to another, successively constraining her freedom in choice and action. On closer look, these problems were interwoven in her life; they did not appear as separate events. The linkages came into focus as we became better acquainted with Mary, her talents, her goals, and her circumstances of living. Indeed, her choice of friends and actvities helped perpetuate the earlier influences. She actively participated in the direction of her own future through her own decisions and the actions she provoked from others. Similarly, her choices were determined in large measure by accceptance into some groups and rejection by others. These social effects provided a catalyst for consistency over time. On this score, Mary's life is not exceptional in that most positive and negative characteristics occur in clusters. For other girls and boys, the clusters operate in a fail-safe fashion to buffer them from some of the hazards of youth.

Packages of problems

At the outset of this investigation, we expected that the problems of aggression could not be divorced from the other issues of living. Correlated outcomes were therefore considered, including those ordinarily viewed as failures in adaptation (i.e. school dropout, suicide attempts, arrests for violence and crime, incarceration) and those viewed as successes (scholarship and academic progress, awards for athletic achievement and/or performing arts, leadership positions, and club affiliations).

We were guided by the idea that the serious problems of living appear in configurations, not as single variables.[1] Extreme maladjustment in acting-out behavior – extreme aggression in school – is ordinarily associated with deficiencies in school performance and, in the school at large, difficulties in getting along with other children and teachers. But the cluster proposal also indicates that there are some persons who do not do well in school and who are not aggressive, and that there are some people who are aggressive who are not deficient in academics. It suggests that the combination of factors is what might be the most constraining of all, not single events taken alone. For example, if we identified highly aggressive children who were also able to make near-normal adaptations in the domains of school performance, such children should have brighter futures than those characterized by the cluster of problems.

More generally, we were as interested in the lives of people who confounded developmental predictions as those who supported them. Slippage in the accuracy of early developmental assessment occurred in two identifiable groups: (1) highly aggressive children who adapted satisfactorily in adolescence when they were not expected to (i.e. "false positive") and (2) nonaggressive children who encountered serious problems in adolescence despite early nonrisk status (i.e. "false negative"). We were also concerned with the developmental events which operated to maintain stability in lifecourse for the majority of children, for good or for ill.

Our longitudinal outcome measures of these high-risk subjects included information about school dropout and retention, arrest records, substance use, instances of severe aggressive acts, marriage and/or parenthood, social achievement, and environmental-family changes. We were thus able to track multiple domains of adjustment, and to track the ups and downs in their lives by our repeated assessments. First we will cover some ground that we traveled earlier in the book on the identification of risk children. Then we will provide a statistical profile of their general adaptation relative to the matched control group in the early stages of the investigation and their current functions. Lastly, we will put these lives back into context, and examine the lifelines that were available to them.

Longitudinal outcomes

In the CLS research, the risk subgroups consisted of those forty children who were judged by school teachers, principals, and/or counselors to be the most assaultive and violent members of the sample at the time of the original selection. An additional group of forty nonaggressive comparison subjects were identified and matched individually on the basis of sex, race, classroom attended, physical size, socioeconomic status, and chronological age.[2] To qualify for the comparison group, the child could not have been nominated for the high-risk group. That is to say, the comparison group did not comprise particularly well-adjusted children; rather, they simply were not the exemplars of aggressive behavior in the school.

Early adjustment

The risk and control groups differed significantly in a number of characteristics related to school performance and social adaptation. To be sure, they were aggressive in peer relationships. But they were also judged by teachers to have lower academic competence than their peers, and to be less popular. In addition, direct classroom observations indicated reliable group differences in the occurrence of aggressive acts in both cohorts. Parallel effects were obtained in girls and boys, and in both cohorts of subjects. Risk children were also less popular than peers in the comparison group, as evaluated by the ICS-T popularity factor scores. Risk subjects were also more disliked by peers, as inferred from nominations of peers who saw themselves as being bothered and bullied by them.

In keeping with our general findings, risk subjects rated themselves as popular as nonrisk subjects in the ICS-S assessment. Moreover, the risk subjects were no more likely than the matched controls to be rejected from the social structure. Risk subjects differed in the types of friends they had, not the number of friends or the reciprocity of friendships. In the general sample, aggressive subjects tended to affiliate with aggressive peers, and vice versa. The effects were replicated in all sex-grade subgroups.

Later adjustment

An overview of adult adjustment for the matched risk and control subjects is shown in Figure 10.1. This composite index reflects problems of young adult adjustment, namely, school dropout, arrests for serious crime, teenage motherhood, psychiatric residential treatment, and mortality. The index ranged from 0 to 5. As shown in Figure 10.1, the summary picture is dismal for over half of the high-risk children of both cohorts when followed up through young adulthood. These are the

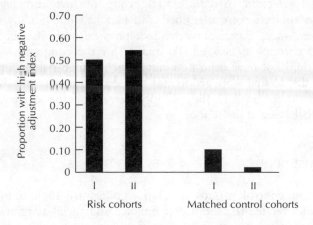

Figure 10.1 Proportion of risk and control subjects in each cohort which obtained high negative indices (3.0) in adulthood.

young people who encountered multiple problems of living, including imprisonment, dropout, and teenage parenthood. Nonetheless, 50% of the risk subjects in Cohort I and 45% in Cohort II avoided problems of adjustment, and 33% (13/40) showed no serious problems in the young adulthood follow up. By contrast, only a small proportion of the control subjects across both cohorts (5%) encountered multiple problems of adjustment in adulthood. Similarly, the majority (70%) showed no serious problems of adulthood in the follow up. The differences between the risk and control subjects in adult adjustment were highly reliable in both cohorts ($p < 0.01$ in Cohort I and $p < 0.001$ in Cohort II). The outcomes in the composite index included early school dropout, criminal offenses, substance use, suicide and psychiatric hospitalization, and teenage parenthood. Each of the domains calls for a careful look.

Early school dropout

The rate of school dropout was significantly higher in the risk group than in the nonaggressive comparison group. Overall, the difference is highly significant, in that three times as many risk subjects (42%) were early school dropouts as control subjects (13%). A closer look at cohort differences indicates that a larger dropout rate occurred among the older risk cohort (47%) than among the younger (36%). There was also a lower dropout rate among the control subjects (0%) in the older cohort than the control subjects in the younger one (25%). The upshot was that the risk-control difference was carried by the subjects who were older at the beginning of the study (13 years of age) than those who were younger (10 years of age).

Two additional factors suggest that dropout rate is a conservative estimate of school difficulties encountered in the highly aggressive subjects. First, subjects in the risk subgroups who remained in school tended to experience more grade failure/grade retention than the matched comparison subjects. Of the twenty-five risk subgroup subjects who remained in school, several (29%) were held back additional years or were placed in special ungraded classes after entering the longitudinal study. Fewer members of the nonrisk comparison group were held back or ungraded (11%). A second and related factor involved pressure by the courts to remain in school. In two instances, the suspension of a prison sentence and/or probation was made contingent by the court upon continued school attendance.

In brief, the risk subgroup has a high level of school problems, reflected both in dropout rates and school retention. The cluster and regression analysis of school dropout and retention in the total sample is presented in Chapter 8. Risk was a major determinant of cluster membership.

Criminal offenses

Significantly more arrests in adolescence for serious offenses (i.e. breaking and entering, assault, drug dealing, vandalism) were observed in the high-risk subgroup than in the nonrisk control subgroup (X^2 (1) = 6.80, $p < 0.01$). Over one-fourth of the high-risk group (26% (10/38)) have been arrested for such offenses compared to one-twentieth of the nonrisk group (5% (2/40)). Three of the high-risk subgroup males have been incarcerated in local state prisons, and two have been fugitives for having escaped or violated probation.

Not all instances of extreme violence observed in this study were prosecuted through the courts. When the assault occurred within the family (such as stabbing the father, mother, brother, or sister), the incident did not usually lead to arrest. When a parent (or stepparent) was the victim, the offending adolescent was typically taken from the home and assigned to a resident psychiatric facility. When another sibling was involved, there was either no change or the victim was taken to another home. Accordingly, a tabulation was made of instances of violence (e.g. stabbing, gun wounds, or assault) regardless of arrest records. This analysis indicates a clear difference between the risk and control groups. No instances of extreme violence were observed in the control group, while approximately one-fourth of the high-risk subjects committed such acts (24%).

Substance use

Since we have not yet reported upon substance use in this book, a brief overview of our general findings are in order. Subjects in the overall CLS were close to the national norms in their use of tobacco, alcohol, and illegal drugs. The proportion of subjects who indicated that they had smoked cigarettes (88%), consumed alcohol (64%), smoked marijuana (19%), and used cocaine (3%) were in line with previous estimates. In general, males were more likely than females to use alcohol and drugs, but the differences were reliable only in the larger cohort (Cohort II). Moreover, there was only one reliable sex difference in tobacco use, regardless of cohort. Equal proportions of boys and girls smoked. But none of the girls regularly chewed tobacco, while 30% of the boys were habitual users of chewing tobacco or dip.

Our subjects were clearly aware when and if substances were legal (e.g. beer drinking was illegal before 21 years of age, and marijuana use was illegal in all but one of the states where our subjects lived). But laws did not preclude the co-occurrence of various substances within persons. In this regard, heavy substance use was correlated across tobacco smoking, alcohol drinking, and marijuana use. The median correlation for girls across the three substances was $r = 0.44$, and the median correlation for boys was $r = 0.31$, and all associations were significant beyond $p < 0.01$. Moreover, cigarette smoking and alcohol drinking were gateways for marijuana use, and marijuana use was a gateway for cocaine and LSD use. In this context, "gateway" means that there exists strong conditional and directional relationships in substance use. For example, if subjects reported marijuana use, the probability was high that they would also report alcohol use ($P = 0.94$). But the relationship was not symmetrical. If subjects reported alcohol use, the probability was $P = 0.30$ that they would also report marijuana use. Denise Kandel and her colleagues have reported elegant analyses of these gateway processes for substance use (Kandel & Yamaguchi, 1993).

A distinctive feature of this investigation was that we could track forward the multiple factors in childhood associated with substance use in adolescence and young adulthood. The patterns with respect to the early diagnosis of risk were clear, even in the younger cohort. On the basis of the correlations among amount of substance use, we derived an index of substance use which was a combination of the three measures of cigarette, alcohol, and drug use. This summary index of substance use, along with the separate measures of tobacco, alcohol, and drug use, constituted criteria for a family of multiple regression analyses. The predictor variables included the subject's risk status at the onset of the study, in addition to demographic variables (sex, socioeconomic status, race) and the ICS social competence ratings. In Cohort 1, two predictors emerged in the prediction of substance use with a multiple correlation of $R = 0.31$ ($p < 0.001$). Race was the first factor to emerge in the stepwise regression solution, in that African-American youths in this sample were less likely than white youths to use substances. High-aggressive risk was the second factor to emerge in the prediction of substance use in high school.

The finding that aggressive risk nominations and ratings were closely linked to substance use in high school was expected (see Anderson, Bergman, & Magnusson, 1989). The race difference was not and it requires comment. First, this reversal of stereotype is not without precedence. Similar findings have been reported on the lower incidence rate of substance abuse among African-American youths (Hawkins, Catalano, & Miller, 1992). Second, the interpretations sometimes offered (i.e. denial and failure of self-disclosure) seem unlikely to hold for the consumption of legal substances as for illegal ones. On this score, we found significant race differences in the reported amount of tobacco smoking and alcohol use as well as illicit substance use. Together, these results suggest that the difference was not a reporting bias. David Hawkins and his colleagues have recently prepared an excellent review of substance use which helps place these results in context (Hawkins, Catalono, & Miller, 1992).[3]

Suicide and psychiatric hospitalization

There were no completed suicides in the risk and comparison subgroups. The three documented suicide attempts all involved hospitalization (two high-risk subjects, one male and one female, and one control female). It should be noted that both suicide attempts in the high-risk subgroup were coupled with stabbing a parent (see Chapter 9). Serious suicidal ideation occurred in the interviews of two other subjects (one control and one risk subgroup).

Consistent with companion analyses, there were no differences between risk and control subjects in psychiatric hospitalization. The two cases for institutional treatment both involved control subjects.

There was no indication in this investigation that the most serious cases of aggressive risk in childhood were associated with heightened risk of residential psychiatric treatment consistent with Magnusson (1988).

Teenage parenthood

The subjects in our study were sexually productive, regardless of their risk status. By June 1992, they were already parents to 198 children, the large majority of which were conceived and born while the parents were themselves still youths and teenagers. In the total sample, 16% of the subjects were teenage parents. In the risk sample, rate of teenage parenthood was twice as high (39%). This propensity for the more aggressive, acting-out youths to become parents is confirmed when the sample of risk youths is extended to include the broader sample of subjects who had been nominated but who, because of the need to equate the groups for sex and classroom, were not included in the risk-control analysis.

These descriptive results were confirmed by a logistic multiple regression analysis of teenage parenthood.[4] We found that being judged at high risk for aggressive behavior at the beginning of the investigation typically emerged as the first predictor of subsequent teenage parenthood. The finding held for both males and females, analyzed separately. Socioeconomic status (SES) was also important for females in both cohorts, but not for males. The factors that did not make it into the equation were measures of popularity and race. Presumably the variance attributable to race in females was captured by SES, in that SES was correlated with both race and early parenthood.

One troubling feature of these results should be noted. In the total sample, only 42% of the infants were living with both biological parents after they were two years of age. At this early state of family development, relationships were unstable for most subjects, regardless of their earlier risk status.

A recent report by Lisa Serbin, Alex Schwartzman, and colleagues in Montreal indicates that the relationship of teenage pregnancy to aggressive behavior is not unique to our sample (Serbin, et al., 1991). In their long-term followup, these investigations found multiple differences in parenthood and risk for their children between girls who were identified as being aggressive in childhood compared to nonaggressive girls. Among other things, the children were more likely to appear in the emergency room for treatment of injury. High aggressive girls (as judged by 7th grade teacher ratings) were also more likely to be treated for sexually transmitted diseases and become pregnant in their late teens and early twenties.

Does it not seem curious that fighting in childhood is related to making love and having children in adolescence? While we can only speculate at this time, three comments are noteworthy. First, the strength of the relationship differed between the sexes. Among males, the aggression-parenthood linkage was robust in both cohorts, analyzed separately. But for females, it was reliable only for the younger cohort. Parenthood is in general more common for females than males. However, being aggressive makes a bigger difference for males than for females. Relative to their nonaggressive counterparts, highly aggressive males are more likely to become teenage parents than are highly aggressive females.

Second, the classification of "aggressive risk" may achieve its predictive power because it indexes a configuration of characteristics – including impulsive expression and antisocial behaviors – rather than aggression, considered alone. Accordingly, the risk judgments in childhood may index a broad spectrum of difficulties, which includes aggressive behavior among other things.

Finally, our preliminary observations suggest that parenthood was very important in the lives of virtually every one of these young people. It provided them not only with responsibility but with a new opportunity to love and to be loved. They see themselves as the most important person in the infant's life. This emotional and psychological aspect of parenthood is difficult to quantify by our available procedures, yet it is nonetheless real. Any evaluation of parenthood, including the parenthood of teenagers, must figure in the personal significance of this accomplishment and this relationship.

Overcoming the odds

In addition to group differences, the data permit a focus on individual trajectories of development and change. Of special interest are the environmental and personal factors which are associated with survival, despite early risk. Recall that a primary aim of our work was to clarify the conditions under which we could demonstrate that the early diagnosis was wrong. On this score, changes from the expected life-course can arise for at least three different reasons in longitudinal work:

1. Developmental novelty. One possibility is that the change may be due to new circumstances that arise during the course of living. That is, people can be entrenched in a given trajectory, then deflected

from it. Once an individual is accurately diagnosed, and the trajectory reliably established, we can observe lives in progress to determine if there are significant deflections from expectations, and why they occur.

2. **Errors in diagnosis.** A second possibility is that what looks to be a developmental change could be an illusion, because the "change" reflected errors in measurement. In the case of measurement error, apparent changes and instabilities would arise because of mismeasurement. For instance, a person may show large fluctuations in a behavior pattern because the procedures employed at the different time points had large errors of measurement, a point emphasized by Block (1977) and Wohlwill (1973). To correct for errors of measurement, the usual solution is to merge across adjacent data points, average across people, and correct for attenuation. Curves become smoother and correlations become larger. While this seems entirely reasonable because of the need to protect against errors of measurement, it creates new hazards. Actual shifts in the lifecourse can thereby be eliminated by the statistical corrections. By aggregating across data points and across people, lives can be made to look a lot more stable than they actually are. It is ironic that statistics which are designed to clarify longitudinal patterns paradoxically can make it harder to recognize changes.

3. Real changes in development. A third possibility is that novelties may arise in development which lead to real changes in the lifecourse. An understanding of how these novelties arise in nature can provide important clues as to how to reproduce them on purpose. After all, this is the goal of education and therapy.

The logical problem in identifying changes in development is similar to the one encountered with "insignificance" in classical hypothesis testing. When you obtain negative effects in research, such as the failure to predict over time, you cannot be certain about interpretation, even when a developmental model may have led you to expect low predictability. The bias in longitudinal research has been to search for statistically significant longitudinal coefficients, not insignificant correlation. How can we escape the dilemma? A first step is to demonstrate empirically that the measures are robust and that regularities over time can be rigorously identified, if they exist. A second step is to formulate with greater clarity the conditions that would lead us to expect changes in development, and precisely when and why changes should occur.

We observed higher levels of stability than we had anticipated. Furthermore, the original categorization was based on a single characteristic of the child, namely, extreme aggressive behavior in school. This stability seems to contradict a belief in the contextual relativity of behavior, and the belief that you should not lift a single variable from its social matrix. The simple diagnostic procedure of asking teachers and principals to identify the most aggressive kids in the school provided a robust prediction for later adaptation beyond the school, even for measures of life and death.

It should be recalled that the figures show an integration of information over a period of six to seven years. These are lives in progress, and the integration obscured the deflections, changes, and experimental starts observed. Indeed, the careful examination of the people whose lives seemed not to change from the early risk predictions indicated that there were plenty of shifts over adolescence. Virtually all of the true-positive "risk" subjects showed major deflections from trajectory, even though it was rare that the changes were maintained.

Why did some shifts in trajectory become enduring while most did not? The answer seems to lie not simply in the person, but in whether the changes were supported by the other forces in the person's life. This brings us back to the folly of divorcing a single trend or shift behavior from the broader contexts in which they are embedded. Developmental theorists, from Magnusson (1988) to Bronfenbrenner (1979) argue for the necessity of considering regulatory constraints across levels, from individual to dyad to social network to society. Furthermore, our data indicate that biases which operate at one level are usually correlated with those that operate at other levels. These systems collaborate rather than compete, and they funnel behavior in the direction best suited for the context in which development occurs.[5] The further we depart from an established trajectory – to a point – the stronger are the forces that push/pull the individual back.

The forces recur and are mutually supportive over the lifecourse, not merely at its beginning. There is often a "catch up" (or "slow down") effect in social development that parallels Tanner's (1962) description of physical development. It is not that potentials for change do not exist, they seem to occur daily. We suggest that they do not endure because of the balance of external and internal constraints. There usually exists a "developmental homeostasis" in social development because of coincident vulnerabilities.[6]

Jane's life does not stand alone. Despite the seeming regularity of outcomes depicted, not one individual was as stable, predetermined, or without hope as the figures suggest. Obscured in the boxscore was the fact that each person had benefited from real changes in their lifecourse. Some of these were momentary, some of them lasted a week; some lasted a year. And some endured.

Overall, we have been struck by the conservatism and regularity in the lifecourse of these subjects, despite the dynamic changes that occur in their lives on virtually a daily basis. When enduring changes in trajectory did occur, they were not in a single characteristic, but in whole configurations of influence. These configurations included drastic changes in family structure (adoption, emancipation), movement to an entirely different region (below the equator in one case), supportive marriages (some of which endure), and influential people at school or home who intervened at multiple levels. A trusting relationship with a responsible adult who is committed to the child is of singular importance in correcting trajectories.

The adjustment–nonadjustment distinction, though useful for gross classification, may be misleading when applied without regard to individual circumstances. On this score, certain girls were classified as making marginal adjustments because they dropped out of school and/or married very early. Nonetheless, some of them are currently living productive lives which belie their background. We have covered some of these lives in the course of this book. One is Lydia who emancipated herself from her family and is now completing a college degree in computer science. Another is Melissa. She was adopted, finished high school, and is completing a community college degree. In each of these cases, the biological parent had abused or neglected the child. Yet the girls were not entirely abandoned in the teenage years. In each case, women unrelated to the girl were willing and able to give a great deal and help the girl through a successful adolescence.

For those boys who remained in an unchanged home and school environment, the development of a distinctive and admired skill seems to have been important. Sports participation was the most accessible avenue for many of the males in this sample, but involvement in the performing arts (e.g. choir, band) provided additional routes for acceptance in the school and the community. To the extent that students excelled in these activities, the likelihood was greatly increased that they would be integrated into the conventional social network. For example, one participant who was the starting quarterback on the football team, was subsequently elected a popular club president and high-school homecoming king. The school invested in him, and he reciprocated.

A comment is in order on the control subjects who encountered serious problems of adaptation in adolescence. Two of the control subjects expressed suicidal ideation and experienced psychiatric distress. The one control male who exhibited problems of externalization (running away, breaking and entering) had high scores on the aggressive factor in the annual teacher and peer ratings. The peer network in which he became involved after elementary school directly supported delinquent activities. The boy's family is intact, though his elderly parents are distressed, they are ineffectual in monitoring and regulating his activities.

Happily, there were also enduring "failures" of expectation; or more accurately, changes in developmental trajectories. About half of the highly aggressive subjects were able to adapt satisfactorily in adolescence, despite odds. Though the reasons for the shifts in developmental trajectory seem diverse, certain commonalities may nonetheless be recognized. For those who remained in school, the development of distinctive skills or talents was a common route to acceptance in the conventional social system by peers or adults. Although athletic ability and/or physical attractiveness are not necessary for gaining status in high school, they are surely not handicaps. Other entry skills included participation in the performing arts, modeling, cheerleading, student government, and scholarship. The emergence of socially desirable personal attributes or skills at adolescence in one domain can strongly influence adaptation in other, seemingly unrelated areas.

But adolescent adaptation is more complex than the stereotypes of the adolescents themselves would have it. External changes of a variety of sorts: a new beginning provided by moving to a new town or across the country, resolution of family problems so more parental attention can be given to the adolescent, adoption by adults who are willing to accept responsibility for guidance and effective mentoring, can have a profound influence on the overall quality of the adolescent's adjustment. Even instances of apparent failure must be viewed in the context of what could have been if no intervention had occurred. Absolute criteria for adaptation can be deceptive if applied without regard to individual circumstances. Even marginal adjustments may be counted as successes, depending upon the person's opportunities.

Adolescence posed hazards for virtually all of the young people in this study, whether or not they had been earlier identified as aggressive. A scan of some of the changes and challenges in the lives of the control sample suggests several were "at risk" according to some criteria (e.g. only 40% of the females in the control group lived continuously with both biological parents, the same as the females in the risk group). For many of these girls, successful progress through adolescence has been a real accomplishment.

The findings suggest that the dynamic forces of development may be balanced from within and without, and most people are kept upon relatively stable behavioral trajectories during adolescence. In this regard, measures of "aggression" appear to index broader problems which, in aggregate, constrain the individual's choices and limit the range of future adaptations. The destinies of the subjects were not wholly fixed; they evolved, and the eventual outcomes were determined by multiple factors (Brim & Kagan, 1980). Looking backward, most major changes in the lifecourse of individuals may be explained (or rationalized) in terms of changes that occurred within the people and/or their environments. It is also clear that some of the primary modifications in personal attributes and circumstances could not have been written in advance, and evolved in the course of living and development. It was, moreover, a process of selective evolution; the modifications were neither happenstance nor void of constraint or direction. These solutions of nature, if understood and reproduced, may generate novel therapeutic strategies and new developmental lifelines.

Comparisons and conclusions

There can be no question about the ability of simple methods to identify children who are likely to encounter grave problems in the course of adolescence. The present techniques from consensus school nominations to peer and/or teacher ratings provide inexpensive but effective assessment procedures. A significant proportion of the subjects who were expected to have difficulties in adolescence did indeed experience them, ranging from school dropout and teenage parenthood to arrest and imprisonment, all the way to death itself.

These outcomes are consistent with other reports which have focused on continuities of problem behaviors from childhood to adolescence and early adulthood (e.g. Elliott, Huizinga, & Menard, 1989; Farrington, 1986; Huesmann, Eron, Lefkowitz, & Walder, 1984; Kagan & Moss, 1962; Loeber, 1982; Magnusson, 1988; McCord, 1979, 1986; Moss & Susman, 1980; Parke & Slaby, 1983; Olweus, 1979; Olweus, Block, & Radke-Yarrow, 1986; Patterson, 1979, 1986; Pulkkinen, 1993). Together, these writers conclude that:

1. Acting-out aggressive behavior in childhood is a significant antecedent for a full range of criminal and substance abuse difficulties at maturity;
2. The pattern of relationship between early social, acting-out difficulties and later problems holds for both males and females.
3. The traditional psychological focus on the pathology of withdrawn, shy behavior seems to be misplaced in the light of the predictive significance of acting-out behavior patterns. Even certain "internalizing" problems have been linked, at maturity, to patterns of early acting-out behaviors.

These convergent results have emerged in longitudinal studies conducted in several disciplines from criminology and sociology to epidemiology and developmental psychology. They tell rather the same story, and their significance cannot be overstated. The longitudinal findings show that there is considerable order in the development of deviant behavior, despite individuality and diversity. Such a system confirms that a developmental science of human behavior is not only possible, but feasible and socially productive.

Lives undergo constant change, and so do forces that operate upon them. We found, for example, in our analyses of social networks that cliques become increasingly segregated as our subjects moved from the 4th and 5th grades to the 7th and 8th grades. Similarly, socioeconomic class became highly salient about the time subjects began to get involved in dating and heterosexual parties. The sociocultural forces of school, home, and the community that were latent in childhood operated like a sledgehammer in adolescence. The "latency period" takes on new meaning when these social influences are considered. Rather than a phase of quiescence, middle childhood may be a phase of life where children are permitted to cross boundaries and explore friendships that become closed to them after they enter adolescence.

Risk is usually seen as a failure in life, and perhaps it is. But for some adolescents, behaviors such as school dropout and aggression may also be part of their plans and expectations. At least some individuals are fitting into the roles for which they have been groomed by their families. The values of the researcher and the larger society are not always the values of subjects and their social networks, and we should be sensitive to the difference.

Even though our findings indicate that for most people there are impressive continuities in social adaptation, we have observed that many children show significant changes over the lifecourse. Where the happy changes have endured, it was because they did not stand alone, and typically involved the commitment of a responsible and supportive adult. In one such case, a sympathetic coach intervened with the boy's parents, other teachers, and inspired the kid himself. In another case, the mother remarried, reclaimed her children from the county residential home, and took them several states away. When they endure, successful interventions were associated with other major and correlated changes in the circumstances of the child's life, including changes in the child's own behaviors and goals. Taken alone, single changes tended not to survive.

Adolescence is popularly viewed as a period of emancipation and freedom with the emergence of a new identity. But for most of our subjects, adolescence has a different message. It is a moment of truth where the constraints of their social and academic opportunities emerge with a heavy hand. For many adolescents, their ideas and attitudes about themselves are more likely to change than are their trajectories of social development.

There has been considerably more regularity in individual lives than we thought we would find, or should find. Lives seem not to be predestined so much as they are kept on course by correlated forces from within and without. Yet there are instances of remarkable and durable shifts in trajectory. In those cases of enduring and productive change, there is an engagement of internal forces coupled with changes in the familial, peer, school, or broader social system. Understanding how these forces operate over time in individual lives is critical for the design of effective social interventions.

ELEVEN

The developmental perspective

Puzzles and proposals

A good scientific theory is under tension from two opposing forces: the drive for evidence and the drive for system. . . . If either of these drives were unchecked by the other, it would issue in something unworthy of the name of scientific theory: in the one case a mere record of observations, and in the other a myth without foundation.

W. V. Quine (1981)

It is time to step back and bring together some of the ideas and findings. Development is concerned with more than events in infancy. In its modern form, development constitutes the backbone for behavioral science and the perspective for a new view on social policy. This chapter is about the implications for scientific structure; Chapter 12 is about concrete interventions and current policies. We believe that our subjects have earned the right to be heard, and the implications of their lives to be made explicit.

One of the robust findings of modern biobehavioral science is that much of the individual's behavior over a lifetime is probabilistic but conservative. Social behavior is a lot more predictable and considerably more organized than many of us had thought it would and should be. One of the stories of this book is that it is constrained by biological background, social circumstances, and physical environment. The closer the investigator peers, the more finely organized are the developmental and evolutionary constraints upon behavior. There may be an important lesson here for us who aspire to understand children and youth and the passages of life. It is a curious finding that most rapid and efficient adaptations in development and evolution arise from constancy and constraint. In other words, flexibility and adaptation

239

grow out of organization and discipline, not out of chaos and inconstancy.

Over the past thirty years, a modern synthesis on behavioral development has emerged that extends across the social and bio-behavioral sciences.[1] The perspective is provocative and, in a quiet way, revolutionary. In one form or another, this developmental view has guided contemporary longitudinal investigations in a drive for relevant evidence. The synthesis reflects the convergence and refinement of ideas from the studies of nonhuman psychobiological development and evolution, human cognitive and social development, and prior longitudinal studies. In this chapter, we offer an introduction to the developmental synthesis and its relevance for solving some puzzles of the transitions of youth. First, we cover why a synthesis was called for.

Talking past each other

Psychologists, sociologists, and other social scientists are rarely at a loss for explanations. This is due in part to the separate evolution of theories, hypotheses, speculations, fanciful ideas, and myths about human behavior that dwell in different lands, with only few guides to distinguish between them. Alfred Baldwin (1967) was right on target when he observed that developmental theories talk past each other. A quarter of a century later, they still do.

The lack of connection of theories to each other and all to the concrete phenomena of living and development seems more than accidental. Basic theories of development in human beings were formulated before there was objective information about the essential phenomena to which the theories were addressed. Precise studies of people over their lifespan is a recent development. In the early stages of the discipline – when the basic theories were formulated – the most influential theory was based upon the clinical retrospections of middle-aged patients, predominantly wealthy women. These retrospections and social constructions were melded with the intuitions, observations, and insights of Sigmund Freud and his collaborators to produce classical psychoanalysis.

In the mid-20th century, experimental psychology became a major player in the theoretical analysis of human development. Psychoanalytic theory was married with the results of short-term experiments and learning concepts to produce an enormously influential set of ideas, labeled social learning theory. After three generations of trans-formation, social learning theory is still alive and influential, and sometimes pitted against other models that give greater attention to mental phenomena, on the one hand, and dynamic and genetic models that focus on emotional states and psychopathology. They mostly talk past each other.

Early in the 19th century, Auguste Comte stimulated the study of social processes and produced the terms "sociology" and "social science". The idea was to bring together and integrate the separate disciplines concerned with human behavior. By the 20th century, social science had become fragmented into a patchwork of disciplines separated by aims, methods, and concepts. Leaving aside theories that have neither a drive for system nor a drive for evidence, contemporary approaches continue to have different goals and objectives. These give rise to different methodologies, observations, and ways of conceptually organizing information.

Which approach to youth and transitions is more accurate? An eclectic answer would be that each model captures some of the truth for some of the issues. The larger problem is that virtually all social behaviors are multiply determined, and, accordingly, it should be possible to find empirical support for any sane proposal on the matter. Researchers in development are usually confronted with networks of relationships, not single antecedent–consequent links. This state of affairs has yielded many positive findings and interpretations. The abundance of "significant" antecedent–consequent linkages in adolescent research has also had a negative side, shifting the responsibility for understanding phenomena away from the data. The findings can become projective tests for the different disciplines, where interpretations are determined as much by theoretical presuppositions as by the total pattern of empirical evidence.

The developmental synthesis

Our longitudinal research was guided by a theoretical synthesis on social development that has gradually gained acceptance in modern accounts of human behavior.[2] This theoretical work is part of a broader movement in developmental science, where the systems approaches of social ecology and developmental psychobiology have virtually displaced competitors. But the developmental perspective goes beyond systems theory in order to address ontogenetic change and resilience. These ideas have large consequences for how one should proceed to understand social development. Seven propositions include:

A child develops and functions psychologically as an integrated unit. Maturational, experiential, and cultural contributions are fused in ontogeny. Single aspects do not develop and function in isolation, and should not be divorced from the totality in analysis.

The holistic view of development addresses the question of how ontogeny is guided. The proposition that the individual develops and functions as a totality and that each aspect of individual functioning gets its functional meaning from the role it plays in the totality is not only a theoretical statement; it has broad empirical support in modern biological science. Thus the optimal functioning of the totality serves as the goal for the development and functioning of the separate parts. No part develops or functions with its own optimal functioning as the sole goal. The cardiac system provides a biological illustration of the operation of self-organizing systems. If one or several components collapse or fail, the remaining components reorganize themselves so that the total cardiac system fulfills its role in the support of the organismic system. Nonetheless, the holistic view has not been dominant in personality and social research. Research traditionally has been designed around single variables and their interrelations with each other. Examples in longitudinal study would include such variables as "aggression" and "intelligence". Within the modern holistic frame-work, such variables (including the effects of age of menarche) cannot be effectively studied if divorced from the social and environmental context in which they occur. In the above instance, what may appear as an outcome of early maturation in girls has been fused with other features of the person and social setting.

> Children develop and function in a dynamic, continuous, and reciprocal process of interaction with their environments, including relations with other individuals, groups, and the subculture.

This second proposition follows directly from the holistic assumption, and should properly be considered a corollary of it. It deals with bidirectionality of social influence and how individuals are synchronized with each other and with their contexts. The idea is embodied in the proposal that the person is an active, purposeful agent in continuous moment-to-moment interaction with the social as well as the nonsocial world.

When we emphasize the reciprocal character of the process in which the individual and the environment have engaged, it is not an interplay of two equal parts. The main organizing principle for a child's active dealing with the outer world is their cognition of the social and physical environment and connected motives, goals, values, and emotions. This mental, mediational system of an individual is framed in the process of interaction with the environment. At each stage, it plays an organizing role in the child's interaction with the environment.

One other question raised by this view of reciprocating persons is the issue of individual integrity and interpersonal synchrony. How does an individual serve two masters at the same time? How is it possible to maintain internal balance, yet adapt to other people? In this regard, reciprocity and synchrony imply constraints on behavior and action. That is, not all forms of synchrony between people and settings are feasible, and most relationships will be resisted to the extent that major changes are required within the person. Bidirectionality does not presuppose mutuality of influence, or that the weights of influence will be equivalent at all stages of ontogeny. On the contrary, one of the more compelling issues is to determine how the bidirectional process operates, and when and why differential influences are observed in infancy, childhood, adolescence, and maturity. This implies an analysis of how the individual's mediating cognitive–emotional subsystems develop through maturation and experience and how they function in the interactional process.

In the accommodations of human development, particularly social patterns, the actions and counteractions of other people constitute major external sources of behavioral organization. When this proposition is taken seriously, the detailed, longitudinal investigation of social behaviors becomes a matter of high priority for the biological sciences and the psychological ones.

> The child's functioning depends upon and influences the reciprocal interaction among subsystems within the individual; namely, the organization of behavioral, cognitive, emotional, biochemical, morphological, perceptual, and biological factors over time.

The point is also a corollary of the holistic proposition. That biological states can affect emotions, cognitions, and behaviors cannot be gainsaid. Nor can effects in the opposite direction be ignored. The feedback loops within and between these systems over development are a broader issue that Gottlieb (1983) refers to as the issue of structure–function bidirectionality.

A methodological implication is that studies in behavioral genetics and neurobiology should begin with detailed accounts of development, especially psychological development. Actions, emotions, and cognitions – the stuff of psychology – have a special status for organismic adaptation and integration. Psychological functioning can be reduced to "biological structure" only in a trivial and misleading sense. It is a mild irony that several areas of biology – sociobiology, ethology, and behavioral zoology

– appreciate the primacy of social behavior, while the point remains unrecognized by many in psychology.

Novel patterns of individual functioning arise during individual ontogeny.

Tracing backward from adulthood to childhood to infancy reveals few novelties in individual functioning. But it is a different story if we reverse the analysis and work forward, beginning from the embryonic and infancy state and advance to childhood, adolescence, maturity, and senescence. In the lifetime of each individual, certain novel behaviors and thoughts emerge. These include the development of the ability to locomote, ingest solid foods, think, to speak, and affiliate in groups. In addition, as the above research illustrates, the onset of the ability to procreate is an emergent, novel function with multiple consequences. Such novelties can reorganize existing patterns, or create entirely new ones.

Standard theoretical constructs and statistical models are poorly equipped to address either type of novelty. Ordinarily this difficulty has been solved by the use of the same trait to describe seemingly similar activities over the life span. But a problem arises when constructs that adequately describe behavior in one stage of development are applied to subsequent stages, despite changes in operational definition. For example, the operations employed to identify aggressiveness in 3–4-year-old children are qualitatively different from 9 to 10 year olds and 17 to 18 year olds. To use the same construct to refer to qualitatively different behaviors can obscure the new phenomena and the mechanisms by which they are established. An equally common temptation is to use quantitative transformations, such standard scores as IQ, that wipe out real differences and create the illusion of a common dimension despite qualitative differences over time. A large effort has been made in traditional methods of psychology to get rid of the effects of time and age.

> Differences in the rate of development may produce major differences in the organization and configuration of psychological functions. The developmental rate of individual components may be accelerated or delayed relative to other features.

Individual development reflects a variety of ontogenetic trajectories. Sexual development is a case in point. Sexual development is not unitary. Some features of the sexual adaptation of humans, such as gonadal structure and function, resist the effects of variations in experience at puberty. Other aspects of sexual behavior, such as preferred sexual activities and partners, may be strongly influenced in the pubertal years. Different features of sexuality call for different epigenetic landscapes, and different formulations of bidirectionality. Acceleration in the age of menarche in humans has been associated with various outcomes, most of which have been viewed as negative for girls and positive for boys (Simmons & Blyth, 1987; Magnusson *et al.*, 1985). Beyond biology, the change in rate of development occasioned by early entry into school (by chance or by geography) has been associated with accelerated cognitive development in children. The advantages are enduring, and they extend beyond scholastic achievement to include advances in basic information processing and intellectual test performance (Morrison, 1991).

These concepts have a common focus upon the rate of development. If modifications in rate occur in the right system at the right time, slight variations can produce manifold differences. The concept extends beyond psychology into neurobiology and evolution, although our present focus is on individual functioning and development.

> Patterns of psychological functioning develop like dynamic systems, in that they are extremely sensitive to the conditions under which they are formed. The emergence of psychological patterns cannot be described as a hierarchical organization, nor can they be reduced to simpler experiential antecedents or more elementary biological units.

According to this proposal, it is an illusion to think of individual functioning as being built up in a hierarchical fashion. It makes no difference whether the hierarchy is presumed to be established upon biological mechanisms or upon early experiences. Instead, elements of experience and biology are seen as undergoing organization or reorganization at key points in ontogeny. During such periods of organization, preexisting features of the child and novel characteristics are brought into alignment and synchronized in ways that enhance individual functioning and accommodation. The nature of the organization is thus mutually dependent upon events within and without.

In modern physical science, this general conception that things change suddenly by fits and starts has been called "catastrophe theory" (Zeeman, 1976). It reflects the proposition that relatively few phenomena in nature are orderly and well behaved; on the contrary, the world is full of sudden transformation and divergence. Nonetheless, there is psychological lawfulness and mathematical order to be found in an analysis of the transformations themselves (Zeeman, 1976).

Conservation in development is supported by constraints from without and from within, and by the correlated action of external and internal forces. The upshot is that social and cognitive organization in development tend to be continuous and conservative, despite continuous change.

Initially, these final two points may appear to negate the earlier propositions of development. After observing that individual development was not strictly hierarchical, we here propose that it is as conservative as it is plastic and malleable. The theoretical problem is to explain how conservatism arises in the midst of change, some of which has been described as "chaotic". The holistic assumption implies conservatism and order. When, for example, two people are synchronized in their actions, the behavior of each provides directions and constraints for the other. Should the constraints be violated, the relationship is itself challenged because of the lack of synchrony. In most relationships and in most social groups, there are strong pressures for conformity in children and youth.

The challenge for contemporary theory in development is to establish a perspective that is broad enough to integrate the multiple subprocesses of behavior, but precise enough to direct the drive for evidence. Without such a model, contemporary research has increasingly relied upon advances in statistical modeling in order to unravel the relevant processes. An attraction of these procedures (e.g. multivariate analyses, linear structural equations) is that they permit the simultaneous evaluation of multiple variables, rank them in weight, and provide guides for eliminating insignificant factors. When the limitations of data or statistics are encountered, assumptions can be made to simplify the model. This analytic strategy has promoted advances in identifying the roles of interactional control, social learning, self-concepts, socioeconomic factors, maturational influences, and psychobiology in behavioral control. Such progress would have been difficult without advanced computer algorithms.

Eight puzzles and the transitions of youth

Some comments are in order on the relevance of the developmental perspective to eight "puzzles" of youth. The puzzles refer to matters that have been debated in the scientific literature and reflect different common-sense beliefs about the nature and properties of the teenage years.

Critical periods of development

Are the first three years critical for the establishment of personality and, if so, why worry about childhood, youth, and early maturity? This question concerns the developmental timing for the organization of human nature. The role of early experience in establishing personality and social behavior patterns has been debated in one form or another since 1897, when J. M. Baldwin wrote that "personality is, after all, a continuously changing thing". Sigmund Freud shortly afterwards made the opposite point. He argued for the primacy of early experience, along with the concepts of fixation, regression, and irreversibility.[3] Ethologist Konrad Lorenz and zoologist John Paul Scott elaborated this theory with direct observations of critical stages in the social development of geese, sheep, and dogs.[4] Recent empirical evaluations of the concept of "critical period" have led to a refinement of the idea. It has been discovered there is considerably more malleability in behavior than was originally recognized.[5]

The matter speaks to a core proposition of developmental theory, namely, the events that trigger the establishment of a behavior pattern are usually different from the events that maintain it. This proposition has a deceptively broad application for behavior. It has been employed to explain diverse phenomena, from the distinctive effects of early maturation *versus* late maturation in girls[6] and prepubertal *versus* post-pubertal castration in cats[7] to the critical period for first language learning and the role of infantile social attachment for friendships in childhood and adolescence.[8] The developmental synthesis holds that both early experiences and later ones may be critical, yet for different reasons. The scientific task is to determine how the effects work in any given behavioral domain, and why they have different impacts at different ages. Urie Bronfenbrenner, whose arguments and ideas paved the way for the adoption of Head Start, has argued that the first three years are important, but so are the next three, and so are the transition years of youth.[9]

The understanding of early relationships presupposes a recognition of new issues arising in development that demand the reorganization of earlier relationships. More broadly, the failure of relationships to undergo major modifications over time could represent a dysfunction of adaptation. Furthermore, these modifications do not occur willy-nilly. On the contrary, universal, predictable and sequential stages in intelligence, physical development, and social behaviors exist. Youth is a stage in life where there is a reorganization in virtually all domains of behavior (Cairns, 1986a). Social development is not fixed, neither by genes nor by earlier experience.

Social synchrony

Psychoanalyst Eric Fromm captured the central point in the title of his provocative book, *Escape from Freedom*.[10] Youth are caught between their need for autonomy and their need for continued dependence. To escape this dilemma, freedom may be reduced, say, by joining a fraternity, converting to Hare Krishna, enlisting in the army, or getting married. In the developmental perspective, the "escape from freedom" is part of a broader dilemma between internal harmony, and synchrony with the acts of other people. At any stage of development, a balance must be achieved between internal harmony and social synchrony. This is the conflict implicit in all social interactions, where two or more people must coordinate their individual goals and behaviors. The remarkable accomplishment of everyday life is that both masters can be served simultaneously. From birth to death, individuals are biased toward social exchanges.

Few teenagers spend their days, or nights, contemplating the existential dilemma of personal autonomy and social dependence. These issues are resolved in the concrete reality of living, usually without awareness. When youths interact, they implicitly provide direction and support for the thoughts and actions of each other. The social actions are thus coordinated with internal direction and goals. When such synchrony fails, the interaction ceases or conflicts arise. These two goals – social synchrony and internal consistency – are simultaneously met when the two individuals adopt common directions. Byproducts of this process include similar patterns of emotional expression, parallel strategies, and/or "thinking along the same lines". That is, biases toward synchrony and similarity are built into the structure and dynamics of exchanges. But accommodations are not inevitable, or there would be no divorces or realignments of friendship.[11]

Following J. M. Baldwin (1897) and H. S. Sullivan (1940), we cannot hope to understand an individual's behaviors and beliefs independently of the social network in which they are embedded. The proper focus for the study of youths is the individual and the social systems in which they are enmeshed, both family and peers. Accordingly, peer groups and social networks should have a pervasive influence upon adolescent behavior, from high levels of academic accomplishment or dropout to athletic achievement or serious drug abuse.

Gordon Allport (1937) pointed out that individuals tend to take on the characteristics, preferences, and styles of the functions they serve in work and life. Novelist Kurt Vonnegut made the same point in *Mother Night*, when his hero observes, "you'd better be careful about who you pretend to be, because that's who you will become".[12] Allport's descriptive label for this phenomenon was functional autonomy. The reciprocity proposal goes beyond description to suggest an explanation for how such actions become part of the self. People who become highly skilled in particular social roles can become captured not only by emergent internal consistencies but by the reactions and expectations of others. Not only can youth become proficient and comfortable in their roles as an "excellent student", "cheerleader", "joker", or "rebel", the reactions of other people help keep them in these roles. To the extent there is continuing internal and external support for particular actions, the term functional autonomy is misleading. "Social synchrony" may better capture both the phenomenon and its mediation.

To what end: perfection or adaptation?

The question of how the goals of development are established speaks to a third puzzle of ontogeny. How are the outcomes of adolescence determined, and how are individual goals established and changed? Taking the second part of the question first, youths may be expected to adopt goals in keeping with the systems of which they are a part, or slightly beyond. Accordingly, the goals and plans of youths seem to reflect in large measure the contexts in which they live.[13] The transition of adolescence requires teenagers to begin to match their plans with their behaviors. For most people, this readjustment seems to be accomplished more readily by the reformulation of expectations or plans than a change in performance. For instance, the below-average girl who planned to become a neurosurgeon in the 7th grade had, by the 11th grade, shifted her career goal to getting a full-time job at $5.50 an hour in the local textile mill.

The issue of goals speaks to a broader matter as well. According to most social-cognitive theories of adolescence, as they age, people reach progressively higher levels of social and ethical maturity. Hence there is a link between moral judgments, social skills, and chronological age, such that advances in one are associated with advances in the others. On the other hand, concepts of "storm and stress" suggest the opposite, that adolescence is associated with increasing difficulties of adjustment.

These two views reflect fundamental differences in how the goals of development may be conceptualized. Which is right? The developmental perspective holds that the concrete "goals" of development are neither within the organism nor within the context. Following von Bertalanffy (1962), it is assumed that direction arises in the course of development. It reflects the continuing fusion of internal processes of the individual with the characteristics of the context in which development occurs. Maturation inevitably involves change, reorganization, and novelty, for good or for ill. Distinctive to adolescence is the sheer rapidity and simultaneity of change in multiple domains, whether outside the self or under the skin.

These perspectives point to the difference in paradigms that guide the study of adolescence. Historically, scientific psychology has two distinct philosophical–scientific roots (Cairns, 1983b). The dominant perspective in psychology from experimental and psychophysics to social and personality is built on the methodological model of physics. This perspective has been traditionally concerned with the link between consciousness, abstract reasoning on morality and ethics, and reality beyond the self. A second perspective in psychology is built upon the methodological and theoretical model of biology. As such, it is concerned with behavioral and biological adaptation in the life history of the individual and in the evolutionary history of the species. Much of the controversy about the nature of adolescence stems from the fact that researchers who represent these two paradigms have different objectives, and investigate different worlds.

The self, the other, and the real

Another puzzle concerns the linkages between people's perceptions of themselves, the attributions of other people, and objective assessments of their behavior. Significant gaps between self-other perceptions have been assumed to be diagnostic of problems.

The developmental synthesis leads to a somewhat different conclusion. Self-concepts must serve at least two masters: internal harmony and external veridicality. We expect that the highest priority for thoughts about the self should be the maintenance of personal integrity and balance. Accordingly, self-concepts do not have to be veridical in order to be functional. As the child reaches adolescence, there are increases in the ability to think abstractly, diagnose relationships, and to perceive discrepancies in behavior, both in others and in him/herself. But there is also an increase in the ability to rationalize, to reconstruct, and compartmentalize one's thinking and beliefs. There is general bias throughout development, including adolescence, to view oneself in a benign and positive light. The cognitive advances that permit abstract rationalizations may be employed to maintain a healthy gap between the social consensus and the internal constructions.[14]

Change and continuity

In growing up, there is a tension between forces that produce change and those that promote stability. On the one hand, developmental reorganizations triggered by the onset of puberty are novel, inevitable, and irreversible. On the other hand, the consolidated habits, predispositions, and social networks in which people are embedded are conservative. They tend to resist modification. Attempts to introduce modest changes in concrete behaviors – in diet, in smoking, in controlling temper – can reveal the grip of the coincident bonds of individual learning, social expectations, subcultural values, and physiological addiction.

Social learning processes deserve special comment. One of the superior mechanisms for short-term adaptation and the consolidation of experience is the learning that occurs in social relationships (Bandura & Walters, 1963; Bandura, 1982). A host of relevant behaviors may be rapidly and effectively modified, at least in the short term. It is not clear, however, whether the effects persist in the long term in the absence of continuing external support. Conversely, there is now ample evidence that the effects of such social learning experiences in development can be modified and cancelled by broader cultural and biological forces, such as "innate drift".[15] These broader forces may involve such factors as the physiological lottery of adolescence, and the prescriptions associated with the assigned sex–age role in the subculture. These constraints are themselves paced by ontogenetic changes and modified as a function of age and function in the society.

The culture and the environment in which the person develops is a significant factor in continuity (Bronfenbrenner & Crouter, 1983). For example, the 15-year-old girl who moves from rural Tulare, California to inner-city Brooklyn, New York, may encounter extreme differences in living circumstances and social influence. Behavioral standards will be different, and so will the penalties for nonconformity. Individual, idiosyncratic factors in the family and her relationships help determine whether she is buffered from the context, or vulnerable to it.

Nature and nurture: dual genesis

Questions on whether behavior is due mostly to genes or to rearing – nature or nurture – refer to one of the most perplexing and beguiling issues in behavioral science. Recent advances in behavior genetics have helped clarify the empirical phenomena. It has been shown, for example, that heritable influences are developmentally regulated, and differential genetic effects are not necessarily observable at birth. Most of the powerful effects of sexual dimorphism are not expressed until puberty. Similarly, the timing of adolescence, and whether the person matures early or late relative to peers, is strongly influenced by heredity. And the impact of these changes upon the person's social and personal adaptation is not automatic; it depends on the social context in which the changes occur and the maturational status of peers. To illustrate, Magnusson (1988) reports that girls who reach physical maturity very early tend to affiliate with older people. But the sexual and social activities which were "normal" for older females were judged to be "deviant" for the early-maturing girls.

Pure or practical science?

The dichotomy between pure and applied concerns is as old as the disaffiliation of academic scientists from G. S. Hall's child study movement in the 1890s, and as fresh as the division between research psychologists and clinical psychologists in the 1990s. In each century, both positions stand to lose. Psychologists as diverse as John B. Watson and Alfred Binet agreed that accounts of human behavior should be clear and robust enough to be related to the pragmatic concerns of society. Binet carried the argument one step further. He proposed that the understanding of certain issues of practical significance for the society can provide the clues for a more powerful science. In that spirit, we will press modern developmental synthesis to inquire how it can assimilate the information contained in the examination of individual lives.

Persons or variables?

A final puzzle concerns the problem of analysis, and whether to employ person-centered or variable-centered analysis. On the one hand, some of the most important advances in understanding development follow from the study of individual changes and adaptation over time. The giants in the discipline – Sigmund Freud, Alfred Binet, Jean Piaget – focused on a few people, studied intensively, over a significant portion of their lives. Yet in most modern statistical analyses in psychology and the social sciences, individual differences are often considered "developmental noise" or error variance.

Magnusson (1988) has recently argued that both person-oriented procedures and variable-oriented ones are required for the systematic study of personality and social forces. In person-oriented models, the focus is upon identifying homogeneous groups of individuals in order to reach the appropriate unit of study. This may be achieved by advances in statistical methodology or by *a priori* theoretical considerations. It is not simply a series of case studies, where nonstandard information is gathered about people on an individual basis. Rather, the first step in the person-oriented analysis is to clarify the appropriate unit for classification, whether it be at the individual, cluster, subgroup, or population level. In contrast, variable-oriented models begin with a focus on specific dimensions (e.g. intelligence, aggression, altruism), not upon people. The interrelations among variables may then be analyzed in the group as a whole, or split according to presumably important characteristics. If samples are sufficiently large, it is possible to employ powerful statistical models to dissect the sources of relationships in the aggregated sample.

We employed both levels of analysis in this volume. We have had to zoom in to focus upon intensive accounts of personal dynamics and zoom out to view the aggregated effects in subgroups, samples, and the population. A coherent view of personality development may be within grasp, but reaching it requires innovations in how research is designed and analyzed.

On research limitations

Although these proposals are quite in line with modern social and behavioral science, they have not been universally adopted. One critique concerns limitations of longitudinal investigations over time and space. For example, in a recent issue of *American Scientist*,[16] it was argued that longitudinal designs should be assigned second-class status, because they are limited to particular samples in particular places at particular times. According to the critique, studies of social development in Sweden or in England cannot be generalized to the United States, and vice versa. On the same ground, the study of social networks among American youths in the southeast can be only of modest value in learning about social networks in the inner cities of Los Angeles, Chicago, and New York. Moreover, all longitudinal studies of human development must be instantly obsolete because they began twenty years ago. Although superficially appealing, this line of reasoning reflects two areas of confusion.

The first misunderstanding concerns the goals of longitudinal study. The aim of intensive study of individuals over time is to *understand* processes in context, not to *predict* context-free outcomes. Processes and principles, once identified, permit the science to transcend time and place. Specific outcomes and specific predictive equations are necessarily conditioned by and relative to particular contexts, samples, and times. The laws of gravity yield quite different outcomes in rate of descent, depending on whether you watch a pebble fall through the water or the air. The scientific task is to specify why contexts make a difference.

The second misunderstanding is more subtle. In order to clarify how development proceeds in different societies and different times, it is necessary to undertake parallel intensive analyses in different settings. It is only through a careful comparison of findings and trajectories across time and place that there is any hope of unraveling what is general and what is specific. Otherwise the science will be trapped by casual observations and common-sense beliefs of what "everybody knows". One of the goals of science is to explain common sense. In this spirit, differences across societies and contexts are just as important for understanding processes as similarities across settings. The challenge is to understand how similarities and differences arise, whether these emerge between the gangs of large cities and the groups of small towns, or between the teenagers of Sweden and the girls who sing the songs of sadness in Nepal.

The criticism turns on two issues. One concerns the temporal relativity of findings and results, no matter how carefully they have been described. The other concerns the cultural and geographic relativity of any specific set of findings. For example, how well might the results of the present investigation survive in other countries? Does the quality of longitudinal research diminish with travel like fine wine, or does it improve with sea voyages like some liqueurs? We offer brief comments on each of these issues of comparative generalization.

Beyond our time?

It helps to place our own investigation in social and educational context. The school-based intervention that has had the broadest impact in this century was initiated by the courts in 1954. This was the year of the landmark *Brown v. Topeka* ruling by the US Supreme Court that established as law that separate was not equal in the classroom. After two decades of disputation and resistance, the decision was fully enacted throughout the southern United States. Racial balance was achieved in southern schools that was rarely matched in any other region of America. People in this investigation may legitimately be called the children of integration. They were among the first generation in the south for whom public school desegregation was firmly in place from the time they entered school until they finished. The integration of African-American, Hispanic, Native-American, and white children in these southeastern schools has been the most complete in the history of the nation. To be sure, this acceptance sometimes coexisted with a strong segregationist influence, but that did not cancel out the opportunities and encouragement for children to attend school. During the period of this study, one African-American girl who had graduated from the high school where we observed was named a Rhodes scholar, and other African-American students were awarded prestigious scholarships to select American universities. The opportunities extended throughout the system; they were not limited to the exceptional few.

Although the court-initiated intervention changed the course of schools, this intervention has not been without cost. It might be argued that the extreme segregation that currently exists within cities is due in part to the movement of majority parents and families to the suburbs and rural areas, where *de facto* segregation could be maintained because of the economic constraints. As matters now stand, there is a crisis of confidence in the public schools. Many social policy recommendations seek to avoid dealing with public schools by establishing alternative educational schemes for private school support, for special "gifted and talented" schools, or for job-preparation programs. Such strategies, while politically attractive in the short run, seem likely to exacerbate the rate of individual failures in education and social disparities in the long run.

Beyond schools as an institution, there were social and economic changes as well. In this regard, there was a serious economic recession that bordered on depression in the early 1980s, when many parents lost their jobs. There were also concomitant reductions in support for further education which cut deeply into lives and families of the young people of this investigation. There were three short-term wars of significance – in Panama, in Grenada, in the Persian Gulf – in which some of our subjects were directly involved and others, indirectly affected. The role of women in the workplace also continued to change dramatically. The national economy shifted gears, so that families required two full-time workers in order to stay above the poverty line or to reach the goals that their parents achieved on one income. Although there have been economic setbacks over the past twelve years, the major changes that affected families in the United States have been linked to the need for more adults in the household to be involved in the workforce in order to survive on a minimal income.

Beyond our place?

Perhaps we should have included "in our place" in the title of this volume. Clearly there are limitations due to geography and context upon the generalizations that might be drawn. This does not mean, however, that all features are equally vulnerable, and it is helpful to try to determine which is which. For that reason we have included summaries of the national and international scenes. By projecting our findings against the backdrop of outcomes obtained in different settings, subcultures, and societies, we can begin to show what is local and specific and general and transcendent for our time.

Of course there is no guarantee on which outcomes and processes are context bound and which transcend geography and society. Those answers will require intensive and longitudinal investigations in multiple settings. Up to this point, the parallels in process have been more striking than the differences. Even where there are large differences in outcome – such as differences in violent deaths in the United Kingdom *versus* the United States, or differences in who is more promiscuous, young teenage girls in Sweden or young teenage boys in the United States, the variance seems to reflect differences in opportunity not differences in process. It is productive to have comparisons across societies to sharpen observations and provide limits to conclusions.

For what purpose?

In everyday life, the developmental idea means that the behaviors of youth are typically lawful and almost certainly functional. Even seemingly self-destructive actions of addiction and violence should be reasonably explained, once the facts are in. We must learn a great deal more about the individual circumstances of their lives than we ordinarily know. To acquire this critical information, we cannot rely only upon what the subjects or their parents tell us. It is an illusion that participants can provide an accurate account of their lives and experiences, if only they wanted to cooperate. The illusion arises because the concepts that all of us have of ourselves serve important functions in personal integration. A mirror image of reality, in personal and interpersonal affairs, is not always given the highest priority.

How can we construct an adequate understanding of social behavior? Is it possible? We think it is, and that a real science of social behavior is within reach. Our reasons for optimism are based more on the advances that have been won in the sister sciences of modern biology than the record of modern behavioral science. What the biology of behavior tells us is that to explain behavior, we must deal with a fusion of the effects. Moreover, it seems important to evaluate assertions on the primacy of genes and early experience in behavior determination. But critical evaluation does not mean rejection, and it is important to permit open-mindedness with respect to ideas that might at first seem foreign or complex.

Childhood and youth are of special importance because there are new things under the sun in every life, and novelties inevitably arise. They emerge from within the person or from the social context, personal relationships, or geographic setting. The family – or what substitutes for a family – is critical if for no other reason than it is one of the continuing influences on the youth's life from childhood through adolescence. But prior choices and experiences combine with continuities in biological constraints and social status to limit changes that are likely to occur. The options for individuals and their behaviors are likely to become increasingly biased in the course of living, except when multiple systems undergo simultaneous transformation in the transition from childhood to adulthood. This is why youth presents special challenges, novel opportunities, and inevitable risks.

TWELVE
___

Extending lifelines

Intervention and prevention

Our Nation is needlessly wasting its most precious natural resource: our children and youth. . . . The lost lifetime productivity of these youngsters, many of whom will never work consistently or live independently, adds significantly to the costs of these disorders.

US Department of Health and Human Services (1990)

We conclude this book by some comments on intervention and prevention. The children of our participants will themselves come of age in the first decade of 2000, and their generation could be the beneficiaries of changes begun in 1994.

Lifelines

Successful individuals are those who pursue productive and happy lives. This standard may apply to all individuals, regardless of their status, abilities, or culture (Freud, 1933). But the pursuit of work and happiness does not guarantee reaching them. The concrete outcomes depend upon events and circumstances that are often beyond individual control. The following six empirical generalizations provide an overview of lifelines, or supports within the individual and in the environment that promote success in living despite the odds against it. They are schools and mentors, social networks and friendships, families and neighbor-hoods, ethnicity and social class, individual characteristics, and new opportunities for living.

258

Schools and mentors

School and school experiences have emerged as key to resilience. At an individual level, school effects are mediated in part by principals, teachers, counselors, and coaches who become personal mentors. At the group level, schools provide the opportunity for children otherwise excluded from conventional society. Although there are individual exceptions, the longer students remain in school, the more adaptive their behaviors and skills become. It is the place where preparation for successful work and careers occurs. The lessons are not restricted to the classroom; they also come from peers, social networks, and friendships.

Any program of intervention and prevention for youth is ill-conceived if it ignores schools and school experiences. School is the place where most children spend most of their time in the first 18 years of their lives. To be successful, individuals must first master the basic communication and computing skills required in schools. They must also develop social patterns, interpersonal strategies, and goals that make it possible for them to qualify for careers. Schooling effects continue; they are not restricted to the child's involvement in a program of Head Start. The first three years of life are important, but so are the years that follow. Windows of opportunity exist throughout the child's school experience. Every school year is important, each one affecting the next. The idea that parents can remove themselves from responsibility for their child's education and development at some magical age is misguided. Independent living does not begin at age five.

Social networks and friendships

Social relationships constitute a primary source of satisfaction or distress. They also serve to convey values and behaviors across people and throughout groups, for good or ill. Although social relationships are fluid, there is consistency in influence, despite changing faces. The ubiquitous role of social networks is seen in virtually all significant areas of personal, social, and academic adaptation. These social networks also contribute to differential mate selection and the construction of the family of the next generation. Nor do the network influences begin and end in adolescence; they persist into adulthood and are re-created in the next generation. This is not a distinctively human characteristic, but that is another story.

Families and neighborhoods

Discussions of the influences of parents and families traditionally focus on their roles in early socialization and the establishment of personality and cognitive patterns in childhood. In the developmental perspective, attention is also given to changes in support during the transition to adulthood. Parental support strategies may be hidden or manifest. Which strategy – the invisible hand or the iron glove – will be effective cannot be specified independent of context. Both are needed for lifelines. For example, we have observed that authoritarian parental constraints have been effective in protecting youths in the inner city. The constraints served as lifelines when anything less would have been hazardous. Although potentially effective in the short term, the iron glove strategy is hazardous, because it may lead to mutual alienation in the long term. A balance is called for in commitment and affection, along with an ability to use whatever strategy is required to be effective. Families may provide support, constraint and protection, or they may join youths in their problems. Individuals, families, and neighborhoods change over time, and the nature of support must be synchronized with these changes.

Ethnicity and social class

Being white, Hispanic, Nisei, or African-American can be a lifeline or a risk, depending on the problem, the context, and the race. On this score, certain findings are counterintuitive to stereotypes. For example, African-American youths are protected from substance abuse rather than being especially vulnerable, and African-American males are less likely than their white counterparts to attempt suicide. There may be a connection. The paradox is that African-American youths score higher on some important risk factors, yet they also show lower levels of substance abuse, dropout, and suicide risk than white youths. Another example of a counterintuitive lifeline concerns first-generation Mexican emigrants to Los Angeles. Children of the first generation have a lower rate of deviance and delinquency than those of the second or third generation. In this case, the problems of crime and delinquency come with enculturation. Yet it would be a mistake to focus only on the violations of ethnic stereotypes. There is an advantage for the majority in American society. Mortality rates of white *versus* African-American youths are markedly lower in virtually all categories, except for motor-vehicle accidents. So are the rates of arrest and conviction for crimes of violence and crimes of youth. The protections of majority status are typically packaged with better educational opportunities, living standards, and higher income.

Individual characteristics and gender

Two of the individual characteristics that qualify as lifelines are the ability to get along with others and the ability to achieve in school.

Having one seems to work well as a lifeline, even when the other is missing. Vulnerability emerges when there is an absence of these two factors. In this regard, it should be recalled that aggression appears as significant in the prediction of subsequent problem behaviors, regardless of the society in which the study was conducted. Cluster analyses indicated that aggression was appropriately seen as having its effect in combination with other factors. In addition, there is good evidence that poor peer relations are not, in themselves, strong predictors of subsequent problem behaviors. It is when this factor occurs in combination with other problems of adaptation that it emerges as a risk.

Gender is something of a lifeline. Girls have some health and behavioral advantages over boys. One advantage appears in lower morbidity and mortality rates of females in childhood and maturity. For example, girls have lower suicide rates, despite higher suicide attempts and lower accident rates. The sex superiority of females shows up in behaviors, in that girls have lower rates of arrests for violence and lower rates of being victims of violence.

Opportunities of a lifetime

There are turning points for lives throughout development, not merely early in life. Parents change, and so do their infants in the passage from birth to maturity. Periods of resilience and plasticity continue to recur throughout development, and some of the major potential turning points occur in entry to school, in the biological lottery of adolescence, in choices of friends and social networks, and in goals for schooling and careers. True, these opportunities in a lifetime are not always exploited. But with support, there can be reorganization of skills and goals. Close relationships seem to be critical in determining whether the opportunities will be seized. These lifelines are relevant, not only for the individuals whom we identified as being individually at risk, but for all.

Risks

In 1904, G. Stanley Hall published a classic volume entitled *Adolescence: Its Psychology and Its Relations to Physiology, Anthropology, Sociology, Sex, Crime, Religion, and Education.*[1] Hall covered all of these issues, and more. He provided a summary of evidence then available and organized it within an encompassing evolutionary model of development. Since then, much has been written about the dismal state of youth in America. The broader problem is that there may be a tendency to scapegoat youth with the problems in the general society. This could lead to a funnelling of resources to the special needs of youth, or it could lead to the devaluation of children and their institutions, including schools and families.

A list of some primary risk factors today covers much of the same ground that G. Stanley Hall originally explored. There are a few new ones as well. Today's risks include violence, family disruption and being poor, deviant social groups and gangs, substance abuse, and school and community disorganization. When the cords of a given lifeline are frayed or weakened, it can become a risk.

Violence

High levels of aggressive behavior, in combination with difficulties in social exchange, constitutes a risk pattern for children and youth. While aggression has traditionally been seen as a male problem, it is equally hazardous for females. Violence has become more frequent in girls, marking a temporal trend that has ominous implications. Aggressive females and males are more likely to become teenage parents than nonaggressive ones, all things considered. There is not only heightened risk for these women as young adults, there is heightened risk for their offspring. In the 21st century it could become more than a familial cycle of violence; it could grow to a social tornado of violence. At the individual level, aggression and hostility look to be as responsible as academic incompetence for removal from education prior to the completion of high school. The upshot is that the track established for early school dropouts is one that retards their participation in the conventional economic system and, instead, places them at odds with it. As the NIH report indicated, the loss in social capital is great. It is especially devastating for poor youths who do not have alternative pathways.

Families, ethnic status, and poverty

Family configurations are undergoing rapid change in the United States. The tracking of the familial structures created by our subjects shows a strong trend toward single parenthood. This is not merely a phenomenon for Americans. For example, Swedish statistical data indicate that the majority of mothers of 25 years or younger are unmarried. Our longitudinal data indicated that 58% of the CLS subjects who became parents as teenagers were unmarried or separated early from the other biological parent. Families that cannot afford to remain in one location and must move lead to higher risk in their offspring. More generally, ethnic status and poverty tend to co-occur, such that many of the negative outcomes associated with being African-American disappear when the effects of economic status are statistically controlled. Assumptions that families will continue to serve as protective agents are an illusion. To the extent that parents are themselves only shortly removed from childhood, questions might be raised on their competence to take care of themselves, much less their children. Economic shifts in this society typically make it necessary for both young parents to work or seek public support. The pattern of benevolent grandparenting itself is rapidly becoming a thing of the past, as young grandparents themselves become economically distressed.

Social networks and gangs

Social networks can be protective or corrosive. It depends upon the group with whom there is an affiliation. Higher risks for aggression and drug abuse arise when there is affiliation with people involved in aggressive behavior and drug use, respectively. This holds for family affiliations as well as peer affiliations. Group affiliations provide the conduit for modifying attitudes and changing values among members. The best predictor of a young person's estimate of their friend's delinquency and use of drugs is the subject's own reported delinquency and use of drugs, not the friend's report. Social networks and perceptions of value structures are woven together to promote behavior organization and to maintain individual goals. A special comment is called for on gang membership as a risk factor. In some areas of the inner city, gangs function as alternative governments in domains where conventional authorities have abdicated control. Among the street children of Mexico City, the gang is synonymous with "family" for some. This is not mere romanticization, it is a recognition of some essential functions served for many 10–18-year-old members. We have observed the same phenomenon among our subjects who have joined gangs, in the inner city or elsewhere. But in all cases it is a marginal family, indicative of high risk.

Substance abuse

Patterns of substance use continue to undergo fads and fashions, as they have for most of this century. Of special importance to us has been the counterintuitive finding that there is a heightened vulnerability among white youths to substance use and abuse. The vulnerability cuts across socioeconomic classes, gender, and levels of academic competence. That is perhaps the reason why federal and local efforts to contain and constrain the activity have been only marginally successful. As it turns out, the risks appear to be broadening to include the majority of youths, even more so than the disenfranchised minority. All this suggests that any successful attempt to intervene will require attention to health education and the values and habits of the youths who use drugs.

School and community disorganization

In the course of this study, we observed certain destructive trends of community disorganization up close. In the trauma center of Los Angeles, most severe traumatic injuries in both females and males were due to violence rather than car accidents. But equally disturbing patterns stood out in small towns and suburban centers, though without the community breakdown. A major risk for the future is the abdication of responsibility by conventional institutions that borders on anarchy in some schools and communities. Abdication of authority does not always mean a lack of organization; it may mean that organization is provided by other sources. The breakdown of the conventional family system may indicate a shift in responsibility to schools, churches, or peers. Similarly, a breakdown of the school and community structures means even fewer lifelines for individual youths.

Implications for prevention

In public health, prevention has the strong positive connotation of the avoidance of disease and decay. Similarly, our concern here is to examine strategies that might invalidate some of the bleak expectations for health and behavior that have emerged from a hard look at the current problems of society as they are reflected in the lives of our 695 subjects.

Various prevention strategies have been proposed for individuals and societies. Given the broad sweep of the difficulties, some people believe that enough is enough as far as research is concerned. They feel that the basic facts about causation are already in, and that one need only to take the next logical set of steps to implement change. A self-evident solution may reflect the biases of the society or investigator rather than the facts of the science. What has been forgotten in such speculations is that individually based psychotherapeutic interventions can claim only modest empirical validity, despite 100 years of practice. Claims that psychological science has evolved effective prevention techniques to change trajectories of development demand careful evaluation.

When common sense fails

Many of the most carefully crafted programs for change based upon self-evident principles have proved to be ineffective. An overview of the results of systematic analyses of treatment programs for adolescence yields findings that are hardly impressive, even when the findings are taken as a whole. Some illustrations of the results indicate that it is folly to lump together all behavior problems and all treatments. Some difficulties are more successfully addressed than others. As in the case of physical illness, what appears as one syndrome may in fact reflect the operation of multiple pathways, each requiring a different strategy of prevention. Two classic examples from different levels of intervention illustrate the hazards of relying upon intuition and incomplete analysis.

The Cambridge–Somerville study was a model prevention program completed in the early 1940s. The goal was to prevent delinquency and crime among youths in a high delinquency area of metropolitan Boston. The program included individual guidance and support, and material guidance in health, school, and family for a large group of youths. The intervention continued over several years for the selected boys and their families. These boys were matched with a sample of control boys who were also followed, but who did not receive the benefits of the prevention program. Joan McCord[2] deserves credit for having conducted careful follow-up studies of these people at different points of adulthood, including late maturity and retirement. An exhaustive analysis indicated that this carefully executed program was a failure in terms of its original goals. It did not prevent crime, alcoholism, or difficulties in living. There was even a dark side, in that the prevention program seemed to have had a reverse effect for some youths. The reasons for the failure and/or reversal have not yet been conclusively specified. But this failure to produce positive effects demands attention and caution.

Another classic failure of prevention has occurred in the cities of the United States, where an effort was made in the 1950s and 1960s to devise programs of urban renewal and provide modern, affordable housing for the disadvantaged, while simultaneously creating the substructure for a new urban society. Accordingly, public housing was created for the disadvantaged minorities. The cities of America and their residents are now paying a huge price for this experiment in social progress. The social effect of this program has been the creation of urban ghettos in virtually every major American city, with the segregation or quarantine of minorities. The upshot, as R. Wallace observes, has been something akin to a nuclear disaster for human potential.[3] By clustering together aggressive youths and gangs, social disorganization was inevitable. As it turns out, the relocation of housing facilitated the breakdown of family links and contributed to the escalation of violence. Short-term gains in the economy and the appearance of cities may have been canceled out by the long-term consequences of social alienation and isolation.

In the light of the magnitude of the problem of violence for modern society in terms of the economic, social, and health costs, we might have anticipated that significant resources have been devoted to understanding its roots and prevention. That has not been the case. In point of fact, only minuscule funds have been devoted to understanding the problems of youth and violence.

The National Institutes of Health is the largest research organization in the world devoted to understanding biomedical and biosocial issues, with an annual budget of more than $10 billion. It is the primary federal agency in the United States that supports research on the study of lifelines and risks in youth. One of the startling findings of this audit of research is shown in Figure 12.1. The thin line depicts the proportion of the National Institute of Health 1992 fiscal year budget devoted to the problems of the development of aggressive and antisocial behavior. This eyelash of resources represents a wink at the problem. Recall from Chapter 9 that violence is the second leading cause of death in all people 15–25 years of age, and the leading cause of death in African-American youths. When compared, in terms of mortality rates, to the resources devoted to other major killers, we find a large inverse correlation between expenditures and significance of the problem for youths ($r = -0.73$). Yet the 1990s political agenda calls for spending large sums on the control and prevention of violent behaviors. There is

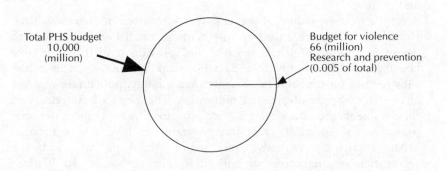

Total PHS budget
10,000
(million)

Budget for violence
66 (million)
Research and prevention
(0.005 of total)

Figure 12.1   Proportion of NIH FY 1992 budget allocated to research for any aspect of aggression, violence, and antisocial behavior.

an urgency about the need to do something expensive and dramatic, on the basis that we already know the answers (e.g. Dryfoos, 1990). That is an illusion. One compelling problem seems to be that programs end just at the time in development that they should continue to ensure their effectiveness.

Lest the errors of the past be repeated, it seems reasonable to wed the implications from the empirical study of lifelines with the information on some programs that seem to work. We first review the implications for prevention, then examine some examples of success.

Towards a solution

Following their review on the comorbidity of behavioral and health problems in adolescence, Earls, Cairns, and Mercy (1993) wrote:

The obstacles of easy availability and access to guns, widespread use of alcohol and drugs, and the decay of central city areas cannot be minimized in any campaign to promote non-violence among today's youth. In the face of these barriers, an effort at health promotion may be equivalent to trying to control an epidemic of tuberculosis in a densely populated area without adequate sanitation. Antibiotics may be of some value in treating individual cases and a vaccine may be of even greater value in protecting some groups of individuals, but the environmental conditions that promote the disease would simply overwhelm public resources in combating it through these means.

Developmental considerations may be critical in pointing to what changes are likely to be most effective in this task. In general, aggressive and violent behaviors are more readily prevented than they are ameliorated, once established. But the conditions for establishment appear not only in early development but in middle childhood and adolescence. Moreover, effective prevention demands attention to the several levels of influence – individual, interactional, familial, peer group, and community-cultural. Efforts at control and prevention cannot be limited to a single time frame of development – either in infancy, preschool, middle childhood, or early adolescence. Waiting until the problems of violence emerge full-blown in adolescence may be too late to be effective.

On this developmental perspective, behavioral interventions designed for a single point in development are not necessarily effective in the long term. One problem is that behavioral systems most readily changed by behavioral intervention programs are, paradoxically, most likely to be vulnerable to rebound to the original state once the prior conditions are reinstituted or treatment is stopped. This observation is consistent with the unstable effects of many delinquency and substance abuse intervention programs which are initially highly successful, but fail in the long term. Once the individual is reintroduced into the community from which she/he was removed, the prior constraints are reintroduced and recidivism occurs. More generally, the social behaviors that seem most malleable in the short run may be the most difficult to shift in the long run, precisely because of their demonstrated dependence upon immediate supporting contextual and social conditions. In such behavioral systems, once the context changes, so should the behaviors.

Yet it is an error to view context only in terms of external events. Each of us has an internal context that is at once dynamic and regulatory. We carry within ourselves distinctive emotions, motives, beliefs, thoughts, and plans across time and space. This personal context promotes behavioral persistence – and self-perceived stability – in the face of external forces for change. What ultimately calls the shots in behavioral regulation – one's internal state or one's environment? One advance of the modern developmental synthesis has been to unravel the apparent dualism between biology and environment. Over development, elements of the internal context can be brought into alignment with elements of the social ecology, and vice-versa. The upshot is that forces under the skin and forces outside become loosely correlated over time, creating a network of constraints and regulatory guides for living., Longterm changes in behavior occur when modifications are sufficiently potent to affect reorganization in both systems.

The longitudinal tracking of persons over time provides a precious resource for understanding how the bidirectional process works in real lives. In overview, we find that there is no single window of vulnerability, and no one point of entry for change. Moreover, the correlations between systems are far from perfect, regardless of age. Opportunities for change – developmental lifelines – exist throughout the lifetime, even among youth at risk.

The prevention strategy that we adopt assumes that the person's behaviors are embedded in the social network and community of individuals of which she/he is a part. In this regard, Baldwin (1897) argued that "each of us is really someone else, even in our own thought of ourselves". By extension, the social network and microcommunity which one is accepted into, or rejected from, typically has certain behavioral, cognitive, and evaluative standards for the person. Failure to attain those criteria in one group/network can, in turn, qualify the person for membership in alternative networks and thereby produce different behavioral trajectories in development (Earls, Cairns, & Mercy, 1993). For example, behavioral interventions that are entirely successful at one stage of childhood and adolescence can be interrupted or reversed at a later stage of adolescence or early maturity if the "social network" is radically changed over that period. Such changes may come about if the effective microcommunity comprises people who have, say, dropped out of school or have serious problems with substance abuse.

All this is to say there are correlated constraints in the trajectories of individual development. That is, configurations of associated internal and external supports are presumed to operate together over time. There is a redundancy of influence. Although one source of influence may change, other elements in the configuration that do not shift can support behavior in a failsafe pattern to maintain personal consistency. In this view, seemingly separate sources of influence must be viewed in terms of their correlated properties.[4]

The preceding discussion leads to five implications on the promotion of health, well-being, and the prevention of serious problems of behavior in youth:

1. Problem behaviors are more readily prevented than ameliorated, once established. Moreover, the conditions for establishment appear not only in early development but in middle childhood and adolescence.
2. Effective prevention demands attention to the several levels of influence: social, cognitive, school, familial, peer group, and community. Given the accessibility of virtually all children in school, and given the traditional role of schools in preparing youth for adaptation to the social and economic institutions of the society, it seems reasonable to prepare intervention programs in collaboration with school systems.
3. Some of the more serious problems of health and behavior can be addressed by heightening the likelihood that youths will have productive and successful experiences in schools. Prevention programs should not be merely an addition or "paste-on" to school activities; they should become an integral part of school organization that is designed to heighten successful academic training.
4. Prevention programs should anticipate the emerging role of developmental constraints, such as the role of peer social networks in adolescence, the emergence of sexual behaviors in adolescence, and the emergent role of economic and social constraints. In this regard, a single age for focal interventions is unlikely to endure.
5. Prevention programs can be designed to influence behaviors and expectations across generations. A successful investment in one generation should have productive outcomes in the next.[5]

Successful interventions

Practical proof lies in whether or not the implications lead to programs that work. For that information, we turn to some recent efforts and their outcomes.

Recent programs that have been successful in demonstrating enduring changes with inner-city youth seem to be consistent with the above proposals. In particular, James Comer has convincingly demonstrated that inner-city "black children could achieve well in a good educational environment" (Comer, 1980, p. 103). He and his team in New Haven demonstrated how "a private university child study center, a public school system, and a community of teachers and parents could establish a long-term collaboration which would primarily benefit the children in the schools" (Comer, 1980, p. xvi). Higher levels of achievement and diminished problems of behavior were shown to be mutually supportive in this study. Other examples of the productive collaboration of academic and behavior programs include demonstrations in Baltimore in the Johns Hopkins Epidemiologic Prevention Research Center (Kellam et al., 1991), in East Harlem, New York, in the Central Park East Secondary School directed by Deborah Meier (Hechinger, 1992), and in Bennett Kew Elementary and Kelso Elementary in the Inglewood area of south-central Los Angeles. There has been, as well, a commitment to achievement where schools are violence free. In the case of the Central Park East Secondary School, there is a shared acceptance by the entire school community "that there is to be no fighting, not even as a game". In each instance, the reduction of violence has been coupled with individual success in academic achievement.

Remedies for the schools by the year 2000 could productively integrate promising programs of multi-level behavioral intervention and conflict resolution (e.g. Olweus, 1994; Prothrow-Stith & Weissman, 1991) with the school curriculum–organization programs that have been shown to work with minority youth (e.g. Comer, 1980; Kellam et al., 1991). To be effective, the program must be concerned with both the child's cognitive development as well as behavioral-health development. Success in addressing one aspect of adjustment should promote success in other areas, including behavior and health.

While such interventions are likely to ensure short-term gains and to be effective as long as they are in progress, three additional steps are to be taken to heighten the likelihood of making enduring changes in adaptation. Following the reasoning of Comer (1980), and Kellam et al. (1991), it seems important to engage the child productively in the activities of conventional institutions. This means, among other things, that children should experience success in aspects of school, including academic progress. This can be achieved in various ways, depending upon the school, community, and the child. Specifically, one goal of the program will be to ensure that the children in the targeted classrooms/schools achieve an acceptable standard of academic competence, given the age-developmental stage of the child. This talent can be recruited both from adults in the community as well as students themselves. In the light of the composition of the schools and the communities, every effort will be made to ensure that there is broad minority representation in this academic assistance role. By providing some financial remuneration for this service, the children, parents, students, and schools should also benefit.

When shared goals are adopted by children, parents, and teachers, there should be greater consistency and coherence in behavioral and academic support. And if parents themselves are brought into close and supportive contact with the school, the lessons learned in the academic context are likely to generalize and be supported outside the school. Bidirectionality also implies that youths should not only be helped, they should be helpers. Accordingly, the children/adolescents who are in intervention programs could be recruited to assist in a variety of programs where they are "expert" relative to others. This assistance may include academic assistance (where at-risk youths help younger or less able students in reading and math), or it may involve areas where the individual has special skills or interests (e.g. art layout in publications, sports assistance with less capable children, help in organizing activities where the youths are put in charge with supervision).

One of the more attractive possibilities for middle-school and high-school students will be to extend the program of assistance to others to community needs and achievements. This is the model that worked effectively in both the east and south-central Los Angeles areas in work with gang members (see Earls, Cairns, & Mercy, 1993). It is proposed that essentially the same principles will operate effectively in dealing with minority youths in other inner-city, suburban, and rural areas. As a footnote to the Los Angeles programs, it should be noted that the recent south-central Los Angeles turmoil reportedly spared buildings/areas in which youths had helped restore. More generally, to the extent that there is both involvement and investment by youths, both the community and the youths stand to gain.

But the serious problems of the future will not be addressed by stop-gap measures. The term "intervention" implies that something must be intervened with and that problems have already taken root. It is more economical and more effective to prevent them in the first place. An excellent example of such an educational–behavioral program designed to promote success and prevent failure is located in Birmingham, Alabama. In the lives of inner-city youth, there is a critical moment of transition that occurs between the time they leave one school and enter the next. In the transition, individuals often drop out of the system and into the void.

In a model Birmingham program, a middle school, a high school, and a junior college creatively linked themselves together to provide an educational pipeline to support students from childhood to maturity. Administrators and teachers at selected middle schools, high schools, and community colleges individually prepare children for the transition from one educational placement to the next. Their goals have been zero school dropout and high levels of performance for all students, not merely a select few. They assume school is for everyone, then anticipate problems and try to prevent them. This is the sort of solution that simultaneously heightens academic performance and diminishes behavioral risks.

Epilogue

Our concern about the success or failure of preventions is not solely academic. Some years ago, one of us was confronted with the care and teaching of a large class of 5th grade students in a San Francisco-area school. About half of the students qualified for placement into special education classrooms, and 80% of them were economically deprived. A 13-year old girl named Bonnie was the class leader, and she controlled much of the rest of the school. Bonnie had been retained for three years. She was the largest, oldest, and the lowest achieving student in the class. She lived in a nearby house of prostitution in the care of her mother's friend. Bonnie was feared, but she was not without friends. Together with a couple of other girls, Beth and Zorrie, she controlled students and teachers. Moreno's question, "Who shall survive?" had special meaning here. The class's two previous teachers left teaching in mid-year rather than remain with these sullen and aggressive youths.

In the course of a year, a remarkable transformation occurred in the class and in Bonnie. For the class, a new policy was instituted where every student performed perfectly on their academic assignments before the end of each week, new focus was given to how they could learn and create rather than why they had earlier failed, individual and whole class achievements were recognized and celebrated by field trips, class visits, and other rewards that were at once fun and educationally enriching, and a supportive structure was provided to ensure that all students met or exceeded the requirements. And all students did, including Beth, Bonnie, and Zorrie. True, expectations were scaled according to ability, but the standards were unbending.

For Bonnie, it was her most successful year in school. Once she was taken into the teacher's confidence, she took the teacher into her confidence. Her peer coercion and domination of other students was coopted for productive teaching purposes, not destructive social ones. Most of the parents were enlisted to support the teaching program. In Bonnie's case, the teacher became a parent surrogate. In the course of the year, Bonnie's performance came up to grade level on all academic subjects. It was demanding for teacher and students alike, but it yielded productive outcomes. These outcomes were maintained the next year the girls were in elementary school, but they unraveled when the girls were promoted to junior high school.

In the years that we kept in contact with Bonnie, her life and prospects became increasingly dismal. After three years of failure in junior high school, she dropped out of school and conventional society. A similar trajectory held for Beth. Following failure and societal dropout, Beth was convicted of homicide and sentenced to life imprisonment for a death that occurred during a robbery. Both lives had been genuinely shifted as children, but the shifts did not square with the constraints they faced the next years.

Our goal in this volume has been to better understand how tragedies like those of Bonnie and Beth can be prevented. But they are not the only ones who are vulnerable. Virtually all teenagers in our time are at risk. The web of events that help regulate their lives become increasingly interwoven over time. To be effective, lifelines that are extended must be kept in place long enough to become opportunities for a lifetime. The fresh and hopeful news is that new opportunities recur and they are not limited to windows that appear early in life.

Notes

Chapter 1

1. See the recent volumes produced by the European Science Foundation's Network on Longitudinal Study under the general direction of David Magnusson (e.g. Baltes & Baltes, 1990; Magnusson & Bergman, 1990a).
2. The definition of developmental science is essential for researchers, but it can be opaque for nonspecialists. Accordingly, "the synthesis is a perspective on individual functioning that emphasizes the dynamic interplay among processes that operate across time frames, levels of analysis, and contexts. The aim is to provide a general framework for linking the concepts and findings of hitherto disparate areas of developmental inquiry. The time frames employed are relative to the lifetime of the phenomena to be understood. The units of focus may be as short as milliseconds and minutes, or as long as years and millennia. In this perspective, phenomena are viewed at multiple levels. Levels refer to the subsystems of the organism and the social and physical environments that are involved in individual functioning. Contexts are inextricable components of individual development, including cytoplasmic, familial, social network, and cultural influences" (Cairns, Elder, Costello, & McGuire, in press).
3. The focus of this volume on risks and protective factors has shaped our selection of topics. But it should be underscored that the sample was representative of all the youth enrolled in public schools of the communities that we sampled.
4. With one exception. The proportion of African-American children (i.e. 25% of the original sample) is approximately twice that found nationally. This over-representation reflects the higher portion of minority children in the region from which the sample was originally selected.
5. We thank Norman Garmezy for this term to describe the unrecognized potential of youth.
6. Beatrix Hamburg (personal communication).

274

Chapter 2

1. This is a real concern, given that the primary theory of personality development in this century (psychoanalysis) was based upon retrospective accounts of patients in psychotherapy (S. Freud, 1933).

2. But not always. There continues to be a debate between theorists who emphasize the enduring properties of traits and those who emphasize developmental changes and transitions.

3. See Kessen (1960) and Wohlwill (1973) for astute overviews of the issues associated with longitudinal research.

4. In addition to the principal study, we have conducted several collateral investigations to clarify methodological and theoretical issues. Two of the collateral investigations are of special interest to this volume. One was a preliminary, two-year investigation with the aim of establishing the measurement properties of the procedures for the CLS study, and providing a dress rehearsal for the design and for our research team. A second investigation was conducted to obtain information about extremely aggressive subjects to corroborate the results of the present investigation. Accordingly, 1,320 extremely assaultive adolescent males and females were studied to determine the generality of the longitudinal "at risk" subgroups. At various points in this volume, we will have occasion to refer to the findings of these collateral investigations.

5. Magnusson (1988).

6. William Kessen (1960) provided a cogent analysis of the conceptual and statistical design issues that confront longitudinal investigators.

7. And the patience paid off. We eventually succeeded in interviewing all subjects who had been "on the run".

8. And international. One subject returned to South America to complete high school. Others were abroad in the military.

9. Farrington et al. (1990); Murphy (1990).

10. Eron & Huesmann (1987); Farrington (1986).

11. It should be noted that parental or guardian permission was required for the children and adolescents to participate in the investigation. We did not wish, however, to limit participation by the direct involvement of parents in the initial stages of the work. Our initial focus was upon the most difficult children and those at greatest risk for aggressive behavior in a normal school population. Accordingly, we did not wish to limit original sampling by an additional requirement for parental participation, on the assumption that some (or many) of the children at risk would not have cooperative parents and insistence on their inclusion would yield a biased sample of youths at risk. Accordingly, the parental and grandparent interviews were conducted systematically when the subjects were in late adolescence, at 19 years of age. The major results of family context will be reported upon in a subsequent volume.

12. Cairns & Moffitt (1992). This paper was prepared to guide measurement selection in the longitudinal study to be undertaken by the MacArthur

Foundation /National Institute of Justice Program on Human Development and Criminal Behavior.
13. Sears *et al.* (1953); Sears, Maccoby, & Levin (1957); Bandura & Walters (1959).
14. Methods and Measures For Longitudinal Study (Cairns *et al.*, 1994) provides further technical information, as do the cited publications.
15. On occasions, participants were reluctant or refused to talk with interviewers to whom they had been assigned on a given year. Under those conditions, we sought permission to return the next year.
16. Lewin (1931).
17. Kuo (1967); Magnusson (1985); Nesselroade & Ford (1985); Wohlwill (1973).
18. This does not mean, of course, that we have not completed standard parametric analyses. We believe that multivariate and regression analyses should be the first step in systematic analysis, not the last. If not carried beyond to person-oriented analyses, they could yield misleading findings.

Chapter 3

1. Following unintentional motor and vehicular accidents, National Center for Health Statistics (1993).
2. See US Department of Health and Human Services, 1991.
3. See Hirschi & Gottfredson (1983).
4. Cairns (1979). T. Hirschi has since discussed the curve at some length in the sociological literature.
5. Hirschi & Gottfredson (1983).
6. Cairns *et al.* (1993).
7. All have been subsumed by the rubric "aggression" (see Bandura, 1973; Cairns, 1973, 1979). The essential problem is that the category is one that requires a social judgment about motives and intentions, and the judgment depends upon whose perspective is taken in determining the provocation and the goal. More generally, actions that interfere with the behaviors of others are inevitable in social exchanges. Such actions are perceived as "aggressive" if they are intense or hurtful, and if there is a judgment of malicious or hostile intent. Violence is the more extreme case. It refers to the exertion of physical force to injure or abuse. In the absence of malice, the hurtful actions may be viewed as accidental, corrective, or therapeutic (e.g. "punishment"). Further, definitional criteria change as a function of the individuals' ages, circumstances, roles, and social and physical contexts.
8. Cairns & Cairns (1986); *Crime in the United States* (1987).
9. Eron *et al.* (1983) (also Huesmann, Lagerspetz, & Eron, 1984). Further, Ferguson and Rule (1980) have identified the rise of a brutality norm in adolescence (i.e. acceptability of physical aggression).
10. Loeber (1982).
11. Ledingham *et al.* (1982).

12. See review by Parke & Slaby (1983).
13. Olweus (1979).
14. See also Feshbach & Price (1984); Kagan & Moss (1962); McCord (1986); Pulkkinen (1993), and Glueck & Glueck (1940; 1950).
15. Frodi, Macaulay, & Thome (1977).
16. Earls, Cairns, & Mercy (1993).
17. The probes included: "Who was involved?" "How did it start?" "What happened?" "How did it end?" "Did anything else come of it?" "How did you feel about it?" "How did the other person feel?"
18. To control for possible effects of repeated testing, a fresh comparison group of 100 7th grade subjects (50 boys, 50 girls) was tested. The comparison subjects were selected from one of the middle schools attended by the longitudinal subjects. In these single-test groups, the gender-by-age effects were parallel to those obtained in the primary longitudinal groups. When differences were observed, the gender-by-age effects for physical aggression were slightly larger in the single-test groups relative to the longitudinal groups.
19. Because of the possible confounding between denial of conflict and failure to report a given theme (i.e. physical aggression, social manipulation), the thematic analyses were computed in two runs, with and without the persons who claimed no conflict had occurred. The same significant findings were obtained, with the exception that proportionately higher levels of physical aggression were obtained in the male–male conflicts (64%) in the 7th grade, and higher levels of social manipulation were obtained in the female–female conflicts (44%) in the 7th grade.
20. See Bloom (1964) and Cairns (1979, Ch. 22).
21. See Pulkkinen (1982); Magnusson (1988); Farrington & West (1990); Rutter (1988); Patterson, Reid, & Dishion (1992); Eron & Huesmann (1987); Elliott, Huizinga, & Menard (1989); Werner & Smith (1992); Block (1971); Masten, Best, & Garmezy, (1990). See also the reanalysis of earlier reports from the Berkeley Growth Study (Elder, Liker, & Cross, 1984).
22. The correlational matrices of stability for males and females over a nine-year period are remarkably consistent. An earlier report of these findings over five years appeared in Cairns *et al.* (1989).
23. Intelligence measures usually involve assessments of an individual's optimal performance under standard conditions; aggressive assessments usually involve judgments of an individual's typical performance in the natural circumstances of her or his life (see Cairns, 1979, Ch. 22).
24. The theme of the 1993 Life History Conference was the development of gender differences. In the three-day meeting at Duke University, attended by many of the active international longitudinal investigators in gender development, a strong consensus emerged on the similarities among males and females in social and developmental processes.
25. Direct evidence for this developmental shift is reported in Cairns *et al.* (1989).
26. Olweus (1979).

27. Extending Olweus' (1979) conclusion for males.
28. Green *et al.* (1980); Cairns & Cairns (1984).
29. Feshbach & Sones (1971).
30. And one can escalate to the other. It is noteworthy that almost as much fighting occurred among females as among males in mid adolescence (though there is a decrease from earlier years in both genders). When the factors leading to female fights in adolescence were examined in the present data, they were typically the outgrowth of prior social aggression (e.g. rumor spreading, social exclusion).
31. Unraveling aggressive behaviors and their development requires simultaneous focus upon theory and assessment. A major hazard in this enterprise has been the propensity to reify the construct of aggression and to expect a single trajectory of growth, development, and decay. That common-sense assumption is misguided. Aggressive behaviors are part of living, and cannot be divorced from the dynamic developmental contexts in which they occur. The properties of the construct of "aggression" change over development. At each developmental stage, the construct reflects the social judgments of society, the social attributions of researchers, and the social constructions of the self. Different developmental trajectories may be described for the separate domains of aggression.

Chapter 4

1. In addition to the forty aggressive subjects matched to the control subjects, an additional group of participants fulfilled all of the criteria for risk selection. This additional subgroup which more than doubled the number of aggressive subjects was not included in the primary risk-control analyses because they were not the subjects of focal observation. Nonetheless, separate analyses of this subgroup and its *post hoc* matched control group supported virtually all of the major analyses reported in this volume for risk-control differences (Cairns, Santoyo, & Holly, in press).
2. Leung (1993).
3. The Birmingham data are reported in Gaines, Cairns, & Cairns (1994) and McDuffie, Cairns, & Cairns (1994). It should be noted, however, that Sheppard Kellam and his colleagues have found large gender differences in aggression by peer reports and teacher ratings in first grade Baltimore inner-city children (Dolan *et al.*, 1993). The reasons for these discrepancies – in the measurement, age, society, generation – remain to be determined. But the point to be emphasized is that gender differences are relative to all three factors.
4. These changes are reviewed in Cairns & Kroll (in press).
5. Cairns & Green (1979).
6. McDuffie, Cairns, & Cairns (1993).
7. Gaines, Cairns, & Cairns (1994).
8. Schlossman & Cairns (1993).

9. There are some exceptions, of course, including the important work of P. C. Giordano and her colleagues (e.g. Giordano, 1978; Giordano, Cernkovich, & Pugh, 1986).
10. See Schlossman & Wallach (1978).
11. See, for example, Cairns (1979), Cairns & Kroll (in press), Maccoby & Jacklin (1974), Whiting & Edwards (1973). But there are some exceptions. Sons are typically not permitted to participate in stereotypic "feminine" behaviors although daughters are often permitted to participate in male-type patterns of play and dress.
12. See Elliott, Huizinga, & Menard (1989); Farrington (1986); Huesmann, Lagerspetz, & Eron (1984); Kagan & Moss (1962); Loeber (1982); Magnusson (1988); McCord (1979, 1986); Moss & Susman (1980); Olweus (1979); Olweus, Block, & Radke-Yarrow (1986); Parke & Slaby (1983); Patterson (1986); Pulkkinen (1993).
13. See Robins and Price (1991) for a careful analysis of the NIMH Epidemiological Catchment Area assessment of the prevalence of mental problems. In this article, the authors observe that conduct disorders in childhood predict both externalizing and internalizing disorders in adulthood for males and females. This is an important revision of Robins's (1986) earlier argument that conduct disorders in childhood predict only externalizing disorders for males and both externalizing and internalizing disorders for females.

Chapter 5

1. See Youniss (1980, 1986); Youniss & Smollar (1985)
2. Cairns & Cairns (1986).
3. Cohen (1955); Sherif & Sherif (1953); Thrasher (1928).
4. Brown (1990).
5. Coleman (1961).
6. Steinberg *et al.* (in press).
7. The role of cheerleading requires special comment on this North American tradition. A colleague whose family moved to the United States from Germany recalled that the academic transition to a Milwaukee high school was a piece of cake. But she experienced a minor culture shock when she went to her first high-school football game. To this European teenager, it was more extravaganza than sporting event.
8. Edwards (1990) has demonstrated that girls in childhood and adolescence tend to form groups of "leaders". According to Edward's study of 159 girls enrolled in a Girl Scout summer camp program, this selective affiliation occurs within a week of residence. We have observed a similar phenomenon in other middle schools and high schools.
9. Elliot, Huizinga, & Menard (1989); Kandel (1978).
10. Bigelow (1977); Youniss (1980).
11. See Cairns *et al.* (in press).

12. Berndt (1982).
13. We thank Lisa Buchanan for her work on these analyses.
14. Jean-Louis Gariépy and Thomas Kinderman collaborated with us toward the solution of this problem (Cairns, Gariépy, & Kinderman, 1990). Man-Chi Leung and Haldor Julinsoon have written computer programs to facilitate the SCM analysis.
15. See Gronlund (1959) for an excellent early review, and McConnell & Odom (1986), for an excellent recent one.
16. Moreno (1934).
17. Bronfenbrenner (1943, 1944).
18. Gronlund (1959).
19. Cairns, Perrin, & Cairns (1985); Cairns & Cairns (1991a).
20. Cairns et al. (1988).
21. Cairns, Gariépy, & Kinderman (1990).
22. See Leung (1993).
23. See Cairns, Perrin, & Cairns (1985).
24. See Leung (1993) for work in Hong Kong and Gaines, Cairns, & Cairns (1993) for research in the the inner city.
25. It should be noted that the intraclass coefficients have been computed for the whole cohort, across all classrooms, separately for males and females. An alternative strategy would be to compute the intraclass coefficients on the basis of each classroom. We have done both. Comparison of the two sets of results (i.e. those for the whole sample, those for individual classrooms), indicates that there is considerable variability among classrooms in the homophily for aggressive behavior. While the results for the total sample are not misleading in the sense that there is a strong propensity toward similarity on the basis of acting out behaviors, some classrooms have considerably higher levels of homophily than others. Preliminary analyses suggest that the most disrupted classrooms are those where the teachers permit the aggressive subjects to form cliques.
26. Homophily has been employed by Kandel (1978) to refer to group similarity phenomenon. Due to the possible ambiguity of the term, we use corresemblance to describe the phenomenon of within-group similarity, and biselection and reciprocation as possible explanatory constructs.
27. Kandel (1978).
28. Cohen (1977); Kandel (1978), Rodgers, Billy, & Udry (1984).
29. Kandel (1978).
30. Rodgers, Billy, & Udry (1984).
31. See also Pulkkinen (1993).
32. Cohen (1977).
33. Cohen (1977) and Kandel (1978) employ "homophily" to refer to the phenomena of coresemblance.
34. Zank (1988).
35. Strayer & Noel (1986). See also Urberg and Kaplan (1989).
36. Feshbach & Sones (1971).
37. Bigelow (1977).

38. Cairns *et al.* (1989).
39. Steinberg *et al.* (in press).
40. See Oden & Asher (1977).
41. Comments we have made about the invisible hand of parents in adolescent social affiliations seem to be equally important in younger children, as Robert Wozniak pointed out to us (personal communication, March, 1990). According to Wozniak, when parents selectively invite, or selectively omit, particular children from weekend parties, the social affiliation patterns of preschool children shift markedly on Monday morning.
42. Hall & Cairns (1984); MacCombie (1978); Patterson (1982); Raush, (1965).

Chapter 6

1. Hirschi (1969); Patterson & Dishion (1985); Thrasher (1928).
2. Hirschi (1969, p. 159).
3. Aichhorn (1935).
4. See Ainsworth (1972); Bowlby (1944, 1952, 1958, 1969, 1973); Sroufe & Waters (1977).
5. Bandura & Walters (1959, p. 375); see Cairns (1961), for a similar argument and a consideration of some of the difficulties in such therapy.
6. Bandura & Walters (1963); Cairns (1961); Mischel (1968).
7. Flavell (1963); Hunt (1961); Miller, (1956).
8. Dodge (1986, p. 283).
9. See also Asher & Dodge (1986); Coie *et al.* (1982); Roff & Wirt (1984).
10. Cohen (1955); Miller (1958); Short & Strodtbeck (1965).
11. Cohen (1955, p. 31).
12. Giordano, Cernkovich, & Pugh (1986); see also Campbell (1980, 1981); Farrington (1986); Hindelang (1976); Jessor & Jessor (1977); Morash (1983).
13. On this count, the youthful gangs of the inner city have some features in common with the fraternal organizations of middle-age and middle-class adult males, including the Freemasons, the Mystic Order of the Shrine, and other fraternal organizations.
14. On the other hand, Simmons & Blyth (1987) found some support for this proposition in a Minneapolis sample of youth. Further study is obviously required before this puzzle is solved.

Chapter 7

1. Mills-Byrd & Cairns (1987).
2. Ross (1989).

3. Ledingham *et al.* (1982); Olweus (1979).
4. See Sears (1965) on masculinity–femininity; Hartshorne & May (1928) and Yarrow, Campbell, & Burton (1968) on conscience; Gewirtz (1972) on dependency.
5. See also Cairns & Cairns (1981; 1988); Epstein (1973, 1980); Greenwald (1980); Wallwork (1982).
6. Different types of interactional measures (e.g. personality ratings and direct behavior observations) may serve different functions, capture different information, and become useful for different purposes in prediction or explanation (Cairns & Green, 1979). The lack of convergence among measures is not necessarily due to unreliability or measurement error; to the contrary, different attributional measures of the "same" thing can capture independent sources of variance (Kelley, 1973).
7. We are thinking of Muhammud Ali, but other boxers could qualify as well.
8. See the excellent recent review by Sedikides (1994). Also, Cairns & Cairns (1988) and Cairns (1990).
9. Boucher & Osgood (1969). These investigators observed that there exist more positive adjectives than negative ones in all languages they investigated using the semantic differential.
10. Paris & Cairns (1972).
11. See Cairns, Cairns, & Neckerman (1989).
12. Even with this self-imposed limitation, we obtained an enormous amount of information on self-concepts and on the reports of others. Our task here is to clarify their relevance for lifelines and risks without burying ideas in numbers and tyrannizing readers with statistics. It is important to note that, with rare exception, the findings reported here are replicated within and between cohorts.
13. The other alternative – which we did not employ in this investigation – would be to have the ratings completed by individuals who know the subjects intimately, such as their parents, mates, or closest friends (Marsh, Parker, & Smith 1983). While that selection criterion has the merit of attempting to establish a human standard for degree of knowledge about the individual, it has the disadvantage of creating nonstandard conditions for interpretation of information. Given the intimate involvement of some "others" with the subject, the same biases reflected in the self-concept would be reflected in the concepts of them provided by the significant other. Such information would be less outside the self than a part of the self.
14. In Lake Wobegone, according to Garrison Keillor, "all the men are strong, all the women are handsome, and all the children are above average". "Lake Wobegone Effect" refers to the third condition.
15. In fact, four definitions of "average" could be offered. Two require information from some normative comparison group. Hence one definition of average is the mean of the scores given the participant population for a particular item or factor by the responses of the other. Another nomothetic definition is the mean of the self-reports of the participant population for a particular item or factor. A third definition of average requires no information from the population: it is the midpoint of the scale item (4.0).

The fourth definition is idiographic, referring to the mean of all items for a given subject.

16. Mean scores are discussed here. In addition, the same self-enhancement bias was obtained when individual scores in each year were analyzed. For example, 82% of the subjects rated themselves in the above average categories of popularity with peers, while only 4% saw themselves as below average or worse on this dimension. This effect held across the nine years of data collection in Cohort I and six years of data collection in Cohort II. The same held for academic competence, where 70–82% saw themselves above average, and 3–7% rated themselves below average across each of the nine years of school.

17. In a recent dissertation, Man-Chi Leung (1993) has provided an informative analysis of the consequences of this regression for understanding self-esteem measures.

18. These statements are based on a family of MANOVA tests, where the self-other by gender interaction was highly reliable from 12 to 16 years of age, but not younger or older.

19. Only the results of aggression are shown here. Parallel findings were obtained for other self-report measures related to competence.

20. See Dryfoos (1990) for a useful review.

Chapter 8

1. Rauch (1989).
2. Annie's explanation was almost identical to the one offered by a New York City dropout interviewed who said, "I didn't drop out, I was thrown out" (Fine, 1986, p. 99).
3. Fine (1987).
4. Whelage (1983); Whelage & Rutter (1986).
5. Pallas (1986).
6. US Bureau of Census (1987).
7. Fine (1984).
8. Wilson (1987).
9. Ensminger & Slusarcick (1992) began with 1,242 subjects and report data on graduation/dropout for 917 subjects. The difference is due to the children who transferred out of the school system, death, or a very small proportion (0.005) who were still in school.
10. McDill, Natriello, & Pallas (1986); Quay (1978); Stroup & Robins (1972).
11. US Bureau of Census (1987).
12. Kaplan & Luck (1977); Steinberg, Blinde, & Chan (1984).
13. US Bureau of Census (1987, p. 2).
14. Ensminger & Slusarcick (1992).
15. These data are taken from Cohort II, the older group of 475 subjects, who are old enough to have dropped out. Cohort I data are consistent, except where noted.

16. These data are based upon the total sample of living subjects. Earlier reported findings in Cairns, Cairns, & Neckerman (1989) summarized the results only from Cohort II. The findings are basically in line with the earlier report, except more white females showed early school dropout in the total sample than in Cohort II. Accordingly, no gender differences in early dropout were identified in the total sample.

17. The problem of configuration analysis was approached by the perspective provided by cluster analysis. A person-cluster analysis was performed on the basis of the behavioral, academic, and demographic information available in the 7th grade. The subsequent rate of early school dropout could then be computed for each cluster. Employing a standard agglomerative hierarchical clustering procedure, seven clusters were identified for both females and males. The clusters were defined on the basis of information obtained in the 7th grade, prior to and independent of school dropout information.

18. The intraclass correlations were statistically reliable for both boys and girls in the 7th grade, but they accounted for only a small portion of the variance. This means that peer associations in the 7th grade provided only modest predictive power for subsequent dropout.

19. Rutter & Quinton (1984).

20. See related work by Stroup & Robins (1972).

21. It should be noted that Ensminger & Slusarcick (1992) report as well upon certain family characteristics, including maternal education and expectations in adolescence.

22. From a forthcoming paper. These statements are based upon an unpublished set of multiple logistic regression analyses that entered the same set of endogenous and exogenous variables employed in the published Cohort II paper (see Cairns, Cairns, & Neckerman, 1989).

23. Magnusson (1988). Correlational and regression analyses do not capture this distinction, in that the homogeneity assumption implies a uniform aggression–dropout relationship across the entire sample.

24. McDill, Natriello, & Pallas (1986), but see Pallas (1986) for a different view.

25. Bureau of Census (1987).

26. The importance of such research cannot be overestimated. Among other things, these data suggest that the *Brown v. Topeka* decision of the US Supreme Court on the desegregation of public schools may have had its greatest effect in southern states, where the proportion of black and white children attending a given school was closely regulated by the federal court. Such supervision was not as close outside the South, even in the major cities. Where the experiment was practiced, in the integration of actual schools of the South, it seems to have begun working in the second generation in terms of school completion. Where it seems to have "failed", notably in the inner cities, there was virtually no experiment (Wilson, 1987).

27. Fine (1986, 1987); Finkelstein (1981).

28. The preliminary nature of these analyses should be stressed. They are based upon only the participants in Cohort I. Additional analyses of the total sample are forthcoming.

Chapter 9

1. Monthly Vital Statistics Report (1982, 1985).
2. Tore Bjerke (1989), unpublished data from the Norwegian Health Council.
3. See also Garfinkel, Froese, & Hood (1982); Goldacre & Hawton (1985); Hawton *et al.* (1982); McClure (1984); Rohn *et al.* (1977); Wexler, Weissman, & Kasl (1978).
4. See Behar (1985). Evaluating clinicians were allowed to make diagnoses using either DSM-III or ICD-9 nosology.
5. Åsberg, *et al.* (1987).
6. Cairns, Gariépy, & Hood (1990).
7. Hocking (1989).
8. Fingerhut & Kleinman (1990); Lee & Livingston (1991); Livingston & Lee (1992); Sadowski, Cairns & Earp (1989).
9. Sadowski, Cairns, & Earp, (1989).

Chapter 10

1. See, for example, Magnusson (1988), Robins (1986), Jessor & Jessor (1977), and Jessor, Donovan, & Costa (1991). We expected, further, that there would be multiple developmental pathways as opposed to a single general problem syndrome.
2. The matching was successful on all variables (e.g. no significant differences were obtained on classroom, race, physical size, SES, age), with one exception. The aggressive–control subjects in the 4th grade did not differ in age (10.1 *versus* 10.3 years in aggressive and control females, and 10.6 *versus* 10.5 years in aggressive and control males, respectively). However, the aggressive–control subjects in the 7th grade differed (13.6 *versus* 13.0 years in aggressive and control females, and 14.1 *versus* 13.3 in the aggressive and control males, respectively). To correct for any effects attributable to the age discrepancy in the older sample, all analyses were conducted with and without age as a covariate. In no instance did covariance analyses (controlling for age) yield outcomes on the relevant variables significantly different than the ANOVA analyses.
3. The findings discussed here on substance abuse are preliminary; a full report is in preparation. See also Earls & Powell (1988), Elliott, *et al.* (1985), and Kandel & Yamaguchi (1993) for further relevant findings.
4. These findings on parenthood are preliminary; a full report is in preparation.
5. The biases that keep individuals on a given developmental trajectory were expected to be multi-level, and they emerge in different forms at the several stages of ontogeny. Our ideas on this matter have been outlined in greater detail elsewhere (Cairns, Gariépy, & Hood, 1990).
6. This investigation was guided by a consideration of the biases that exist social development. Specifically, we anticipated that there would be

evidence for developmental homeostasis in behavioral development akin to
genetic homeostasis in phylogeny (Lerner, 1954).

Chapter 11

1. Cairns (1979); Magnusson (1988).
2. The developmental model has its foundation in the social-cognitive theory
   of J. M. Baldwin (1897), and the developmental psychobiology of T. C.
   Schneirla (1966) and Zing-Yang Kuo (1967), with modern systematic
   statements provided by Cairns (1979, 1986a, 1991, 1992), Bronfenbrenner (1993), Gottlieb (1983, 1992), Magnusson (1988), and Sameroff
   (1983). This section borrows from Magnusson & Cairns (in press).
3. Freud (1933).
4. Lorenz (1965); Scott (1977).
5. Bateson (1979); Gottlieb (1979).
6. Magnusson (1988).
7. Rosenblatt (1965).
8. Bowlby (1973).
9. Bronfenbrenner's concept of the continuing impact of experience in
   adolescent development has been extended in recent works, including the
   important volumes by Feldman & Elliott (1990) and Csikszentmihalyi,
   Rathunde, & Whalen (1993).
10. From (1941).
11. There are limits, as noted in Brown (1965), Cairns (1979), and Homans
    (1950).
12. Vonnegut (1967).
13. Baldwin (1897).
14. Cooley (1922).
15. The concept of "innate drift" was introduced by Breland and Breland
    (1961) to refer to how the lessons of operant conditioning could be
    eliminated by developmental changes in structure and motivation.
16. Ospiow (1993).

Chapter 12

1. This was not Hall's only pioneering effort. He was the first president of the
   American Psychological Association, the first professor of psychology in
   the United States (at Johns Hopkins University), the editor of the first
   American journal devoted to psychology, a founder of the child study
   movement in North America. At 83 years of age, he published the first
   textbook on behavioral aging, entitled *Senescence*.
2. McCord (1991).
3. Wallace (1990).
4. Recent longitudinal findings indicate that there is significant continuity and
   organization in individual social patterns across ontogeny (e.g. Cairns &

Cairns, 1991b; Coie & Dodge, 1983; Elder *et al.*, 1986; Farrington & West, 1990; Magnusson, 1988; Olweus, 1979; Patterson, DeBaryshe, & Ramsey, 1989; Rutter, 1988; Sampson, & Laub, 1993; Stattin, 1990; Werner & Smith, 1986). Such continuities over time seem to reflect the operation of correlated constraints, including those within the person as well as those outside the self (i.e. in his/her social, economic, and physical environment). Such longitudinal research findings on the conservative nature of development are wholly consistent with the results of intervention programs, which find that key social behaviors are highly resistant to change and modification (Loeber & LeBlanc, 1990; McCord, 1986). Resistance to modification is particularly apparent for aggressive, violent behaviors (Earls, Cairns, & Mercy, 1993).

5. These implications are consistent with the recent recommendations of the Carnegie Council on Adolescent Development with regard to the programs needed to promote health in adolescence (Hechinger, 1992). In brief, the Council recommends that: (1) adolescents should have health education and life skills training that give special attention to conflict resolution and responsible decision making; (2) adolescents should have access to health services through student health clinics and adequate care; (3) adults should be willing and able to provide responsible direction, in part through becoming embedded in a network of supportive community and youth organizations, and efforts should be made to improve the social and environmental conditions in which youths live, including more adequate control of illicit substances and firearms, and better connections to "the world of work". See also the recent recommendations of a special panel of the National Academy of Science (Reiss & Roth, 1993). McCord and Tremblay (1992) and Earls, *et al.* (1993) contain useful discussions of contemporary violence intervention and prevention programs

References

Adams, H. B. (1918). *The education of Henry Adams: An autobiography.* New York: Houghton-Mifflin.

Aichhorn, A. (1935). *Wayward youth.* New York: Viking Press.

Ainsworth, M. D. S. (1972). Attachment and dependency: A comparison. In J. L. Gewirtz (Ed.), *Attachment and dependency* (pp. 97–137). New York: Wiley.

Ainsworth, M. D. S., Blehar, M., Waters, E., & Wall, S. (1978). *Patterns of attachment: A psychological study of the strange situation.* Hillsdale, NJ: Lawrence Erlbaum Associates.

Allport, G. W. (1937). *Personality: A psychological interpretation.* New York: Holt, Rinehart, & Winston.

Anderson, T., Bergman, L. R., & Magnusson, D. (1989). Patterns of adjustment problems and alcohol abuse in early adulthood: A prospective longitudinal study. *Development and Psychopathology, 1,* 119–131.

Asberg, M., Shalling, D., Traskman-Bendz, L., & Wagner, A. (1987). Psychobiology of suicide, impulsivity, and related phenomena. In H. Y. Meltzer (Ed.), *Psychopharmacology: The third generation of progress* (pp. 655–668). New York: Raven Press.

Asher, S. R., & Coie, J. D. (1990). (Eds) *Peer rejection in childhood.* New York: Cambridge.

Asher, S. R., & Dodge, K. A. (1986). Identifying children who are rejected by their peers. *Developmental Psychology, 22,* 444–449.

Baldwin, A. L. (1967). *Theories of child development.* New York: Wiley.

Baldwin, J. M. (1897). *Social and ethical interpretations in mental development: A study in social psychology.* New York: Macmillan.

Baltes, P. B., & Baltes, M. M. (1990). (Eds) *Successful aging: Perspectives from the behavior sciences.* Cambridge, UK: Cambridge University Press.

Bandura, A. (1973). *Aggression: A social learning analysis.* Englewood Cliffs: Prentice Hall.

Bandura, A. (1982). Self-efficacy mechanism in human agency. *American Psychologist, 37,* 122–147.

288

Bandura, A., & Walters, R. H. (1959). *Adolescent aggression*. New York: Ronald Press.

Bandura, A., & Walters, R. H. (1963). *Social learning and personality development*. New York: Holt, Rinehart, & Winston.

Bateson, P. P. G. (1979). How do sensitive periods arise and what are they good for? *Animal Behaviour, 27*, 470–486.

Behar, L. (1985). Changing patterns of state responsibility: A case study of North Carolina. *Journal of Clinical Child Psychology, 14*, 188–195.

Bergman, L. R., & Magnusson, D. (1990). General issues about data quality in longitudinal research. In D. Magnusson & L. R. Bergman, *Data quality in longitudinal research* (pp. 1–31). Cambridge, UK: Cambridge University Press.

Berndt, T. J. (1982). The features and effects of friendship in early adolescence. *Child Development, 53*, 1447–1460.

Berndt, T. J., & Hoyle, S. G. (1985). Stability and change in childhood and adolescent friendships. *Developmental Psychology, 21*, 1007–1015.

Bertalanffy, L. V. (1962). *Modern theories of development: An introduction to theoretical biology*. New York: Harper & Brothers. (First published in 1933.)

Bigelow, B. J. (1977). Children's friendship expectations: A cognitive-developmental study. *Child Development, 48*, 246–253.

Block, J. (1971). *Lives through time*. Berkeley: Bancroft Books.

Block, J. (1977). Advancing the psychology of personality: paradigmatic shift or improving the quality of research. In D. Manusson & N. D. Endler (Eds.), *Personality at the crossroads: Current issues in interactional psychology* (pp. 37–63). Hillsdale: Erlbaum.

Block, J. (1983). Differential premises arising from differential socialization of the sexes: Some conjectures. *Child Development, 54*, 1335–1354.

Block, J. H., & Block, J. (1980). The role of ego-control and ego-resiliency in the organization of behavior. In W. A. Collins (Ed.), *Minnesota symposium on child psychology* (Vol. 13) (pp. 39–101). Hillsdale: Erlbaum.

Bloom, B. (1964). *The stability of human characteristics*. New York: Wiley.

Boucher, J., & Osgood, C. E. (1969). The Pollyanna hypothesis. *Journal of Verbal Learning and Verbal Behavior, 8*, 1–8.

Bowlby, J. (1944). Forty-four juvenile thieves: Their characters and homelife. *International Journal of Psychoanalysis, 25*, 19–52 and 107–127.

Bowlby, J. (1952). *Maternal care and mental health (2nd ed.)*. Geneva: World Health Organization.

Bowlby, J. (1958). The nature of the child's tie to his mother. *International Journal of Psychoanalysis, 39*, 350–373.

Bowlby, J. (1969). *Attachment and loss*. New York: Basic Books.

Bowlby, J. (1973). *Attachment and loss. Vol. 2. Separation*. New York: Basic Books.

Breland, K., and Breland, M. (1961). The misbehavior of organisms. *American Psychologist, 16*, 681–684.

Brennan, T., Huizinga, D., & Elliott, D. S. (1978). *The social psychology of runaways*. Lexington, MA: D. C. Heath.

Brim, O. G., Jr., & Kagan, J. (1980). (Eds). *Constancy and change in human development*. Cambridge, MA: Harvard University Press.

Bronfenbrenner, U. (1943). A constant frame of reference for sociometric research. *Sociometry, 6,* 363–397.

Bronfenbrenner, U. (1944). A constant frame of reference for sociometric research: Part II. Experiment and inference. *Sociometry, 7,* 40–75.

Bronfenbrenner, U. (1979). *The ecology of human development: Experiments by nature and design.* Cambridge, MA: Harvard University Press.

Bronfenbrenner, U. (1993). The ecology of cognitive development: Research models and fugitive findings. In R. H. Wozniak & K. Fischer (Eds), *Development in context: Acting and thinking in specific environments.* Hillsdale: Erlbaum.

Bronfenbrenner, U., & Crouter, A. C. (1983). The evolution of environmental models in developmental research. In W. Kessen (Vol. Ed.) & P. H. Mussen (Gen. Ed.), *Handbook of child psychology* (Vol. 1) pp. 357–414, 4th edn. New York: Wiley.

Brown, B. B. (1990). Peer groups and peer cultures. In S. S. Feldman & G. R. Elliott (Eds), *At the threshold: The developing adolescent* (pp. 171–196). Cambridge, MA: Harvard University Press.

Brown, R. W. (1965). *Social psychology.* New York: Free Press.

Cairns, C. B., Neimeyer, J., Neiman, J., & Cairns, R. B. (1991). Aggressive and violent injury among children and young adults. *Ann. Emerg. Med., 20,* 951.

Cairns, R. B. (1961). The influence of dependency inhibition on the effectiveness of social approval. *Journal of Personality, 29,* 466–488.

Cairns, R. B. (1979). *Social development: The origins and plasticity of social interchanges.* San Francisco: Freeman.

Cairns, R. B. (1983a). Sociometry, psychometry, and social structure: A commentary on six recent studies of popular, rejected, and neglected children. *Merrill–Palmer Quarterly, 29,* 429–438.

Cairns, R. B. (1983b). The emergence of developmental psychology. In P. H. Mussen (Gen. Ed.) & W. Kessen (Vol. Ed.), *Handbook of child psychology: Volume 1: History, theory, and methods* (pp. 41–102, 4th edn). New York: Wiley.

Cairns, R. B. (1986a). A contemporary perspective on social development. In P. S. Strain, M. J. Guralnick, & H. M. Walker (Eds), *Children's social behavior: Development, assessment, and modification* (pp. 3–47). New York: Academic.

Cairns, R. B. (1986b). Phenomena lost: Issues in the study of development. In J. Valsiner (Ed.), *The individual subject and scientific psychology* (pp. 97–112). New York: Plenum Press.

Cairns, R. B. (1990). Developmental epistemology and self knowledge. In E. Tobach, L. Aronson, & G. Greenberg (Eds), *Levels of development: Schneirla Symposium* (Vol. 4). Hillsdale: Erlbaum.

Cairns, R. B. (1991). Multiple metaphors for a singular idea. *Developmental Psychology, 27,* 23–26.

Cairns, R. B. (1992). The making of a developmental science: The contributions and intellectual heritage of James Mark Baldwin. *Developmental Psychology, 28,* 17–24.

Cairns, R. B., & Cairns, B. D. (1981). Self-reflections: An essay and commentary on "Social cognition and the acquisition of self". *Developmental Review*, *1*, 171–180.

Cairns, R. B., & Cairns, B. D. (1984). Predicting aggressive patterns in girls and boys: A developmental study. *Aggressive Behavior*, *11*, 227–242.

Cairns, R. B., & Cairns, B. D. (1986). The developmental-interactional view of social behavior: Four issues of adolescent aggression. In D. Olweus, J. Block, & M. Radke-Yarrow (Eds), *Development of antisocial and prosocial behavior: Research, theories, and issues* (pp. 315–342). New York: Academic.

Cairns, R. B., & Cairns, B. D. (1988). The sociogenesis of self concepts. In N. Bolger, A. Caspi, G. Downey, & M. Moorehouse (Eds), *Persons in social context: Developmental processes* (pp. 181–202). New York: Cambridge University Press.

Cairns, R. B., & Cairns, B. D. (1991a). Social cognition and social networks: A developmental perspective. In D. Pepler & K. Rubin (Eds), *The development and treatment of childhood aggression* (pp. 249–278). Hillsdale: Erlbaum.

Cairns, R. B., & Cairns, B. D. (1991b). Sociogenesis of aggressive and antisocial behaviors. In J. McCord (Ed.), *Facts, frameworks, and forecasts: Advances in criminological theory* (pp. 157–192). New Brunswick: Transaction Press.

Cairns, R. B., Cairns, B.D., Leung, M.-C., & Ladd, T. R. (1994). *Measures and methods for the CLS longitudinal study.* Chapel Hill, NC: Center for Developmental Science.

Cairns, R. B., Cairns, B. D., & Neckerman, H. J. (1989). Early school dropout: Configurations and determinants. *Child Development*, *60*, 1437–1452.

Cairns, R. B., Cairns, B. D., Neckerman, H. J., Ferguson, L. L., & Gariépy, J.-L. (1989). Growth and aggression: I. Childhood to early adolescence. *Developmental Psychology, 25, 320–330.*

Cairns, R. B., Cairns, B. D., Neckerman, H. J., Gest, S., & Gariépy, J.-L. (1988). Social networks and aggressive behavior: Peer support or peer rejection? *Developmental Psychology*, *24*, 815–823.

Cairns, R. B., Elder, G. H., Jr., Costello, E. J., & McGuire, A. (Eds) (in press). *Developmental science.* New York: Cambridge University Press.

Cairns, R. B., Gariépy, J.-L., & Kindermann, T. (1990). *Identifying social clusters in natural settings.* Unpublished manuscript, University of North Carolina at Chapel Hill, Chapel Hill, North Carolina.

Cairns, R. B., Gariépy, J.-L., & Hood, K. E. (1990). Development, microevolution, and social behavior. *Psychological Review*, *97*, 49–65.

Cairns, R. B., & Green, J. A. (1979). How to assess personality and social patterns: Ratings or observations? In R. B. Cairns (Ed), *The analysis of social interaction: Methods, issues, and illustrations* (pp. 209–226). Hillsdale: Erlbaum.

Cairns, R. B., & Kroll, A. B. (1994). A developmental perspective on gender differences and similarities. In M. L. Rutter, D. F. Hay, & S. Baron-Cohen (Eds), *Developmental principles and clinical issues in psychology and psychiatry.* Oxford: Blackwell Scientific Publications.

Cairns, R. B., Leung, M-C., Buchanan, L. D., & Cairns, B. D. (in press).

Friendships and social networks in childhood and early adolescence: Short-term stability and fluidity. *Child Development.*

Cairns, R. B., & Moffitt, T. (1992). *Task force on individual and family measures: I. Rationale and criteria for selection.* Cambridge, MA: Harvard University School of Public Health Program on Human Development and Criminal Behavior.

Cairns, R. B., Perrin, J. E., & Cairns, B. D. (1985). Social structure and social cognition in early adolescence: Affiliative patterns. *Journal of Early Adolescence, 5,* 339–355.

Cairns, R. B., Peterson, G., & Neckerman, H. J. (1988). Suicidal behavior in aggressive adolescents. *Journal of Clinical Child Psychology, 17,* 298–309.

Cairns, R. B., Santoyo, C., & Holly, K. A. (in press). Aggressive escalation: Toward a developmental analysis. In M. Potegal & J. Knutson (Eds), *Escalation of aggression: Biological and social proceses.* Hillsdale, NJ: Lawrence Erlbaum Associates.

Campbell, A. (1980). Friendship as a factor in male and female delinquency. In H.C. Foot, A.J. Chapman, & J.R. Smith (Eds), *Friendship and social relations in children* (pp. 365–390). Chichester: John Wiley.

Campbell, A. (1981). *Girl delinquents.* New York: St. Martin's Press.

Caplan, P., MacPherson, G., & Tobin, P. (1985). Do sex related differences in spatial abilities exist? *American Psychologist, 40,* 786–799.

Caspi, A., & Moffitt, T. (1991). *Puberty and deviance in girls.* Symposium paper read at the Biennial Meeting of the Society for Research in Child Development, Seattle, Washington, April.

Census of population (1980). General population characteristics. (1983). *1980 census of population. Volume 1. Characteristics of the population.* Washington, DC: US Department of Commerce, Bureau of the Census.

Choquet, M., Facy, F., & Davidson, F. (1980). Suicide and attempted suicide among adolescents in France. In R. D. T. Farmer & S. Hirsch (Eds), *The suicide syndrome* (pp. 73–89). London: Cambridge University Press.

Cobb, B., Cairns, R. B., Miles, M., & Cairns, B. D. (1994). The role of gender, risk-taking, and aggression in adolescent injury: A longitudinal perspective. Presented at the 8th Annual Conference of the Southern Nursing Research Society. Chapel Hill. (published abstract).

Cohen, A. K. (1955). *Delinquent boys: The culture of the gang.* Glencoe: Free Press.

Cohen, J. M. (1977). Sources of peer group homogeneity. *Sociology of Education, 50,* 227–241.

Coie, J. D. (1990). Toward a theory of peer rejection. In S. R. Asher & J. D. Coie (Eds), *Peer rejection in childhood* (pp. 365–398). New York: Cambridge University Press.

Coie, J. D., & Dodge, K. A. (1983). Continuities and changes in children's social status: A five-year longitudinal study. *Merrill–Palmer Quarterly, 29,* 261–282.

Coie, J. D., Dodge, K. A., & Coppotelli, H. A. (1982). Dimensions and types of social status: A cross-age perspective. *Developmental Psychology, 18,* 557–569.

Coleman, J. S. (1961). *The adolescent society.* New York: Free Press.

Comer, J. (1980). *School power: Implications in an intervention project.* Free Press: Collier Macmillan.

Cook, P. J. (1991). The technology of personal violence. In M. Tonry (Ed.), *Crime and justice: A review of research* (pp. 1–71). Chicago: University of Chicago Press.

Cooley, C. H. (1922). *Human nature and the social order.* Rev. Edn. Glencoe: Free Press.

Crime in the United States. (1992). Washington, DC: Government Printing Office.

Csikszentmihalyi, M., Rathunde, K., & Whalen, M. (1993). *Talented teenagers: The roots of success and failure.* New York: Cambridge University Press.

Davis, P. A. (1983). *Suicidal adolescents.* Springfield: Charles C. Thomas.

de Ribaupierre, A. (1989). (Ed.) *Transition mechanisms in child development: The longitudinal perspective.* Cambridge, UK: Cambridge University Press.

Dodge, K. A. (1986). Social information-processing variables in the development of aggression and altruism in children. In C. Zahn-Waxler, E. M. Cummings, & R. Iannotti (Eds), *Altruism and aggression: Biological and social origins* (pp. 280–302). Cambridge, UK: Cambridge University Press.

Dolan, L. F., Kellam, S. G., Hendricks-Brown, C., Werthamer-Larsson, L., Rebok, G. W., Mayer, L. W., Laudolff, J., & Turkkan, J. S. (1993). The short-term impact of two classroom-based preventive interventions on aggressive and shy behaviors and poor achievement. *Journal of Applied Developmental Psychology, 14,* 317–345.

Dryfoos, J. G. (1990). *Adolescents at risk: Prevalence and prevention.* New York: Oxford University Press.

Earls, F., & Powell, J. (1989). Patterns of substance use and abuse in inner-city adolescent medical patients. *Journal of Biology and Medicine, 61,* 233–242.

Earls, F., Cairns, R. B., & Mercy, J. (1993). The control of violence and the promotion of non-violence in adolescence. In S. G. Millstein, A. C. Petersen, & E. O. Nightingale (Eds), *Promoting the health of adolescents: New directions for the twenty-first century* (pp. 285–304). New York: Oxford University Press.

Edwards, C. A. (1990). *Leadership, social networks, and personal attributes in school age girls.* Unpublished doctoral dissertation, University of North Carolina at Chapel Hill, Chapel Hill, North Carolina.

Elder, G. H., Jr., (1974). *Children of the Great Depression: Social change in life experience.* Chicago: University of Chicago Press.

Elder, G. H., Jr. (in press). Life course development. In R. B. Cairns, G. H. Elder, Jr., E. J. Costello, & A. McGuire (Eds), *Developmental science.* New York: Cambridge University Press.

Elder, G.H., Jr., Caspi, A., & Van Nguyen, T. (1986). Resourceful and vulnerable children: Family influences in hard times. In R. Silbereisen & H. Eyferth (Eds), *Development as action in context: Problem behavior and normal youth development* (pp. 167–186). New York: Springer.

Elder, G. H., Jr., Liker, J. K., & Cross, C. E. (1984). Parent-child behavior in the great depression: Life course and intergenerational influences. In P. B.

Baltes & O.G. Brim, Jr. (Eds), *Life-span development and behavior* (Vol. 6, pp. 111–159). New York: Academic Press.

Elliott, D. S., Huizinga, D., & Ageton, S. S. (1985). *Explaining delinquency and drug use.* Beverly Hills: Sage.

Elliott, D. S., Huizinga, D., & Menard, S. (1989). *Multiple problem youth: Delinquency, substance use, and mental health problems.* New York: Springer-Verlag.

Ensminger, M. E., & Slusarcick, A. L. (1992). Paths to high school graduation or dropout: A longitudinal study of a first-grade cohort. *Sociology of Education, 65,* 95–113.

Epstein, S. (1973). The self-concept revisited: Or a theory of a theory. *American Psychologist, 28,* 404–416.

Epstein, S. (1980). The stability of behavior: II. Implications for psychological research. *American Psychologist, 35,* 790–806.

Eron, L., & Huesmann, L. R. (1987). The control of aggressive behavior by changes in attitudes, values, and the conditions of learning. In R. J. Blanchard & C. Blanchard (Eds), *Advances in the study of aggression* (Vol. 2, pp. 139–171). New York: Academic Press.

Eron, L., Huesmann, L. R., Brice, P., Fischer, P., & Mermelstein, R. (1983) Age trends in the development of aggression, sex typing, and related television habits. *Developmental Psychology, 19,* 71–77.

Farrington, D. P. (1986). Stepping stones to adult criminal careers. In D. Olweus, J. Block, & M. Radke-Yarrow (Eds), *Development of antisocial and prosocial behavior: Research, theories, and issues* (pp. 359–384). New York: Academic.

Farrington, D. P., Gallagher, B., Morley, L., St. Ledger, R. J., & West, D. J. (1990) Minimizing attrition in longitudinal research: Methods of tracing and securing cooperation in a 24-year follow-up study. In D. Magnusson & L. R. Bergman (Eds), *Data quality in longitudinal research* (pp. 122–147). Cambridge, UK: Cambridge University Press.

Feldman, S. S., & Elliott, G. R. (1990). *At the threshold: The developing adolescent.* Cambridge, MA: Harvard University Press.

Ferguson, T. J., & Rule, B. G. (1980). Effects of inferential set, outcome severity, and basis of responsibility on children's evaluation of aggressive acts. *Developmental Psychology, 16,* 141–146.

Feshbach, N. D., & Sones, G. (1971). Sex differences in adolescent reactions to newcomers. *Developmental Psychology, 4,* 381–386.

Feshbach, S. (1970). Aggression. In P. H. Mussen (Ed.), *Carmichael's manual of child psychology* (3rd edn, Vol. 2). New York: Wiley.

Feshbach, S., & Price, J. (1984). Cognitive competencies and aggressive behavior: A developmental study. *Aggressive Behavior, 10,* 185–200.

Fine, M. (1986). Why urban adolescents drop into and out of public high school. *Teachers College Record, 87,* 89–105.

Fine, M. (1987). Silencing in public schools. *Language Arts, 64,* 157–174.

Fingerhut, L. A., & Kleinman, J. C. (1990). International and interstate comparisons of homicide among young males. *Journal of the American Medical Association, 263,* 3292–3295.

Finkelstein, B. (1981). Private conflicts in public schools: The sabotage of educative possibilities? *Phi Delta Kappa*, *75*, 326–328.
Flavell, J. H. (1963). *The developmental psychology of Jean Piaget*. Princeton: Van Nostrand.
Freud, S. (1933). *New introductory lectures on psycho-analysis*. New York: Norton.
Friedrich-Cofer, L. (1989). *Parental abdication: A problem in search of a policy*. Paper read at the Biennial Meeting of the Society for Research in Child Development. Kansas City, Missouri, April.
Frodi, A., Macaulay, J., & Thome, P. R. (1977). Are women always less aggressive than men? A review of the experimental literature. *Psychological Bulletin*, *84*, 634–660.
Fromm, F. (1941). *Escape from freedom*. New York: Farrar & Rinehart.
Gaines, K. R., Cairns, R. B., and Cairns, B. D. (1994). *Social networks and risk for school dropout*. Paper presented at the Society for Research in Adolescence, San Diego, California, March 1994.
Garfinkel, B. D., Froese, A., & Hood, J. (1982). Suicide attempts in children and adolescents. *American Journal of Psychiatry*, *139*, 1257–1261.
Gewirtz, J. L. (1972). *Attachment and dependency*. Washington: V. H. Winston.
Giordano, P. C. (1978). Research note: Girls, guys, and gangs: the changing social context of female delinquency. *The Journal of Criminal Law and Criminology*, *69*, 126–132.
Giordano, P. C., Cernkovich, S. A., & Pugh, M. D. (1986). Friendship and delinquency. *American Journal of Sociology*, *91*, 1170–1202.
Gleick, J. (1987). *Chaos: Making a new science*. New York: Penguin Books.
Glueck, S., & Glueck, E. (1940). *Juvenile delinquents grown up*. New York: The Commonwealth Fund.
Glueck, S., & Glueck, E. T. (1950). *Unraveling juvenile delinquency*. Cambridge, MA: Harvard University Press.
Goldacre, M., & Hawton, K. (1985). Repetition of self-poisoning and subsequent death in adolescents who take overdoses. *British Journal of Psychiatry*, *146*, 395–398.
Gottlieb, G. (1979). Comparative psychology and ethology. In E. Hearst (Ed.) *The first century of experimental psychology* (pp. 147–176). Hillsdale: Erlbaum.
Gottlieb, G. (1983). The psychobiological approach to developmental issues. In M. M. Haith, J. J. Campos, & P. H. Mussen (Eds), *Handbook of child psychology, Vol 2: Infancy and developmental psychobiology* (pp. 1–26). New York: Wiley.
Gottlieb, G. (1992). *Individual development and evolution: The genesis of novel behavior*. New York: Oxford University Press.
Green, K. D., Beck, S. J., Forehand, R., & Vosk, B. (1980). Validity of teacher nominations of child behavior problems. *Journal of Abnormal Child Psychology*, *8*, 397–404.
Greenwald, A. G. (1980). The totalitarian ego: Fabrication and revision of personal history. *American Psychologist*, *35*, 603–618.
Gronlund, N. E. (1959). *Sociometry in the classroom*. New York: Harper.

Gulliksen, H. (1950). *Theory of mental tests*. New York: Wiley.

Hall, G. S. (1904). *Adolescence: Its psychology and its relations to physiology, anthropology, sociology, sex crime, religion, and education* (2 vols). New York: D. Appleton.

Hall, W. M., & Cairns, R. B. (1984). Aggressive behavior in children: An outcome of modeling or reciprocity? *Developmental Psychology*, 20, 739–745.

Hankoff, L. D. (1982). Suicide and attempted suicide. In E. S. Paykel (Ed.), *Handbook of affective disorders* (pp. 416–428). New York: Guilford Press.

Hartshorne, H., & May, M. A. (1928). *Studies in the nature of character. Vol. l: Studies in deceit*. New York: Macmillan.

Hawkins, D. A., Catalono, R. F., & Miller, J. Y. (1992). Risk and protective factors for alcohol and other drug problems in adolescence and early adulthood: Implications for substance abuse prevention. *Psychological Bulletin, 112*, 64–105.

Hawton, K., O'Grady, J., Osborn, M., & Cole, D. (1982). Adolescents who take overdoses: Their characteristics, problems and contacts with helping agencies. *British Journal of Psychiatry, 140*, 118–123.

Hechinger, F. M. (1992). *Fateful choices: Health, youth for the 21st century*. Carnegie Council on Adolescent Development, Carnegie Corporation of New York: New York.

Hindelang, M. J. (1976). With a little help from their friends: Group participation in reported delinquent behavior. *The British Journal of Criminology, 16*, 109–125.

Hirschi, T. (1969). *Causes of delinquency*. Berkeley: University of California Press.

Hirschi, T., & Gottfredson, M. (1983). Age and explanation of crime. *American Journal of Sociology, 89*, 552–584.

Hocking, M. A. (1989). Assaults in south east London. *Journal of the Royal Society of Medicine, 82*(5), 281–284.

Holland, D. & D. Skinner (in press). Contested ritual, contested feminities: (re)forming self and society in a Nepali women's festival. *American Ethnologist*.

Homans, G. C. (1950). *The human group*. New York: Harcourt, Brace.

Huesmann, L. R., Eron, L. D., Lefkowitz, M. M., & Walder, L. O. (1984). The stability of aggression over time and generations. *Developmental Psychology, 20*, 1120–1134.

Huesmann, L. R., Lagerspetz, K., & Eron, L. D. (1984). Intervening variables in the TV violence-aggression relation: Evidence from two countries. *Developmental Psychology, 20*, 746–775.

Hunt, J. McV. (1961). *Intelligence and experience*. New York: Ronald.

James, W. (1890). *The principles of psychology, Vol.1*. New York: Macmillan.

Jessor, R. (1982). Critical issues in research on adolescent health promotion. In T. J. Coates, A. C. Petersen, & C. Perry (Eds), *Promoting adolescent health: A dialogue on research and practice* (pp. 447–465). San Francisco: Academic Press.

Jessor, R., Donovan, J. E., & Costa, Frances M. (1991). *Beyond adolescence: Problem behavior and young adult development*. New York: Cambridge University Press.

Jessor, R., & Jessor, S. L. (1977). *Problem behavior and psychosocial development: A longitudinal study of youth.* New York: Academic.

Kadanoff, L. P. (1986). Chaos: A view of complexity in the physical sciences. In *The great ideas today: 1986.* Chicago: Encyclopaedia Britannica, Inc.

Kagan, J., & Moss, H. A. (1962). *Birth to maturity: A study in psychological development.* New York: Wiley.

Kandel, D.B. (1978). Homophily, selection, and socialization in adolescent friendships. *American Journal of Sociology, 84,* 427–436.

Kandel, D. S., & Yamaguchi, K. (1993). From beer to crack: Developmental patterns of drug involvement. *American Journal of Public Health, 83,* 851–855.

Kaplan, J. L., & Luck, E. D. (1977). The dropout phenomenon as a social problem. *Educational Forum, 47,* 316–318.

Kellam, S. G., Brown, C. H., Rubin, B. R., & Ensminger, M. E. (1983). Paths leading to teenage psychiatric symptoms and substance use: Developmental epidemiological studies in Woodlawn. In S. B. Gunn, F. J. Earls, & J. E. Barrett (Eds), *Childhood psychopathology and development* (pp. 17–51). New York: Raven Press.

Kellam, S. G., Werthamer-Larrson, L., Dolan, L. G., Brown, C. H., Mayer, L. S., Rebok, G. W., Anthony, J. C., Laudolff, J., Edelsohn, G., & Wheeler, L. (1991). Developmental epidemiologically-based preventive trials: Baseline modeling of early target behaviors and depressive symptoms. *American Journal of Community Psychology, 19,* 563–584.

Kelley, H. (1973). The processes of causal attribution. *American Psychologist, 28,* 107–128.

Kessen, W. (1960). Research design in the study of developmental problems. In P. H. Mussen (Ed.), *Handbook of research methods in child development* (pp. 36–70). New York: Wiley.

Kosky, R. (1982). Suicide and attempted suicide among Australian children. *Medical Journal of Australia, 1,* 124–126.

Kuo, Z-Y. (1967). *The dynamics of behavioral development: An epigenetic view.* New York: Random House.

Ledingham, J. E., Younger, A., Schwartzman, A., & Bergeron, G. (1982). Agreement among teacher, peer, and self-ratings of children's aggression, withdrawal, and likeability. *Journal of Abnormal Child Psychology, 10,* 363–372.

Lee, M. W., & Livingston, M. M. (1991). Prevalence and accessibility of firearms among Louisiana students: Implications for firearm safety instruction. *LAHPERD Journal, 53,* 20–21.

Lerner, R. I. (1954). *Genetic homeostasis.* New York: Wiley.

Leung, M-C. (1993). *Social cognition and social networks of Chinese school children in Hong Kong.* Unpublished doctoral dissertation. University of North Carolina at Chapel Hill, Chapel Hill, North Carolina.

Lewin, K. (1931). Environmental forces in child behavior and development. In C. Murchison (Ed.), *A handbook of child psychology* (pp. 590–625, 2nd edn). Worcester, MA: Clark University Press.

Livingston, M. M., & Lee, M. W. (1992). Attitudes toward firearms and reasons for firearm ownership among nonurban youth: Salience of sex and race. *Psychological Reports, 71,* 576–578.

Loeber, R. (1982). The stability of antisocial and delinquent child behavior: A review. *Child Development, 53,* 1431–1446.

Loeber, R., & LeBlanc, M. (1990). Toward a developmental criminology. In M. Tonry & N. Morris (Eds), *Crime and justice: A review of research* (Vol. 12, pp. 375–473). Chicago: University of Chicago Press.

Lorenz, E. N. (1983). *Irregularity: A fundamental property of the atmosphere. The Crafoord Prize in the Geosciences: 1983.* Stockholm: The Royal Swedish Academy of Sciences.

Lorenz, K. Z. (1965). *Evolution and the modification of behavior.* Chicago: University of Chicago Press.

Lytton, H. & Romney, D. (1991). Parents differential socialization of boys and girls: A meta-analysis. *Psychological Bulletin,* 109, 267–296.

Maccoby, E. (1990). Gender and relationships – a developmental account. *American Psychologist,* 46, 513–520.

Maccoby, E. E., & Jacklin, C. N. (1974). *The psychology of sex differences.* Stanford: Stanford University Press.

MacCombie, D. J. (1978). *The development of synchrony in children's interchanges.* Unpublished doctoral dissertation, University of North Carolina at Chapel Hill, Chapel Hill, North Carolina.

Magnusson, D. (1966). *Test theory.* Reading, MA: Addison-Wesley.

Magnusson, D. (1985). Implications of an interactional paradigm for research on human development. *International Journal of Behavioral Development, 8,* 115–137.

Magnusson, D. (1988). *Individual development from an interactional perspective.* Vol. 1. In D. Magnusson (Ed.), *Paths through life: A longitudinal research program.* Hillsdale: Erlbaum.

Magnusson, D., & Bergman, L. R. (1984). On the study of the development of adjustment problems. In L. Pulkkinen & P. Lyytinen (Eds), *Human action and personality: Essays in honour of Martti Takala, Jyväskylä studies in education, psychology, and social research.* Jyväskylä, Finland: University of Jyväskylä.

Magnusson, D., & Bergman, L. R. (1990a). (Eds) *Data quality in longitudinal research.* Cambridge, UK: Cambridge University Press.

Magnusson, D., & Bergman, L. R. (1990b). A pattern approach to the study of pathways from childhood to adulthood. In L. N. Robins & M. Rutter (Eds), *Straight and devious pathways from childhood to adulthood* (pp. 101–115). Cambridge, UK: Cambridge University Press.

Magnusson, D., & Cairns, R. B. (in press). Developmental science: An integrated framework. In R. B. Cairns, G. H. Elder, Jr., E. J. Costello, & A. McGuire (Eds), *Developmental Science.* New York: Cambridge University Press.

Magnusson, D., Bergman, L. R., Rudinger, G., & Törestad, B. (1991). (Eds) *Problems and methods in longitudinal research: Stability and change.* Cambridge, UK: Cambridge University Press.

Magnusson, D., Stattin, H., & Allen, V. (1985). Biological maturation and social development: A longitudinal study of some adjustment processes of mid-adolescence to adulthood. *Journal of Youth and Adolescence, 14,* 267–283.

Marsh, H. W., Parker, J. W., and Smith, I. D. (1983). Preadolescent self-concept: Its relation to self-concept as inferred by teachers and to academic ability. *British Journal of Educational Psychology, 53,* 60–78.

Masten, A. S., Best, K. M., & Garmezy, N. (1990). Resilience and development: Contributions from the study of children who overcome adversity. *Development and psychopathology, 2,* 425–444.

McClure, G. M. G. (1984). Recent trends in suicide amongst the young. *British Journal of Psychiatry, 144,* 134–138.

McConnell, S. R., & Odom, S. L. (1986). Sociometrics: Peer-referenced measures and the assessment of social competence. In P. S. Strain, M. J. Guralnick, & H. M. Walker (Eds), *Children's social behavior: Development, assessment, and modification* (pp. 215–284). New York: Academic.

McCord, J. (1979). Some child-rearing antecedents of criminal behavior in adult men. *Journal of Personality and Social Psychology, 37,* 1477–1486.

McCord, J. (1986). Instigation and insulation: How families affect antisocial aggression. In D. Olweus, J. Block, & M. Radke-Yarrow (Eds), *Development of antisocial and prosocial behavior: Research, theories, and issues* (pp. 343–358). New York: Academic.

McCord, J., & Tremblay, R. E. (1992). *Preventing antisocial behavior: Interventions from birth through adolescence.* New York: Guilford Press.

McDill, E. L., Natriello, G., & Pallas, A. M. (1986). A population at risk: potential consequences of tougher school standards for student dropouts. *American Journal of Education, 94,* 135–181.

McDuffie, K. Y., Cairns, R. B., & Cairns, B. C. (1994). *The development of attributions and competence among urban boys and girls.* Paper presented at the Society for Research in Adolescence, San Diego, California, March 1994.

McIntire, M. S. (1980). The epidemiology and taxonomy of suicide. In M. S. McIntire & C. R. Angle (Eds), *Suicide attempts in children and youth* (pp. 1–23). New York: Harper and Row.

Miller, G. A. (1956). The magic number seven, plus or minus two: Some limits on our capacity for processing information. *Psychological Review, 63,* 81–96.

Miller, W. B. (1958). Lower class culture as a generating milieu of gang delinquency. *Journal of Social Issues, 14,* 5–19.

Mills-Byrd, L., & Cairns, R. B. (1987). Life satisfaction in elderly, poor, widowed, Black women. Unpublished manuscript, University of North Carolina at Chapel Hill.

Mischel, W. (1968). *Personality and assessment.* New York: Wiley.

Monthly Vital Statistics Report, 31, Supplement (1982). Washington, DC: US Department of Health and Human Services, Public Health Service.

Monthly Vital Statistics Report, 34, Supplement 2 (1985). Washington, DC: US Department of Health and Human Services, Public Health Service.

Morash, M. (1983). Gangs, groups, and delinquency. *The British Journal of Criminology, 22,* 97–111.

Moreno, J. L. (1934). *Who shall survive? A new approach to the problem of human interrelations.* Washington, DC: Nervous and Mental Disease Publishing Co.

Morrison, F. J. (1991). Learning (and not learning) to read: A developmental framework. In L. Ruben & C. A. Ferfetti (Eds), *Learning to read: Basic research and its implications* (pp. 163–174). Hillsdale. Erlbaum.

Moss, H. A., & Susman, E. J. (1980). Longitudinal study of personality development. In O. G. Brim, Jr. & J. Kagan (Eds), *Constancy and change in human development.* Cambridge, MA: Harvard University Press.

Murphy, M. (1990). Minimizing attrition in longitudinal studies: Means or end? In D. Magnusson & L. R. Bergman (Eds), *Data quality in longitudinal research* (pp. 148–156). Cambridge, UK: Cambridge University Press.

National Advisory Mental Health Council (1990). *National plan for research on child and adolescent mental disorders.* Rockville: US Department of Health, National Institute of Mental Health.

National Center for Health Statistics (1989), *Vital and health statistics of the National Center for Health Statistics, 1989.* Washington, DC: US Printing Office.

National Center for Health Statistics. (1993). *Vital Statistics of the United States, 1989,* (Vol. II, Mortality part A). Washington, DC: Public Health Service. DHHS Pub. No. (PHS) 93–1101. US Government Printing Office.

Neckerman, H. J. (1992). *A longitudinal investigation of the stability and fluidity of social networks and peer relationships of children and adolescents.* Unpublished doctoral dissertation. University of North Carolina at Chapel Hill, Chapel Hill, North Carolina.

Nesselroade, J. R., & Ford, D. H. (1985). P-technique comes of age: Multivariate, replicated, single-subject designs for research on older adults. *Research on Aging, 7,* 46–80.

Oden, S., and Asher, S. R. (1977). Coaching children in social skills for friendship making. *Child Development, 48,* 495–506.

Olweus, D. (1979). Stability of aggressive reaction patterns in males: A review. *Psychological Bulletin, 86,* 852–875.

Olweus, D. (1994). *Bullying at school.* Cambridge, UK: Blackwell Publishers.

Olweus, D., Block, J., & Radke-Yarrow, M. (1986). (Eds) *Development of antisocial and prosocial behavior: Research, theories, and issues.* New York: Academic.

Ospiow, S. (1993). Review of female life careers: A pattern approach. *American Scientist, 81,* 94.

Pallas, A. M. (1986) School dropouts in the United States. In J. D. Stern & M. F. Williams (Eds), *The condition of education: Statistical Report Center for Education Statistics – 1986 Edition* (pp. 158–174). Washington, DC: US Government Printing Office.

Paris, S. G., & Cairns, R. B. (1972). An experimental and ethological investigation of social reinforcement in retarded children. *Child Development, 43,* 717–729.

Parke, R. D., & Slaby, R. G. (1983). The development of aggression. In P. H. Mussen (Gen. Ed.) & M. Hetherington (Ed.), *Handbook of child psychology*

(Vol. 4). (pp. 547–642, 4th edn). New York: Wiley.

Patterson, G. R. (1979). A performance theory for coercive family interaction. In R. B. Cairns (Ed.), *The analysis of social interactions: Methods, issues, and illustrations* (pp. 119–162). Hillsdale, NJ: Erlbaum.

Patterson, G. R. (1982). *Coercive family process.* Eugene: Castalia.

Patterson, G. R. (1986). Performance models for antisocial boys. *American Psychologist, 41,* 432–444.

Patterson, G. R. & Dishion, T. J. (1985). Contributions of families and peers to delinquency. *Criminology, 23,* 63–79.

Patterson, G. R., DeBaryshe, B. D., & Ramsey, E. (1989). A developmental perspective on antisocial behavior. *American Psychologist, 44,* 329–335.

Patterson, G. R., Reid, J. B., & Dishion, T. J. (1992). *Antisocial boys.* Eugene: Castalia.

Piaget, J. (1926). *The language and thought of the child.* New York: Harcourt Brace. (Originally published, 1923.)

Prothrow-Stith, D., & Weissman, M. (1991). *Deadly consequences.* New York, NY: Harper Collins.

Pulkkinen, L. (1993). Continuities in aggressive behavior from childhood to adulthood. *Aggressive Behavior, 19,* 249–263.

Quay, H. C. (1978). Behavior disorders in the classroom. *Journal of Research and Development in Education, 11,* 8–17.

Quine, W. V. (1981). *Theories and things.* Cambridge, MA: Belknap Press.

Rauch, J. (1989). Kids as capital. *Atlantic Monthly* (August), 56–61.

Raush, H. L. (1965). Interaction sequences. *Journal of Personality and Social Psychology, 2,* 487–499.

Reiss, A. J., Jr., & Roth, J. A. (1993). (Eds) *Understanding and preventing violence: Panel on the understanding and control of violent behavior.* Washington, DC: National Academy Press.

Robins, L. N. (1986). The consequences of conduct disorder in girls. In D. Olweus, J. Block, & M. Radke-Yarrow (Eds), *Development of antisocial and prosocial behavior: Research, theories, and issues* (pp. 385–414). New York: Academic.

Robins, L. N., & Price, R. (1991). Adult disorders predicted by childhood conduct problems: Results from the NIMH Epidemiologic Catchment Area project. *Psychiatry, 54*(2), 116–132.

Rodgers, J. L., Billy, J. O. G., & Udry, J. R. (1984). A model of friendship similarity in mildly deviant behaviors. *Journal of Applied Social Psychology, 14,* 413–425.

Roff, J. D. & Wirt, R. D. (1984). Childhood aggression and social adjustment as antecedents of delinquency. *Journal of Applied Social Psychology, 12,* 111–126.

Rohn, R. D., Sarles, R. M., Kenny, J. J., Reynolds, R., N., & Heald, F. P. (1977). Adolescents who attempt suicide. *Journal of Pediatrics, 90,* 636–638.

Rosenblatt, J. S. (1965). Effects of experience of behavior in male cats. In F. A. Beach (Ed.), *Sex and behavior* (pp. 416–439). New York: Wiley.

Ross, M. (1989). Relation of implicit theories to the construction of personal histories. *Psychological Review, 96, Vol. 2,* 341–357.

Rutter, M., & Casaer, P. (1991). (Eds) *Biological risk factors for psychosocial disorders*. Cambridge, UK: Cambridge University Press.

Rutter, M., & Giller, H. (1983). *Juvenile delinquency: Trends and perspectives*. New York: Penguin.

Rutter, M., & Quinton, D. (1984). Long-term follow-up of women institutionalized in childhood: factors promoting good functioning in adult life. *British Journal of Developmental Psychology, 18,* 225–234.

Sadowski, L. S., Cairns, R. B., & Earp, J. A. (1989). Firearm ownership among nonurban adolescents. *American Journal of Diseases of Children, 143,* 1410–1413.

Sameroff, A. J. (1983). Developmental systems: Contexts and evolution. In P. H. Mussen (Gen. Ed.) & W. Kessen (Vol. Ed.), *Handbook of child psychology: Vol. 1: History, theory, and methods* (pp. 237–294). New York: Wiley.

Sampson, R. J., & Laub, J. H. (1993). *Crime in the making: Pathways and turning points through life*. Cambridge, MA: Harvard University Press.

Sanger, C. (1989). *Parental misappropriation of the statutory emancipation procedure*. Paper read at the Biennial Meeting of the Society for Research in Child Development, Kansas City, Missouri, April.

Schlossman, S., & Cairns, R. B. (1993). Problem girls: Observations on past and present. In G. H. Elder, Jr., R. D. Parke, & J. Modell (Eds), *Children in time and place: Relations between history and developmental psychology* (pp. 110–130). New York: Cambridge University Press.

Schlossman, S., & Wallach, S. (1978). The crime of precocious sexuality: Female juvenile delinquency in the progressive era. *Harvard Educational Review, 48,* 65-94.

Schneirla, T. C. (1966). Behavioral development and comparative psychology. *Quarterly Review of Biology, 41,* 283–302.

Scott, J. P. (1977). Social genetics. *Behavior Genetics, 7,* 327–346.

Sears, R. R. (1951). A theoretical framework for personality and social behavior. *American Psychologist, 6,* 476–483.

Sears, R. R. (1965). Development of gender role. In F. A. Beach (Ed.), *Sex and behavior* (pp. 133–163). New York: Wiley.

Sears, R. R., Maccoby, E. E., & Levin, H. (1957). *Patterns of child rearing*. Evanston: Row, Peterson.

Sears, R. R., Whiting, J. W. M., Nowlis, V., & Sears, P. S. (1953). Some child-rearing antecedents of aggression and dependency in young children. *Genetic Psychology Monographs, 47,* 135–234.

Sedikides, C. (1994). Motivated self-perception: To thine own self be true, to thine own self be good, and to thine own self be sure. Unpublished manuscript, University of North Carolina at Chapel Hill.

Serbin, L. A., Peters, P. L., McAffer, V. J., & Schwartzman, A. E. (1991). Childhood aggression and withdrawal as predictors of adolescent pregnancy, early parenthood, and environmental risk for the next generation. *Canadian Journal of Behavioural Science, 23,* 318–331.

Shaffer, D. (1974). Suicide in childhood and early adolescence. *Journal of Child Psychology and Psychiatry, 15,* 275–291.

Shaffer, D. (1985). Depression, mania and suicidal acts. In M. Rutter and L. Hersov (Eds), *Child and Adolescent Psychiatry*, 2nd ed. (pp. 698–719).

Shaffer, D., & Fisher, P. (1981). The epidemiology of suicide in children and young adolescents, *Journal of the American Academy of Child Psychiatry*, 20, 545–565.

Sherif, M., & Sherif, C. W. (1953). *Groups in harmony and tension*. New York: Harper.

Short, J. F., Jr., & Strodtbeck, F. L. (1965). *Group process and gang delinquency*. Chicago: University of Chicago Press.

Simmons, R. C., & Blyth, D. A. (1987). *Moving into adolescence: The impact of pubertal change and school context*. New York: Aldine.

Sroufe, L. A., & Waters, E. (1977). Attachment as an organizational construct. *Child development*, 48, 1184–1199.

Stattin, H. (1990). *The development of anti-social behavior*. Unpublished manuscript, Stockholm University.

Stattin, H., & Magnusson, D. (1990). *Pubertal-maturation in female development*. Hillsdale: Erlbaum.

Steinberg, L., Blinde, P. L., & Chan, K. S. (1984). Dropping out among language minority youth. *Review of Educational Research*, 54, 113–132.

Steinberg, L., Darling, N., Fletcher, A., Brown, B., & Dornbusch, S. (in press). Authoritative parenting and adolescent adjustment: An ecological journey. In P. Moen, G. Elder, Jr., & N. Kluscher (Eds), *Linking lives and contexts: Perspectives on the ecology of human development*. Washington: American Psychological Association.

Strayer, F. F., & Noel, J. M. (1986). The prosocial and antisocial functions of preschool aggression: An ethological study of triadic conflict among young children. In C. Zahn-Waxler, E. M. Cummings, & R. Iannotti (Eds), *Altruism and aggression: Biological and social origins* (pp. 107–131). Cambridge, UK: Cambridge University Press.

Stroup, A. L., & Robins, L. N. (1972). Elementary school predictors of high school dropout among black males. *Sociology of Education*, 45, 212–222.

Sullivan, H. S. (1940). Some conceptions of modern psychiatry. *Psychiatry*, 3, 1–117.

Tanner, J. M. (1962). *Growth at adolescence*. Oxford: Blackwell Scientific Publications.

Thrasher, F.M. (1928). *The gang*. Chicago: University of Chicago Press.

Toch, H. (1969). *Violent men*. Chicago: Aldine.

US Bureau of the Census (1984). *Statistical abstracts of the United States: 1985* (105th edn) Washington, DC: US Department of Commerce.

US Bureau of Census (1987). *Current Population Reports*, Series P-20, No. 413, *School enrollment – Social and economic characteristics of students: October 1983*. Washington, DC: US Government Printing Office.

US Congress Office of Technology Assessment (1991). *Adolescent health. Vol. 1, Summary and policy options*. OTA-H-468. Washington, DC: US Government Printing Office.

US Department of Health and Human Services, Public Health Service (1990). *Healthy people 2000: National health promotion and disease prevention objectives.* (PHS)91-50212. Washington, DC: US Government Printing Office.

Urberg, K., & Kaplan, M. (1989). An observational study of race, age, and sex: heterogeneous interaction in preschoolers. *Journal of Applied Developmental Psychology, 10,* 299–311.

Vonnegut, K. (1967). *Mother night.* New York: Avon Books.

Wallace, R. (1990). Urban decertification, public health and public order: 'Planned shrinkage', violent death, substance abuse, and AIDS in the Bronx. *Social Science and Medicine, 31,* 801–813.

Wallwork, E. (1982). Religious development. In J. M. Broughton & D. J. Freeman-Moir (Eds), *The cognitive developmental psychology of James Mark Baldwin: Current theory and research in genetic epistemology* (pp. 335–388). Norwood: Ablex.

Werner, E. E., & Smith, R. S. (1986). *Kauai's children come of age.* Honolulu: The University of Hawaii Press.

Werner, E. E., & Smith, R. S. (1992). *Overcoming the odds: High risk children from birth to adulthood.* Ithaca: Cornell University Press.

Wexler, L., Weissman, M. M., and Kasl, S. V. (1978). Suicide attempts 1970-75: Updating a United States study and comparisons with international trends. *British Journal of Psychiatry, 132,* 180–185.

Whelage, G. G. (1983). *Effective programs for the marginal high school student.* Bloomington: Phi Delta Kappa.

Whelage, G. G., & Rutter, R. A. (1986). Dropping out: How much do schools contribute to the problem. *Teachers College Record, 87,* 374–392.

Whiting, B. B. (1976). The problem of the packaged variable. In K. F. Riegel & J. A. Meacham (Eds), *The developing individual in a changing world: Vol. 1: Historical and cultural issues* (pp. 310–321). Chicago: Aldine.

Whiting, B. B., & Edwards, C. P. (1973). A cross-cultural analysis of sex differences in the behavior of children three through eleven. *Journal of Social Psychology, 91,* 171–188.

Willemsen, E. & Sanger, C. (1991). Statutory emancipation of minors: Use and impact. *American Journal of Orthopsychiatry, 61,* 540–551.

Wilson, W. J. (1987). *The truly disadvantaged.* Chicago: University of Chicago Press.

Wohlwill, J. F. (1973). *The study of behavioral development.* New York: Academic Press.

Wozniak, R. H., & Fischer, K. (1993). (Eds) *Development in context: Acting and thinking in specific environments.* Hillsdale: Erlbaum.

Yablonsky, L. (1962). *The violent gang.* New York: Irvington Publishers.

Yarrow, M. R., Campbell, J. D., & Burton, R. V. (1968). *Child rearing: An inquiry in research and methods.* San Francisco: Jossey-Bass.

Youniss, J. (1980). *Parents and peers in social development.* Chicago: University of Chicago Press.

Youniss, J. (1986). Development in reciprocity through friendship. In C. Zahn-Waxler, E. M. Cummings, & R. Iannotti (Eds), *Altruism and aggression: Biological and social origins* (pp. 88–106). Cambridge, UK: Cambridge University Press.

Youniss, J., & Smollar, J. (1985). *Adolescent relations with mothers, fathers, and friends.* Chicago: University of Chicago Press.

Zank, S. (1988). *Zur Entwicklung des Lösungsmittelschnüffelns bei Jungendichen und jungen Erwachsenen.* Berlin: Verlag Arno Spitz.

Zeeman, E. C. (1976). Catastrophe theory. *Scientific American, 234,* 65–83.

Author index

Adams, H. B., 97, 288
Ageton, S. S., 285, 294
Aichorn, A., 132, 281, 288
Ainsworth, M. D. S., 281, 288
Ali, Muhammud, 282
Allen, V., 245, 298
Allport, G. W., 42, 248, 288
Anderson, T., 229, 288
Anthony, J. C., 270, 297
Asberg, M., 285, 288
Asher, S. R., 131, 281, 288, 300

Baldwin, A. L., 240, 288
Baldwin, J. M., 37, 90, 100, 107, 247,
    248, 286, 288
Baltes, M. M., 11, 274, 288
Baltes, P. B., 11, 274, 288
Bandura, A., 34, 132, 151, 251, 281, 288,
    289
Bateson, P. P. G., 286, 289
Beck, S. J., 73, 278, 295
Behar, L., 285, 289
Bergeron, G., 88, 277, 282, 297
Bergman, L. R., 10, 11, 37, 42, 229, 274,
    288, 289, 298, 299
Berndt, T. J., 96, 97, 280, 289
Best, K. M., 277, 299
Bigelow, B. J., 280, 281, 289
Billy, J. O. G., 280, 301
Binet, A., 37, 252
Bjerke, T., 195, 285
Blinde, P. L., 185, 283, 303
Block, J., 11, 62, 161, 232, 236, 277, 279,
    289, 300
Block, J. H., 289
Bloom, B., 277, 289

Blyth, D. A., 145, 245, 281, 303
Boucher, J., 282, 289
Bowlby, J. 132, 281, 286, 289
Breland, K., 286, 289
Breland, M., 286, 289
Brennan, T., 187, 289
Brice, P., 277, 294
Brim, O. G. Jr., 236, 289
Bronfenbrenner, U., 233, 247, 251, 280,
    286, 290
Brown, B. B., 91, 279, 281, 290, 303
Brown, C. H., 183, 270, 297
Brown, G., 34
Brown, R. W., 286, 290
Buchanan, L. D., 280, 292, 304

Caesar, P., 11
Cairns, B. D., 34, 35, 39, 73, 91, 103, 139,
    157, 174, 177, 210, 212, 277, 278,
    279, 280, 281, 282, 284, 287, 291,
    292, 295, 299
Cairns, C. B., 214, 290
Cairns, R. B., 3, 11, 33, 34, 35, 41, 42, 73,
    85, 91, 103, 105, 106, 108, 110,
    133, 135, 139, 157, 174, 210, 212,
    214, 247, 250, 267, 268, 271, 274,
    276, 277, 278, 279, 280, 281, 282,
    284, 285, 286, 287, 290, 291, 292,
    293, 295, 296, 298, 299, 300, 302
Campbell, A., 281, 292
Campbell, J. D., 282, 304
Cantril, H., 148
Caspi, A., 142, 287, 292, 293
Catalano, R., 229, 296
Cernkovich, S. A., 279, 281, 295
Chan, K. S., 185, 293, 303

Choquet, M., 200, 292
Cobb, B., 212, 292
Cohen, A. K., 119, 136, 279, 280, 281, 292
Cohen, J. M., 279, 292
Coie, J., 131, 281, 287, 288, 292
Cole, D., 285, 296
Coleman, J. S., 91, 279, 293
Comer, J., 241, 270, 293
Cook, P. J., 215, 217, 293
Cooley, C. H., 286, 293
Coppotelli, H. A., 281, 292
Costa, F. M., 285, 296
Costello, E. J., 274, 291
Crime in the United States 48, 277, 293
Cross, C. E., 277, 293
Crouter, A. C., 251, 290
Csikszentmihalyi, M., 286, 293
Current Population Reports, School Enrollment, 169

Darling, N., 279, 281, 303
Davidson, F., 200, 292
Davis, P. A., 200, 293
DeBaryshe, B. D., 287, 301
de Ribaupierre, A., 11
Dishion, T. J., 277, 281, 301
Dodge, K. A., 281, 287, 288, 292, 293
Dolan, L. F., 88, 270, 293, 297
Donovan, J. E., 285, 296
Dornbusch, S., 279, 281, 303
Dostoevski, F., 5
Dryfoos, J., 147, 148, 267, 283, 293

Earls, F., 85, 267, 268, 271, 277, 285, 287, 293
Earp, J. A., 285, 302
Edelsohn, G., 270, 297
Edwards, C. A., 113, 279, 293
Edwards, C. P., 279, 304
Elder, G. H., 145, 274, 277, 287, 291, 293
Elliott, D. S., 34, 62, 187, 131, 236, 277, 279, 280, 285, 289, 294
Elliott, G. R., 286, 294
Ensminger, M. E., 183, 283, 284, 294, 297
Epstein, S., 161, 282, 294
Eron, L., 11, 29, 53, 62, 66, 236, 275, 277, 279, 294, 296

Facy, F., 200, 292
Farrington, D. P., 11, 62, 236, 275, 277, 279, 281, 287, 294

Feldman, S. S., 286, 294
Ferguson, L. L., 278, 281, 291
Ferguson, T. J., 157, 277, 294
Fernandez, G., 206
Feshbach, N. D., 80, 123, 281, 294
Feshbach, S., 277, 294
Fine, M., 168, 169, 283, 285, 294
Fingerhut, L. A., 199, 217, 285, 294
Finkelstein, B., 285, 295
Fischer, K., 277, 294, 304
Fisher, P., 199, 303
Flavell, J. H., 281, 295
Fletcher, A., 91, 279, 281, 303
Ford, D. H., 276, 300
Forehand, R., 73, 278, 295
Freud, S., 37, 52, 240, 247, 252, 258, 275, 286, 295
Friedrich-Cofer, L., 188, 295
Frodi, A., 277, 295
Froese, A., 285, 295
Fromm, E., 248, 286, 295

Gaines, K. R., 139, 278, 279, 280, 295
Gallagher, B., 277, 294
Garfinkel, B. D., 285, 295
Gariepy, J. L., 11, 105, 106, 110, 278, 280, 281, 285, 286, 291
Garmezy, N., 62, 274, 277, 299
Gesell, A., 37
Gest, S., 280
Gewirtz, J. L., 282
Giordano, P. C., 137, 279, 281, 295
Gleick, J., 4, 295
Glueck, E. T., 277, 295
Glueck, S., 277, 295
Goethe, J., 52
Goldacre, M., 285, 295
Gottfredson, M., 276, 296
Gottlieb, G., 243, 286, 295
Green, J. A., 279, 282, 291
Green, K. D., 73, 278, 295
Greenwald, A. G., 282, 296
Gronlund, N. E., 280, 296
Gulliksen, H., 161, 296

Hall, G. S., 252, 261, 262, 286, 296
Hall, W. M., 281, 296
Hamburg, Beatrix 274
Hankoff, L. D., 200, 296
Hartshorne, H., 282, 296
Hawkins, D., 229, 296
Hawton, K., 285, 295, 296

Heald, F. P., 285, 301
Hechinger, F. M., 270, 287, 296
Hendricks-Brown, 88, 293
Hindelang, M. J., 281, 296
Hirschi, T., 132, 281, 296
Hoshing, M. A., 214, 285, 296
Holland, D. 154, 296
Holly, K. A., 278, 292
Homans, G. C., 108, 286, 296
Hood, J., 285
Hood, K. E., 11, 285, 286, 291
Hoyle, S. G., 96, 289
Huesmann, L. R., 29, 62, 236, 275, 277, 279, 294, 296
Huizinga, D., 34, 62, 131, 187, 236, 277, 279, 280, 285, 289, 294
Hunt, J. McV., 281, 296

Jacklin, C. N., 80, 279, 298
James, W., 45, 52, 296
Jessor, R., 212, 281, 285, 296, 297
Jessor, S. L., 281, 285, 297
Juliusson, H., 280

Kadanoff, L., 4, 296
Kagan, J., 236, 277, 279, 289, 297
Kandel, D. B., 118, 228, 270, 280, 285, 297
Kaplan, J. L., 283, 297
Kaplan, M., 281, 304
Kasl, S. V., 285, 304
Keillor, Garrison, 282
Kellam, S. G., 88, 183, 270, 278, 293, 297
Kelley, H., 282, 297
Kenny, J. J., 285, 301
Kessen, W., 9, 10, 275, 297
Kindermann, T., 11, 105, 106, 110, 280, 291
Kleinman, J. C., 199, 217, 285, 294
Kosky, R., 200, 297
Kroll, A. B., 110, 279, 291
Kuo, Z-Y., 37, 276, 286, 297

Ladd, T., 34–5, 291
Lagerspetz, K., 277, 279, 296
Langmeyer, D., 206
Laub, J. H., 287, 302
Laudoff, J., 88, 270, 293, 297
LeBlanc, 10, 287, 298
Ledingham, J. E., 88, 277, 282, 297
Lee, M. W., 285, 297
Lefkowitz, M. M., 236, 296

Lerner, R. I., 286, 297
Leung, M-C., 34, 35, 80, 278, 280, 283, 291, 292, 297
Levin, H., 276, 302
Lewin, K., 40, 41, 276, 297, 302
Liker, J. K., 277, 293
Livingston, M. M., 285, 297
Loeber, R., 10, 33, 230, 277, 279, 207, 299
Lorenz, K., 4, 247, 286, 298
Luck, E. D., 283, 297
Lytton, H., 110, 298

Macaulay, J., 277, 295
Maccoby, E. E., 80, 110, 276, 279, 298, 302
MacCombie, D. J., 281, 298
Magnusson, D., 10, 11, 41, 42, 62, 66, 141, 145, 161, 184, 233, 236, 242, 245, 252, 229, 274, 275, 276, 277, 279, 284, 285, 286, 287, 288, 289, 298, 299, 303
Marsh, H. W., 282, 299
Masten, A., 62, 277, 299
May, M. A., 282, 296
Mayer, L. W., 270, 293, 297
McAffer, V., 230, 302
McClure, G., 200, 285, 299
McConnell, S. R., 280, 299
McCord, J., 236, 265, 277, 279, 287, 299
McDill, E. L., 283, 284, 299
McDuffie, K. Y., 278, 279, 299
McGuire, A., 274, 291
McIntire, M. S., 200, 299
Meier, D., 270
Menard, S., 34, 131, 236, 277, 279, 280, 294
Mercy, J., 85, 267, 268, 212, 271, 277, 287, 293
Mermelstein, R., 277, 294
Miles, M., 212, 292
Miller, G. A., 281, 299
Miller, J. Y., 229, 281, 296
Miller, W. B., 281, 299
Mills-Byrd, L., 282, 299
Mischel, W., 281, 299
Moffitt, T., 33, 142, 276, 292
Monthly Vital Statistics Report, 285, 299
Morash, M., 281, 299
Moreno, J. L., 100, 272, 280, 299
Morley, L., 277, 294
Morrison, F., 245, 300
Moss, H. A., 62, 236, 277, 279, 297, 300

Murphy, M., 275, 300

National Center for Health Statistics, 196, 198, 201, 276, 300
Natriello, G., 283, 284, 299
Neckerman, H. J., 42, 91, 108, 122, 123, 174, 177, 277, 278, 280, 281, 282, 284, 291, 292, 300
Neiman, J., 214, 290
Neimeyer, J., 214, 290
Nesselroade, J. R., 276, 300
Noel, J. M., 110, 281, 303
Nowlis, V., 276, 302

Oden, S., 281, 300
Odom, S. L., 280, 299
O'Grady, J., 285, 296
Olweus, D., 53, 62, 64, 66, 236, 270, 277, 278, 279, 282, 287, 300
Osborn, M., 285, 296
Osgood, C. W., 282, 289
Ospiow, S., 286, 300

Pallas, A. M., 283, 284, 299, 300
Paris, S. G., 282, 299, 300
Parke, R. D., 236, 277, 279, 300
Parker, J. W., 282, 299
Patterson, G. R., 62, 236, 277, 279, 281, 287, 301
Perrin, J. E., 103, 157, 280, 292
Peters, P., 230, 302
Petersen, A., 272
Piaget, J., 37, 90, 252, 301
Powell, J., 285, 293
Preyer, W., 37
Price, J., 277, 294
Price, R., 279, 301
Prothrow-Stith, D., 270, 301
Pugh, M. D., 279, 281, 295
Pulkkinen, L., 11, 62, 236, 277, 279, 280, 301

Quay, H. C., 283, 301
Quine, W. V., 151, 239, 301
Quinton, D., 284, 302

Radke-Yarrow, M., 236, 279, 300
Ramsey, E., 287, 301
Rathunde, K., 286, 293
Rauch, J., 167, 283, 301
Raush, H. L., 281, 301
Rebok, G., 88, 270, 293, 297
Reid, J. B., 277, 301

Reiss, A. J. Jr., 287, 301
Reynolds, R. N., 285, 301
Robins, L. N., 279, 283, 284, 285, 301, 303
Rodgers, J. L., 280, 301
Roff, J. D., 281, 301
Rohn, R. D., 285, 301
Romney, D., 110, 298
Ross, M., 10, 150, 282, 302
Rosenblatt, J. S., 286, 301
Roth, J. A., 287, 301
Rubin, B. R., 183, 297
Rudinger, G., 11, 299
Rule, B. G., 157, 277, 294
Rutter, M., 11, 34, 62, 277, 283, 284, 287, 302
Rutter, R. A., 283, 304

Sadowski, L. S., 285, 302
St. Ledger, R. J., 277, 294
Sameroff, A. J., 286, 302
Sampson, R. J., 287, 302
Sanger, C., 188, 302, 304
Santoyo, C., 278, 292
Sarles, R. M., 285, 301
Schlossman, S., 3, 85, 279, 302
Schneirla, T. C., 37, 286, 302
Schwartzman, A. E., 88, 230, 270, 282, 297, 302
Scott, J. P., 247, 286, 302
Seavy, D. G., 276, 302
Sears, R. R., 34, 276, 282, 302
Sedikides, C., 282, 302
Serbin, L., 230, 302
Shaffer, D., 199, 206, 211, 303
Shalling, D., 285, 288
Sherif, C. W., 279, 303
Sherif, M., 279, 303
Short, J. F. Jr., 281, 303
Simmons, R. C., 145, 245, 281, 303
Skinner, D., 154, 296
Slaby, R. G., 236, 277, 279, 300
Slusarcick, A. L., 183, 283, 284, 294
Smith, I. D., 282, 299
Smith, R. S., 277, 287, 304
Smollar, J., 279, 305
Sones, G., 278, 281, 294
Sroufe, L. A., 281, 303
Stattin, H., 141, 142, 144, 145, 245, 287, 298, 303
Steinberg, L., 91, 124, 185, 279, 281, 283, 303

Strayer, F. F., 110, 121, 281, 303
Strodtbeck, F. L., 281, 303
Stroup, A. L., 283, 284, 303
Sullivan, H. S., 248, 303
Susman, E. J., 62, 236, 279, 300

Tanner, J. M., 143, 233, 303
Taylor, J., 192
Thome, P. R., 277, 295
Thrasher, F. M., 100, 279, 281, 303
Toch, S., 74, 303
Torestad, B., 11, 299
Traskman-Bendz, 285, 288
Tremblay, R. E., 287, 299

Udry, J. R., 118, 280, 301
Urberg, K., 281, 304
US Bureau of the Census, 283, 284, 303
US Census Report, 48
US Department of Health & Human
        Services, 258, 276, 304

Van Nguyen, T., 287, 296
von Bertalanffy, L., 249, 289
Vonnegut, K., 248, 286, 304
Vosk, B., 73, 278, 295

Wagner, A., 285, 288
Walder, L. O., 236, 296
Wallace, R., 265, 287, 304
Wallach, S., 279, 302

Wallwork, E., 282, 304
Walters, R. H., 34, 132, 151, 251, 276,
        281, 289
Waters, E., 281, 288, 303
Watson, J. B., 252
Weissman, M. M., 270, 285, 301, 304
Wendt, M., 192
Werner, E. E., 62, 277, 278, 304
Werthamer,-Larsson, L., 88, 270, 293,
        297
West, D. J., 62, 277, 287, 294
Wexler, L., 285, 304
Whalen, M., 286, 293
Wheeler, L., 270, 297
Whelage, G. G., 283, 304
Whiting, B. B., 279, 304
Whiting, J. W. M., 276, 279, 302, 304
Willemsen, E., 188, 304
Wilson, W. J., 169, 283, 285, 304
Wirt, R. D., 281, 301
Wohlwill, J., 9, 232, 276, 304
Wozniak, R., 281, 304

Yablonsky, L., 131, 275, 304
Yamaguchi, K., 228, 285, 297
Yarrow, M. R., 282, 304
Younger, A., 88, 277, 282, 297
Youniss, J., 90, 279, 280, 304

Zank, S., 120, 281, 305
Zeeman, E., 245, 305

Subject index

Aggression (see also violence)
  across time, 87–8
  age difference, 55
  anatomy, 73
  antisocial, 76
  causes, 4
  clustering, 74
  cohort differences, 82
  conflict reports, 45–6, 54–9
  contagion, 74
  cycling, 76
  definition, 276
  delinquency, 130–1
  development of, 2, 54
  direct confrontation, 56
  gangs, 138–40
  gender differences, 55, 64–5
  geographic comparisons, 83
  growth of, 53, 65–6
  hostile behavior, 82
  indirect, 57, 67
  individual differences, 53, 62
  inner-city, 83–4
  low threshold, 76
  methods of study, 51, 54
  national problem, 195–6, 198–200
  nature of, 53
  prediction 62, 80, 114, 239
  problem girls, 85–7
  projection and external blame, 55
  rejection, 131–2
  social support for, 133–6
  stability, 61–4
  timing, 76
  why aggression? 52
At risk youth, 6, 35, 68, 69–71, 221–3,

236–8
  adult adjustment, 225–6
  correlated outcomes, 223–4, 236, 238
  criminal offenses, 227–8
  failures of expectation, 224, 235–6
  false negative, 224
  false positive, 224
  fluidity of risk, 222–3
  hidden competence, 7, 222
  longitudinal outcomes of CLS, 224–5
  methods for research, 236
  overcoming the odds, 231–6
  problems in identification, 232
  psychiatric hospitalization, 229–30
  real change in development, 232
  risk/control comparisons, 225
  school dropout, 226
  SES effects, 230
  substance use, 228–9
  suicide attempts, 229–30
  teenage parenthood, 230–1
  unstable family, 230
Attrition, 10, 12, 23, 25–30, 44, 275
  cooperation and trust, 24
  dropped out of school, 26, 29
  foster families, 27
  illegal activities, 27
  lost, 27, 29
  mobility, 19
  moved, 26
  not random, 30
  permission, 27
  risk/lifelines, 29
Average child myth, 40
  aggregation, 40
  unit of analysis, 41

311

Behavioral observations, 35, 38–9, 44, 71–6
  aggressive cycles, 76
  hostile interchanges, 74–6
  prosocial behavior, 76–7
Behavior, actions and cognition, 32
  constraints, 32
  multiple social contexts, 32
  organizations, 32, 239
  predictable 239
  synchrony, 32
Biological lottery, 7

Carolina Longitudinal Study (CLS), 2, 13
  CLS research effort, 254–6
  extended sample, 17
    grandparents, 18
    parents, 18
  geographic influence, 255
  institutional cooperation, 21–3
  measures, 30-3
  mobility, 19
  original settings, 18–21, 255
  participants, 24
  participation, 21
  permission, 21
  purpose, 256
  teacher payment/gifts, 21
  understand individual circumstances, 256
Change and continuity, 250
  consolidated habits, 251
  culture and environment, 251
  'innate drift', 251
  reorganizations, 250
Correlated constraints, 4, 32, 41, 69, 74, 93, 99,108, 111, 115–21, 122–7, 148, 151, 190, 222, 232–8, 239–40, 242–6, 251–2, 255, 257, 259–60, 267–9, 273
Critical periods, 247
  early vs. later experiences, 247
  reorganization of stages during youth, 247

Data quality, 37–40
  data tyranny, 11
  phenomena lost, 12
  replication 12, 13
  slippery scales, 12, 24
Delinquency and crime, 36, 130–1
Developmental context, 200–1

context, 249
context-free outcomes, 253–4
culture and environment, 251
external veridicality, 250
time in history, 254
Developmental homeostasis, 233
Developmental perspective, 239–57
  basic theories in humans, 240–1
  biobehavioral science, 239
  biological states, 243
  catastrophe theory, 245
  conservatism and order in development, 246
  developmental synthesis, 240, 241–2
  experimental psychology, 240
  goals and adaptations, 249
    age effects on maturity 249
  holistic nature, 4, 6
    multiple measures required, 31
  holistic view, 242
  novelty in development, 244
  rate of development, 244
  research limitation, 253–4
    context-free outcomes, 253–4
    processes in context, 253–4
  self, other, and real, 250
    external veridicality, 250
    internal harmony, 250
  social behavior, 256
  social context, 254
  social learning, 251
  social science background, 241
  statistical modeling, 246
  synchrony of individuals and context, 242–3
  systems theory, 241
  theoretical problems, 240
  time in history of CLS, 254–5
  transitions, 257
  understanding processes, 253
  understanding social behavior, 256–7
Developmental science, 2, 4, 52
  chaos of youthful development, 5
  correlated constraints, 4
  definition, 274
  developmental synthesis, 240, 241–2
  resilience, 6

Ethics, 2, 90, 249–50
  development and, 249–50
  parents and guardians, 275
  peers and, 90

Ethics (*continued*)
  research, 2

Families, 27, 114, 124–7, 178, 230, 248
  functional emancipation, 188–9
  intact, 12
  marriage, 36, 38, 178
  parental abdication, 188–91
  parents and networks, 124-7
  post-modern, 13
  runaways, 36, 187–8
  statutory emancipation, 189
  teen parents, 36, 38, 230–1
Friends, 90, 94–5, 97
  functions of fickleness, 98–100
  importance of a friend, 94–5, 97
  peers, 90
  relationship fluidity, 95–6
  value of peers, 91

Gender differences, 12, 55, 64–5, 78–80,
    80, 89, 85–6, 141, 277–9, 141,
    142–5, 260–1
Girls
  aggressive, 78-80
  determinant of deviance, 141
  early maturation, 141
  forgotten, 12
  menarche, 142–3
  social adaptations, 142–5
Guns (firearms), 05, 215 19

Hidden competence, 7, 222
History of psychology, 249
  biology model, 249
  physics model, 249
Homicide, 49, 52, 197–8
Hong Kong, 16, 80

Interpersonal Competence Test, 35, 38,
    59–61
Intervention/Prevention, 258–72
  attention to age/development, 271
  Baltimore, Kellam, 270
  Birmingham, Middle Schools, 272
  Cambridge–Somerville, 265
  configurations of influence, 268
  developmental constraints, 269
  effectiveness of school programs, 269
  enduring changes, 268
  engagement in conventional activities,
    270

ethnicity, 260
  examples, 270
  failure of common sense, 265
  family, 6, 259–60, 262
  friends, 6, 259
  gender, 260-1
  individual characteristics, 260–1
  influence behavior across generations,
    269
  Inglewood, CA, 270
  internal and external supports, 269
  lifelines, 258
  neighborhood, 259-60, 262
  New Haven, CN, 270
  New York, NY, 270
  NIH resources for research, 266–7
  opportunities for change, 268
  opportunities in life, 261
  prevention, 264
  programs in community, 271
  risks, 261-4
  schools, 6, 259, 260, 264
  shared goals, 271
  social class, 260, 262
  successful interventions, 270–2
  urban renewal, 265
Interviews, 33–4, 35, 45, 38–9

Longitudinal design, 12, 13–16
  cross-generational link, 12
  cross-sectional, 9
  life-course, 1, 42
  retrospective, 9
  social history, 9
Los Angeles, 16, 213–5

Maturation, 36, 38, 113, 141–5
  biological lottery, 7
  biophysical status, 6
Morbidity, 49, 212–15, 218–20
Mortality, 36, 49, 52, 88, 194–5, 197–8,
    229–30

Nature/nurture, 251–2
  genetic effects and, 251
  timing, 251
Newspapers, 34
  official reports, 36
Novelty in development, 11, 54, 231, 244,
    246, 250

Pathways of living, 1, 2

Peer nominations, 36
Person oriented analysis, 14, 18, 21, 40–3,
    83, 119, 173–6, 178–82, 223–4,
    231–8, 252–3
  configurations, 43
  variable analysis, 252–3
Pure vs. practical science, 252

Risk-taking behavior, 204, 212
Runaways, 36, 187–8

School Dropout, 167–93
  age, 172–3
  contributing factors, 184–6
  definition, 170–1
  education and training of, 186–7
  GED/diplomas/alternative, 179
  involuntary, 170
  job picture, 178-9
  life after, 178–9
  marriage, 178
  national picture, 168–70
  overcoming dropout, 182
  parenthood, 178
  peer group effects on, 176-8
  prevention and educational policy,
    186–7
  problems with authority, 179
  race, 172, 184–5
  reasons/rationalizations, 179-80
    correlations with causation, 183
    self-reflections, 179–81
  re-entry, 181-2
  remedies for, 191–3
    continuity of programs, 193
    curriculum, 191
    peer groups, 191
    social support of schools, 192–3
    suspension issues, 192
  vulnerability, 173–6
SCM (Social Cognitive Map), 100–7, 121,
    217
  recall matrix/co-occurrence matrix,
    102–6
Self, 147–66
  adaptability and flexibility, 152–4
  adaptive processes, 164–5
  age-related, 152
  of aggressive youth, 163–5
  biophysical, 153
  brutalization norm, 157
  cluster membership and self, 160

cognitive constructions of 165–6
concepts, development of, 152, 250
correspondence of thoughts, 151
dual masters of the, 150–2, 165
harmony vs. veridicality, 151
ICS, 154–5
Lake Wobegone effect, 155–6
life satisfaction, 148–50
longitudinal findings, 154
Pollyanna Law, 153
public vs private, 153
rate/content of change, 153
reports, 147, 153–62
self esteem, 148
self-other correspondence, 160–3
self-other enhancement, 156, 157–60
self-scale enhancement, 156, 166
Social Networks
  academic achievement, 113
  adolescent culture, 91
  age, 113
  aggression, 112
  athletics, 113
  attractiveness, 113
  birds of a feather, 109
  co-resemblance in behavior and
    interests, 112–14
  crowds, 91
  dropout, 114
  early maturing girls, 141–5
  existence, 11
  fluidity of groups, 91, 92–4, 95–7,
    122–4
  formation of groups, 116, 127
  functions of groups, 116–19, 127–9, 138
  gang formation, 138–41
  gangs as family, 263
  homogeneous groups, 109–12
  homophilies, 115
  isolates, 130, 135–6
  leadership, 113
  maturation, 113
  nature of stability, 92
  parents, 124–7
  popularity, 113
  predictive associations, 114
  prevention, 259, 260, 263
  propinquity, 107–9
  reciprocal socialization, 117–19
  rejection and social deficits, 131–3, 136
  relationships, 40, 95–7
  reorganization of groups, 122–4

Social Networks (*continued*)
  research participation, 113
  shadows of synchrony, 130
  sharing perspective, 91
  similarities in deviance, 119–21
  social clusters, 101, 121–2, 127–9
  social cognitive maps, 100–7
  social networks and gangs, 139
  stability of groups, 92–4, 122–4
  teenage parents, 114
Social synchrony, 248–9
  autonomy, 248
  independence, 248
  research base is family and peers, 248
Statistical Abstract of Sweden, 2
Substance use, 228–9, 263–4
Suicide, 88, 195, 198, 229–30
  aggression, 202, 206–11, 219
  attempt rates, 200
  behavioral neurobiology, 211
  clusters of, 203
  Conduct Disorder, 210
  destructive dyscontrol, 210
  personal relationships, 205
  provocation of, 204–5
  reciprocation process, 204
  relative isolation, 204
  "risk-taking", 204, 212
  social alienation, 202
  social networks, 202, 218

Willie M. program, 206–10

Taiwan, 16
Teenage parenthood, 36, 38, 230–1
  school dropout and, 114–15, 167–8
Trauma injury and violence, 213–15

US Census Bureau, 2, 18–20

Violence (see also aggression)
  African–American, 84
  comorbidity, 68
  developmental pathways of, 50
  epidemic, inner-city, 83, 89
  guns and violence, 215–18
  homicide, 49, 52
  in society, 46–7
  murder/victimization, 48
  national picture, 47–9
  research design to study, 51
  sex difference increase, 89
  sex differences, 80, 85–6
  sexual promiscuity, 87, 89
  status offense, 87
  suicide risk, 88
  trauma and violence, 213–15

Woodlawn project, 183–4

Yearbooks, 34